A TALE OF TWO MONASTERIES

A TALE OF TWO MONASTERIES

WESTMINSTER AND SAINT-DENIS
IN THE THIRTEENTH CENTURY

William Chester Jordan

PRINCETON UNIVERSITY PRESS

PRINCETON AND OXFORD

Library of Congress Cataloging-in-Publication Data

Jordan, William C., 1948–

A tale of two monasteries : Westminster and Saint-Denis in the thirteenth century /
William Chester Jordan.

p. cm.

Includes bibliographical references and index.

ISBN 978-0-691-13901-2 (hardcover : alk. paper) 1. Westminster Abbey—History.

2. Abbaye de Saint-Denis (Saint-Denis, France)—History. 3. Great Britain—Politics and
government—1216–1272. 4. France—Politics and government—1226–1270.

5. Richard, de Ware, d. 1283. 6. Mathieu, de Vendôme, d. 1286. I. Title.

DA687.W5J67 2009

271'.1042132—dc22   2008033066

British Library Cataloging-in-Publication Data is available

This book has been composed in Galliard

Printed on acid-free paper. ∞

press.princeton.edu

Printed in the United States of America

3   5   7   9   10   8   6   4   2

Ad Tonitrum Purpureum
(a.k.a. Purple Thunder)

CONTENTS

ILLUSTRATIONS

PREFACE

W ALKING THROUGH the Dean's Yard at Westminster Abbey, dedicated to Saint Peter the Prince of the Apostles and King Edward the Confessor, one soon approaches the east cloister, next to the medieval Chapter House.[1] Tourists mill about. Signs—routinely ignored—caution them to keep their voices down. A great many visitors appear uncertain as to where to proceed, while others, simply exhausted by sightseeing, sit wearily on the old low walls. A few strain to read the inscriptions on the stone walkways that, worn down from age and steady traffic, mark the burials of monks and abbey officials. Visitors scarcely notice a plain dark wooden door beside the Chapter House, but a small sign instructs the potential guest to ring the bell for entry. Once pressed, the bell provokes someone inside to respond over an old-fashioned intercom. The disembodied voice, pleasingly educated and welcoming, inquires as to the guest's business and, once assured on this score, buzzes him in. Entry is by mounting a plain stone staircase to a darkish, appropriately musty, and altogether lovely chamber, impressive with books shelved in parallel stacks and old portraits decorating the walls. The books are more striking than the portraits. They are venerable looking volumes, true tomes, books for scholars who yearn to delve into the minds of the ancient Catholic Fathers and the Protestant divines. But the voice that permitted entry, now possessed of a body, beckons from the top of a spiral staircase at the far end of the chamber. The stairs lead to a cramped set of rooms where the guest can consult the abbey muniments, as he has requested.

"Muniments" is a very old word for archives, but appropriate in this context, where history seems to weigh so heavily. Thousands upon thousands of medieval documents, by one estimate 57,500, rest in Westminster Abbey's incomparable archives.[2] The guest sits, presents his credentials,

---

[1] Westminster, that is to say, the ecclesiastical complex of buildings (minster) on the west, is alleged to have been a designation that came into common use to distinguish the abbey from Saint Paul's, sometimes known as Eastminster; Fuller, *History of the Worthies of England*, 2:411 (citing Bale, *De Scriptoribus Britannicis*).

[2] For the figure cited, see Tanner, "Nature and Use of the Westminster Abbey Muniments," p. 72. Elsewhere (p. 43), Tanner writes, "No English Cathedral or Abbey Church has so complete a collection of documents dealing with its history and internal administration." On the process of organization of the muniments in the eighteenth and nineteenth centuries, see the *First Report of the Royal Commission on Historical Manuscripts*, 1:94–97. While the vast majority, with a few exceptions (cf. London, BL, Cotton Faustina A III, "Registrum Cartarum ecclesiae B. Petri Westmonasteriensis"), of the voluminous administrative records are in situ, the abbey's medieval literary manuscripts have not survived in great abundance, and those that have survived have often migrated to other collections; e.g., London, BL, Royal 5 B VIII, an anthology of patristic and postpatristic texts, and London, Lambeth Palace Library, MS 761, a Life of Saint Edward the Confessor. Either that or they

attends to the explanation of procedures, then consults old handwritten and typewritten catalogs, fills out forms, and waits in silence. A few minutes later the first of the requested documents of the mid-thirteenth century appear. They come typically four or five at a time—letters, charters, memoranda, account rolls, loan agreements, receipts, notaries' instruments, deeds—nearly all composed in the vigorous Latin of the medieval monks and their correspondents.

Across the Channel a visit to the royal abbey of Saint-Denis, though interesting, is less charming. The French Revolution offered great promise to nation and people while wreaking its havoc on this celebrated monastery as on hundreds of others. The keepers of the national patrimony now require that the restored remnants of the building complex at Saint-Denis be respected. Unfortunately, this requirement and the historical sensibility that underlies it came late; one of the consequences of the abbey's desecration in earlier centuries was the destruction of large amounts of its once copious archives and the migration of the vast majority of the still considerable surviving portions to governmental repositories, like the Archives Nationales (AN) and the Bibliothèque nationale de France (BnF). There is at least something to be said for working on thirteenth-century parchments in the manuscript room of the old Bibliothèque Nationale (BN) on rue Richelieu, where they remain stored and available for consultation despite the construction of the impressive but coldly austere steel-and-glass BnF on the Quai François Mauriac. To enter the very handsome room of the old BN is to step far back in time—heavy oaken desks, small color-coded plaquettes for seat assignments and for ordering manuscripts, a sense of intimacy with the artifacts and of silent, almost monastic, community with the other scholars.

No one, to my knowledge, has made a sustained attempt to compare the two institutions—Saint-Denis and Westminster—despite their obvious similarities in the thirteenth century and the competition that characterized their relations until the French Revolution.[3] Both were Benedictine in the rule the monks followed; both were under the direct and unmedi-

---

have somehow been overlooked, like WAM, no. 9468, a deed of the mid-fourteenth century, which was unknown until Christmas 1909, when it was discovered "in a secret coffer in the old 'Ark' chest in the Muniment Room. This coffer was unknown to Widmore and Burtt [earlier catalogers], and was accidentally found by the carpenter during repairs" according to the present index slip.

[3] For an incomplete but suggestive comparison of the early modern institutions, see the articles by Le Gall, "Nécropole dynastique des Bourbons," pp. 61–80, and Ruggiu, "Westminster, nécropole royale," pp. 81–112, in a dedicated section of *Revue historique* (January 2006), titled "Deux nécropoles royales à l'âge moderne: Saint-Denis et Westminster."

ated jurisdiction of the Holy See in terms of their relations with other ecclesiastical authorities; both were under the special protection and patronage of their respective crowns. And while one (Saint-Denis) already was, the other (Westminster) aspired to be the preferred site for their kings' burials. Other similarities come to mind as well. Both were located in privileged "suburbs" of the greatest city in each realm, London and Paris. And both were almost unimaginably wealthy. There were contrasts, too, of course. While the writing of the official history of France was centered in Saint-Denis, it was not the monks of Westminster but the inmates of the monastery of Saint-Albans, sometimes in the service of the Westminster community, who had the strongest claim to be the official chroniclers of English history.[4] Indeed, it has rightly been said that Westminster "[A]bbey had no great reputation for scholarship," historical or otherwise, or for the products of its scriptorium in general.[5] On the other hand, Saint-Denis, despite repeated efforts to claim the privilege, never succeeded in permanently wresting the coronation of the French king from the cathedral of Reims. Westminster may not have written much history, but, in the recurrent ceremonies of coronation, it made a certain sort of history.

Remarkably, in the same year, 1258, two men achieved the headship of the two abbeys, and they would, each of them, rule for a quarter of a century. They came to know each other well because the histories of the two realms were so deeply enmeshed in these years. And their careers, though at odds in many details and emphases, have, like the character of the monasteries they ruled, a great deal in common. One noteworthy feature of both lives was their unceasing devotion to the kings whom they served for much of this period: Louis IX and Philip III of France had their Mathieu de Vendôme, and Henry III and Edward I of England had their Richard de Ware. The idea of writing—or trying to write—the story of two great abbeys and the two men who headed them in a time of enormous change in two rival kingdoms was too attractive to resist. This book is the result.

---

[4] The *Flores historiarum*, a chronicle compilation begun at Saint-Albans, was sent to Westminster in 1265, and edited and continued there. Cf. Binski, *Westminster Abbey and the Plantagenets*, pp. 121–22.

[5] Sharpe et al., *English Benedictine Libraries*, p. 609; Lancaster, "Henry III, Westminster Abbey, and the Court School of Illumination," pp. 85–95.

ACKNOWLEDGMENTS

M Y DEBTS OF GRATITUDE will never be paid, but at the very least I want to make a public declaration of the names of the people to whom I owe them: Thomas Boeve, Princeton University; David Carpenter, King's College, University of London; Guy Geltner, University of Oxford; Barbara Harvey, Somerville College, Oxford University; Christine Kenyon (Hershey) Jordan (for the idea of the book); Lauren Lepow, Princeton University Press; Richard Mortimer, Westminster Abbey; Terri O'Prey, Princeton University Press; Kenneth Pennington, Catholic University of America; Richard Pfaff, University of North Carolina, Chapel Hill; Clara Platter, Princeton University Press; Gyan Prakash, Princeton University; Robert Stacey, University of Washington; Brigitta van Rheinberg, Princeton University Press; and Nicholas Vincent, University of East Anglia.

TECHNICAL MATTERS:
CURRENCIES, CALENDARS, NOMENCLATURE

THIRTEENTH-CENTURY ENGLAND and France had different currencies and monies of account. The French had pounds of Tours, *livres tournois* (l. t.), and pounds of Paris, *livres parisis* (l. p.). Four l. p. was the equivalent of 5 l. t. The English pound sterling (£) had a nominal exchange rate of 4 l. p., although it actually exchanged for 3 l. p. in the period covered by this book. Each pound had 20 shillings (Latin *solidi*, French *sous*), abbreviated s., and each shilling 12 pennies or pence (Latin *denarii*, French *deniers*), abbreviated d. Of course, the shillings and pence of England related to those of France at the same rate of exchange as their pounds, as was true of the marks of the two countries, which were equivalent to two-thirds of a pound or 160 d.

The calendars of the two kingdoms also differed. English calendars began the year generally on 25 March, the feast of the Annunciation to the Virgin, also known as Lady Day; the French year typically began on the movable feast of Easter, as early as 22 March or as late as 25 April. I have silently converted all dates to "new style" according to the calendar common today. So, for example, 12 February 1260 according to the medieval French or English reckoning "old style" would be 12 February 1261 as we now think of it.

One last technical point: the central personal rites of passage of the historic Christian church have no place for last names. One is baptized with given names, offered and taken in marriage in the same way, and likewise committed to eternal rest. The man who became a monk in the Middle Ages or now becomes a monk symbolically lost (or loses) his connections with his earthly biological family. One should properly speak of the English abbot whose career is one of the focuses of this book solely as Abbot Richard. Adding the tag "of (*or* de) Ware" gives specificity and provides some welcome stylistic variety, and with these purposes in mind, I have not hesitated to use it, just as people in the Middle Ages fairly often did. Nevertheless, I have resisted the current English convention of referring to Abbot Richard interchangeably as Abbot Ware, which would have been meaningless in his own time. I have seen no such usage in documents contemporary with his rule of Westminster Abbey, and even if a few escaped my notice, the weight of the evidence would still be against conventionalizing it. Abbot Richard he was in his lifetime; Abbot Richard he is in the pages of this book. It goes almost without saying that the reader will

also not find Richard's French counterpart—the other focus of study—
Mathieu de Vendôme, the abbot of Saint-Denis, masquerading as Abbot
Vendôme in these pages.

A TALE OF TWO MONASTERIES

I

ENGLAND AND FRANCE

IN THE EARLY THIRTEENTH CENTURY

I N ONE SENSE the story of this book opens in the year 1258 when two relatively obscure monks, Richard de Ware and Mathieu de Vendôme, were elected rulers of Westminster Abbey and the Abbey of Saint-Denis. In another sense, however, the monks' story commences more than a half century earlier, when war broke out between King John of England and King Philip II of France. The failure of the two kings and their advisers to resolve the conflict and the persistent turmoil that their failure generated in the ensuing decades provide the essential introduction to the two abbots' history and that of their monasteries in their lifetimes. For it was an almost inevitable consequence of their election to such influential positions that Richard and Mathieu became partisans in the continuing diplomatic and political drama affecting their countries.

It was in the year 1200 that King John of England (1199–1216) took a young girl, Isabelle d'Angoulême, as his wife.[1] Isabelle attracted him because she was pretty and pert, or, in another, duller but no less well-argued interpretation, because marriage to her provided the key to a strategic opportunity. Her family ruled the Angoumois, a principality in western France about 150 kilometers south of the Loire River. Its location and power offered a means to check the rise to prominence of an ambitious baron, Hugues, count of La Marche, but Hugues was already engaged to Isabelle when John decided to act. Thus it was in a preemptive move that he carried Isabelle off and married her himself. The action did not so much secure an alliance with Isabelle's family as it put in jeopardy John's continued possession of the vast array of French lands he had inherited in 1199 on the death of his brother, Richard the Lionhearted (1189–1199). Count Hugues of La Marche owed faithfulness to John, but only as long as the latter treated him justly. The taking of his intended bride was unjust, and when the count gave up trying to obtain satisfaction directly from John, he turned to their mutual overlord, the Capetian king of France Philip II (1179/80–1223), a man who had long coveted the territories in

---

[1] On Isabelle, see Vincent, "Isabella of Angoulême," pp. 165–219, and Jordan, "Isabelle d'Angoulême," pp. 821–52.

his realm that were, to his infinite displeasure, under the direct control of the wearer of the English crown.[2]

The French ruler commanded John to appear before him and his High Court to answer the charges levied against him and to receive Philip's judgment. John categorically refused even though he held his lands in France from and had pledged his faith to the French king. Philip and his court therefore solemnly declared John's French lands forfeit to the crown. War ensued, and by 1204 French troops had subjugated Normandy. By the end of 1206 they had extended their master's control to most of the lands John claimed that were situated north of the Loire River.

Soon afterward John provoked an equally dangerous personage, Pope Innocent III. The issue, the English king's refusal to admit the papal candidate to the see of Canterbury after a disputed election, ultimately led the king and the pope to take actions against each other, the former confiscating ecclesiastical property and sending hostile English churchmen into exile, the latter imposing a kingdomwide interdiction of religious services in 1208. It would not be until 1212 that John extricated himself from this struggle, promising as part of the settlement to accept the overlordship of the pope for his own royal lordship of England.

The line of demarcation established in 1206 between areas of French and English rule on the Continent, to resume the military narrative, was generally stable until the early 1220s, when large additional territories south of the Loire were successfully annexed by Philip's heir and successor, Louis VIII (1223–1226). To be sure, the half century following the initial French conquests saw John and, thereafter, his son Henry III (1216–1272) attempt to regain their lands. Their lack of success had enormous repercussions in English history. The lifting of the papal interdict in late 1212 was the one really bright spot for King John, allowing him to concentrate his efforts on the war with France, but popular disappointment during the year 1214 with his most intensive but wholly ineffective effort to recover his Continental patrimony was a major cause for the great revolt of the heavily taxed English barons that led to the acceptance of Magna Carta in 1215. Magna Carta failed to bring more than a temporary cessation of the revolt, but it did lay the foundation for a longer-term modus vivendi between the crown and the English aristocracy—one often contested, but in the end quite constraining and enduring.[3]

---

[2] This chapter draws substantially throughout on the narratives of Powicke, *Loss of Normandy*; idem, *Thirteenth Century*; Carpenter, *Minority of Henry III*; Baldwin, *Government of Philip Augustus*; Petit-Dutaillis, *Etude sur la vie et le règne de Louis VIII*; and Richard, *Saint Louis*.

[3] Carpenter, *Minority of Henry III*, p. 412. For a comprehensive treatment of the politics surrounding the creation of Magna Carta, see Holt, *Magna Carta*.

After his father's death Henry III continued to assert the Plantagenets' claims to the lost French lands, although his attempts, like John's, to enforce these claims by specifically military action never achieved success. His principal opponent for most of his reign was Louis IX (1226–1270), and the two men's opposition sparked a rivalry that lasted until the end of their lives. Yet that rivalry itself gradually transmuted over the years, as it became evident that war was not the English king's best game, and as the French king focused more and more of his attention on the desire to distinguish himself as a crusader. The progressive infrequency and relatively low intensity of Henry III's threats to mount a military expedition to compel acknowledgment of the justness of his territorial claims in France led to the illusion of peace between the two kingdoms in the mid- and late 1240s. It remained to turn the illusion into legal reality, but the most hopeful moments in this process did not come until the 1250s. The two kingdoms remained technically at war until late in that decade.

If the initial shock and the ever-lengthening reality of the loss of the French lands transformed the kingdom of England, the French victories no less profoundly transformed the nature of French society and domestic politics. Success ultimately turned this one among many military, diplomatic, and economic principalities in western Europe into the most powerful kingdom in Christendom. It provided additional substance to the French crown's claims to superiority among Catholic monarchies. And it fed a nascent but deepening patriotism in a realm that until then had been scarcely more than a congeries of loosely attached principalities.[4]

The loss of most of their territories in France in the early thirteenth century did not mean that the English kings or their subjects were wholly estranged from the Continent. English aristocrats, many of whom were descendants of men who had conquered the kingdom in 1066, constituted a community comfortable in French and in regular contact with Francophone Continental kin and friends.[5] Henry III also retained direct political control of the lands of the southwest that the Capetians did not seize in the thirteenth century, the duchy of Aquitaine (with its capital at Bordeaux and one of its greatest ports at Bayonne) and small adjacent territories. Britain's proximity to the Continent assured that in peacetime trade relations formed an important bond. Wine exported to the island kingdom now, with the loss of Anjou and Poitou, came more dispropor-

---

[4] See the collection, edited by Bedos-Rezak, *Polity and Place: Regionalism in Medieval France*, and Dunbabin's *France in the Making*. See also Iogna-Prat, "Constructions chrétiennes," pp. 55–60.

[5] Lodge, "Language Attitudes and Linguistic Norms," p. 78. Cf. Iglesia-Rábade, "Multi-Lingual Pulpit," pp. 479–92.

tionately and in larger quantities from the Bordelais.[6] Finally, travels back and forth of clergymen and pilgrims were never infrequent.

Except, however, for making plans of reconquest, only to execute them unsuccessfully, and strengthening the administration of the much-reduced Angevin Empire, the English king's council devoted far less time to affairs on the Continent after 1215 than had been the case earlier.[7] In a famous quip, the historian George Sayles once said that King Henry III, "debarred" by his military and political fortunes from replicating his predecessors' travels "to the Continent, was determined to redress the balance by having the Continent come to England."[8] He meant that those of Henry's Continental relatives who came to the kingdom held a favored place in his sentiments. Critics may have exaggerated the power and danger of these so-called aliens, especially Henry's half siblings from his mother's remarriage. Nonetheless, after a time these kinfolk from Poitou and its environs, the Poitevins, together with the king's relatives by marriage (to Eleanor of Provence) from both Provence and Savoy, did command a sizable portion of royal benefactions.[9]

The king was also an extravagant man. He was enormously wealthy, as most medieval kings were, but not even a monarch's wealth was limitless. Henry lavished gifts not only on the aliens but also his other friends. Some of his tendencies were kept under control in his youth (he was only nine when he came to the throne in the aftermath of his father's unsuccessful repudiation of Magna Carta). At first, dominion in his government lay with a grand old man, William Marshal, the Earl of Pembroke, but when the earl died only a few years into the reign, control over Henry passed to a triumvirate, a sort of regency council, that included Pandulph, the papal legate; Peter des Roches, the bishop of Winchester; and Hubert de Burgh, the justiciar.[10] William Marshal and, after him, the triumvirate engineered the rebels' appeasement, the face-saving departure of a French invasion force that had come to support them against John, the spiriting away of Henry's mother (in the view of many, the cause of all woes) to her homeland, Magna Carta's prudent reissue, and the enactment of the companion Charter of the Forest in 1217. The new government managed to achieve a level of stability thereafter, even when strains appeared in the regency in the 1220s.

---

[6] Boutoulle, "Vigne," p. 293.

[7] Studd, "Reconfiguring the Angevin Empire," pp. 31–41.

[8] Sayles, *Medieval Foundations of England*, p. 416.

[9] Vincent, *Peter des Roches*, p. 37. The now standard biography of Henry's consort is Howell's *Eleanor of Provence*.

[10] There are good modern biographies of two of these men: Crouch, *William Marshal*, and Vincent, *Peter des Roches*. Carpenter's *Minority of Henry III* is also essential.

The king gradually assumed the reins of power, starting in 1223, and in 1225 he reissued the Great Charter. But no scholar has made much of a case that Henry's interest in governance made him an effective ruler. His great advantage was that the people around him, like Hubert de Burgh, who emerged as the dominant presence, were themselves well-schooled administrators, and that the administrative routines established in the twelfth century persisted into the thirteenth. England remained a small well-governed country, as the commonplace has it. To be sure, intermittent squabbles among individual barons, baronial factions, and alien lords hampered the government's operations, and the difficulties that ensued were marked from time to time by politic reissues of Magna Carta as a kind of ritual—a promise on the king's part and, by implication, on the government's to do better.[11] Even real lapses in direction from the center had less deleterious implications than they might otherwise have had, thanks to the quality and clever inventiveness of crown administrators working in the long tradition of Plantagenet governance. Thus, for example, in response to the Fourth Lateran Council's interdiction of priests' sanctifying the ordeals hitherto used to try accused felons, it was the judges, not the crown, who worked out a new way of proceeding—namely, trial by petty jury, a unanimous verdict of twelve good men and true to replace the ordeals.[12]

The real crisis in English governance did not begin until the 1240s, and it accelerated in the 1250s. It was occasioned by a fiscal logjam.[13] First, the period was one during which the king began to expend huge sums on artistic patronage, particularly that associated with Westminster Abbey's rebuilding.[14] Second, in 1242, during an ill-planned and ill-executed regional rebellion against the French king, Louis IX, Henry tried and failed for the last time in a costly £40,000 attempt to reconquer his Continental dominions.[15] Third, he increasingly bestowed honors and wealth, including heiresses, on the aliens in the country, especially the Poitevins.[16] Fourth, Magna Carta and indeed the whole panoply of good customs that the king formally and ritualistically espoused limited his willingness to try to raise money in ways that some of his predecessors had employed.[17] In

---

[11] Cf. Vincent, *Peter des Roches*, p. 443.

[12] Cf. Groot, "Early-Thirteenth-Century Criminal Jury," pp. 3–35.

[13] Substantial context is provided in Stacey, *Politics, Policy and Finance*.

[14] On the early stages of the thirteenth-century phase of the Westminster Abbey construction project from 1245 to 1259, see Binski, *Westminster Abbey and the Plantagenets*, pp. 13–29.

[15] Jordan, "Isabelle d'Angoulême," pp. 841–47; Powicke, *Thirteenth Century*, p. 103.

[16] Waugh, "Marriage, Class, and Royal Lordship," pp. 181–207; Carpenter, "King, Magnates, and Society," pp. 39–70.

[17] Waugh, *Lordship*, pp. 83–104; Stacey, *Politics, Policy and Finance*, pp. 201–37; Turner, *King and His Courts*.

particular, he or, rather, his agents could be grasping, but his government was never as arbitrary or as exacting as his father's had been in its financial practices, except possibly with regard to the exploitation of the Jews, which, not surprisingly, was particularly intense in the 1240s.[18] Perhaps the elements of the system of governance and domestic political relations could have been maintained in tremulous equilibrium despite these fiscal demands and constraints, but a fifth set of factors intervened in a powerful and determinative way. They can be summed up in one word, Sicily, or the *Regno* as it was also known.[19]

From the early days of the thirteenth century the popes were concerned with the possibility that a strong and potentially hostile Holy Roman Emperor might control not only the political and financial resources of Germania, but those of the Italian peninsula to the north and south of the Papal States and those of the island of Sicily.[20] Whoever controlled these resources could threaten the integrity of the Papal States and the freedom of the papacy itself. The emperor who had the best hereditary claims to these lands and who appeared—at least in the eyes of Popes Gregory IX (1227–1241) and Innocent IV (1243–1254)—to fulfill the worst of their forebodings in this regard was the Hohenstaufen Frederick II (1215–1250).[21] Intermittent violence between the emperor and the popes culminated in 1245 in the papacy's relocation to Lyon on the borders of medieval France, where it enjoyed the protective proximity of French military power. At the First Council of Lyon and in the same year Pope Innocent IV solemnly deposed the emperor. Since Frederick did not meekly accept his deposition, the pope looked for a secular champion to fight what he regarded as a just war—a Crusade—against the Hohenstaufen.[22]

Innocent's French protector, Louis IX, was unwilling to engage in hostilities, partly for juridical and moral reasons, for he was uncertain as to the legality and righteousness of the pope's deposition of Frederick.[23] His reluctance also stemmed partly from strategic considerations. The French king had recently made a commitment to go on Crusade to the eastern Mediterranean. Indeed, the Council of Lyon gave ecclesiastical blessing to his planned enterprise. War with the empire would have delayed, perhaps prevented, the Crusade, and a favorable outcome was far from certain in any case. Consequently, Pope Innocent IV needed to turn to others, in-

---

[18] Stacey, "Royal Taxation," p. 207; Carpenter, *Minority of Henry III*, p. 111.

[19] Weiler, *Henry III of England and the Staufen Empire*, pp. 147–71, provides the most up-to-date synthesis, but his assessment of the king's policy as essentially sound sometimes seems to me to involve special pleading.

[20] Abulafia, *Frederick II*, pp. 136, 164.

[21] Ibid., pp. 165, 368.

[22] Ibid., pp. 380–89; Jordan, *Louis IX*, pp. 26–29.

[23] Jordan, *Louis IX*, pp. 27–29.

cluding members of the French king's family, but in their case, too, pressure from Louis was sufficient to restrain them from seeking glory and the crowns that theoretically had become available as a result of the papal bull of deposition.[24] Moreover, pressure on Innocent IV continued to come from the French king to negotiate or compromise to end the imperial-papal strife, strife that did no good for what was seen as the Catholic powers' proper undertaking, armed resistance to Muslim advances in the Holy Land and its environs.[25]

When Louis IX went on Crusade in 1248, the situation was still unresolved. Nor did matters improve in 1250 when Frederick II died, for his family stubbornly but quite understandably refused to acquiesce in their disinheritance.[26] Papal intransigence or wherewithal (it depends on one's point of view) led to increasingly shrill denunciations of the whole Hohenstaufen family—a brood of vipers that had to be put down. Even the eventual failure of Louis IX's Crusade was by some laid in part at the dead emperor's door. He had done nothing to help Louis; and he was alleged to have connived to keep the French king, who was briefly taken prisoner in Egypt in 1250, in captivity, in order to give himself a free hand against the pope—free, that is, of the French ruler's meddling and verbal warnings.[27]

Louis IX returned from Crusade only in 1254. In the interval between the emperor's death and the French king's return, the pope continued to cast about for a champion to confront Hohenstaufen forces, in Italy in particular, where his own supporters and their mercenaries, backed by increasingly depleted papal funds, were sorely beleaguered. It was in these circumstances that Innocent IV and his successor Alexander IV (1254–1261) began assiduously to sound out the English as possible collaborators in the defense of the church against the viperous brood of Hohenstaufen threatening it.[28] King Henry III was under some pressure himself. He was supposed to go on Crusade, but though he had taken the vow in 1250, he had not done so. He reaped no prestige from this inactivity.[29]

These circumstances made the imperial business all the more intriguing and attractive—a just and holy war that promised a crown (though not all of Frederick's crowns; the pope's desire was that no one man should ever have such authority again) and the vast wealth and patronage accompanying the rule of a kingdom. In Henry III's case, the imperial

[24] Berg, "Manfred of Sicily and Urban IV," p. 120.
[25] For general background on the Crusades, see Riley-Smith, *Crusades*.
[26] Abulafia, *Frederick II*, pp. 410–14.
[27] Jordan, *Louis IX*, pp. 29–30.
[28] Powicke, *Thirteenth Century*, pp. 120–22.
[29] Tyerman, *England and the Crusades*, pp. 111–18.

business transmuted into the Sicilian business. After sensitive negotiations, the English king in 1254 accepted the Sicilian crown on behalf of his second son, Edmund. The climate of opinion in England was not entirely favorable to this new royal enthusiasm. "I do not think the king acts wisely" (*Jo ne quid ke li rois face sagement*), one English clerical poet wrote or, rather sang, around 1256: "He who seeks an example, / look to the king of France" (*Ke vot aver semblance, / regarde le rois de France*), who still refused to get involved or let his brothers get involved in the Sicilian business.[30]

Did Henry have any real sense of the possible complications and problems that would plague his decision? The Italian Franciscan chronicler Salimbene hinted that the English king was incapable of the systematic critical thought necessary to make informed choices.[31] And a modern interpreter, Simon Lloyd, was moved after his examination of the evidence to muse about the king's personality and abilities in foreign affairs in these words: "Henry's capacity to play for high stakes, yet lose" so often, was "truly remarkable."[32] Another has described the rather moody king as "always a slow learner."[33] Though more sympathetic in general to Henry than many other historians, even Carpenter and Stacey are harsh. The former describes the king as "impulsive, enthusiastic and ignorant of political realities."[34] The latter uses the word "inept" to characterize him and judges the Sicilian policy "utter lunacy."[35] Other scholars have rejected these judgments as too severe.[36] On one matter, nevertheless, there is universal consensus: the king of England underestimated the destructive repercussions of becoming involved in the tangle of Italian politics, diplomacy, and war.

All this was in the future in 1254. The delighted pope now had a champion to secure the prize of Sicily.[37] Henry agreed to guarantee the papacy's debts up to 135,000 marks, but payments were demanded more swiftly than they could be made, even with the enormous pressure put on the English church to contribute. If the debts were not paid, it was hard to imagine a Sicilian campaign being mounted. Henry's prolonged failure to fulfill his promise of aid, thus, could not sit well with the pope, and the threat of papal excommunication hung like the Damoclean sword above

---

[30] Wright, *Political Songs*, p. 44.

[31] Salimbene de Adam, *Cronica*, 1:445.

[32] Lloyd, "King Henry III, the Crusade and the Mediterranean," p. 119.

[33] Vincent, *Peter des Roches*, pp. 454–55, 463.

[34] Carpenter, *Minority of Henry III*, p. 390.

[35] Stacey, *Politics, Policy and Finance*, p. 258.

[36] Clanchy, "Did Henry III Have a Policy?" pp. 203–16; Weiler, "Henry III and the Sicilian Business," pp. 127–50; idem, "Henry III through Foreign Eyes," pp. 137–61.

[37] Powicke, *Thirteenth Century*, p. 122.

the English king's head.[38] Moreover, Henry's agents in Italy kept coming under pressure to make additional promises; total obligations, partly because of the accrual of interest, came to exceed the originally promised 135,000 marks.[39] The king's was a nasty chicken-and-egg conundrum. The conquest of Sicily would open the door to the appropriation of the island's wealth to the Plantagenet and papal cause, but the invasion of the *Regno* required spending money that Henry would not have at his disposal until after the invasion's success.[40]

Although the king continued to do his best to raise money and mollify the pontiff, accumulating the necessary resources was slow and got slower over time.[41] As early as 1257 it became excruciatingly clear that there was no way fully to achieve the crown's goal without recourse to a special general aid or levy—taxation—in England. In 1215 Magna Carta had mandated that the king receive consent to taxation from the common counsel of the realm. The chapter of the Great Charter that imposed consent was omitted in the official reissue of 1225 that became the standard text of the document, but it remained good law all the same.[42] If Henry was going to levy a tax, he was going to have to call a council of his magnates and barons, who, as he and his advisers were well aware, would use the occasion to air their own grievances against the government. It only added to the king's and the kingdom's misery that the years 1255–1258 were very bad in terms of weather, harvests, and high prices.[43] It was almost inevitable that the council would refuse the king's requests unless and until he answered some of their charges of bad governance.[44] One of their leaders was the powerful and influential Earl of Leicester, Simon de Montfort, the king's brother-in-law and erstwhile confidant.[45]

Already in May of 1258 the king, in order to secure a subsidy, agreed to the reform of the realm through a committee of twenty-four.[46] At Oxford in June 1258 the king and his party, which included his eldest son

---

[38] Lunt's chapter on Sicilian finances is very informative. I have necessarily simplified an extremely complex story. Lunt, *Financial Relations*, 1:255–90.

[39] Ibid., pp. 282 and 288.

[40] See, for example, ibid., p. 288: by the spring of 1258, "the most which [Henry III] would promise a cardinal who claimed to have spent in the promotion of Henry's Sicilian interests 2,000 marks not covered by the 135,541 marks was reimbursement from the revenues of Sicily when he should have obtained possession of the kingdom."

[41] Ibid., pp. 272–90.

[42] McKechnie, *Magna Carta*, pp. 233–34; Lyon, *Constitutional and Legal History*, pp. 385–88.

[43] Titow, *English Rural Society*, p. 97; Bridbury, "Thirteenth-Century Prices," p. 20.

[44] Treharne, *Baronial Plan of Reform*, pp. 1–69.

[45] On Simon de Montfort's relations with Henry III at this stage, see Maddicott, *Simon de Montfort*, pp. 154–62.

[46] Powicke, *Thirteenth Century*, p. 135.

and heir, Prince Edward, and the longtime abbot of Westminster, Richard de Crokseley, met with the barons in a great court or council, the famous Oxford Parliament. The barons made considerable demands, ultimately including the expulsion of aliens.[47] Henry reluctantly agreed, and the baronial plan of reform, the Provisions of Oxford, was born: at its heart were the principles articulated a half century before in Magna Carta.[48] The plan provided for the establishment of a council of fifteen to be appointed jointly by the king and the barons and intended to advise Henry on policy matters and practical matters of governance. It also called for the establishment of a committee of twelve, appointed by the barons alone, to meet with the council of fifteen regularly at full meetings, thrice a year, of the king's Parliament. The meetings' ostensible purpose was to give oversight to the work of the council of fifteen.

The Provisions enacted limitations on the powers of the heads of governmental departments, like the chancellor, and reinstituted the justiciar's office, which Hubert de Burgh had once held. Hubert had fallen out with the king in the early 1230s and was accused of an array of seditious crimes.[49] Although he managed to keep his estates until his death in 1243, Hubert was witness in 1234 to Henry's suppression of the justiciarship, long regarded as the highest office in the realm, for the justiciar, besides formally heading up the justice system implicit in his title, often served as the king's stand-in when the monarch was traversing his Continental lands in the twelfth and early thirteenth centuries.[50] The barons saw the reconstitution of the office and its occupation by an ally as an additional check on the king.[51]

There were many other chapters in the Provisions of Oxford. Sheriffs, for example, were to be selected from among provincial dignitaries, a clear attempt to localize power, but their terms were supposed to be limited to one year, as well. And they and other local officials were to undergo systematic regular investigation of their activities in office. With these and other reforms enacted, the committee of twenty-four agreed to consider the grant of an extraordinary aid for the Sicilian business.[52] Whether the royal humiliation would be redeemed by Sicily's conquest remained to be seen, but there was no doubt as to the reality of the humiliation in June

---

[47] Treharne, *Baronial Plan of Reform*, pp. 69–81; Powicke, *Thirteenth Century*, pp. 134–40.

[48] On the Provisions of Oxford, see Treharne, *Baronial Plan of Reform*, pp. 82–101. On the statute-like status of the Provisions, even though no official text survives, see Valente, "Provisions of Oxford," pp. 25–41.

[49] Carpenter, "Fall of Hubert de Burgh," pp. 1–17.

[50] West, *Justiciarship*.

[51] Treharne, *Baronial Plan of Reform*, pp. 90–91.

[52] Ibid., p. 100.

1258. Many of the so-called aliens and their allies rightly saw in the humbling of their royal patron a threat to their own physical welfare and fled the country.[53] Precious few in power seemed anymore to heed the distraught king.

The political history of France could not have been more different, although in a catalog of extraordinary triumphs for the crown there was to be one shattering disappointment. The triumphs began with the conquest of Normandy in 1204 and further victories by 1206 in other territories John of England claimed north of or bisected by the Loire River (including Maine, Anjou, and Touraine).[54] These conquests received military confirmation, after several years of de facto truce, in King Philip II Augustus's great victory at Bouvines on Sunday, 27 July 1214, when he defeated the coalition that King John had assembled from German allies for the northern front of a two-front war against the French.[55] Meanwhile, toward the southwest, on the second front, Philip's son and heir, the future Louis VIII, moved against King John's own forces. The English monarch beat a hasty retreat rather than fight a prolonged war. The price of his withdrawal to his island kingdom, as remarked earlier, was the rebellion that would produce Magna Carta and later a short and abortive French invasion led by Prince Louis.[56]

The minor setback of the unproductive invasion of England aside, the French went from triumph to triumph. King Philip undertook no further major military endeavors himself after 1214, either to seize lands held by the English south of the Loire or to take possession of territories in the deep south of the country where another confused situation did offer opportunities. There, in the deep south, northern Frenchmen had been involved since 1209 in a violent struggle on the papacy's behalf to dispossess those native political authorities who were regarded as protectors of the so-called Cathar heretics. Throughout southern France (Languedoc and Provence) "good men and women," as they were known, had been articulating beliefs and engaging in devotional practices that already in the middle of the twelfth century struck many prelates as heretical. Seeking to understand the present threat in terms of the heresies of the past, theologians identified certain beliefs of these rebels against the church as dualist or Manichaean.[57] It was not simply lack of success in countering the here-

---

[53] Ibid., p. 104.

[54] Baldwin, *Government of Philip Augustus*, pp. 191–96.

[55] Ibid., pp. 207–19; Duby, *Legend of Bouvines*.

[56] On Magna Carta, see above. On Louis's invasion, see Sivéry, *Louis VIII*, pp. 133–95.

[57] In general, see Lambert, *Cathars*, but one of the best correctives, separating what we know about the beliefs and activities of the good men and women and what orthodox churchmen and most later historians have imputed to them, is Pegg's *Corruption of Angels*.

tics by peaceful means that provoked a Crusade against them and their alleged protectors in 1209, but a series of incidents, culminating in the murder of a papal legate, that did. Pope Innocent III blamed the greatest lord in the south, Count Raymond VI of Toulouse, for the murder (a charge the count always denied) and implicitly for the failure of the various missions to prevent the slide away from orthodox Catholicism. With violence being used against the church, the pontiff believed himself justified in retaliating with a holy war, the Albigensian Crusade, so named from the town of Albi, regarded as a particular hotbed of heresy.[58] Innocent III promised that those who took part in the war on the papal side (these turned out to be mainly northern Frenchmen) would benefit spiritually and materially from their commitment.

Philip Augustus made modest gestures in support of the war, and his son more vigorous ones, but neither the French nor the English, who were not indifferent to heresy in and about their remaining Continental lands, committed significant resources at this stage.[59] Thus initially and for several years thereafter the military situation in the south was under the command of northern French barons, most importantly Simon de Montfort (the elder) and, after his death in 1218, his son Amaury. Simon enjoyed significant temporary successes, and at the Fourth Lateran Council of 1215 the pope recognized his ascendancy by deposing Raymond VI and vesting the county of Toulouse and its extensive lands in Simon's hands. However, the military situation degenerated after the close of the council, as Raymond of Toulouse's heir and namesake steadily made inroads against the northern occupiers. By 1223, a year after his father's death and his own formal recognition by his supporters as Count Raymond VII, he had managed to recoup most of his father's losses. Raymond VII also proclaimed his orthodoxy (not that his father had ever acknowledged his heresy or his support of heretics, despite the papacy's charges against him). The situation became so precarious that, hopeless for his personal cause, Amaury de Montfort ultimately ceded his rights in his father's conquests to the new Capetian king, Louis VIII, in January 1226.

Louis VIII accomplished two great feats in his short reign, 1223–1226.[60] First, he renewed the hot war with England in 1224, conquering a significant swath of territories south of the Loire, including Poitou and its borderlands. He made feints even further into the southwest but for

---

[58] For narrative treatments of the war(s), consult Strayer, *Albigensian Crusades*, and Sumption, *Albigensian Crusade*. See also, Pegg, *Most Holy War*.

[59] For Philip, see Baldwin, *Government of Philip Augustus*, pp. 336–39; for Louis, see Sivéry, *Louis VIII*, pp. 129–31, 206–10. Cf., on England, Vincent, "England and the Albigensian Crusade," pp. 67–97.

[60] Sivéry, *Louis VIII*, pp. 239–60, 363–400.

strategic and tactical reasons did not pursue the conquest of the duchy of Aquitaine and its cities, the last great territory in France under English control. Even without seizing Aquitaine, he added thousands of square kilometers to his father's conquests before calling off the campaign. His second achievement was the enforcement of his newly acquired rights in the deep south. Following Amaury's concessions he became the head of the Albigensian Crusade and in a brilliant campaign in 1226 succeeded in inflicting a string of defeats that effectively brought large parts of Languedoc under the French crown's direct control. When Louis VIII died on 8 November 1226 still on campaign, none of these conquests— in the west or south—was absolutely assured. Everything depended on the new king, Louis IX, a boy of twelve, and his mother, Blanche of Castile, the regent.

Faced with resentments over the fact that the dying Louis VIII had assigned the regency to a Spaniard—and a woman at that—and widespread sentiment that a boy king would succumb to a self-aggrandizing aristocratic faction, those who wanted to assure the succession had their work cut out for them.[61] The history of the next several years was fraught with plots, yet the government consistently managed either to disrupt them by playing one faction off against another or, when deflection and appeasement were impossible, using force selectively but effectively to frustrate the plotters. Those French aristocrats who wanted to upend the late king's arrangements were stymied at every turn, and Louis IX under Queen Blanche's tutelage emerged as a decisive and capable ruler as he approached manhood.

Nor were the achievements of conquest in the west or south overturned in this period. The English failed to mount any effective counteroffensive to win back lands either south or north of the Loire. Their most powerful potential ally, Count Raymond VII of Toulouse, even came to recognize that the best hope of retaining his title and at least some portion of his ancestral lands was to compromise with the Capetians. The French royal army's relative success in Languedoc, despite Louis VIII's death, in overcoming native insurgencies and in thwarting more organized resistance made this choice grow all the more attractive to Raymond. And the prospect, on the French side, of ending the Albigensian Crusade, with an agreement favorable to it, even one that recognized the count of Toulouse's retention of a large though much reduced block of lands, was also attractive. The end result was the Treaty of Meaux-Paris of 1229.

The year 1229 thus saw a large area of southern France come under direct Capetian administration.[62] While Raymond VII's principal patri-

[61] Richard, *Saint Louis*, pp. 36–49.
[62] Ibid., pp. 96–101.

mony, the county of Toulouse, was formally recognized by treaty as his of right, the count nevertheless lost to the crown and to other princes and lords considerable lands his father had once held, including large territories in Provence. He also had to agree that his heir, a girl, Jeanne, would marry Louis IX's younger brother, Alphonse. Such a marriage, in the best-case scenario for the French crown, presaged an eventual Capetian, though not necessarily royal, succession in the county of Toulouse. It is a matter of debate whether Count Raymond VII thought these agreements were written in stone, or just felt that he would have to bide his time until more favorable circumstances allowed him to renegotiate or wholly undo them.

The French crown found it costly to keep armies in the field to resist possible English military action and to pacify the south, while at the same time performing the routine tasks of governance and practicing the traditional largesse that bound aristocratic groups and ecclesiastics to the dynasty. One way of raising the money needed was the imposition of confiscatory taxation on the Jews.[63] Jews in France belonged to the great lords, and the greatest of the lords, the lord with the most Jews, tens of thousands of Jews, was the king. Philip Augustus had once expelled the Jews from royal lands, at a time very early in his reign when his direct lordship extended over a small geographical region. Sixteen years later, in 1198, he reversed his decision, permitting Jews to resettle in the royal domain. With the considerable expansion of direct royal rule through the conquests in the west and south in the next three decades, new and large Jewish populations also came under the crown's *dominium* either in direct subjugation or indirectly by the subjection of their Catholic lords to Capetian authority.

It was the Jews under the crown's direct *dominium* who were periodically obliged to render to the royal fisc their assets from moneylending to Christian debtors. Typically, royal agents seized the Jews' bonds and fiscal registers, sometimes discounted the loans recorded in them by one-third, regarded as excessive interest or usury (so the holy monarchy of France was not besmirched in this respect), and made the debts payable to the royal fisc. Often enough, the Jews' other liquid assets—money, plate, and jewels—were appropriated to the fisc as well in what were known as *captiones*, takings. The French government had numerous sources of revenue from feudal dues to sales taxes; and it could count on enormous yearly revenues in normal times. War and putting down civil strife, however, put extraordinary demands on any government, as Henry III in England was also well aware, so that recourse to the confiscation of Jewish wealth was

[63] For the information provided in the next several paragraphs, see Jordan, *French Monarchy and the Jews*, pp. 128–32.

conceived as legitimate and, however conceived, was a great fiscal benefit. It was certainly one of the most important factors in securing the regency in the difficult early years of Louis IX's reign.

Yet there is no doubt that in royal circles there was continuing concern about benefiting from a business, usurious moneylending, that was in itself sinful. Once the government defeated initial resistance to the regency—and, even more important, once the ratification of the Treaty of Meaux-Paris appeared to assure real continuity between the achievements of the monarchy in the past and its hopes for the future—royal councilors in consultation with the king and his mother took stock of the relationship of France, conceived as a holy Catholic kingdom, and the Jews' status within it. The year 1230 saw a great meeting of the secular and ecclesiastical barons and the king's publication of an edict or statute, the Ordonnance of Melun, to which they subscribed and which absolutely forbade lending money at interest in the realm.[64] It did not forbid pawnbroking, but reduced the profits for Jews by essentially turning it into a used-goods business in which the proprietor of a pawnshop could make a profit only if the pledge left with him failed to be redeemed within the specified time. It then became his to sell. The statute went on to stigmatize as rebels any Christian lords in France who defied these provisions by continuing to allow Jews to lend money at interest.

Anti-Jewishness and its counterpart, the continuing effort to hallow the dynasty and kingdom, and attempts to harness the nobility to the political vision of the crown persisted hand in hand in the 1230s and 1240s, sometimes perhaps fortuitously, at other times because of substantive connections among royal policies. In 1239 the king, who was ruling in his own name but still with his mother as his closest adviser, solemnly received into France the precious Passion relic, the Crown of Thorns, that had been in the possession of the Byzantine emperors since the first mention of the relic in a nonsacred or semisacred text.[65] The Latin emperor, Baldwin II (1228–1261), who now ruled precariously in Constantinople, which the Franks had conquered during the Fourth Crusade in 1204, needed money in general and needed to pay off his Italian creditors in particular. Thus he agreed to let his cousin, the French king, redeem the Crown of Thorns, which the imperial government had pledged to merchants. In France elaborate efforts were undertaken to craft a liturgical and symbolic interpretation of the relic's presence, one that would leaven the already considerable sacred mythology of the kingdom. France, symbolized by the lily, for example, was now a lily among thorns, to mention a trope that was adopted

---

[64] Jordan, "Jews, Regalian Rights, and the Constitution," pp. 4–7; idem, *French Monarchy and the Jews*, pp. 132–33.

[65] Jordan, *Louis IX*, pp. 107–9; Le Goff, *Saint Louis*, pp. 140–46.

and adapted to this end.[66] Soon after the reception of the Crown and many other relics from the Byzantine hoard, the king made the decision to build a sanctuary especially for them. It would take years to complete but would be consecrated in April 1248 as the Sainte-Chapelle, a splendid and costly Gothic architectural reliquary erected next to the royal palace on the Ile de la Cité in Paris.[67]

The aggressive Catholicity of the monarchy was further instanced in 1240, when, responding to a request of Pope Gregory IX, the government summoned northern French rabbis to answer charges that the Talmud contained slurs against Christianity and silly fables that offended the truths of the Bible—so an apostate from Judaism had informed the pontiff.[68] After the investigation in Paris and what appears to have been some disagreement about the extent of the material in the Talmud that could be interpreted as absurd or as denigrating Christ, Mary, and the tenets of the Catholic faith, the French government ordered the burning of as many copies of the work as possible, an act accomplished in 1242.

It was almost precisely at this time that the crown had to face another rebellion. Louis VIII had intended to provide for his younger sons by assigning appanages when they came of age, territories whose revenues would allow them to rule as great lords and thereby help administer the realm.[69] Louis IX and his mother saw to the application of the late king's wishes. In 1237 Louis IX's brother Robert received the northern county of Artois as his appanage. In 1241 Alphonse was invested with the county of Poitou, one of the western conquests. And in 1246 Charles received two more conquered western territories, the counties of Anjou and Maine. Although some technical implications of the transfer remained unclear, as was bound to be the case with any new jurisdictional and fiscal arrangement like the appanage system, Artois's transfer to Robert went quite smoothly in terms of what was really critical, the politics of the process. Artois, of course, was an older part of the royal domain lands, not a region that had come under direct royal domination as a result of a relatively recent and bitter war.

Poitou's transfer was different—and potentially so would be that of Anjou and Maine—for the barons of these counties had not necessarily shed their loyalty to the Plantagenets who still claimed overlordship. Even if loyalty was fairly weak toward the former rulers, as it most probably was, local barons also had personal grievances against the Capetians. The

[66] Mercuri, "*Stat inter spinas lilium*," pp. 497–512.

[67] Le Goff, *Saint Louis*, pp. 146–48.

[68] Jordan, "Marian Devotion and the Talmud Trial," pp. 61–76; idem, *French Monarchy and the Jews*, pp. 137–41.

[69] Wood, *French Apanages*, is comprehensive.

experience of being conquered in the campaigns of 1202–1206, 1214, and 1224, no matter what the barons' basic inclinations, inevitably created ripe soil for disputes with the new overlord. Moreover, Capetian kingship, which constructed itself increasingly as sacred, put implicit if vague constraints on local barons' freedom of action. One need only think back to the Ordonnance of Melun that declared any magnate who disobeyed the regulations on Jewish life and status to be a rebel. The claim to superiority implicit in the ordinance is the reason that legal historians have come to regard it as a statute, perhaps the first real piece of legislation in Frankish history since around Charlemagne's time.

At first, Poitou's transformation into an appanage in 1241 and the transfer of authority over it from the crown to Louis IX's brother Alphonse seemed to go smoothly.[70] Barons who were to come under the new order were invited to attend a great festival at the castle town of Saumur to celebrate the transition and to swear allegiance to Alphonse as the new count. They did so with alacrity and displays of good feeling. But resentments rose to the surface soon afterward, in part instigated by King John's widow and Henry III's mother, Isabelle d'Angoulême, who had been forced to return to the Continent on her husband's death. It was Isabelle's several children from her remarriage who would become the alien beneficiaries of enormous and envied amounts of largesse from Henry III. At this juncture Isabelle inspired her husband, Hugues de la Marche (son of the original fiancé from whom John had snatched her), to join with a number of other disgruntled magnates and rebel against Louis IX. It was this conspiracy that Henry III decided to join; Count Raymond VII of Toulouse and other southern barons also thought of joining and in some cases did.

Efforts to stave off a violent confrontation were unsuccessful. The French—regarding the rebellion, let alone the intervention of Henry III and a few other barons, as nothing less than an attempt to unwrite the triumphant history of the last forty years—sent an army as numerous as the locusts of the air and led by Louis IX himself to overwhelm the enemy. It did so in a brilliant series of campaigns in the early summer of 1242 that not only humiliated the opposition militarily (chivalrous though the French forces were in allowing them honorable withdrawal), but also scared many as yet wavering barons into maintaining their neutrality or even supporting the Capetians. The rebellion was crushed. Alphonse became the unchallenged count of Poitou, and a few years later Charles the unchallenged count of Anjou and Maine. The triumphs of the great and holy French monarchy seemed never ending.

[70] On the events being narrated in the text, see Jordan, "Isabelle d'Angoulême," pp. 842–48, and Richard, *Saint Louis*, pp. 136–41.

The tribulations, on the other hand, of the distant Crusader States—the
Latin East—seemed equally ceaseless, and the long tradition of French
participation in the Crusades worked its magic on the still youngish king
of France.[71] News of the ravaging of Jerusalem in 1244 by Khorazmian
Turks focused Louis IX's attention on the East. His recuperation from a
near fatal illness late in the year persuaded him that his prayers for a return
to health had been answered, and those prayers included a vow to go on
Crusade. Not everyone was pleased with his decision. In particular, his
mother was in despair in what was the first important public disagreement
between them.

It is likely, though, that they had not always seen eye to eye before 1244.
For instance, historians have surmised that they differed in their attitude
about the necessity of burning the Talmud, and they also disagreed on
the household role of Louis's wife, Marguerite de Provence, whom he
had married in 1234.[72] The marriage was a political one, encouraged and
arranged by the king's mother, but Blanche disliked Marguerite (a sentiment returned in full), while Louis, at this point in his life, found his
wife to be quite pleasing. To be sure, he later came to have misgivings
about Marguerite's political instincts and judgment. She was the sister
of Eleanor of Provence, whom Henry III married in 1236, which perhaps gave these misgivings greater weight at this historical moment.
Moreover, as Louis IX matured and became ever more penitential in his
piety, Queen Marguerite changed less dramatically in the externals of her
devotions and to some extent regretted aspects of her husband's devotional journey or, rather, the material manifestations of it, like his disdain
for exquisite clothing.[73]

Neither the alleged disagreements between Louis and his mother over
the fate of the Talmud nor their personal differences about Marguerite,
however, had much publicity at the time. Louis's barons still harbored the
impression that the king was firmly under his mother's guidance when her
vocal but ineffective opposition to the Crusade became public knowledge.[74] She engaged the bishop of Paris, Guillaume d'Auvergne, an erudite
theologian and former professor, to caution her son that a vow taken while
under the strain of physical suffering was not necessarily binding. Instead
of using this as a way to repudiate the intent of the vow, however, the
recuperated Louis reswore it. One of the more gossipy chroniclers delighted in describing the emotional and tearful scenes in which Blanche
later implored her son to remain in France and attempted frenetically to

---

[71] Richard, *Saint Louis*, pp. 159–80, and, for further background and context, Phillips,
"Latin East," pp. 112–40.

[72] The most comprehensive biography of Louis's queen is Sivéry's *Marguerite de Provence*.

[73] Jordan, "Case of Saint Louis," pp. 215–16.

[74] Jordan, *Louis IX*, p. 5.

restrain him from leaving the kingdom when preparations were complete in 1248. It is clear that Louis, who departed anyway, had a great deal at stake in going on Crusade: the honor and glory of the French kingdom, the tradition of his crusader ancestors (Louis VII, Philip II Augustus, and Louis VIII), his own recognition as a champion of holy church, and, using modern terminology, coming into his own as an adult.[75]

The period from the taking of the crusader's vow until the departure for Crusade was packed with activity.[76] The Sainte-Chapelle was being built at enormous cost after the already enormous monetary outlay for the relics that it was to enshrine; one estimate is that the total expenditure was about 100,000 l. t. An almost completely new port was being constructed in the south at Aigues-Mortes in part to facilitate the embarkation of the crusaders—and this created another enormous financial demand on the crown.[77] Former rebels were encouraged to take the crusader's vow, rather than stay behind and do mischief in the king's absence; encouragement sometimes took the form of cash advances to help pay for their Crusade contingents and pressure on them from the Inquisition to do penance.[78] Efforts were made both to persuade Henry III to renounce the idea of attacking France while Louis was abroad and to take the crusader's vow himself, while at the same time stockpiles were accumulated in the western territories, like those recently in rebellion, to be available just in case either a nativist uprising or an English invasion became a reality during Louis's absence.[79]

Meanwhile, less costly but time-consuming and anxious undertakings were also dominating French royal circles. Royal demesne towns (communes) were cajoled into offering monetary aid to the looming holy war, as were seigneurial towns to their lords.[80] Louis responded positively to aristocratic demands that he lobby the pope to restrain ecclesiastical encroachments on their jurisdiction and, evidently, the use of mendicant friars as fiscal agents.[81] He did so probably on principle but also obviously to secure aristocratic support for the Crusade.[82] Envoys acting in Louis's

---

[75] Ibid., pp. 3–13.

[76] Ibid., pp. 14–110; Richard, *Saint Louis*, pp. 181–204.

[77] Jehel, *Aigues-Mortes*, is comprehensive, if sometimes jumbled.

[78] Maier, *Preaching the Crusades*, p. 69.

[79] Jordan, "Cutting the Budget," pp. 307–18; idem, *Louis IX*, pp. 25–26.

[80] On the royal communes, see Sivéry, *Capétiens et l'argent*, pp. 140–44. On seigneurial towns—in this case, the Auvergnat urban policy of Louis's brother Alphonse—see Teyssot, "Mouvement communal," p. 203.

[81] The so-called Protest of Saint Louis of 1247; Maier, *Preaching the Crusades*, pp. 129–30.

[82] Aristocratic support was very considerable (Jordan, *Louis IX*, pp. 18–24, 66–68), but less so among the Bretons than I estimated (p. 67); see the corrective provided in Jones, "Les Bretons et les croisades," pp. 371–72.

behalf tried with uneven success to convince other princes, like the king of Norway, to contribute to the Crusade, but it was always the case that a great many more rulers made plans to go on Crusade than actually went.[83] Efforts to broker peace between the papacy and Emperor Frederick II, however, enjoyed no success at all.[84] Not even secret face-to-face discussions between Louis and Pope Innocent IV brought about any significant softening of papal policy toward the emperor, despite Frederick's often expressed willingness, whether genuine or not, to join the French monarch's expedition.[85] Frederick would not commit resources before the fact of reconciliation, the lifting of his excommunication, and the annulment of his deposition.

Louis IX's government cut costs everywhere possible in the colossal effort to raise an army, secure shipping, build the port, finish the Sainte-Chapelle, and do all the other business a medieval principality was supposed to do.[86] At the pope's command it got fundamental financial help from the French church.[87] The king himself also authorized a thoroughgoing investigation of the realm in 1247, the intention being to streamline administration and make it more effective fiscally, and to atone for injustices that royal officials had accidentally or deliberately committed against his subjects during his reign. The results of these extraordinary investigations, largely but not exclusively carried out by nonadministrators, Franciscan and Dominican friars and a few other men without any obvious self-interest in hiding the administration's failings, were sobering. The king discovered that levels of corruption, inefficiency, cronyism, and brutality were higher than he had imagined.[88] It was revealed that there was a deep well of resentment against government, particularly its failure to restrain Jewish moneylending, which, because of bribery of local officials, appeared to be flourishing throughout the country despite the legislation of 1230. Louis fired or forced the retirement of several administrators in 1247 and 1248, transferred others, sent troubleshooters into

---

[83] For Louis's solicitation of Norway and the broad context of Norwegian foreign policy at this time, see Gelsinger, "Thirteenth-Century Norwegian-Castilian Alliance," pp. 55–80. For further illustrations of unfulfilled plans, see also Rodríguez García, "Henry III (1216–1272), Alfonso X of Castile (1252–1284) and the Crusading Plans of the Thirteenth Century," pp. 99–120.

[84] Kienast, *Deutschland und Frankreich*, 3:609–13.

[85] Baaken, "Verhandlungen von Cluny (1245)," pp. 531–79.

[86] Jordan, "Cutting the Budget," pp. 307–18. See also Murray, *Notre-Dame Cathedral of Amiens*, p. 76.

[87] Jordan, *Louis IX*, pp. 79–82. Whether churchmen desired to or even thought it fair that they should contribute may be doubted; see Buc, *Ambiguïté du Livre*, pp. 279–80.

[88] Jordan, *Louis IX*, pp. 46–63; idem, *French Monarchy and the Jews*, pp. 133–37, 144–46; Sivéry, "Mécontentement dans le royaume de France," pp. 3–4; Bartlett, "Impact of Royal Government," pp. 83–96.

those provinces most poorly governed, reimbursed enormous numbers of petitioners, and cracked down hard and systematically on Jewish money-lenders—all to cleanse himself and his government of the pollution that came from failing to provide justice. How could the Crusade but succeed under such circumstances?

Despite his mother's unhappiness with his going on the expedition, she served as regent in his absence, since his brothers, otherwise likely candidates for the job, accompanied him. He left his eldest son, still a young boy, and his other children behind with Blanche in Paris. Yet Louis took his wife Marguerite along with him. One might speculate that this is evidence of his concern that the two women had to be kept apart to avoid disruption at the court. That he obliged his spouse to leave her children behind in the care of their grandmother, a woman she so disliked (even though Louis's more friendly sister, Isabelle de France, would also be there) could also be seen as another step in what would be an ever-increasing personal distance between the king and his wife.

The Sainte-Chapelle was new to the spiritual landscape in 1248 but was incorporated into the rituals that accompanied the king's departure on Crusade.[89] The Crown of Thorns was exposed to elite and possibly nonelite faithful at the chapel dedication ceremony in late April of the year.[90] The real focus of ceremonial action, however, remained the traditional site outside the city at the royal abbey of Saint-Denis. So, after solemnly receiving the purse (scrip) and staff of a pilgrim at Notre-Dame cathedral in Paris, Louis processed barefoot the few kilometers to the abbey. It was there on 12 June 1248 that, having taken communion, he received the pilgrim's sash and took up the *oriflamme*, the battle flag, from the patron and martyr's tomb amid his entourage's shouts of *Montjoie Saint-Denis! Montjoie Saint-Denis!* Mount Joy—symbolically, Zion. Hardly could an acclamation have been more appropriate.[91]

This solemn association of the French crown and Zion, the Holy Land, made the failure of the king's Crusade and his brief captivity even harder

[89] On the relevance of the Sainte-Chapelle's decorative motifs to the joint theme of righteous kingship and crusading, see the excellent and wide-ranging study of Alyce Jordan, *Visualizing Kingship*.

[90] Billot, "Saintes-Chapelles," pp. 229–48, emphasizes the traditional view of the Sainte-Chapelle of Paris as a private aristocratic family chapel, which it certainly was, like many other similar saintes-chapelles, but Cohen has shown ("Indulgence for the Visitor") that the public nature of the royal chapel and its attendant open spaces has gone unappreciated because of architectural modifications that for a long time have masked this aspect of the building.

[91] A lavish treatment of the slogan and its relation to the cult of Saint Denis is Lombard-Jourdan's *"Montjoie et saint Denis!"* See also her "Munjoie," pp. 35–64, and "'Montjoies,'" pp. 65–98.

to bear. Louis had traveled south paralleling the Rhône River before heading west for the port of Aigues-Mortes. Many other French crusaders and their contingents joined him; still others arrived later or left from different ports. They rendezvoused at the island of Cyprus, where supplies had been accumulating for two years, and made preparations for an amphibious landing in Egypt.[92] Their strategy, a wise one, was to disable Egypt, perhaps even conquer it, which would effectively eliminate one of the greatest threats to the Crusader States' survival.[93]

When their preparations were complete, the French launched their invasion and on 6 June 1249 met with initial success, conquering the port city of Damietta. After securing the city, they decided to defer any major advance for several months, an interval that promised to bring additional men and matériel. It was early the next year that the army proceeded up the Nile, only to be outfought by their Muslim opponents in a series of engagements that lasted until April 1250. Louis's brother Count Robert of Artois died at Mansurah in the campaign, and Louis and the survivors of his army were captured. Queen Marguerite, back in Damietta, rallied those who wanted to abandon the city when they heard the news. She did so even though she had just given birth to a baby boy, Jean, Jean Tristan because he was born in *tristesse*, sadness. Her success in stabilizing the situation in Damietta was crucial. The Muslims wanted Damietta back—preferably without a fight. Disputes among Muslim leaders opened the way to negotiations and ransom—money for the release of Louis's troops and Damietta for the king himself. All was arranged within the first weeks after the defeat. Then Louis and his now far smaller army departed Egypt (6 May 1250) and sailed to the Crusader States where he spent four years doing his best with reduced resources to shore up their defenses and heal the internal political struggles that were plaguing them.

Back home in France word of the king's defeat and his captivity provoked a kind of popular Crusade in 1251, which briefly appears to have had Blanche of Castile's support, but as it spent itself in class violence in France she suppressed the so-called Shepherds who constituted it.[94] Her other living sons, Alphonse and Charles, also released from captivity, did not remain in the Holy Land with their elder brother but returned to France. They made gestures, perhaps sincere gestures, to return to their brother with help, but failed to do so. Alphonse suffered from a serious eye ailment, relieved only by a Jewish doctor's intervention. Charles got himself involved in a succession struggle in Flanders and Hainaut that he hoped would win him the latter fief. He even managed to secure large

[92] Dianoux de la Perrotine, "Saint Louis à Chypre," pp. 13–16.

[93] Richard, *Saint Louis*, pp. 215–16.

[94] Kerov, *Narodnye vosstaniia*, pp. 42–51; Barber, "Crusade of the Shepherds," pp. 1–23. Cf. Beaune, "Messianesimo regio e messianesimo popolare," pp. 114–36.

loans and gifts from northern French towns for the undertaking, money that was therefore not available to refinance the Crusade, although the towns managed both before and during the Crusade to raise enormous sums for the king's expedition.[95]

Through all this period England was largely an absent actor. Fears that Henry III might choose to exploit Louis's desperate plight abroad or disturbances at home, like the rising of the Shepherds or, in late 1252, the regent Blanche of Castile's death, were never realized. Perhaps in addition to Henry's taking the crusader's vow in 1250 the participation of a contingent of Englishmen on Louis IX's expedition was a factor that deterred him from deciding to launch an invasion of France.[96] Nevertheless, it did become clear to the crusaders in the Holy Land that they could not remain there forever. The news that Blanche was dead did not reach the French king until mid-1253, almost six months after her death. A deeply shaken Louis IX decided he had to return to France. There was still business to finish and arrangements for the Crusader States to be made, but when these were completed, he embarked. The remnants of the great army that had departed Europe in 1248 with such hope landed in Provence in the early summer of 1254 with a king at their head who accepted responsibility for the disaster. He was a sinner, and he had to atone, because he intended to try again and fulfill his—and France's—God-ordained role as defender of Christendom.[97]

From 1254 on, Louis IX, historians agree, set himself on a path of penitential kingship, but this does not mean that the chief features of his rule were his religious devotions. True, he was assiduous in his practice of the Catholic faith.[98] He incorporated into his devotions rituals—like allowing himself to be whipped with chains and getting up several times a night for prayers—that his friends thought were extreme and his detractors thought were absurd and unkingly. Yet this new Joseph the Patriarch, new Moses, new Solomon, and new Josiah, to name a few of many images his behavior evoked, also spent an extraordinary amount of time governing his kingdom.[99] His activity in this regard, by almost any

[95] Jordan, "Communal Administration in France," pp. 293–94.

[96] On the English contingent and Henry's vow, see Tyerman, *England and the Crusades*, pp. 109–16. See also Maier, *Preaching the Crusades*, pp. 150–51.

[97] Cf. Schneidmüller, *Nomen Patriae*, pp. 122–23, 208; Le Goff, "Saint Louis and the Mediterranean," pp. 21–43.

[98] Le Goff, "Saint Louis et le prière," pp. 85–94.

[99] For the images, see Jordan, "Psalter of Saint Louis," pp. 65–91; idem, "The 'People' in the Psalter of Saint Louis," pp. 13–28; Le Goff, "Royauté biblique," pp. 157–67; idem, "Roi dans l'Occident," p. 4; idem, "Coronation Program," pp. 46–57; Guest, "The People Demand a King," pp. 1–27; Weiss, "Three Solomon Portraits," pp. 15–36; idem, "Biblical History and Medieval Historiography," pp. 710–37; idem, "Architectural Symbolism," pp. 308–20; and Jordan, "Seeing Stories in the Windows of the Sainte-Chapelle," p. 47.

measure, would be considered obsessive and compulsive, although it was a commonplace that a king, even a sinful king, who treats his subjects well will have God's aid in governance.[100]

Relations between the two kingdoms, England and France, and the two kings, Henry III and Louis IX, had something of an unresolved quality about them in the decade of the 1250s, which any serious observer would have noticed. The most striking anomaly was the war, in that it was now a war in name only. And yet, the long truces notwithstanding, it was the pervasive suspicion and hostility between the two realms that remained powerful, occasionally acute, and almost wholly sterile. Henry's desire to win Sicily and Louis's to relieve the Holy Land made the animosity between their two countries doubly counterproductive. Neither ruler could realistically hope to achieve his goal in the absence of a resolution of the fundamental issue, the war. It was a fact of life, too, that as long as the war remained unconcluded, all sorts of other problems would continue to evade solution and would thereby have a destabilizing impact on many other weighty aspects of the history of the two realms. We shall have to return to this matter in chapter 3. Now, however, it is time to look away from the centers of political power and authority and refocus on the other major actors in this story, two churchmen, and also on the two ecclesiastical institutions that helped shape their lives.

---

[100] Montgomery, *Chastoiement*, pp. 43 and 150–51 (lines 3859–68). For details on his governance in the latter period of his reign, see below, chapter 4.

II

TWO GREAT MONASTERIES

AND TWO YOUNG MEN

T HE YEAR 1258 ushered in dramatic changes in the lives of Brother
Mathieu de Vendôme and Brother Richard de Ware. Mathieu,
probably the slightly older of the two men, was born around 1222
in Vendôme, a castle town and capital of a seigneurie in western France
about two hundred kilometers southwest of the village of Saint-Denis.
There is no direct evidence that he was of the noble line of the counts of
Vendôme, which is almost proof positive that he was not. Nevertheless,
local enthusiasts have long asserted his kinship to the comital family, and
at least one of the commune's Web sites advertises the supposed relationship as fact.[1] After many years as a simple monk, Mathieu became abbot
of Saint-Denis in 1258 at age thirty-six.[2] Why did he choose—or why was
he invited—to become a monk in the first place at a house so far from his
birthplace, and why had such an elite institution embraced him, if one
cannot invoke his nobility of birth as the factor trumping geography?

The likeliest possibility is that as a boy Mathieu was enchanted by the
cult of Saint Denis (Dionysius in Latin)—the first bishop of Meaux and
thereafter the first bishop of Paris—as a result of youthful visits to one of
the martyred prelate's cult sites in Vendôme's neighboring village of
Thoré. The village and the parish church of Thoré, since 1060 in the
possession of the Benedictine monastery of La Trinité of Vendôme, had
earlier belonged to the abbey of Saint-Denis and retained their dedication
to Denis throughout the centuries to come. The church celebrated his
cult and probably had frescoes, a devotional art form widely distributed
in the Vendômois, depicting his legend.[3] Through this means the saint's
history and passion were known to locals, all of whom had access to the

---

[1] http://www.francebalade.com/vendome/ctvendome.htm. The opinion, however, despite the absence of proof, goes back to the learned fathers of *Gallia christiana*, *GC*, vol. 7,
col. 391.

[2] On the date of his election, see the abbey's so-called chronicle *ad cyclos paschales* (*HF*,
23:144), and *GC*, vol. 7, col. 391. See also Carolus-Barré, *Procès de canonisation*, pp. 223–
24, and Richard, *Saint Louis*, p. 553.

[3] On the town, parish, and parish church of Thoré, see Saint-Venant, *Dictionnaire topographique . . . du Vendômois*, p. 434. On the prevalence of Romanesque wall painting in the
Vendômois, see Davy, "Connaissance de la peinture murale romane," pp. 35–41.

little church, and, if they captivated the boy, contributed to his desire to become a monk at Saint-Denis and his later assiduous efforts to enhance the martyr's cult at the royal abbey.[4] One other thing seems secure in this reconstruction: the Vendômois, according to Meredith Lillich's brilliant argument, stayed in Mathieu's thoughts the rest of his life. He may have professed at La Trinité, and it is to Mathieu that one should turn, still following Lillich, to explain later Capetian efforts to enhance the great monastery there.[5]

In any case, vivid and even a little creepy, the legends of Saint Denis most certainly would have captivated a pious boy. They told of how soldiers beheaded Denis and two companions, Rusticus and Eleutherius, in a persecution that local pagan priests instigated and the Roman governor carried out during imperial times. They recounted, too, how Denis's corpse carried its own severed head some distance to his and its burial place. Is it any wonder that the head-clutching martyr came to be invoked to relieve migraines?[6] The spot the corpse chose for his grave was on the outskirts of Paris. Local Christians, led by a woman named Catulla, soon erected a shrine dedicated to the martyr. Another pair of companions, Sanctinus and Antoninus, who evaded the persecutors but who saw the martyrdom and its remarkable aftermath, were said to have taken all this amazing news to the pope.

It was an added attraction of the legends by Mathieu de Vendôme's time that, despite Abelard's valid but largely unsuccessful historical criticism in the early twelfth century, Denis, in truth a third-century saint, was conflated with two other quite distinct persons with the same name. One was the first-century Greek convert from paganism whom the apostle Paul persuaded of the truth of the Christian faith on the Areopagus in Athens (Acts 17.34). The second was the fifth- or sixth-century Syrian, now known as the Pseudo-Areopagite, who claimed in his Greek-language mystical works to be the Pauline convert in order to give those works quasi-apostolic authority. It is unlikely that any of the skepticism about the identity of the head-carrying saint reached Mathieu while he was still a boy in Vendôme. Bright and an enthusiastic devotee of the famous martyr, and thus probably known by pilgrims to and by the keepers of Saint-Denis de Thoré who had contacts with the great abbey two hundred kilometers distant, the youth would have seemed a worthy recruit.

There is no certainty to this scenario, but in this or some other similar way Mathieu de Vendôme did come to the favorable attention of the prestigious community and was permitted to become a member. He was a

---

[4] Below, p. 34.
[5] Lillich, *Armor of Light*, pp. 241–50.
[6] *Lives of the Saints*, 10:111.

monk at Saint-Denis for a considerable period before his elevation to abbot. Toward the end of his life he recalled a time when King Louis IX visited the abbey to make an offering to its patron saint, and this had taken place a good decade before his election as head of the community.[7] He succeeded to the leadership of the abbey at a moment when the community, under the leadership of his predecessor, Henri Mallet (1254–1258), was beginning to get a reputation for lax discipline.[8] And Mathieu would be remembered in part as the man who reestablished order at the celebrated monastery.[9]

The village of Saint-Denis, a northern suburb of Paris, and the modest chapel-shrine first built there to honor the martyr and his companions became a famous pilgrimage site by Saint Geneviève's time (d. 512), more than one hundred years before the seventh-century founding of an abbey there, reputedly by the Frankish king Dagobert (628–639).[10] The first monks to take up residence rapidly accumulated privileges that made them and their monastery nearly free of all spiritual jurisdiction except the pope's, a status that would later be described as exemption. By a series of definitive eleventh- and twelfth-century papal confirmations, this status was and remained unassailable through the end of the Middle Ages.[11] As the abbey's renown grew and royal interest continued, there were periodic improvements in its facilities, including a building campaign in the eighth century intended to replace the first monastic church. Yet it was not until the abbacy of the justly famous Suger in the twelfth century that a radically remodeled church arose that set the monastic sanctuary apart from churches throughout Christendom.[12] For it was Suger's abbey church of Saint-Denis that has traditionally been regarded as the first full instantiation of what is now called the Gothic style.[13]

Saint-Denis became an immensely rich and influential monastery over the centuries.[14] This was in part on account of royal and aristocratic patrons who lavishly endowed it with rural properties, urban real estate, and

[7] He referred to Louis's visits before his Crusade of 1248–1254 and immediately thereafter in his testimony before commissioners appointed in 1282 to inquire into the king's sanctity (below, pp. 202–3). As the testimony the witnesses gave was ideally constituted of what they knew directly and immediately, Mathieu was already a monk at Saint-Denis in the middle 1240s (cf. Sivéry, *Philippe III*, p. 93).

[8] Bruzelius, *13th-Century Church*, p. 134; Carolus-Barré, *Procès de canonisation*, p. 224.

[9] Carolus-Barré, *Procès de canonisation*, p. 224.

[10] See Spiegel, *Chronicle Tradition of Saint-Denis*, p. 14, and, more generally, Lombard-Jourdan, *"Montjoie et saint Denis!"*

[11] Berkhofer, *Day of Reckoning*, pp. 42, 46, 60.

[12] The most comprehensive history of the church until Suger's death is Crosby's *Royal Abbey of Saint-Denis*.

[13] Panofsky, *Abbot Suger*, p. 36, for the classic formulation.

[14] Nebbiai dalla Guarda, "Des rois et des moines," p. 357.

money and precious objects. From the thirteenth century onward the abbey also organized a spiritual *confrérie* or confraternity of laypeople and ecclesiastics, who shared worship and prayers, and through whose connections the monks gained increased authority and greater ability to secure benefactions from the members' kin. This confraternity responded to an older one associated with the cathedral of Paris that restricted membership to only twelve people from Saint-Denis, six lay and six religious.[15] But, regardless of the insult of a quota on Saint-Denisiens enforced by a rival institution, such combined lay and ecclesiastical confraternities, spiritual in avowed purpose, but also financially beneficial, were common. Westminster Abbey had one too.[16]

Pilgrims' oblations were another major source of income for the monastery. A succession of formidable abbots, like Suger, consolidated estates and ran the abbey quite ably from a financial point of view, as recent scholarship has shown.[17] Because of its proximity to Paris, the abbey was also in the particularly fortunate position, economically speaking, of being adjacent to one of the densest concentrations of consumers in Western Europe. Saint-Denis, the town and abbey, serviced these consumers profitably. The services were concentrated in but not limited to the so-called royal fair of Lendit, a profitable entrepôt that from 1124 on was in the abbey's possession.[18]

True, many merchants made special demands of the Lendit fair (which had to be adjudicated by the crown in 1215) or preferred to do business in Paris and, thus, strove to obtain trading privileges within the city, rather than in suburban or slightly more distant fairs, of which there were a number like Saint-Denis's Lendit.[19] For Paris had emerged definitively as the capital city in the late twelfth century and grew enormously as a result.[20] Moreover, villagers and abbey alike in Saint-Denis suffered from the competition of the other suburban fairs and markets since local producers could choose from any number of sites as their principal sales outlet and did not always choose the abbey village. Effectively, indeed, this meant that merchants plying their wares at the Lendit fair came almost exclu-

[15] Lombard-Jourdan, "Confrérie de Saint-Denis," pp. 377–87.

[16] Below, chapter 4, p. 97.

[17] This is the thrust of Berkhofer's *Day of Reckoning*, which shows that the same efficiency and success attended both Saint-Denis and a number of neighboring Benedictine houses.

[18] Ibid., p. 68. To obtain a comprehensive picture of Saint-Denis's fairs, including Lendit, see Lombard-Jourdan, "Foires de l'abbaye de Saint-Denis," pp. 99–159, and idem, "Naissance d'une légende parisienne," pp. 161–78.

[19] On the royal adjudication, see Baldwin, *Government of Philip Augustus*, pp. 347–48. Another such fair was that at Pontoise; *Register of Eudes of Rouen*, p. 180.

[20] A useful recent history of medieval Paris is Roux, *Paris au moyen âge*. See also Baldwin, *Paris, 1200*.

sively from very nearby, a relatively small hinterland north of the Seine River and west of the Oise.[21] Still, the capital was simply so large, probably one hundred thousand in population on the eve of Mathieu's abbacy and steadily growing, that there was always a greater need for goods among the city's inhabitants than the municipal markets could provide.

There was also some specialization among the markets and fairs in the city and suburbs. Unmilled cereals tended to be marketed directly in Paris, while Saint-Denis's Lendit fair offered almost no commerce in such grains. The same can be said of financial services. These were much more significant in the city, with its numerous financiers and moneylenders, than in any of the suburban fairs, including Saint-Denis's, even though the abbey did have ownership over a few Jewish villagers who were money-lenders. Most likely, these Jews had sufficient resources to provide only small consumption loans in the mid-thirteenth century, however rich they may once have been.[22] The Lendit fair, more importantly, saw vending in and contracting for local artisans' metalwork and marketing in textiles and draft animals on a relatively modest scale. However, the chief products, and those on which, therefore, Saint-Denis collected most of its sales taxes during the fair, were closely tied to the Parisian population's consumption needs: clothing, flour, and meat, especially lamb, since parchment was also a main commodity furnished to stationers providing for the needs of the university.[23] Every sheep without its "parchment" was table food. Income was also generated from stall and booth charges, lodging rented by the abbey, and the profits of administering justice.[24]

Material wealth gave Saint-Denis heft, but the monastery was more than wealthy. It was unique in its relationship with the church at large and with the French crown. With regard to the church, exemption from episcopal jurisdiction distinguished Saint-Denis from many Benedictine monasteries, though by no means from all, but as they did with other exempt houses, popes used Saint-Denis as a preferred conduit at times to publish their bulls of protection of the crown and its privileges.[25] Yet, among monasteries in the West, it was one of very few that enjoyed a real reputation

[21] Cf. Fossier's analysis of the "Dit du Lendit," a late thirteenth-century poem on the fair, penned by what he calls "a talentless rhymester" (*un rimailleur sans talent*); *Histoire économique et sociale*, pp. 362–64.

[22] The best study is Graboïs, "Abbaye de Saint-Denis et les juifs," pp. 1187–95. On the weakening economic role of northern French Jews in general in the thirteenth century, see Jordan, *French Monarchy and the Jews*, pp. 92–176.

[23] For the evidence of the "Dit du Lendit" and Fossier's comments, which make the point about parchment, which is not stressed in the poem, see his *Histoire économique et sociale*, p. 364, and the *Atlas historique de Saint-Denis*, p. 390.

[24] *Atlas historique de Saint-Denis*, p. 389.

[25] *Layettes*, 4:28–29, 131, 181 nos. 4720, 4726, 5034, 5172.

among the Greeks. Denis, after all, according to the legends was a Greek saint—and it was he, reputedly the apostle Paul's disciple—who lay in France. The Greeks sent copies of the Areopagite's works to the abbey in the ninth century.[26] On their side, Saint-Denis's monks celebrated a Greek mass on the octave of their patron saint, 16 October. They continued to do so deep into the modern period, long after most of the few other French institutions known to have celebrated Greek masses gave up the practice.[27]

Details about the liturgical life, the real estate holdings, and the relations of Saint-Denis with other institutions are extensively recorded. The monastery's thick cartularies, for example, meticulously inscribe its gifts, along with a staggering number and variety of other acts. The *Cartulaire blanc*, the most famous of these, is the record of no fewer than twenty-six hundred transactions and memoranda (see figs. 1 and 2). An abundance of individual charters also set down in writing gifts made by aristocrats and bourgeois, the abbey's purchases and exchanges, and many other activities, making Saint-Denis, like Westminster, one of the best-documented institutions in medieval Europe. And these records show that its network of relations with different social groups from the crown right down to unfree peasants was intensive at every level.

And yet it was the crown, far more than any other group, that was preeminent in the abbey's relations. Kings—like Louis IX—regularly visited, but each year, in Mathieu's time, the ruler made one highly symbolic pilgrimage in order to offer the saint four *besants d'or*, Byzantine or Byzantine-imitation gold coins.[28] An appropriate oblation this was for the Greek holy man who protected France (in modern parlance, one would describe him as the realm's patron saint). This is also why French medieval kings who went to battle would come to the abbey to receive its ensign, the *oriflamme*, as their battle standard.[29] What better place, then, for the burial of the French kings and other members of the royal family than the abbey crypt: Saint-Denis, by Mathieu's time, had established itself as the principal royal necropolis.[30] The abbey scriptorium memorialized the royal line's deeds by writing the increasingly official histories of the kings and kingdom.[31] Finally, the great sanctuary also sheltered some of the

---

[26] Waldman, "Denis," p. 292.

[27] Robertson, *Service Books*, pp. 285–98.

[28] Sivéry, *Philippe III*, p. 41.

[29] Waldman, "Denis," p. 293. For a more comprehensive treatment of the *oriflamme*, see Lombard-Jourdan, *Fleur-de-lis*, pp. 152–61.

[30] Clark, "Saint-Denis," p. 838.

[31] Spiegel, *Chronicle Tradition of Saint-Denis*. The use of monasteries as archival depositories, closely related to the historiographical function, was commonplace for lay aristocrats and monarchs across Christian Europe: Crouch, "Norman 'Conventio,'" p. 299; Demurger, *Templiers*, p. 377.

most treasured items of French regalia—royal crowns, including the coronation crown, the sword and sheath used in the rite of royal consecration, and the golden spurs, gilded scepter, *main de justice* (a short baton topped by a creamy white ivory hand symbolizing kingly equity), silken purple slippers, and the tunic and surcoat of the same color, also employed in the ceremony.[32]

Despite the presence of so much of the coronation regalia at the abbey, however, Saint-Denis was not the coronation church.[33] The great monastery had rivals in France, and it was as rivals that the abbot and monks thought of institutions like Reims cathedral, the coronation church. Perhaps the feeling of rivalry peaked at those moments during the coronations when the abbot of Saint-Denis was obliged to take his part in the ceremony. He carried the regalia from Saint-Denis and watched over the objects at the cathedral's high altar during the rite.[34] He even helped place the crown on the monarch's head. But the master of ceremonies, formally speaking, was the archbishop of Reims. And the ceremony itself emphasized the subordinate place of the abbey. The royal offering to Saint-Remi on this occasion, according to the Coronation Ordo of 1230, was set at thirteen gold coins. Late in the reign of Louis IX, a revised ordo coming out of Reims specified that these thirteen coins were to be *besants d'or*, a pointed effort, according to Richard Jackson, to privilege the Remois ceremony above the annual Saint-Denis feast day royal oblation of four *besants d'or*.[35]

Saint-Denis's monks, despite tradition's being against them, did argue in favor of their better right to host the coronation ceremony. And, exceptionally to be sure, they could in the mid-thirteenth century point to Philip II Augustus's second coronation as evidence that the abbey was at least a fit site for the ritual. Philip, like every Capetian king in the continuous line since 987, was crowned twice, first during his predecessor's lifetime, and again after his predecessor's death. (Philip was the last king for which this was the case.) Philip's first coronation took place at Reims in 1179; his second, at Saint-Denis in 1180. This was hardly compelling evidence that Saint-Denis ought to be vested with the sole right of coronation, but "throughout the thirteenth century, the abbey continued to represent an entitlement to the coronation ceremony."[36] If this claim had ever

---

[32] Le Goff et al., *Sacre royal*, pp. 270–71.

[33] In many countries besides France, the coronation regalia were kept in a monastic or quasi-monastic house, whether or not the coronation took place there. Such was the case in Portugal and Aragon, where Templars kept the regalia; Demurger, *Templiers*, p. 377.

[34] Le Goff et al., *Sacre royal*, pp. 165, 270–71.

[35] Jackson, *Vive le Roi!*, pp. 49–50.

[36] The quotation is from Abou-El-Haj, "Structure of Meaning," p. 147. See also Robertson, *Service Books*, p. 98 n. 233.

been recognized, the monks would have found that hosting the coronation was a significant drain on monetary resources and an endless source
of fiscal dispute among crown, abbot, and local layfolk, to judge from the
experience at Reims.[37]

Reims cathedral was by no means Saint-Denis's only rival in France.
The cathedral of Notre-Dame of Paris staked a claim to specialness that
the monks of Saint-Denis also appear to have spiritedly resented. In the
early thirteenth century the abbey had among its relics a holy nail from
Christ's Passion, but the nail attracted limited interest from the faithful.[38]
A similar nail in Notre-Dame's possession enjoyed a more popular cult,
and it has been argued that this imbalance peeved the monks, and that
they acted out an imaginative scenario to redress it.[39] First, they brought
attention to their nail by claiming in 1233 that it had disappeared, was
lost or stolen.[40] This in turn led to a phony but ostensibly frenzied hunt
for it that resulted in its recovery. (The pattern is an old one: a saint's body
or relic that does not want to change its home will frustrate all attempts
to force it to; a saint or relic that wants a change of home will find a way
to depart no matter what measures are employed to prevent the move.)[41]
The recovery of Saint-Denis's nail in 1233 proved that the relic, although
nettled by the lack of attention it had been receiving before going into
hiding, was still by and large content to remain at the royal abbey if wor-
shippers became a little more solicitous of it. As a thank offering the monks
commemorated the "invention" or finding of the nail with a new liturgical
ceremony. The Passion nail expressed its satisfaction by staying put for the
rest of the Middle Ages and by helping out in time of need, as when the
monks brought it out to process, along with other relics, to the Seine
during a period of severe flooding in 1280.[42] Whether the monks succeeded in undermining the pride of place until then given the Passion nail
at Notre-Dame of Paris is, however, unknown.[43]

Machinations like the Passion nail's secreting away and pseudomiracu-
lous recovery, if scholars' accusations are on the mark, do suggest that
controlling the large, wealthy, and prestigious community of monks at
Saint-Denis was a difficult charge. Henri Mallet, Mathieu de Vendôme's
predecessor, had not been up to the task. His sexual dalliance with a

---

[37] Petit-Dutaillis, *Etude sur la vie et le règne de Louis VIII*, p. 222 and appendix 6; Langlois, *Règne de Philippe III*, p. 55 n. 4.

[38] Lombard-Jourdan, *Fleur-de-lis*, pp. 178–203, is a comprehensive history of the relic.

[39] Robertson, *Service Books*, pp. 73–74.

[40] Lombard-Jourdan, *Fleur-de-lis*, pp. 193–96.

[41] Cf. Geary, *Furta Sacra*.

[42] *HF*, 23:145.

[43] For the later history of the nail and its cult until the Revolution, see Lombard-Jourdan,
Fleur-de-lis, pp. 196–203.

woman exposed the monastery to ridicule.[44] And he left usurious debts for his successor. Frère Mathieu (or Maci or Mahé, as he was more familiarly known) got down to business quickly. Papal confirmation of election was a requirement for exempt abbeys.[45] It was obtained for him expeditiously by a delegation sent to Rome; he does not seem to have traveled with it. The confirmation was accompanied by a papal release from having to pay Henri Mallet's debts.[46] The archbishop of Sens's formal consecration of Mathieu as the new abbot of Saint-Denis was also accomplished before the end of the year 1258.[47] The solemnities of confirmation and consecration provided a nice moment for the king to relieve the abbey of its onerous obligation to provide hospitality (*gîte*) for the monarch and his retinue during the frequent royal visits to the monastery.[48]

From Mathieu's viewpoint the papal and royal gestures were welcome both for their substance and for the indication they gave to him and to his monks that he enjoyed the favor of the powerful in his plans to improve life at the monastery. Immediately, however, he focused less on the disciplinary aspects of his project than on the religious and ceremonial aspects. Unlike the regime in some Benedictine monasteries, for example, where the devotional role of the abbot was severely limited, protocols at Saint-Denis allowed the abbot to play a very active role in formal devotions, especially on the high feast days, including Christmas, Easter, and, of course, Saint Denis's day (9 October). On these days, accompanied by a cadre of elder monks (*priores*) wearing highly decorated copes in testimony to the great jubilation of the occasions, he presided at the devotions. It was also his job to lead the way in the processional journeys to the high altar on all the highest feast days. He had a large number of other duties related to chanting, either solo or as the leader of the chanting, as well.[49]

These duties alone might have inspired Mathieu to correct, where correction was needed, and improve liturgical practices at the abbey, but another factor, somewhat more penitential in flavor, played into the project of reform. For it was only a few days after his first joyous celebration of

---

[44] Cf. Sivéry, *Philippe III*, p. 93.

[45] Lawrence, *Medieval Monasticism*, p. 119.

[46] *GC*, vol. 7, col. 391.

[47] Carolus-Barré, *Procès de canonisation*, p. 224.

[48] *GC*, vol. 7, col. 391; Brussel, *Nouvel examen de l'usage général des fiefs*, 1:541.

[49] Robertson, *Service Books*, p. 309: the abbot, "along with four of the most senior monks (*priores*) chanted the solo portions of the eighth responsory at Matins on the *annuale* feasts of Christmas and Saint Denis, and he also intoned the antiphon to the Benedictus at Lauds on Christmas and on Easter. He likewise sang the V. *Viderunt omnes* in the nave of the church during the procession after Terce on Christmas. Because of his senior rank, the abbot headed the procession to the altar at Mass on the highest feasts." Robertson addresses the wearing of copes on p. 315.

Christmas as the new abbot and, a week later, the feast of Christ's Circum-
cision that Mathieu was faced with a major tragedy. On 3 January 1259,
the feast of Saint Geneviève, the patroness of Paris, an abbey wall col-
lapsed, crushing twelve monks to death.[50] Following the obsequies, the
new abbot initiated permanent repairs, confiding the work to the care of
the realm's leading master mason, Pierre de Montreuil.[51] It would turn
out to be the first step in a refurbishment campaign at the monastery that
would continue for two decades.

Partly in response to the tragedy Mathieu commenced an effort to enhance the cult of the monastery's protector, its patron saint. To this end,
he and the community of monks at Saint-Denis humbly petitioned the
cathedral chapter of Meaux for relics of the two confessors, Sanctinus and
Antoninus, buried there who were reputed to have witnessed Saint Denis
and his companions' martyrdom and carried the news to Rome.[52] Later
in their lives the men became successive bishops of Meaux. According to
the Dionysian legend, Sanctinus was Denis's successor at Meaux when the
future martyr moved to Paris to become its initial bishop, and Antoninus
followed Sanctinus. After their deaths their bodies came to be venerated at
the cathedral. Now, Abbot Mathieu wished to symbolically and spiritually
reunite the martyrs at Saint-Denis (Dionysius, Eleutherius, and Rusticus)
with the witnesses to their passion. The clergy of Meaux responded with
remarkable goodwill and alacrity by offering the community one of Sanctinus's ribs and an arm bone from Antoninus's body in 1259. The two
saints' feast was thereafter kept at the abbey of Saint-Denis on 19 October,
ten days after the feast of the martyrs.

Orchestrating his action to coincide with the translation of the two
confessors' relics from Meaux, Abbot Mathieu translated to new tombs
within the monastic precincts the remains of a number of former abbots,
including the celebrated Suger.[53] Since translation was almost a declaration of and certainly a claim for the sanctity of the deceased abbots, these
acts supercharged the holiness of Saint-Denis. In concert with the various
translations, moreover, Mathieu commissioned an array of service books
to record the forms and schedule of devotional practices, including those
now to be associated with the cults of Sanctinus and Antoninus. Anne
Robertson has identified two of these books. One is the oldest surviving
ordinary from the abbey, setting out the standard services. Its earliest

---

[50] Carolus-Barré, *Procès de canonisation*, p. 224. Cf. Bruzelius, *13th-Century Church*, pp.
134–35.

[51] Carolus-Barré, *Procès de canonisation*, p. 224.

[52] I follow Robertson's reconstruction, *Service Books*, pp. 76 n. 134 and 249; *GC*, vol. 7,
col. 391.

[53] *HF*, 23:144; *GC*, vol. 7, col. 391. Bruzelius, *13th-Century Church*, p. 135.

written portions date from the very commencement of Mathieu's rule, while the calendar included in it was inscribed soon after to incorporate the new feast. The other is a lavishly illustrated missal, whose date is less secure, but possibly also as early as 1259 in its initial inscriptions, and which Mathieu appears to have commissioned to take the place of an older book of the same sort that was the worse for wear.[54]

The first year of Mathieu de Vendôme's headship of Saint-Denis, fraught with difficulties and challenges for the new abbot, mirrors that of his counterpart in England, Richard of Westminster. Richard hailed from Ware, a small but lively Hertfordshire market town that was a stopover for thousands of annual pilgrims traveling north to the Virgin's shrine at Walsingham and south to Saint Thomas Becket's at Canterbury.[55] Growing up in the town offered a boy the opportunity to hear stories about the two great pilgrimage centers and the ecclesiastical institutions that served them, and to dream of traveling to them. There were, of course, ecclesiastical institutions in Ware itself, the parish church as well as a priory established after the Conquest (and dependent on the Benedictine monastery of Saint-Evroult in the *pays d'Ouche* region of Normandy), where an intelligent boy or ambitious young man could receive training in Latin and apparently an excellent introductory religious education, and might also partly satisfy his curiosity about the land of France.[56] The careers of William de Ware, an almost exact contemporary of Richard, and Nicholas de Ware, a slightly younger man, bear some of this out. After his early lessons, William was taken from Ware and entered the Franciscans as a child oblate. (There was no Franciscan convent at Ware until the mid-fourteenth century.) He went on to become a distinguished theologian, known as *doctor fundatus* and occasionally as *doctor praeclarus* and *doctor profundus*. One of his pupils was the great Scholastic philosopher Duns Scotus.[57] Nicholas de Ware also entered the church and in the later thirteenth century became prior of Saint Bartholomew's, Sudbury, in Suffolk, a priory depen-

[54] Robertson, *Service Books*, pp. 355, 379–83. The early date for the second book is conjectural; a less risky guess for dating it is the interval 1259–1275. The books are now in Paris (BnF: MSS lat. 976 and 1107). The second, besides being lavishly illustrated, is musically notated.

[55] The cook, one of the pilgrims in the *Canterbury Tales*, hails from Ware; *Riverside Chaucer*, p. 84. The desire of certain antiquaries to associate Richard with the noble family of Warren was misguided, or, in Fuller's words, "pretending his honour, but prejudicing the truth thereby" (*History of the Worthies of England*, 2:43). Fuller's own index (3:589) prejudices the truth in a different way, by referring to Richard de Ware as a bishop.

[56] Reference to Ware Priory, a dependent of Saint-Evroul, may be found in "Parish Church of Eaton," pp. 52–63.

[57] So surmises John Marenbone, "almost certainly," in the *Oxford Dictionary of National Biography*, 57:389–90.

dent on Westminster Abbey.[58] Still another contemporary Ware native, a different Richard, ended up in Westminster as well, but as chaplain of the royal chapel there.[59]

It is unknown at what date the future Abbot Richard departed Ware either for Westminster Abbey, which had a great deal of property in the vicinity of his birthplace, or perhaps for some more advanced educational or religious institution preparatory to his profession at the royal monastery. What seems a reasonable inference from later evidence documenting his monastery's purchase of the Hertfordshire manor of Amwell is that Richard maintained his contacts with Ware. This transaction, managed by Richard during his abbacy, involved several burgesses of Ware directly and indirectly.[60] And men from Ware at several other times transacted business with the abbot, thus offering him opportunities, if he wished to exploit them, to stay abreast of the lives and fortunes of friends and family in his not-too-distant hometown.[61]

Richard's name first occurs in a monastic record, as far as is known, in the forty-second year of the reign of King Henry III (between 28 October 1257 and 27 October 1258). It notes that Brother Richard de Ware appeared in the royal court at Westminster, a stone's throw from the monastic cloister, in the place of the then abbot, Richard de Crokesley (*petentem per fratrem Ricardum de Ware monachum suum positum loco suo*).[62] Richard de Ware's selection to represent the absent abbot testifies to his creditable execution of routine monastic duties prior to his election as abbot and the confidence that Richard de Crokesley placed in him, but his brother monks had not come to look upon him as the latter's obvious successor. Indeed, to some extent his advancement to the abbacy so early in his career was a fluke.

Richard de Crokseley, after all, was neither incapacitated nor ill when he traveled to the grim Oxford Parliament of June 1258, where the disagreements between the king and his barons about the governance of the realm and the Sicilian business were addressed. A learned man with elegant man-

[58] Knowles, Smith, and London, *Heads of Religious Houses*, 2:131.

[59] *Close Rolls, 1268–1272*, p. 83, records the royal gift of a robe to this Richard de Ware in 1269.

[60] For men of Ware (Roger and William) involved in various aspects of the transactions at Amwell in Abbot Richard de Ware's time, see WAM, nos. 4227, 4242; and WD, fols. 234b–235, 377.

[61] I list some instances of inhabitants of Ware involved in business with Westminster, but no attempt has been made to be comprehensive: WD, fols. 135 (dating from 1268; John de Ware, a witness to a transaction); 233b (year 1263; Robert de Ware, another witness); 236 (between 1258 and 1263; Solomon de Ware, another witness); 491b–492b (datable to 1276; Sir John de Ware and his son, Roger de Ware).

[62] WAM, no. 1202.

ners and a firm royalist partisan, Abbot Richard de Crokseley enrolled as one of the king's twelve chief official delegates (balancing the baronial party's twelve) at the Parliament.[63] After the assembly concluded its business, the abbot joined the king's son, Prince Edward, over drinks in a convivial but serious reflection on the events and personages of the fractious meeting. According to the annalist of Burton, an exact contemporary to the events (his chronicle ends in 1262), an unknown evildoer, Hell's very offspring (*quidam perditionis filius*), managed to breach security and poison the abbot's drink and those of other members of the party. Richard de Crokseley had no suspicion of the danger and drank his fill. Whether or not one credits the accusation of poisoning, it is a fact that Richard de Crokseley sickened and died soon after the party—on 18 July. His body was brought back to Westminster and laid to rest in the abbey church in a marble coffin.[64] He had made elaborate arrangements as to how and by means of which revenues he should be remembered. As he had been assiduous in accumulating properties for a manor at Hampstead (*per suam industriam se adquissivisse*), he desired that the mass to be said on the anniversary of his death and the charities to be distributed, including food for the poor, be paid for out of income from these properties.[65] Such arrangements were not unusual and in this case were ratified both by the crown and by the Holy See, although the unsettled times associated with King Henry's struggle with his baronage in the long wake of the Oxford Parliament made it difficult until much later on to fulfill them as regularly and conscientiously as the late abbot would have hoped and expected.[66]

The monks at Westminster then proceeded to elect a new abbot. They settled not on Richard de Ware but on their prior, Philip de Lewisham, although perhaps he did not relish assuming the job.[67] Was he "too fat to

[63] *Select Documents of English Constitutional History*, p. 57. Matthew Paris, *Chronica majora*, 5:700, in his character assessment of Richard noted his genial subservience to the king. See also the *Chronicon domini Walteri de Heminburgh*, 2:307, which describes Richard de Crokseley as "vir utique nobilis et discretus."

[64] "Annals of Burton," in *Annales Monastici*, 1:460. See also the "Annals of Winchester" and the "Annales of Dunstable," in *Annales Monastici*, 2:97, and 3:211, and the *Chronicon domini Walteri de Heminburgh*, 1:306–7. Matthew Paris, *Chronica majora*, 5:700, mentions the death (signifying it with a drawing of the abbatial miter and staff inverted in the margin) as well as Richard's burial at Westminster but not the poisoning. The coffin was excavated on 12 July 1866; Stanley, *Historical Memorials of Westminster Abbey*, 2:130.

[65] WAM, no. 5400. I am quoting from a copy of a letter from Abbot Adam of Waltham that includes the contents of a papal letter permitting the abbot and convent of Westminster in the year 1267 to provide the appropriate funds, ten marks, which were to support the anniversary mass as well as the doles to the poor for Abbot Richard de Crokseley's salvation ("certis diebus certa refectio pauperum et quedam alia salubria pro anime sue remedio").

[66] See also below, p. pp. 95–96.

[67] Matthew Paris, *Chronica majora*, 5:701.

move," that is, to make the trip to Rome for confirmation? It is true that he sent proxies to the Holy City. But the jocular locution, "too fat to move"—the coinage of Arthur Stanley, the erudite nineteenth-century dean of the abbey, summarizing the contemporary chronicler Matthew Paris's notice of the prior's corpulence—strikes me as a silly way to put it.[68] Indeed, Dean Stanley's easy inference that Philip de Lewisham fit the modern caricature of the obese monk and lazy glutton may be downright uncharitable. The fact that he died before the confirmation could take place suggests that Philip was unhealthy at the time of his election, though perhaps not considered in immediate danger of dying. Corpulence in later life is as often evidence of a pathological retention of liquids as it is of gluttony. It typically aggravates pain in the joints and makes walking, let alone long-distance travel even in modern vehicles, agonizing.

In any case Philip de Lewisham met his end before his confirmation but not before a delegation set off to Rome to seek it. A new election was therefore necessary. On 1 December three Westminster monks representing the abbey—Brother John, the precentor; Brother William, the sacristan; and another Brother William, the keeper of the infirmary—received royal permission for the convent and the subprior (the temporary head of the abbey, with the old abbot dead and the prior, alias abbot-elect, also dead) to proceed to this election.[69] The monks settled on Brother Richard de Ware by way of compromise.[70] Soon afterward, on the 15th of December, the king accepted the election and sent notification of it to the pope.[71] Another delegation, this one including the newly elected abbot, then set out for Italy to obtain papal confirmation.

Westminster Abbey, which Richard would rule for a quarter of a century, owed some of its importance, as Saint-Denis in France did, to its proximity to the realm's greatest city. Except for relatively brief periods in which the king took the administration of London into something like modern receivership, the city was less directly governed by the English crown than was Paris by its royal lord.[72] That said, London was still a very important object of concern and interest to the English kings. It was the bustling demographic center of the realm, although certainly not as large as Paris in population.[73] Westminster was a contiguous suburb where both the

---

[68] Stanley, *Historical Memorials of Westminster Abbey,* 2:131.

[69] *Patent Rolls, Henry III, 1258–1266,* p. 6.

[70] Matthew Paris, *Chronica majora,* 5:701.

[71] *Patent Rolls, Henry III, 1258–1266,* p. 7.

[72] In general on the governance of London, see Tout, *Beginnings of a Modern Capital,* and Barron, *London in the Later Middle Ages.*

[73] Cf. Keene, "London," pp. 25–28, and Barron, *London in the Later Middle Ages,* p. 238.

royal abbey and Westminster palace were located. As the site of the central law courts and the intermittent but frequent meetings of the royal council, Westminster had displaced Winchester as the realm's chief administrative center and enjoyed a secular prestige that the village of Saint-Denis could not claim.[74] Many businessmen were drawn to make donations to the abbey.[75] Many others among London's citizens resented the power of Westminster and the privileges of its Benedictine abbey, including its fairs, which by their proximity offered more competition to London's merchant elite than Saint-Denis's Lendit fair did to Paris's; the English kings were not averse to favoring Westminster's fairs when London burghers showed disrespect or too much independence of spirit for their taste.[76]

A church, later an abbey, existed from relatively early Saxon times.[77] It came to be dedicated to Saint Peter, who reputedly descended from heaven to consecrate the sanctuary. In the mid-tenth century, in the period of the monastic reforms of Dunstan, the zealous archbishop of Canterbury under King Edgar (959–975), the community of monks expanded and the complex of monastic buildings was augmented. But it was Edward the Confessor (1042–1066), the last Anglo-Saxon king, who embarked on a major rebuilding of the abbey complex. The centerpiece, his church, was dedicated on 28 December 1065, a year before the Norman Conquest of England and the coronation of William the Bastard (William the Conqueror, 1066–1087) as king on Christmas Day 1066. Since then the abbey church has remained the preferred coronation site, although in exceptional circumstances of political uncertainty and the need for swift action, other sites have served. It was in the 1240s, long into the reign of Henry III, who gradually came to claim Edward as his ideal, that most of the Confessor's church was razed so that the edifice could be further expanded and modernized in the Gothic style—the style pioneered at Saint-Denis in the mid-twelfth century, which had become dominant for monumental buildings throughout western Europe by the thirteenth. The rebuilding became Henry's obsession and of necessity one of the chief concerns of the succession of abbots at Westminster.

The Anglo-Saxon Edward, who had spent his early years in Normandy while the Danish royal family ruled in England, had had a reputation for holiness. He was renowned for his piety, and he lived in a virginal union

---

[74] Barron, *London in the Later Middle Ages*, p. 47.

[75] Rasmussen, "Monastic Benefactors," pp. 80–81.

[76] Cf. *Cambridge Urban History of Britain*, 1:214–15; Carpenter, *Struggle for Mastery*, p. 378.

[77] For overviews of the medieval history of Westminster Abbey, from which most of the information in the next several paragraphs is summarized, see Aveling, "Westminster Abbey," pp. 3–84.

with his wife. Although his formal canonization did not take place until nearly one hundred years after his death, he was widely considered a confessor or saint in royal and aristocratic circles after the Conquest. Not surprisingly, the abbey church, within whose precincts he was laid to rest in 1066, came in time to enjoy a double dedication—to Saint Peter and to him. No monarch from William the Conqueror on ignored Westminster Abbey, though some, notably Henry III, more than others lavished it with benefactions, and it consequently became an extremely well-endowed and much envied institution.

The documentary base to reconstruct its endowment and the administration of its estates is, also like Saint-Denis's, immense: original charters, individual authentic copies, notarial records, and a great cartulary called Westminster Domesday (along with related collections, like the *Liber Niger*).[78] Although there are excerpts from William the Conqueror's eleventh-century register conventionally referred to as Domesday Book copied into the 655 folios of Westminster Domesday (at fols. 29b–34b), the earliest that the abbey collection came to be known by this name seems to have been the mid-sixteenth century. Gabriel Goodman, dean in the years 1561–1601, authenticated sometime during these years a much earlier grant to the abbey that one Robert Abbatt copied from the cartulary, here named "Domesdaie boke"; and either before or after this, on 23 June 1571, Dean Goodman made several extracts from documents in the archives, including the cartulary he again referred to as "Domesday booke," to determine the obligations of the abbot and convent "to cleanse and scour the sewers and watercourses on their lands at South Lambeth . . . leading into the River Thames."[79] The misleading name has stuck (see fig. 3).

Westminster Abbey was a very privileged institution, as even the most cursory glance at Westminster Domesday confirms, but in contrast to the

---

[78] Mason, *Westminster Abbey Charters*, p. 5, provides a list, dates, and comments on the various collections. First and foremost is Westminster Domesday (Westminster Abbey Muniments Book, no. 11, referred to in short form by Mason as WAD, rather than WD, which I am using); it was largely written in the early years of the reign of Edward II. A second collection, predating WD by a few years but much more limited in content, namely, to "charters chiefly of notables—such as kings, popes, bishops" is British Library (BL), MS Faustina A III; this is Mason's F. MS Cotton Titus A VIII of the BL, dated to the earlier part of the fourteenth century, is a similar collection; Mason gives it the *sigillum* T. The BL's MS Cotton Claudius A VIII, dating from the mid-fifteenth century (Mason's C), includes extracts from John Flete's history of the abbey. *Liber Niger* (Westminster Abbey Muniments Book, no. 1; Mason's LN) is also fifteenth-century but occasionally contains material not available elsewhere. Westminster Abbey Muniments Books nos. 3 and 12 and the College of Arms MS Young 72 (Mason's CAY; cf. *Abstract of Charters*), according to Mason, add little information not available elsewhere or in better or earlier texts.

[79] WAM, nos. 1808 and 1874, preserve the two sets of extracts discussed.

history of Saint-Denis it was not definitively established until the thirteenth century, despite some forged charters of the century before, that it was fully exempt from all ecclesiastical authority but the pope's.[80] Indeed, as late as the 1220s, a newly confirmed bishop of London marshaled documents that supported his see's claim to exercise jurisdiction over Westminster Abbey. The monks resisted, and as a result of the arbitration of a very weighty panel including the archbishop of Canterbury, the bishop of Winchester, and the bishop of Salisbury, among others, the monks prevailed. The year 1222 was a good year: the arbiters decided, upon having made a few modest property adjustments in the see of London's favor in order (in Emma Mason's opinion) to soften the blow, that Westminster Abbey was subject neither to the bishop nor to any other ecclesiastical authority whatsoever, excepting only the supreme pontiff.[81] The phrase "ad Romanam ecclesiam nullo medio pertinens" and variants thereof, though by no means unknown before then, frequently recur in the abbey records thereafter.[82]

Partly symbolizing the abbot and convent's exemption, even before the arbitrated judgment, was the permission granted to the community from the first decade of the thirteenth century to chant the angelic hymn, the *Gloria in excelsis*, on days that otherwise fell within penitential seasons when singing it was ordinarily forbidden. These days included two Marian feasts. The first was that of the Virgin's Purification, 2 February, a feast that sometimes fell after Septuagesima, the third Sunday before Lent, which was the day, rather than Ash Wednesday, that commenced the Lenten fast for monks. The second of the Marian feasts specified was Annunciation, 25 March, which usually fell in Lent. Finally, the abbot and his monks, as Benedictines, were permitted to intone the *Gloria in excelsis* on the feast of Saint Benedict, 21 March, which always fell in Lent, since Easter can never occur before 22 March. These privileges, granted in the pope's name by a legate sometime between 1200 and 1210, are said to have been bestowed because Westminster was dedicated to Saint Peter (and, therefore, implicitly had a spiritual relationship with the see of Saint Peter), and because Westminster's dependence on the Holy See was direct and unmediated.[83] Exemption's payoff for the papacy was the unusual de-

---

[80] On the forgeries and thus the prehistory of authentic exemption, see Lunt, *Financial Relations*, p. 106 n. 9.

[81] Mason, *Westminster Abbey and Its People*, pp. 81–82; Pearce, *Walter de Wenlock*, p. 26.

[82] See, for example, WAM, no. 5400.

[83] WAM, no. 12733, "liceat vobis in purificatione beate virginis si venerit post septuagesimam et in die annunciationis eiusdem et in festo beati Benedicti ymnum Angelicum scilicet Gloria in excelsis deo solenniter cantare." Saint Benedict had several feast days, but 21 March was commemorated as the date of his death. The dating of the privilege is based on the period of time during which John of Salerno, cardinal priest of Saint Stephen in Celiomonte and papal legate in Ireland and Scotland, was traveling in the British Isles. See also WD, fol. 11.

gree of loyalty institutions enjoying the privilege gave the supreme pontiff. Often preferentially it was exempt institutions to which the popes turned to carry out their orders.[84]

The abbey's portfolio of secular privileges was also thick and diverse. Many of the powers vested in it were judicial and revenue-generating.[85] For example, in Hertfordshire, where there was an array of its estates, Westminster enjoyed the right to receive both the chattels of men who were executed for capital crimes and those of fugitives from justice, their taking flight being tantamount to conviction. A brief thirteenth-century report later copied into Westminster Domesday noted the abbot's (in fact, Richard de Ware's) receipt of 5s. 6d. from the sheriff of Hertford for the chattels of one Adam Wygod, who was executed by hanging. The same report provides evidence of the abbot's receipt of 5s. 3d. and 40d. for the chattels of two fugitives from the law.[86] Counterbalancing the abbot and his monks' profits from executions was the effective role that Westminster monks played as intercessors with the crown for the pardon of convicted felons who would otherwise hang, and as providers of sanctuary for fugitive felons.[87]

The income generated from the profits of estates, judicial rights, and oblations was meant to maintain a community that scholars believe amounted to about fifty or sixty monks in the thirteenth century.[88] In the twelfth century, this income was insufficient for the style of living and hospitality deemed appropriate; an aggressive series of campaigns for the acquisition of property and, in particular, increasing royal patronage in the thirteenth century ameliorated this situation.[89] The monks in the period of our interest would have been supported by an even larger number of service personnel. Each new monk pledged *stabilitas morum, conversio et obedientia secundum Regulam Benedicti*, a phrase that suggests a certain prescribed gravity and order to life and a turning away from vain secular

[84] Cf. *Original Papal Documents*, nos. 677, 695–96, 698, 833, for instances of both Westminster and Saint-Denis being employed in this manner.

[85] The abbey's immense "soke," to use the legal language, and the resentments it led to are noted in Williams, *Medieval London*, p. 81.

[86] WD, fol. 113b (dated 1280/81).

[87] On pardons, see, for example, *Patent Rolls, Henry III, 1258–1266*, p. 539; *Patent Rolls, Henry III, 1266–1272*, p. 628, which record one pardon requested (26 January 1266) by John de Lira and Henry de Evesham, monks of Westminster, for Samuel son of William for the death of Walter Onywond and another (21 February 1272) at the instance of John sacristan of Westminster, for William son of John of Chalden for the death of Luke de Massinges. For sanctuary, see Mason, *Westminster Abbey Charters*, pp. 22, 195–96, and Jordan, "Fresh Look at Medieval Sanctuary."

[88] Harvey, *Obedientiaries of Westminster Abbey*, p. xx; Moorman, *Church Life in England*, p. 404.

[89] Platt, *Abbeys and Priories*, pp. 67, 69.

concerns. From Richard de Ware's time there survive "21 small pieces of parchment, being the original professions of their vows. . . . Each has the mark of the cross."[90] If this reflects all the professions that were made during his abbacy (and in the absence of an epidemic it must be close to all), it would mean that a place in the monastic community became open as a result of a death on the average of about once a year.

Of the roughly sixty monks at any one time in the mid-thirteenth century, thirty-five to forty were obedientiaries, men assigned to offices with carefully prescribed duties and who, in order to carry them out, could claim income at specified proportions or from particular endowments among the abbey revenues.[91] The genuinely major officials, besides the abbot, prior, and subprior (the number one, two, and three men) were the cellarer, who saw to the provisioning of the monastery; the sacristan, who supervised the abbey's precious possessions; and the abbot's steward, also known as collector or receiver of revenues—these are the ones mentioned in financial records in Richard de Ware's time.[92] Others, like the keeper of the infirmary, were also important figures. Among the *in-firmarius*'s regular income in Richard de Ware's time were annual gifts of deer from royal forests for sick monks.[93] Ill brothers were relaxed from the vow not to eat meat.

To the extent that the sources allow one to judge, the abbots of Westminster were somewhat more autonomous within or, negatively put, more cut off from their community than the abbots of Saint-Denis were from theirs in the High Middle Ages. Barbara Harvey concludes that they were "well advanced" in their "withdrawal from the common life of the monastery by 1100," although the abbots, in Emma Mason's words, were "expected to attend almost all of the daily offices (except prime), and the daily chapter, and to dine in the refectory."[94] Even among those who believed the abbots should attend (and many monks may have felt no particular desire to have them present), expectation of their attendance was mere wishful thinking considering the abbots' other tasks.

From at least 1225 strict division of goods between the abbot and convent was agreed.[95] There was also an equally strict apportionment of income-producing estates or manors between the two.[96] No such division

---

[90] WAM, no. 12890 A–U. *Fourth Report of the Royal Commission on Historical Manuscripts*, pt. 1, p. 187.

[91] Harvey, *Obedientiaries of Westminster Abbey*, p. xix.

[92] Ibid., pp. 35, 178, 223.

[93] *Close Rolls, 1256–1259*, p. 259 (the example cited is from 1258).

[94] Harvey, *Obedientiaries of Westminster Abbey*, p. 2; Mason, *Westminster Abbey and Its People*, pp. 83, 87.

[95] Harvey, *Obedientiaries of Westminster Abbey*, pp. xxv and 3.

[96] Stern, *Hertforshire Demesne of Westminster Abbey*, pp. 48–49.

could be absolute or without a few disputes especially during the vacancies between one abbot's death or resignation and the election, confirmation, and installation of a new one.[97] But these intervals were also occasions for restating the theoretical strictness of the division, for during such times the crown had exclusive rights of custody over the abbot's property.

An entry on the Close Rolls in 1258 recalls the strictness of the division of goods (*bona prioris et conventus Westmonasterii penitus separata a porcione abbatis ejusdem loci*).[98] However, an entry soon after on the same Rolls reveals the complications that could arise. The prior and convent of the abbey entered a claim to the standing autumn grain in two carucates of land, perhaps two hundred acres, at Stanwell that the late abbot, Richard de Crokesley, had held in guard for a limited term. The term had not expired by the time of his death. Whose goods were these? Who should receive them, the king in fulfillment of his role as custodian during the vacancy or the corporation that constituted the abbey? In this case, the crown anticipated a somewhat protracted legal argument and ordered a view of the grain—a precise determination of the property in dispute—prior to a full settlement. The sheriff of Middlesex on the crown's behalf and an appointee, unnamed, on the abbey's side were to make the view.[99]

Richard de Ware, informally on the eve of his trip to Rome for his confirmation as abbot, acknowledged the validity of the division of goods and, on the eve of a second trip a little more than a year later, also pledged that he would not have the arrangements modified by appeal to the pope.[100] More formally and comprehensively a few years later, in letters dated 30 May and 11 June 1262, he accepted the full legitimacy of the division (*acceptamus omnino*), specifying for good measure certain of the monastic subunits (*super camera, celarium et coquina*) whose income was set apart from his.[101] He further promised not to lodge any protests to the crown with regard to these arrangements.[102] The best estimate is that toward the end of the thirteenth century the abbot's portion of Westminster's income amounted to about £520; the convent claimed slightly more than twice as much, about £1,120.[103] Taken together, these sums—the equivalent of

---

[97] Cf. Pearce, *Walter de Wenlock*, pp. 139–41.

[98] *Close Rolls, 1256–1259*, p. 249. Westminster's *custos* or guard at the time was one Adam de Aston.

[99] *Close Rolls, 1256–1259*, p. 259. The carucate was a variable measure, but an estimate of two hundred acres for two carucates is a moderate, not a high one.

[100] WD, fol. 637b.

[101] WAM, no. 5673 (this formal acceptance is dated Thursday before the Feast of Saint Barnabas the Apostle, that is to say, 11 June); WD, fols. 634–634b. See also the *Fourth Report of the Royal Commission on Historical Manuscripts*, pt. 1, p. 174, and Pearce, *Walter de Wenlock*, p. 142.

[102] WD, fol. 634b.

[103] Harvey, *Obedientiaries of Westminster Abbey*, p. xxvi.

about 8,000 l. t.—made Westminster Abbey very rich but still less well-off than the wealthiest cathedrals and monastic houses in Europe.[104]

Soon after his accession the abbot-elect secured, in a royal instrument dated 16 December 1258, freedom of passage to go to Rome for confirmation.[105] He would tarry seven months on the Continent.[106] In this he was no different from many Englishmen who, as Donald Matthew noted, enjoyed spending time on the Continent.[107] Presuming this was his first ever trip abroad, it would have been during this time that he became aware firsthand and an ardent admirer of Continental artistic styles. It was in Italy that the new abbot encountered the so-called Cosmati work, intricate marble inlay that several years later he contracted craftsmen to install at Westminster.[108] Either on his trip through France to Italy or on the way back, he also decided to have a personal seal made in the French manner (see fig. 4). "Unlike other English abbots and bishops," writes T. A. Heslop, Richard de Ware does not appear on his seal "with his weight evenly distributed and facing forward but with a slight sway at the hips and looking a little to his right" and with vestments showing naturalistic, "free-falling folds."[109] This stylistic mode, Heslop adds, originated in the early thirteenth century and became all the rage in northern French ecclesiastical circles in the 1250s. Whether Richard, as abbot-elect on his way to Rome or as abbot on his return journey, hired a French craftsman in France to cast the seal-die, had a French native do so at Westminster (a "tantalising" possibility, in Heslop's view), or employed an Englishman cognizant of the French style has not been ascertained, but the abbot was using his cosmopolitan new seal by the fall of 1259.[110]

The trip to Rome was expensive, and although the abbot's yearly income was quite substantial, not all of it was available for the purpose. Some was earmarked for routine expenditures associated with the abbatial office. Some of what should have been available was simply not forthcoming—a common enough occurrence during vacancies. The latter was the case with

---

[104] Cf. the figures assembled in Jordan, *Unceasing Strife*, p. 82.

[105] *Close Rolls, 1256–1259*, p. 35.

[106] Cf. Carpenter, "King Henry III and the Cosmati Work," p. 191.

[107] Matthew, *English and the Community of Europe*, pp. 13–14.

[108] Foster, "Context and Fabric," pp. 50–51; for much more on this below, pp. 47, 105–8.

[109] Heslop's description is given in the catalog prepared by Alexander and Binski, *Age of Chivalry*, p. 318 no. 282. The reverse of the seal shows the Confessor and the Pilgrim, that is, a scene from the story of Edward's gift of a ring to a pilgrim who turns out to be John the Evangelist. More generally on English seals (of which as many as thirty thousand survive from the thirteenth and fourteenth centuries), see Heslop, "English Seals," in Alexander and Binski, *Age of Chivalry*, pp. 114–17.

[110] WAM, no. 12802, dated Tuesday next after the feast of All Saints, or 4 November, 1259. See also Alexander and Binski, *Age of Chivalry*, p. 318 no. 282, and Binski, "Cosmati at Westminster," p. 29.

the revenue from certain of the lands of Richard Goscelin and Ralph, his heir. These lands were in the abbot's portion because the Goscelins had mortgaged them for a term of six years to Abbot Richard de Croxeley in order to raise money to pay debts they owed Jewish moneylenders in London. The six years were almost elapsed, but not quite. In this case, however, the abbot's treasury was temporarily disadvantaged during the vacancy, because the crown on 25 November 1258 granted the Goscelins seisin of their lands, implying the collection of revenues, until such time as a new abbot was available with whom they could complete the earlier arrangements.[111] The income that would otherwise have accrued to the abbot's treasury in the interval before Richard de Ware's abbacy went instead to them.

What seems to be an uglier case involved a vineyard in the pretty village of Pershore in the county of Worcester. Relations between Westminster Abbey and Pershore Abbey, the principal ecclesiastical institution in the village, were stormy, for Edward the Confessor had partly endowed his monastery of Westminster on lands that Pershore was successfully encouraged to alienate for the purpose. A vestige of this concession was the fact that within the village, the very center of Pershore's lordship, Westminster possessed two-thirds of the profits of justice and numerous income-producing properties.[112] All this sustained the smoldering disgruntlement of the inmates of the Worcester abbey. The situation was made worse when Pershore fell on hard times after a number of devastating fires among its abbey buildings. The accusation the crown made, sometime before 6 June 1259, when attorneys for Pershore answered the charge, was that the abbot of Pershore had caused or ordered, or so it was alleged (*ut dicitur*), the destruction of a vineyard, likely including the seizure of grapes and wine, hard by the village "in contempt of the king and the prejudice of Westminster Abbey while it was vacant and in the king's hand" after Richard de Croxeley's death.[113] It was one thing for the crown to exploit its own rights during vacancies in ways that offended the houses under its custody and future abbots (and there is plenty of evidence of its officials' doing so), but it was quite another to countenance a third party acting in a similar way to the royal dishonor.[114]

Yet the chance of exercising a contested right and getting away with it (thus establishing a precedent and the basis for litigating a future claim) was too attractive to dissuade all would-be challengers. Another instance

---

[111] *Close Rolls, 1256–1259*, p. 346.

[112] Cam, *Hundred and the Hundred Rolls*, pp. 170, 284.

[113] *Close Rolls, 1256–1259*, p. 480.

[114] The best study of the often ruthless exploitation of these so-called regalian rights by the English crown during vacancies is Howell's *Regalian Right in Medieval England*.

involved the administration of advowsons, that is to say, the presentation of candidates to offices or benefices in the abbot's gift that came open during vacancies. On Westminster's behalf, during the vacancy that preceded Richard de Ware's confirmation as abbot and his return from Rome and enthronement at the abbey in August 1259, the crown made many such appointments—it appears almost routinely and without contestation—in various dioceses (Winchester, London, and Lincoln).[115] At least one such appointment, however, was still challenged by the bishop of London as a usurpation of his own prerogative. To be sure, the challenge failed when the king declined to withdraw it, but the claim itself might be used as evidence at a subsequent appointment.[116] All the royal appointments to benefices in Westminster's gift ceased around the time of this dispute, more precisely on 17 August 1259, when Henry III ceded his rights of presentation and ordered the subprior and convent, to whom he had handed over the exercise of his rights of custody (in return for a monetary gift), to cede theirs to the newly vested abbot.[117]

One of the reasons his trip to Italy was so expensive was that Richard did not spend all of his time in Rome. He and his retinue were peripatetic like the papal court, and their travels and changes of lodging cost money. It was not at Rome but at Anagni in March, for example, that he would see the glistering Cosmati floors, reminiscent of mosaics, that so captivated him. David Carpenter surmises that the new abbot, after his return to England, gave "King Henry first-hand information about the Cosmati."[118] It was also at Anagni on the 11th of March that Pope Alexander IV appointed Richard to the position of papal chaplain, the customary honorific office bestowed on abbots of Westminster.[119]

Only two days later, on 13 March, in order to pay for the gifts and other expenses of his own confirmation and promotion to papal chaplain and the debts incurred by his entourage's travels and sustenance within Italy and for their return to England, Richard de Ware received papal permis-

---

[115] For instances of royal appointments to benefices until Richard de Ware's enthronement at Westminster, see *Patent Rolls, Henry III, 1258–1266*, pp. 11, 30, 35, 38; the four presentations referenced here occurred on 8 February, 15 July, 2 August, and 13 August 1259.

[116] The refusal was not formally conveyed to the bishop until 4 July 1260; *Patent Rolls, Henry III, 1258–1266*, p. 81. The dispute generated a large number of records: see, for example, WAM, no. 8581, for the appointment of the abbot of Waltham as papal judge in the matter. (Other relevant records indexed for the year 1260 at WAM are nos. 8577, 8582, 8583–8585, and 8589–8590.) Much, much later, 19 September 1266 (*Patent Rolls, Henry III, 1258–1266*, p. 640), an assize of darrein presentment confirmed the abbot of Westminster's seisin of the advowson and thus the king's legal right to have made the appointment during the vacancy.

[117] *Patent Rolls, Henry III, 1258–1266*, p. 39.

[118] Carpenter, "King Henry III and the Cosmati Work," p. 191.

[119] *Calendar of Entries in the Papal Registers*, 1:364.

sion to borrow 1,000 marks (£666 12s. 16d.) from a consortium of Florentine merchant bankers.[120] He also renegotiated a schedule of payments for the loans that Italian moneylenders had earlier made to cover the expenses of Philip de Lewisham's aborted confirmation.[121] Complex protocols partly redacted in Italy and completed in London vested the English crown with enforcement by distraint in case of default. The protocols were received by the crown in the persons of Brother Robert of Scotland, one of the royal chaplains; Edward of Westminster, a king's clerk; and William de Boncoeur, a knight who made a career in the royal administration.[122] King Henry III confirmed them on 5 November. Incidentally, the confirmation was one of the last official documents to refer to his royal majesty not only as the ruler of the English and the Irish but also as duke of the Normans and count of the Angevins. For later, almost a month to the day (4 December 1259), and as the culmination of an extraordinary series of negotiations in Paris, Henry would cede these once treasured titles to the Capetian king of France, Louis IX.[123]

---

[120] Ibid. For a fuller discussion of the abbot's dealings with Italian moneylenders, see Jordan, "Westminster Abbey and Its Italian Bankers."

[121] WAM, no. 12802; see also nos. 12804 and 12808 (a late copy).

[122] WAM, no. 12802; the names, in the original, adjusted to the nominative case, are rendered as "Frater Robertus de Scotia, domini Regis capellanus; Dominus Edwardus de Westmonasterio, eiusdem Regis clericus; et Dominus W. bon quer, miles."

[123] For Henry's confirmation, see WAM, no. 12803. On the change in the use of titles and the fabrication of a new English royal seal to reflect the change, see *De antiquis legibus liber*, p. 43, with discussion in Chaplais, *Essays in Medieval Diplomacy:* essay 1, "The Making of the Treaty of Paris (1259) and the Royal Style," pp. 248–50.

III

THE TREATY OF PARIS

KING HENRY III was in the duchy of Aquitaine in November of 1254. Problems in the duchy and a relatively recent falling out with Simon de Montfort, his sister's husband, whom he had entrusted with affairs there, had brought him to the Continent. Conditions somewhat improved during his stay, and the king decided to return home, to England, through French royal lands, some of which he still laid claim to. He wanted to meet his counterpart, Louis IX, who was newly returned from Crusade. And Louis IX was eager to meet him. They were brothers-in-law: their wives were sisters, Marguerite and Eleanor, coheiresses of the county of Provence. Both had brothers who were married to the two other coheiresses of the county, Richard of Cornwall, Henry's brother, to Sanchia, and Charles of Anjou, Louis's sibling, to the fourth and youngest child of the family, Béatrice. Familial ties were complemented by the two kings' similar outlook on life, especially the depth of their piety and devotion to the Catholic Church. And though Henry had not yet fulfilled his crusader's vow, taken in 1250, and, because of domestic political complications, never would, the men shared in 1254 a continuing concern with the fate of Christian arms in the Holy Land. There was only one serious problem. They were at war.[1]

Henry first made a pilgrimage to the Loire Valley abbey of Fontevraud, one of the major necropolises for the Plantagenet dynasty.[2] It was here that his grandfather, King Henry II, and his grandmother, Eleanor of Aquitaine, were interred, and his famous uncle, Richard I the Lionhearted, had his tomb. The body of Henry III's mother Isabelle of Angoulême (d. 1246) also rested in the abbey precincts. During his pilgrimage he oversaw the translation of her body to a more honorable tomb in the church. Then, he departed to the Cistercian abbey of Pontigny, more than 250 kilometers to the northeast in Champagne where he prayed at the shrine of the late archbishop of Canterbury and saint, Edmund Rich (Edmund of Abingdon), who had died not far from the monastery in 1240. Rumor had it that the archbishop, angry with his king, died in exile. Henry wanted to

---

[1] A lovely comparative portrait of the two kings and their extrication of their realms from war is Carpenter's "Meetings of Kings Henry III and Louis IX," pp. 1–30; he devotes a few pages to the relations of the spouses as well (22–24).

[2] Powicke, *Thirteenth Century*, pp. 118–19.

put the rumor, which had little truth in it, to rest and to clear his own reputation. In this he was not successful, but not for lack of trying.[3]

When he completed his devotions at Pontigny, it was time for Henry to meet the king of France. They rendezvoused about 150 kilometers west of Pontigny at Orléans in the shadow of the great cathedral dedicated to the Holy Cross there.[4] The well-mannered Capetian invited Henry to accompany him to Paris to see its sights, including the reliquary sanctuary next to the royal palace, the Sainte-Chapelle. All four sisters of Provence and their mother were in the capital. The setting and company generated comradely feelings and an opportunity for Louis's wife, Marguerite, to tell her sisters about her sad yet thrilling adventures in the East.[5] Sir Maurice Powicke put it simply and nicely in summing up the state of mind of England's king: "Henry was very happy."[6] The anomaly of the two realms' being in a state of war achieved a new level of incongruity. That Louis IX was also in train at exactly the same time to dislodge his brother Charles from the war of succession in Flanders and Hainaut, and, slightly later, to end long-standing territorial disputes with France's southern neighbor, the Crown of Aragon, which would culminate in the Treaty of Corbeil in May 1258, added emphasis to the incongruity of the long cold war with England.[7]

This did not mean that peace between the northern kingdoms was inevitable. It was the Sicilian business that assured this. "English barons who were in favour of the peace with France, indirectly and perhaps unwittingly brought pressure upon Henry III by refusing the grant of a subsidy for the Sicilian affair."[8] Finish one war before starting another seems to have been the operative wisdom. "Because we [Henry III] have the business of the kingdom of Sicily much at heart and wish to see it brought to a happy conclusion, behold, we are prepared, in accordance with your counsel [that of the pope and the cardinals] and that of the Roman Church, to make peace and concord with the illustrious king of the Franks."[9] Active formal negotiations toward a peace treaty

---

[3] Jordan, "English Holy Men of Pontigny," pp. 66–73.

[4] Powicke, *Thirteenth Century*, p. 119.

[5] Hamilton, "Eleanor of Castile," p. 95.

[6] Powicke, *Thirteenth Century*, p. 119.

[7] On Louis IX's efforts on Flanders and Hainaut, see Jordan, *Louis IX*, p. 141, and Kienast, *Deutschland und Frankreich*, 3:624–31. On the negotiations leading to the Treaty of Corbeil (11 May 1258), see Hillgarth, *Spanish Kingdoms*, 1:243, and O'Callaghan, *History of Medieval Spain*, p. 363. More generally for assessments of Louis IX's quest for peace in the period 1254–1258, see Buisson, "Saint Louis et l'Aquitaine," pp. 1–19, and Barber, *Trial*, p. 38.

[8] Chaplais, *Essays in Medieval Diplomacy*: essay 1, "The Making of the Treaty of Paris (1259) and the Royal Style," p. 239.

[9] Cuttino, *English Medieval Diplomacy*, p. 59.

began in the wake of Henry's first meeting with Louis. One of the English ambassadors in the negotiations was Richard de Crokesley, the abbot of Westminster.[10]

While Henry's desire to conquer Sicily was an incentive to make peace with France, the baronial troubles accompanying his efforts to raise money for the project had a negative and enduring financial impact on the royal resources that could be devoted to the continuation of major construction work at Westminster Abbey, work that had been going on since the mid-1240s.[11] The king tried his best; he continued, under the resented tutelage of his barons, to provide funds for the abbey to the extent possible and to fulfill his customary obligations, like providing annual renders of deer (venison) and wine.[12] And the magnates themselves reckoned it useful to continue supporting the abbey's rebuilding, if not entirely at earlier levels. A subsidy of one thousand marks, for example, was offered to the abbey for the building work in August 1258 during the vacancy following Richard de Crokesley's death "by the counsel of nobles of the council."[13] The nobles thereby wanted to make their own statement, namely, that they saw the saint in heaven, Edward the Confessor, as smiling benignly on *their* view of the community of the realm.[14] If David Carpenter is correct, they went further in articulating this claim by authorizing their armorials' placement in the wall arcades of the choir as a form of appropriation of the church.[15]

The barons' continuing allocation of funds to the abbey, even though typically at the king's behest, can also be read as an effort to secure this impression. In February 1259 by the "counsel of the magnates of the council" Alice de Lacy was granted wardship of the lands of her late husband, the Earl of Lincoln, in return for a payment of £362 per year to the keepers of the works of Westminster Abbey. Her heir was eight years old, meaning that these annual renders would continue for thirteen years. By October 1269 she had contributed £3,754 to the building works. The

[10] Chaplais, *Essays in Medieval Diplomacy*: essay 1, "The Making of the Treaty of Paris (1259) and the Royal Style," p. 238; Cuttino, *English Medieval Diplomacy*, p. 8.

[11] Carpenter, "Westminster Abbey and the Cosmati Pavements," pp. 37, 39–40.

[12] In general, see, especially for an assessment of the king's behavior with regard to funding construction, Carpenter, "Westminster Abbey in Politics," p. 53; idem, "Westminster Abbey and the Cosmati Pavements," p. 38. For customary renders in 1259—eight deer, a cask of wine for the abbot and convent at the Confessor's feast—see *Close Rolls, 1256–1259*, pp. 425, 445.

[13] Carpenter, "Westminster Abbey in Politics," p. 50.

[14] Ibid., pp. 50, 52; Carpenter, "Westminster Abbey and the Cosmati Pavements," p. 40.

[15] Carpenter, "Westminster Abbey in Politics," pp. 52–53; idem, "Westminster Abbey and the Cosmati Pavements," pp. 40–41.

council refrained from appropriating the income for the king's debts.[16] On the 3rd of June 1259 the council committed itself to the last major phase of work at the abbey. Another large section of the eleventh-century church was ordered to be razed. The principal addressees for this order were Brother Edward, the subprior, the highest-ranking official then resident at the abbey (Richard de Ware was not yet returned from Italy) and the sacristan. The king and council jointly asked the men to see to the commencement of replacement work.[17]

July and September 1259 witnessed two similar interventions from the baronial council or the king imploring a councilor to act. July saw the council approve the assignment of one thousand marks due from the Chaworth wardship to the works at the abbey, with the license of Hawise, the widow of Patrick de Chaworth, who died in 1258. The Chaworth family was part of a wealthy lineage that had done service to the crown for years and was destined in the centuries to come to achieve greater distinction and accumulate greater honors. The goods to be capitalized to produce the assigned sum were to be collected on the feast of Saint Martin, 11 November, with the payment being rendered in fifty-mark installments beginning at Michaelmas (29 September) 1259 and continuing thereafter on every Easter and Michaelmas until the obligation was discharged.[18] It was in September that the king implored Hugh Bigod, then occupying the recently revived office of justiciar, to give one hundred pounds for the abbey works before he came for a visit there.[19] One of the projects that these funds were to go for was the immediate (*sine dilacione*) reassembly of an iron lectern (*lectrinum*) in time for the king's arrival at the abbey in anticipation of a trip to France to finish the peace negotiations. The subprior, Edward of Westminster, was charged with the task.[20]

Nevertheless, despite the barons' gifts to the abbey, Westminster remained for the time being very much a royal monument—commemorating the royal dead, offering encouragement to the king in fiscally difficult times, and providing a site for festive celebrations that enhanced the image of the monarchy. A few examples will make this clear. On 14 January 1259 the king ordered the delivery of fifty marks for cloth with pearls (*perulis*)

---

[16] Carpenter, "Westminster Abbey in Politics," p. 50; idem, "Westminster Abbey and the Cosmati Pavements," p. 38. Colvin, *Building Accounts*, pp. 416–32, published some of the evidence of these payments.

[17] *Close Rolls, 1256–1259*, p. 390. Carpenter, "Westminster Abbey in Politics," p. 50.

[18] *Patent Rolls, Henry III, 1258–1266*, p. 32; Colvin, *Building Accounts*, pp. 416–32. Cf. WAM, no. 12808. Carpenter, "Westminster Abbey in Politics," p. 51.

[19] Carpenter, "Westminster Abbey in Politics," p. 53.

[20] *Close Rolls, 1259–1261*, p. 112. The lectern at the time of the order was in a state of disassembly (*disjunctum per frustra*); Brother Edward was to see to its being assembled and set up in the new chapter room (*conjungi et erigi faciat in novo capitulo*).

for an altar frontal for the tomb of his young daughter, Katherine. The little Katherine, born deaf, had died only three years old on 3 May 1257 at Windsor Castle. She was further commemorated at the abbey with a gift of painted icons for the altar of the Blessed Virgin.[21] A few months after the gifts in Princess Katherine's memory, on 13 May 1259, the abbey stood surety for royal debts—at least one thousand marks—and Henry III deposited the Plantagenet family's jewels there as a pledge.[22] In reality, the abbey's gesture was a continuation of a surety issued six months before on 3 November 1258 when it guaranteed a loan that the king had contracted in order to pay the arrears he owed of the annual renders England made to the Holy See.[23] And, as the final example, on 13 October 1259, Saint Edward the Confessor's feast day, in the presence of an immense array of notables, the king knighted John, the duke of Brittany's son, who would later wed the royal daughter Beatrice.[24]

Not long afterward, Henry III undertook another trip to France, this time to take part in the closing sessions of the negotiations that had been initiated to end the war. In October, just before he left, a parliament was held at Westminster, in line with the Provisions of Oxford.[25] The barons' confidence was far greater than it had been when they entered upon their revolutionary challenge to royal authority a little more than a year before. Now they issued the Provisions of Westminster, directives that further regulated government and administration, especially with regard to the operation of the justice system. They also authorized a comprehensive judicial eyre. Judges whom they chose were soon after sent into the counties on circuit to hear cases of malfeasance, usurpation, extortion, bribery, and on and on. In this way the reforms initiated at the center of government began to make an impact in the realm at large and helped shaped a wider public opinion about the proper execution of lordship at all levels.

Henry departed for the Continent in November 1259, intending to be present in the French capital on 4 December for the formal publication of what would be known as the Treaty of Paris. I follow Pierre Chaplais and, after him, George Cuttino in using the term "publication" rather than "ratification."[26] Ratification occurred by proxy in October 1259 before Henry's departure, even though a few points still remained to be settled

---

[21] *Calendar of the Liberate Rolls*, 4:448. See also Carpenter, "King Henry III and the Cosmati Work," p. 187.

[22] *Calendar of the Liberate Rolls*, 4:459.

[23] Ibid., p. 437.

[24] "Annals of Oseney," in *Annales Monastici*, 4:124. Carpenter, "Meetings of Kings Henry III and Louis IX," p. 20.

[25] Powicke, *Thirteenth Century*, pp. 147–50.

[26] Chaplais, *Essays in Medieval Diplomacy*: essay 1, "The Making of the Treaty of Paris (1259) and the Royal Style," p. 238; Cuttino, *English Medieval Diplomacy*, p. 10.

and were not finally resolved until 3 December.[27] Henry attended the publication and then remained in France, at various locations, after the ceremony until April of the next year. He had asked the new abbot of Westminster to join him. Richard de Ware and the property pertaining to his office as abbot came under royal protection in an order dated 7 November 1259, since he acceded to his suzerain's request. Probably Henry, who took ship on the 14th, envisaged from the beginning that the abbot would stay with him during the entire period of the royal sojourn in France, no matter how long it lasted, since the order of protection was not to expire until Easter.[28]

At first the trip went as expected. The 19th of November saw a veritable avalanche of letters from Montreuil-sur-Mer that anticipated a speedy return to England after the diplomatic formalities. Brother Edward, back at Westminster, in his capacity as supervisor of the Confessor's shrine (*custos operacionum feretri Beati Edwardi*), was directed to obtain fifty marks for precious stones and cameos (*camautos*) for the saint's reliquary an to arrange for their inlaying in time for the king's return.[29] (He would later be rewarded for his good service with a nice robe.)[30] Similar orders in confirmation of the directive were sent the same day to various royal officials back home.[31] But in fact Henry's visit was prolonged, partly because of his desire to attend the funeral of Louis IX's seventeen-year-old eldest son who died unexpectedly in January 1260. The depth of the French king's hurt touched the royal court and the delegation from England as well.[32]

For much of their stay during December 1259 and January 1260 in France, Henry certainly and Richard, it would seem plausible to suppose, enjoyed apartments at the royal abbey of Saint-Denis and the hospitality of its new abbot, Mathieu de Vendôme.[33] It was presumably the first meeting of the abbots, whose similar offices in similar institutions, and whose relative inexperience in those offices, gave them so much in common. Moreover, both were beset by considerable problems from the first—Mathieu de Vendôme with the tragedy of the accidental deaths of twelve monks and the need to rebuild the part of the abbey that had caused their deaths, and Richard de Ware with Westminster's vulnerability in the agonizing struggle between the king and his barons for control of the

---

[27] Chaplais, *Essays in Medieval Diplomacy.* Essay I, "The Making of the Treaty of Paris (1259) and the Royal Style," pp. 238–247; Cuttino, *English Medieval Diplomacy,* p. 10.

[28] *Patent Rolls, Henry III, 1258–1266,* p. 59.

[29] *Close Rolls, 1259–1261,* p. 223.

[30] Ibid., p. 318.

[31] Ibid., p. 224.

[32] Le Goff, *Saint Louis,* p. 268.

[33] See the itinerary prepared in Treharne, *Baronial Plan of Reform,* pp. 384–85.

realm. Neither man was destined by noble birth to play a role in the politics of kings, but both were now obliged to do so. There was some basis for mutual sympathy here.

Yet Henry and Richard's reception at Saint-Denis would certainly have been less welcoming if what may be called *l'affaire Deerhurst*—a strange incident or, rather, series of strange incidents that brought a prominent member of the English episcopate and the monastery of Saint-Denis into conflict—had not recently been resolved. Certain lands and buildings in Deerhurst, on the Severn River in the English county of Gloucester and the diocese of Worcester, constituted a dependency of a non-English abbey, in this case, Saint-Denis. It was none other than the French-reared Edward the Confessor who had endowed the Capetian royal monastery at Saint-Denis with its first grant of property in Deerhurst.[34]

A few other French monasteries also received such grants in Anglo-Saxon times, but especially after the Norman Conquest of England in 1066 many more, especially Norman abbeys, obtained holdings in the island kingdom.[35] The endowments were characterized by two forms of organization.[36] In one scenario, the endowments were used to support cells, dependent priories, of the mother houses. These so-called conventual priories were simply small abbeys themselves, but they sent regular payments to the mother houses testifying to their dependency. Their priors were either elected by the inmates and then confirmed by the various mother houses or were directly appointed by the mother houses from among the monks in the Continental institutions. The conventual priories were real corporations. They had seals and could make contracts (with the permission of their mother houses), and they followed the monastic rule of their owners.[37]

In the other scenario, the endowments remained purely and simply income-producing property for the Continental owners, which typically sent or appointed managers to see to their administration. Although these managers, unfortunately, were often called priors and the buildings on the endowed property priories, the managers did not have to be monks, their priories were not corporate bodies, and monastic life was not necessarily practiced in them. Of course, it was always possible for a Continental mother house to create a conventual priory on its English properties long after it first acquired them. Taken together, whether in the conventual form or not, these endowments and institutions are known as the alien

[34] *GC*, 7:364. New, *History of the Alien Priories*, p. 2.

[35] Heale, *Dependent Priories*, p. 20, with references to detailed studies.

[36] The information in the next several paragraphs on the various forms of organization that evolved from these endowments is paraphrased from New, *History of the Alien Priories*.

[37] Ibid., p. 37.

priories, and they continued to be a feature of English ecclesiastical life until the English government repudiated the institution during the later phases of the Hundred Years War.[38]

Soon after the Confessor made his grant of the Deerhurst properties to Saint-Denis, the French monastery sent a small group of monks to establish a cell.[39] Saint-Denis did not permit the new conventual priory of Deerhurst to elect its own prior. Instead, the mother house appointed him from its own ranks.[40] Like any landed endowment to a church, at least any without a restrictive clause to the contrary in this period, Saint-Denis's Deerhurst lands constituted a perpetual, that is to say, an inalienable gift and are referred to as such in a charter of 1059 (*donum in perpetuum sancto Dionysio*).[41] They formally belonged to the saint in heaven, and Denis had no intention of selling them. Only the pope as the Vicar of Christ and the direct lord of the exempt abbey of Saint-Denis could act extraordinarily and permit their sale. All these facts make certain events involving Deerhurst in the 1250s appear very, very strange.

For the chronicler Matthew Paris reported a quite surprising occurrence at the beginning of these years.[42] King Henry III's brother, Richard, Earl of Cornwall, is said to have visited Saint-Denis in 1250 and bought Deerhurst Priory from the monastery and to have done so after having received papal approval in Italy. Moreover, Matthew Paris explained, when Earl Richard returned to England, he put the resident monks to flight (*monachis effugatis omnibusque dirutis*). He felt no compunction for doing so or for inconveniencing the lives of Deerhurst's neighbors—he especially feared no monk—as he formulated his plans for transforming the priory property, because he was under the protection of the pope, at least according to our typically antipapal chronicler (*Nec postea timuit aliquem vicinum, praecipue religiosum, quin omnia pro libitu tractaret, Papali tutus protectione*). Thereafter the small priory buildings started to go to seed (*sic diatim coepit conditio ecclesiae deteriorari*), but the earl was still unconcerned, for he intended in the near future to build a castle where they stood anyway, presumably to protect traffic on the Severn River (*proposuitque ibidem castrum aedificare pro fluvio Savernae*).

---

[38] These two "scenarios" depend on New's distinction. Heale (*Dependent Priories*, pp. 4–5) argues that the distinction, though adopted by modern scholars from late medieval administrative terminology, may misrepresent the thirteenth-century situation. I recognize the persuasiveness of his argument, but the status of Deerhurst would fall into the first category, either by New's (and late medieval administrators') or by Heale's definition.

[39] New, *History of the Alien Priories*, p. 2.

[40] Ibid., pp. 37–39, 43.

[41] *GC*, 7:364.

[42] Matthew Paris, *Chronica majora*, 5:112, 118.

Noël Denholm-Young, Earl Richard's scholarly biographer, concluded that this "remarkable transaction never took full effect."[43] Matthew Paris cannot help us further; he died in 1259. However, it can be argued that one of Abbot Mathieu de Vendôme's first acts, which would have been unknown to the Saint-Albans chronicler, was an effort to undo the Deerhurst alienation. Indeed, it is clear that in 1259 he did so. How? Despite Earl Richard's desire to fortify the Severn at Deerhurst, he never carried out his plan and instead permitted or did not interfere with the scattered monks' return, for too much other business was intruding on his life.[44] He was completing the building of the famous monastery he endowed at Hailes, also in Gloucester. He was investing resources in constructing a major castle in Wiltshire. Before his royal brother had accepted the crown of Sicily for his son, Edmund, Earl Richard was in negotiations about accepting it for himself, which came to nothing personally but occupied a great deal of his time. Richard in the same busy years of the 1250s was also putting forth his candidacy for the imperial throne by standing for election as king of the Germans, a more successful but equally time-consuming and far costlier endeavor. Finally, as the baronial crisis worsened in England, Richard was more and more drawn into it. He was sympathetic to the barons' criticisms of his royal brother's governance, but he remained loyal to the crown. Tugged by all these forces in the 1250s, Deerhurst receded in importance and, to repeat Denholm-Young's words, the priory's transformation "never took full effect."

Unfortunately, the monks were in a kind of limbo, seemingly severed from their dependency on Saint-Denis for a time and, as a consequence of this, bereft of the exempt status, implied—arguably—in their former dependency on an exempt abbey. When Deerhurst's sale to Earl Richard was undone, as it later was, the monks assumed that their return to dependence on Saint-Denis restored their exemption. They began to live and act as they had before any of Earl Richard's interference. In 1256, for instance, the prior presented before the justices of the forest one Pagan de Mobray as the priory's woodward of Taynton, where the monks had a manor given to Saint-Denis by Edward the Confessor. The justices swore him without incident.[45] Yet when the prior died in 1258 or perhaps early 1259, the bishop of Worcester, Walter Cantilupe, contested the monks' status and claimed jurisdiction.[46] From across the Channel Saint-Denis

<hr />

[43] Denholm-Young, *Richard of Cornwall*, p. 74 n. 2.

[44] The standard modern biography, from which the following information has been extracted, is Denholm-Young's *Richard of Cornwall*.

[45] *Oxfordshire Forests*, pp. 47 and 79 no. 76 and n. 28.

[46] The details on the events chronicled in this paragraph have been reconstructed from entries in *Close Rolls, 1259–1261*, pp. 21, 47, 226.

protested vigorously, but, spurred on by the bishop of Worcester's not exactly disinterested entreaties, Henry III took Deerhurst into his hand, a move that further outraged the monastic community at Saint-Denis. The king's decision was unconsidered and unfortunate at a time when he was trying his best to soften every possible tension between England and France and negotiate a final peace between the countries. It was probably under the influence of Abbot Richard de Ware—who knew a great deal about Deerhurst, since Westminster had a manor there and collected significant revenues—that Henry soon changed his mind.[47]

With some determination, therefore, the king sought to bring the dispute between Bishop Walter Cantilupe and the new abbot of Saint-Denis, Mathieu de Vendôme, to an end. To make a show of doing so he withdrew the royal *custos* of the priory and restored the cell to Saint-Denis. The documents that describe these events demonstrate that the matter had reached only a temporary settlement, though. A final decision was put off until Michaelmas, shortly before the king left for France. The decision, not surprisingly, was favorable to Saint-Denis: Deerhurst was treated as an ordinary conventual alien priory of Saint-Denis in the decades to come. Which is not to say there were no further disputes. The status of alien priory was always an anomalous one in England's monastic universe, but Deerhurst was now anomalous in the same way the other alien priories were.[48]

It also now makes sense in part why Richard de Ware was invited to join the king's entourage. It was not only his position as abbot of Westminster but his facility in advising the king on the Deerhurst dispute with Saint-Denis. Abbot Mathieu de Vendôme warmly welcomed the English king and Abbot Richard when they arrived in Paris for the publication of the treaty. He not only provided them with nicely appointed apartments but greeted them with the full splendor of his monks in procession and, together with Louis IX, underwrote a large share of their expenses during

[47] On Westminster's properties and rights at Deerhurst and relations with the village and priory in Richard de Ware's time as monk and abbot, see WD, fols. 316–320, and *Curia Regis Rolls*, vol. 19, nos. 1297, 2025, 2404, and vol. 20, nos. 243, 814, 1341, 1864. See also Harvey, *Obedientiaries of Westminster Abbey*, p. 3; Mason, *Westminster Abbey and Its People*, p. 84; Cam, *Hundred and the Hundred Rolls*, p. 267.

[48] See, for example, the disputes cataloged in *English Episcopal Acta*, vol. 13, no. 109 (dated 28 October 1264), and *Parliament Rolls*, 1:150 (dated Michaelmas 1283), both demonstrating the continued institutional tie between Deerhurst and Saint-Denis. In the first, three monks of Saint-Denis were contumacious excommunicates dwelling at the priory against the will of the bishop of Worcester, who was seeking royal intervention; in the second, "amercements [were] pardoned to the prior of Deerhurst at the request of the abbot of Saint-Denis."

the stay.[49] The English king attentively carried out his devotions at the great French abbey.[50]

Richard de Ware was to make numerous, often leisurely, trips to France and through France to Italy during the remainder of his life. There is every likelihood that he interrupted his itinerary several times with sojourns at Saint-Denis, regularly renewing his acquaintance with his brother abbot, Mathieu. The Frenchman and his monks were congenial hosts. The archbishop of Rouen, Eudes Rigaud, once recalled in his daybook spending time at the abbey of Saint-Denis on the martyr's feast day. He noted the community's "generosity and graciousness" as well as its willingness to shoulder all the expenses of hospitality for him and for the French king, for a visiting papal legate, and for many other prelates at the same time.[51]

Of course, Richard de Ware was not dependent on Mathieu's hospitality during his travels to and through France. His entourage also had a claim on the hospitality of the famous Augustinian canonry of Saint-Victor of Paris. A *confederacio* of mutual prayers for the deceased brothers of the two houses, Westminster and Saint-Victor, had been established in the twelfth century, initiating a comradely relationship that implied reciprocal hospitality.[52] By and large, however, I am inclined to believe—or, rather, it is my hunch and only a hunch—that, unless Westminster were having particular problems that would have embarrassed Abbot Richard to discuss, he preferred to stay at Saint-Denis, which was the real counterpart of his own royal abbey.

The Treaty of Paris of 1259 brought the war that began in 1202 to an end.[53] Its heart, though not the opening section, is a pledge of mutual forgiveness. Louis forgave the English kings for all the harms that they had inflicted on the kingdom of France since the war began, and Henry forgave the French kings for all the harms that they had brought upon England. Comely sentiments and hopes, however, had to be translated into technical language: Henry III renounced his claims to Normandy, Anjou, Maine, Touraine, and Poitou. Louis IX in turn recognized Henry's direct authority over a huge swath of territory in the southwest, the duchy of Aquitaine (Bordeaux, Bayonne, and their environs, Gascony, and all

---

[49] On the underwriting of expenses, see Carpenter, "Meetings of Kings Henry III and Louis IX," p. 9, who argues back from Henry's household account rolls. In general on these accounts, see Carpenter, "Household Rolls," pp. 22–46.

[50] Carpenter, "Meetings of Kings Henry III and Louis IX," pp. 15, 19–20.

[51] *Register of Eudes of Rouen*, p. 730.

[52] For a discussion, see Mason, *Westminster and Its People*, p. 242.

[53] For most of what follows on the Treaty of Paris, I paraphrase Cuttino, *English Medieval Diplomacy*, pp.10–13.

the coastal islands that were *of* the kingdom of France).[54] He also ceded what was his to cede in the sees and cities of Limoges, Cahors, and Périgueux. Where there was documentary evidence, however, that made the cession of property in these regions difficult (as, for example, if a gift or feoffment had been granted to a vassal of the crown with reversion to the donor's line), he promised either to make a fair substitution of rights elsewhere or, if possible, to purchase the rights (say, of reversion). What was fair was to be determined by mutually agreeable arbiters—all by All Saints 1260.

A more complicated situation in the Agenais led to Louis's promise to render an annual payment, equal to the county's value (itself determined by mutually agreeable arbiters), to the English government in twin installments. The complications, centering on the nature of inheritance claims in the fief, would become extremely troubling in the 1270s because of arguments about the residual rights of Louis's brother Alphonse of Poitiers and his wife, Jeanne, the heiress of Toulouse. Still, the essence of the agreement here as everywhere in the treaty was that men of good faith could resolve the complicated issues, and that Louis and his successors would not maliciously cause Henry and his successors to suffer the perpetual loss of the fief or its equivalent. A similar agreement was made with regard to lands in Saintonge that would be held by Alphonse until his death.

To retain the duchy of Aquitaine for himself and his successors Henry III agreed to do liege homage to Louis IX and future kings of France. This was not the reimposition of a relationship that had lapsed during the years of hot and cold war, 1202–1259. It was, if Pierre Chaplais was correct, the recognition on Henry's part that "allodial Gascony," that is, a land once freely possessed, was now in a dependent relationship to the French crown. Gascony was *in* and *of* the kingdom. Its duke held it conditionally, namely, on the proper provision of services, including military and judicial services, to the French crown. For Chaplais this placed Louis IX, who had extracted the submission, firmly in the line of his territorially expansionist predecessors, Philip II Augustus and Louis VIII.[55] It also opened up the possibility of appeals to the French king's court for defect of justice from rear vassals in the duchy or on the march between the duchy and the French king's direct holdings, but no one at the time anticipated how thorny this issue would become.[56]

---

[54] On Louis IX's understanding of his authority with regard to Aquitaine, see Buisson, "Saint Louis et l'Aquitaine," pp. 1–19.

[55] Chaplais, *Essays in Medieval Diplomacy*: essay 2, "Le Traité de Paris de 1259 et l'inféodation de la Gascogne allodiale," pp. 121–37.

[56] Cf. Studd, "'Privilegiati,'" pp. 175–85.

For a few other small territories, like Armagnac, Bigorre, and Fézensac, that had distinct tenurial and inheritance customs, Henry also promised to do the appropriate homage. As a nice touch, he and his predecessor were forgiven for any failures to do such homage during the long war; this served to obviate the issue of whether any such homage had even been due. For if it could be proved that it had been due, the question of a penalty for failure would have arisen. Surely, Louis would have forgiven Henry and his predecessors, but multiple one-sided acts of forgiveness could come across as condescension, when the whole thrust of the negotiations was to produce a document that looked like a cordial agreement of equals. Of course, this face-saving strategy fooled no one in France and perhaps no one in England. French humorists (vernacular street comedians) joked about how the English barons would try to sabotage the stinking "fart" (French *pes*, a pun on *paix*, peace) that Louis, the "rich man of Paris," had imposed on their king.[57]

Another of the treaty's provisions helps explain the reference to the French king as a rich man; it stipulated that Louis IX provide the funds to maintain a force of five hundred knights for two years in the English king's service. Mutually agreeable arbiters would determine the appropriate sum to raise and maintain this force, which was to be paid over a two-year period, with three payments per year. The total eventually came to more than 100,000 l. t. It was almost as if Louis were paying for the lands his predecessors conquered. His hope was that the knights would be used in God's service, the Crusade, but he conceded that in the English king's galaxy of concerns, the welfare of the realm was equally deserving. Baronial influence on this issue is also revealed here: determining England's welfare was to be vested in men named by Henry in consultation with the English magnates who dominated government.

The treaty concluded with an elaborate series of guarantees, along with the statements alluded to of general forgiveness on each side. Louis promised to uphold the treaty, as did Henry. Henry's two sons, Edward and Edmund, joined their father in the promise and in renouncing their rights to the conceded territories. It was expected that the promises would be renewed every ten years. Nevertheless, despite hopes to the contrary and the good feelings of the moment, it was also explicitly acknowledged that, God forbid, the treaty might break down, that Henry III, a future king, or an heir to the English kingship might wish to repudiate the concession of such vast territories as once constituted a major part of what history has come to call the "Angevin Empire." All the sureties—the knights in the lands affected by the treaty who took oaths to support it

---

[57] Symes, *Common Stage*, p. 255.

after its ratification in October or in the wake of its publication on 4 December 1259—were thus obligated to raise arms against future repudiators and in favor of the French crown and its rights under the agreement. This provision in fact recognized that not everyone affected by the treaty's provisions was entirely happy. Earl Richard of Cornwall, for example, reserved his claims to the lands of his late mother Isabelle d'Angoulême, despite the treaty and Isabelle's dying wish that her second set of children have these as their inheritance.[58]

Richard de Ware and Mathieu de Vendôme were very much junior players in the dramatic negotiations of the Treaty of Paris. Even though they were observers of the closing act of this drama and were rapidly becoming familiar with some of the major political actors of the day in the two kingdoms, neither was as yet personally close to the monarch he served, though that, too, was rapidly changing. If there was a churchman on the English side who was important in achieving the treaty, it had been the late abbot of Westminster, Richard de Crokesley. If there was a French prelate who had genuine influence, it was Eudes Rigaud, since 1248 the Franciscan archbishop of Rouen and primate of Normandy and therefore a man ardently concerned about a treaty touching the dominium of the duchy.[59] Richard de Crokesley's death in 1258 left the way open for the growing role of Richard de Ware. Eudes Rigaud, on the contrary, continued to be Louis IX's friend right up until the king's death on the Crusade on which the archbishop accompanied him more than ten years later.[60] Nevertheless, the political status of Normandy was resolved in 1259, and thus Eudes thereafter spent most of his time on clerical business in the archdiocese. He made only occasional trips to Paris, mainly to attend Parlement. The reverse was the case for Mathieu de Vendôme. Occasional trips took him away from Paris.[61] Mostly, he was in close spatial proximity to the king and court. True, the Benedictine abbot never superseded the Franciscan archbishop in the hierarchy of the king's closest friends, but he did do so as a political councilor. In Parlement his seat, first in rank *after* the bishops, belied his political influence, which eventually far exceeded theirs.[62]

Henry III's satisfaction with the outcome of the negotiations emboldened him. Distance from England and from the constant admonitions of his baronial keepers appears, following David Carpenter, to have contrib-

---

[58] Denholm-Young, *Richard of Cornwall*, p. 97.

[59] On Eudes's role in the negotiations, see Gavrilovitch, *Etude sur le Traité de Paris*, pp. 25, 37, 58; Davis, *Holy Bureaucrat*, pp.164–66.

[60] Davis, *Holy Bureaucrat*, pp. 160–69.

[61] For example, he made brief trips in 1259 and 1260 to Champagne; *GC*, vol. 7, col. 391.

[62] The reference to his seat (*GC*, vol. 7, col. 391) is dated 1260: *habito in saltu Vincennarum primus ab episcopis sedisse legitur.*

uted to his resolve to face down the magnates or at least to stop rolling over so readily for them. Until the 25th of January 1260 (the feast of the Conversion of Saint Paul), he issued a torrent of assertive letters from the monastery of Saint-Denis and thereafter from several other locations in France, many dealing with his seemingly perpetual shortage of resources and the needs of Westminster Abbey for funds to continue the refurbishing of the fabric.[63] But although he accomplished a considerable number of tasks through the orders issued in these "more assertive" letters in this period, he was loath to hold formal judicial sessions of the English royal court on French soil, which might be repudiated by those in charge back home.[64]

When Henry III finally decided to leave the abbey of Saint-Denis, though not France, Richard de Ware did not travel with him. The king had business for his newfound confidant. He had already, on 20 December 1259, issued a royal order allowing the prior (in the place of the abbot, who was still in France with him) and the convent of Westminster to pay their outstanding debts to Italian merchant moneylenders from money raised through a levy imposed on the tenants and their properties.[65] Thereafter, under a writ of protection of 19 February 1260, Abbot Richard set out on another lengthy trip to Rome on Westminster's and the king's business.[66] Besides reassuring his own Italian creditors, Richard had the opportunity and unquestionably the charge to bring the supreme pontiff up to date on several crucial matters: the outcome of the treaty negotiations in Paris and the initial pace of their implementation, of course, but also Henry's continuing insistence that he intended to go on Crusade and, as soon as possible, fulfill his promised commitment to a Sicilian cam-

---

[63] For English royal letters dated at Saint-Denis in this period, see *Close Rolls, 1259–1261,* pp. 233–34, 261–63, 266–68; *Calendar of the Liberate Rolls,* 4:521. In a letter to Hugh Bigod (*Close Rolls, 1259–1261,* pp. 267–68), the English justiciar, who was acting as regent during Henry's absence, the king remarked that he and the queen had departed Saint-Denis in fine fettle on the feast day mentioned (*Nos autem et regina nostra sani et incolumes die Conversionis Beati Pauli de Sancto Dyonisio recessimus*). On his apparent assertiveness, cf. Carpenter, "Westminster Abbey and the Cosmati Pavements," p. 41.

[64] Henry's reluctance to do justice is expressed in a memorandum (*Close Rolls, 1259–1261,* p. 261) concerning a dispute which came before him at Saint-Denis that he declined to judge outside the realm (*extra regnum Anglie*). The claim that he was "more assertive" in this period and the explanation provided are David Carpenter's, "Westminster Abbey in Politics," p. 54.

[65] *Patent Rolls, Henry III, 1258–1266,* p. 109. Westminster was not unique in its problems or in seeking royal permission to tax in order to deal with them. The same missive permitted the exempt abbot of Bury Saint-Edmunds, its prior, and the convent to levy an aid on their tenants in order to obtain the funds necessary to pay off the monastery's merchant creditors.

[66] *Patent Rolls, Henry III, 1258–1266,* p. 117. Carpenter, "King Henry III and the Cosmati Work," p. 191.

paign. It would have been the abbot's task, too, to explain the Provisions of Oxford and his king's attitude toward them in order to find out how far the pope was willing to go to help Henry overcome the restrictions they placed on his rule.

While the abbot of Westminster went on his Rome mission, the English king spent what was eventually several months in Louis's realm. Perhaps it was the relative repose of his life that kept him there. To read some of his correspondence is to be convinced that he extended his trip day by day. For example, despite the financial exigencies that still encumbered him, he continued to favor Westminster Abbey from abroad.[67] Yet in one of the letters, dated 14 January 1260, that demonstrates his concern, he issued an order to Brother Edward, the subprior, which detailed the preparations that the monk should see to in anticipation of his return to England and his bestowal of offerings on the monastery. The language makes it seem as if he conceived of an immediate departure but then changed his mind. In any case, he ordered the subprior to have some rich saffron-yellow silk that he had earlier sent to him by a royal clerk fashioned into a chasuble, the sleeveless drape for the celebrant of the mass, and a choir cope or long ceremonial outer garment of the same material ornamented with gold fringe, presumably for his new friend the abbot. They were to be ready by the time the king arrived, and Henry authorized the disbursement of money from the treasury to pay for the work.[68] Ten days later he had not departed France. Instead he wrote home to try to get some more money sent to him to prolong his stay.[69]

In late February he was still in France. On the 24th, from Saint-Omer, he directed that one mark of gold be made ready for an oblation at the shrine of the Confessor. He was in arrears in making gifts to the saint because of his delay in returning. He wanted the gold there so that he could make a formal offer of it at the shrine when he reached England. The expert goldsmith William of Gloucester was charged with the arrangements.[70] This was one of many such gifts of gems and of gold in 1260 in which the royal goldsmith exercised his expertise, presumably by assaying the gold and other precious metals.[71] All the gifts were costly; one purchase, for a single jewel, was authorized for up to fifteen or twenty marks.[72] Yet still the king did not return.

Indeed, it was not until April that Henry III embarked for England. Much of his time in the immediate aftermath of his return he spent in and

---

[67] *History of the King's Works*, 1:146.
[68] *Close Rolls, 1259–1261*, pp. 233–34.
[69] Ibid., p. 266.
[70] ibid., p. 243.
[71] See, for example, ibid., p. 258.
[72] Ibid., p. 314.

near Westminster.[73] Mostly this was for business. Westminster Palace was the center of government. But Westminster Abbey was not far from his thoughts. A record from 9 June 1260 reminds us, as Henry did not have to be reminded, that every time he returned from beyond the seas he was formally obligated as king to offer a mark of gold at the Confessor's shrine.[74] This was the sort of activity he prized, as is plainly evidenced by his loving preparations since February to make sure the gift was worthy, but the harsh and topsy-turvy reality of politics is what really took up his time after his return from France, where he had been "very happy." It would be long before he was quite so happy again.

---

[73] See the itinerary for 16 May–3 June in Treharne, *Baronial Plan of Reform*, p. 385.
[74] *Calendar of the Liberate Rolls*, 4:509.

IV

THE BEST OF TIMES, THE WORST OF TIMES

EVEN IF LOUIS IX did not quite find in Mathieu de Vendôme, as he found in the Franciscan Eudes Rigaud, the perfect match for his own devotional enthusiasms, he nonetheless admired the Benedictine and showed it in numerous ways, starting early in his abbacy. Already in 1260 he specially entrusted three royal crowns to Mathieu and his abbey's safekeeping to be added to the regalia.[1] These included the two large gold crowns set with gemstones that Philip II Augustus had commissioned for the coronation of future kings and queens. The third was a smaller gold circlet (*coronula aurea*) that Louis IX wore when he dined formally on the anniversary of his coronation.[2] The king's satisfaction with the monastery's stewardship had its resonance in the abbot's admiration for the ruler: in the course of his rule at Saint-Denis, Mathieu constructed an "abbatial palace decorated with portraits of kings of France with apartments reserved for the sovereign."[3]

The evidence of goodwill between the two men does not imply that the abbey's relations with the royal *government*, let alone with other powers, were necessarily or always congenial. It did genuinely matter that the two men, the king and the abbot, respected each other. It meant that they strove to soften disputes between the crown and the monastery, as men who were not friendly or were positively unfriendly at the personal level might not have done. It meant, too, that each might offer his good offices when conflicts arose between one of them and some other secular or ecclesiastical power. Nonetheless, given the mind-boggling complexity of tenurial relations in law and practice in medieval France and the existence of multiple intersecting lordships and claims of rights in the country, disagreements and disputes were inevitable and frequent between institutions like the abbey and the state, and between it and other influential propertied institutions below the level of the crown.

One of the more surprising characteristics of the cases dealing with disputes between the abbey and the crown is the clear superiority in record keeping that the abbey possessed. The archivist-monks, those in charge of

[1] Guillaume de Nangis (*vita* of Philip III), *HF*, 20:468–69. Tanz, "Saint-Michel contra Saint-Denis," pp. 108–9; Brown, *Saint-Denis*, p. 312; Bruzelius, *13th-Century Church*, pp. 10–11.

[2] *Layettes*, 3:552 no. 4640; *GC*, vol. 7, col. 391.

[3] Brown, *Saint-Denis*, p. 312.

the parchments, appear to have had an extraordinary document retrieval system, which often made it possible to present written authenticated proofs for rights that the king's men contested on the basis of a much less adequate parchment record or retrieval system. Or perhaps it would be somewhat fairer to say that the royal archives were more difficult to control, since they were immensely larger than any abbey's, even Saint-Denis's. However that may be, little of the monastery's system was owed to Mathieu de Vendôme's abbacy per se. Modes of retrieval based on filing by subject in individual receptacles, reference to chronological and donor and charter-issuer lists (papal grants and confirmations, royal grants and confirmations, and so on), quick-check references, like the comprehensive cartularies with standard summaries of parchments and extensive indexing and highlighting (by rubrication and signs), were all available before Mathieu's time as abbot.

Availability and practice are two different matters, however. When, as the record of one case he actually lost in court reveals, Abbot Mathieu was still new to his job, the system, however superb in theory, was not working well: although the final decision in this case dates from February 1264, well into Mathieu's abbacy, what brought about the loss was the failure of the preparers of his brief to produce sufficient records, as the masters of the king's court bluntly put the matter, to prove its position when the case first—soon after his election—entered litigation.[4] Never again during Mathieu's tenure, so far as I have been able to establish, do such explicitly disparaging remarks intrude into the records of the abbey's cases before Parlement, and I am convinced as a result that it was he who disciplined the archivist-monks and got them to improve their practices.

At Pentecost 1264, for example, the abbot and convent of Saint-Denis were allowed to retain their justice in Osny (in the present-day department of Val d'Oise) because, as the masters of Parlement put it, it was the king's case that was not sufficiently proved.[5] At the All Saints term 1264, to give a second example, the abbot and the convent retained their justice in the village called in Latin *Ad Loca* (or *Locum*) *ultra rivulum*, the present Vauréal, also in the department of Val d'Oise, because the king's case was not sufficiently fortified by record evidence, whereas the abbey's was.[6] Under Mathieu de Vendôme the abbey of Saint-Denis emerged as a document-submitting juggernaut in its legal disputes—in comparison to the crown and every other institution with which it came into conflict. This fact did not mean that Saint-Denis inevitably won its cases, but it gave the abbey an extraordinary advantage in litigation.

---

[4] The case is discussed in more detail below, pp. 69–70.
[5] *Olim*, 1:190 no. III; *Actes du Parlement de Paris*, 1:79 no. 859.
[6] *Olim*, 1:197 no. VI; *Actes du Parlement de Paris*, 1:81 no. 893.

This was important because rights, lucrative and prestigious for those who exercised them, were challenged and defended all the time. Two illustrations will suffice. On 12 June 1267 Pierre Boucher, though a man and *serviens* (servant or sergeant) of the abbot of Saint-Denis, was adjudicated for homicide by the king's men in the royal court at Senlis. The abbot protested, but since Pierre was only a *serviens*, there was little Saint-Denis could do.[7] Men of this status or rank did not automatically enjoy the cover of ecclesiastical exemption.[8]

At Pentecost 1269 a decision of Parlement accorded to the abbot of Saint-Denis, against the king, the justice of the river port of Gennevilliers (Hauts de Seine). This judgment was rendered following a series of events that attended an accident on the river. A ferryboat coming down the Seine had broken the cable rope that was employed to facilitate communication at Gennevilliers between the two banks of the river. When the cable snapped, it caused the death of the mistress of the ferry. The author of this misfortune, the man whose action caused the cable to break, was arrested by the abbot's men, but the king's officers intervened and seized him, claiming royal justice on the river. In fact, justice at the port (including this part of the river) would be found to lie with the abbot; it was this usurpation that the court rectified.[9]

The variety of disputes with other institutions and lords, others besides the crown, in which the abbey of Saint-Denis was involved in the first few years of Mathieu's headship, is quite large. And the pattern is the same, that is, less legal and documentary surefootedness at the start of Mathieu's abbacy than was the case several months later. The first part of the pattern played out very precisely on 14 February 1259, shortly after he became abbot and only a few weeks after the collapse of the abbey wall in early January. On that date arbiters announced a compromise settlement between Saint-Denis and the monastery of Notre-Dame de la Roche over a tithe that both institutions claimed. The settlement was recorded with the *officialis*, the bishop of Paris's judicial representative. The tithe in question was on five arpents of a grange known as Beaurain (department, Yvelines). Beaurain was not a priory dependent on Saint-Denis, but Saint-Denis's monks and lay workers had long before helped clear the area where it was located, and the buildings erected there sometimes served the abbey's men as housing. Workers under the jurisdiction of other establishments, notably Notre-Dame de la Roche, had taken part in the labor and also had access to the buildings, or presumably there would have been no

---

[7] *Olim*, 1:674–75 no. XXI; *Actes du Parlement de Paris*, 1:104 no. 1132.

[8] Cf. the distinction later made between the Templars and their servants by the masters in theology at the University of Paris: Jordan, *Unceasing Strife*, pp. 30–31.

[9] *Actes du Parlement de Paris*, 1:125 no. 1401.

question as to how the tithe should be apportioned. Whatever the customary practice, the compromise stipulated that Notre-Dame de la Roche was thenceforth to pay Saint-Denis the portion of tithe generated from four arpents, 80 percent, rather than all of the clearing. Notre-Dame received 20 percent and also alleviation of arrears and charges that might otherwise be claimed against it because of its excessive appropriations, greater than 20 percent, of the tithe in the past.[10] The monks in charge of Saint-Denis's archives had failed to provide Abbot Mathieu with the documents that would make an ironclad case in favor of the royal monastery's full ownership, even though customary practice indicated its preponderant rights. Indeed, whether they ever drafted the appropriate documents for what appears to have been a rather informal set of arrangements may be doubted. In either case, this constituted a notable lapse on the monks' part.

Later in the year, to provide another example of this sort, the abbey's representatives came to court once more. The 15th of September 1259 heard them assert that the men of Argenteuil (department, Val d'Oise) had knowingly given false testimony—had perjured themselves by bearing false witness—in an earlier dispute. Saint-Denis had won the earlier case, probably because its own witnesses were weightier and more consistent. The point in dispute here was rather different. It was the abbot himself, Mathieu de Vendôme, who insisted on inflicting a punitive fine on the community of Argenteuil. Parlement, in this instance, conceded that Mathieu had the authority to do so; it was his by right. But, in the absence of a privilege bestowed on the abbot or his predecessors to the contrary, the court insisted that he could not exercise this power without procuring an order from the court.[11] He could not muster the documentary evidence, if it existed, that countered this claim.

However, it is a third example, a judgment delivered by Parlement at Candlemas, 2 February, 1264 that cements the case for the limited competence of the abbey archivists early in Mathieu's abbacy. This litigation from 1264 has already been referred to. Though they did not render their judgment until 1264, the masters of the court indicated that the matters in dispute went back to the opening days of the abbot's headship. The masters condemned Mathieu to pay to Jean, the butler of France, one of the great honorific officers of state, one hundred shillings as of right for support of the butlership. The abbot countered by invoking his monastery's exemption from payment, but the judges dismissed the claim on the basis of insufficient evidence. A second claim that Mathieu made, namely, that his predecessors had not paid the sum, also proved to be inexact ac-

---

[10] *Série L . . . L829 à L839B*, p. 71, L838 no. 24.
[11] *Olim*, 1:456 no. XXIII; *Actes du Parlement de Paris*, 1:32 no. 370.

cording to the examination of relevant royal records (*per regia scripta*).[12] As I suggested and as the language of the judgment itself appears to confirm, this case, which probably began in 1259, like the others from 1259 already described, reveals an archival apparatus at the abbey of only limited energy and effectiveness, conditions that were remedied soon after.

The evidence for the remediation? A few cases are certainly suggestive. On the 6th of April 1260 Saint-Denis requested that a priest by the name of Morand relinquish, within a year and a day, a rent he was collecting, which a woman had assigned for a chaplaincy in his church at Montmagny (department, Val d'Oise). The woman had since died, and because the rent was collected on a fief dependent on the abbey of Saint-Denis, the community retook possession so that it would not fall under the regime of the dead hand (*mortmain*).[13] If the monastery had not done this and secured the documentary materials saying it had done it, Morand or a later incumbent could have refused to render the ordinary feudal dues owed from the fief. The attention to this matter was characteristic of monastic administration after the cluster of mismanaged court cases of 1259.

Very similar are two other actions taken by the abbey that also reveal the heightened and meticulous attention to administrative detail, no matter, by the way, how small the property involved. One is the relinquishment that the monastery forced the canons of Saint-Denis-du-Pas of Paris to make in November 1262 of *capitalis census*, a levy on the heads of households, in a small district where this right of collection pertained to the canons. The problem was that the district in question fell under the jurisdiction of the great monastery, and to avoid the possibility of its authority's being compromised by *mortmain*, the abbey obliged the canons to cede the right to collect the levy and others in similar districts in return for an annuity, in this case, of only 12s.[14] The second example is an exchange arranged in 1262 (or possibly early 1263) when a married couple for 50 l. p. sold to the abbey an annual rent of five casks (*muids*) of wine that they collected from abbey properties at Cormeilles (department, Val d'Oise). The couple themselves had earlier purchased the rent from another married couple, and therefore the children of the former owners were persuaded to recognize the validity of the sale and to cede any residual rights they might otherwise claim.[15]

Arrangements like the foregoing leading to the protection and the legal vindication of the abbey's and its dependents' rights were the norm in the mid- and late 1260s. Sometimes the data are laconic, but they confirm the

---

[12] *Actes du Parlement de Paris*, 1:76–77 no. 833.

[13] *Cartulaire blanc de Saint-Denis*, Rueil no. 42.

[14] Ibid., Rueil no. 43.

[15] Ibid., Rueil no. 45, dated 1262, old style.

general observation. The year 1268, for instance, saw the successful defense of the dependent priory of Vaux's right to justice over against the claims of a lay lord, Bouchard de Mirmendie, in the territory known as *Rebotis*.[16] On 9 February 1269 a husband and wife, having claimed that the abbot and convent had taken possession of a vineyard in Argenteuil which was theirs by succession, were rebuffed. The abbot and convent proved their case, indeed with records showing that they had continuously possessed the vineyard for more than thirty years.[17] At the same session of Parlement the same aggrieved couple, Hugues Le Gantier and his wife Julianne, also attacked the judgment that Abbot Mathieu had rendered in his court over a dispute they had with another party about the ownership of a house that they also claimed by hereditary succession. Their appeal to Parlement led instead to the affirmation of the abbot's decision as good and just (*determinatum fuit et pronunciatum quod judicium abbatis bonum erat et justum*).[18] The successes at this session of Parlement were not over. A murderess had fled to Grand-Puits (in the present department of the Seine-et-Marne), a town over which Saint-Denis's almoner claimed high justice. The king's men seized her, claiming that the crown had high justice there. The abbot proved the almoner's right by showing a royal charter (*visa eciam carta quadam regia ab abbate Sancti Dyonisii exhibita*).[19]

The decade closed with another very firm affirmation of the abbey's rights. The evidence is preserved in a "compromise." I use the quotation marks because the weight of the agreement overwhelmingly favored Saint-Denis. Dated February 1270, the compromise was consented to before the *officialis* of Paris and involved Guillaume Tristan, a knight of Champigny. According to its provisions Guillaume renounced all claim to collect levies on produce (*herbage*) and on transport (*rouage*) undertaken by Saint-Denis's dependent peasants (*hôtes*) dwelling at Champigny. He renounced his claim to have fishing rights in the River Marne. He acknowledged that he was not entitled to levy winepress fees on the vineyard of the old taxable quarter (*censive*) of Champigny pertaining to Saint-Denis. In the future he would also forgo his claim to receive the oath of the guard of the vineyard and vintages. The only privilege the knight retained was that of fishing in the pools or puddles (*flaques*) of water remaining on the abbey's territory after the recession of the Marne to its course following the spring flood (*crue*).[20] Tristan was regarded as a variant of *triste*, sad (although

[16] *Olim*, 1:273–75 no. I; *Actes du Parlement de Paris*, 1:117 no. 1302.

[17] *Olim*, 1:282–83 no. III; *Actes du Parlement de Paris*, 1:120 no. 1343.

[18] *Olim*, 1:742 no. IX; *Actes du Parlement de Paris*, 1:119 no. 1322.

[19] *Olim*, 1:285–86 no. VII; *Actes du Parlement de Paris*, 1:120 no. 1347 and 336 no. 232A.

[20] *Série L . . . L829 à L839B*, p. 72, L838 no. 26.

historical linguists argue for the Celtic origin of the name of Isolde's lover). In this case, the popular etymology seems apt. Guillaume Tristan could not have been very happy with this so-called compromise.

Even with regard to issues of property and jurisdiction, the first decade of Mathieu's abbacy was not devoted solely to defending the monastery's standing claims and existing rights and ensuring against future counter-claims in a more thorough fashion than had characterized the period of his predecessor's rule. It was also a time for the abbot to undo earlier concessions and accumulate wholly new privileges and properties both for the monastery and for its dependents. Thus the 9th of April 1263 saw notification given by the official of the archdeacon of Poissy of the sale to (or, more technically, recovery by) the dependent priory of Argen-teuil of five pecks (*mines*) of wheat and oats taken annually from the priory's grange at Bourdonné. Up until the time that he let the priory recuperate the render, one Guillaume Galopin, a knight from Bourdonné, received this produce every year.[21] Another acquisition, this one for the abbey directly, occurred in April 1265. It saw the abbot and monks of Saint-Denis purchase annual rents totaling 8 l. p. from a husband and wife (the woman had inherited the rents). The purchase price was 120 l. p. The bulk of the rents, 6 l. p., was drawn on property constituting part of the endowment of the abbey's office of chamberlain (*cambellania*); a much smaller portion, amounting to 40s. p., was generated from scattered properties at Rueil (department, Hauts-de-Seine).[22] In February 1267 a cleric of Saint-Magloire of Paris gave the abbey another piece of property in Rueil, a vineyard.[23] It was on 16 October 1269 that one Pierre Bodart sold to Saint-Denis approximately five *quarteria* of arable land at Tremblay (department, Seine-Saint-Denis) for 10 l. t.[24] And on 8 February 1270 notification was given by the *officialis* of Paris of the sale to Saint-Denis, by Renoud de Chambly, *civis* of Paris, and his wife Gile, of the mill "dit de Saint-Denis," situated in the parish of Notre-Dame of Pontoise for 280 l. p.[25]

To go through recoveries, donations, and purchases of this sort would be tiresome, though. Recoveries were generally motivated on the abbot's part by the simple desire to undo past and legally dubious alienations, which is not to say that Mathieu could not be induced to concede this or that monastic holding or modest privilege, if there was a greater benefit to be obtained, like the king's blessing. Thus in 1266 he made some politic

---

[21] Ibid., pp. 65–66, L837 no. 73.

[22] *Cartulaire blanc de Saint-Denis*, Rueil nos. 46–47.

[23] Ibid., Rueil no. 38.

[24] Ibid., Tremblay no. 31

[25] *Série L . . . L829 à L839B*, p. 76, L839A no. 11.

minor concessions to the newly established nunnery of Longchamp, founded by Louis IX's sister.[26] This sort of thing was rare, however. Most transactions, the gifts in particular, found their origin in the mutual desire of the abbot for the property and of the donors for a means to honor the martyr Saint Denis and assure requiem masses to their own benefit. The purchases often seem to have been stimulated by the abbot's wish to consolidate properties and reconstitute them as compact domains. The fact is, as Carolus-Barré showed, that Mathieu eventually acquired domains in the abbey hinterlands at Chars, Cormeilles, Laversines, Marival, Monerville, and Mucecourt.[27] He exchanged property, in order to acquire and consolidate domains, at Gouvieux, Plailly, and Montmélian.[28]

The story I have told of Mathieu de Vendôme and his abbey's prosperity could only have unfolded in a peaceful world where churchmen like himself did not have to fear or even imagine unfettered aristocratic usurpation of their rights or violence against them. No king could assure the continuity of the positive economic climate of the midcentury, and nothing Louis IX did, given the nature of medieval states' intervention into economic life, could have much stimulated the economic growth that was so beneficial to France in his reign. Certain failures to act, however, could have inhibited this growth, especially failure on his part to punish aristocratic and other forms of class violence. The simple fact, however, is that in this he did not fail. What marked Louis IX as a great king were his effective reforms of government, reforms assuring that disputes were adjudicated in courts rather than settled by violence and that the functionaries of government themselves respected the rights of property holders. In this environment the enduring security of Saint-Denis and Mathieu de Vendôme's achievements for the abbey are not surprising.

A great deal has been written on Louis IX's reforms, especially the so-called Great Reform Ordinance of December 1254, and much effort has been expended in assessing their efficacy. A very brief summary of this research is required here, partly because Mathieu de Vendôme counseled the king on the reforms that constructed the new moral order in France, and partly because Louis's magisterial effort to be a true medieval "champion of moral repression" (Le Goff's apt phrase) will have to be contrasted to the content and implementation of the new order generated in England.[29] In England, of course, the new order was imposed in the first instance by the baronial reformers, and it or parts of it were variously

---

[26] Field, *Isabelle of France*, p. 219 n. 16.
[27] Carolus-Barré, *Procès de canonisation*, p. 225.
[28] Ibid.
[29] For the phrase quoted, see Le Goff, *Saint Louis*, p. 425.

and inconsistently contested, rejected, or accepted grudgingly by the king, Henry III, and his advisers, like Richard de Ware.

The roots of Louis IX's reforms go back to the investigations into corruption and administrative incompetence that the king launched on the eve of Crusade. The reports the investigators generated formed the basis for a large number of personnel changes before he departed in 1248 and in the first year or so of his absence under the regent, Blanche of Castile.[30] After the sobering lesson of defeat and captivity on Crusade and his return, Louis reinstituted investigations of this sort and regularized them.[31] He continued to favor the Franciscans and Dominicans as investigators because of their evangelical zeal and their outsider status with regard to the administration itself. At every level of the royal and provincial government there were periodic inquiries by these selected and zealous friars and a few other men, lay and ecclesiastical, into administrative performance. These typically accompanied the appointment of new administrators. That is to say, the deaths, retirements, and transfers of officeholders offered opportunities to assess the recent incumbents' work. Huge numbers of both complainants and character witnesses were interrogated as the system took shape, and many of the records of their testimony survive.

The availability of effective and honest administrators to fill openings was a problem Louis also addressed, since he favored moving high officials to new posts or reassigning regional officials after about five years in office to ensure against their developing overly strong ties with the districts they governed. (He also would not permit regional administrators to acquire landed property in these districts, enroll their children in religious institutions in them, or let their offspring marry locals.) Royal administration was very hierarchical. The benefit of this structure was that it implied a kind of table of ranks, a system of promotion. Men worked their way to the top. True, few of the lowest-level officials (subsergeants, beadles, sergeants, guards, foresters), mostly of lower-class birth, ever moved up very much, for the ranks of the genuinely powerful administrators—*prévôts*, *châtelains*, *viguiers*, *vicomtes*, *baillis*, and *sénéchaux*—were reserved for wealthy bourgeois families, in the case of the *prévôts*, and knightly and slightly higher-born noble families, in the case of the others. But it was possible for a *châtelain* to become a *bailli* or a *viguier* to become a *sénéchal*, if he did exemplary work in the lower office. Louis IX had a well-deserved reputation for personally keeping attuned to reports of good administration and consulting that information when requests were made on behalf of candidates for office.

[30] Above, pp. 20–21.
[31] Le Goff, *Saint Louis*, pp. 216–20, and for the details in the next several paragraphs, Jordan, *Louis IX*, pp. 135–213.

The king also issued a set of guidelines for the governance and administration of the royal towns.[32] Paris as the capital commanded his special
attention with regard to the conduct of the municipal watch, the regulation of the gilds, and the proper relationship between the royal and municipal authorities.[33] His more comprehensive concern with urban corporations arose from the provision of the Treaty of Paris that obligated him
to provide Henry III with funds sufficient to raise a force of five hundred
knights and maintain it for two years. He requested financial aid from
royal towns to fulfill his obligation but encountered in the first instance
respectful opposition. The mayors and aldermen chiefly drew Louis's attention to what they had already given the crown—grants before the Crusade for that expedition, additional grants during the war, even some afterward to help clear government debts. They not only enumerated but
complained about having given or lent Charles of Anjou money when he
became involved in the war of the Flemish succession after the regent
Queen Blanche's death and before the king's return from the Holy Land.
Moreover, they claimed that they themselves had already had to borrow
to make these expenditures and numerous others, and they were drowning
in the payment of usurious interest. They desired to (and would eventually) come through and help the king raise the money he needed, but their
complaints, though framed in submissive language, were insistent.

Louis wanted to know more. He ordered the towns to prepare full
accountings of their income and expenditures as well as of their old
debts. These were to be submitted, in the case of the Norman towns, to
the Exchequer in Falaise; other towns were to submit their accounts to
the masters of the king's court in Paris. After these accounts were evalu-
ated, the king was persuaded that his good towns had not been entirely
good. The auditors thought that municipal administrators, despite their
heavy legitimate fiscal obligations, were overspending on things like gifts
to visiting dignitaries and junkets to Paris, masquerading as business trips.
They were also appalled, as the king was, that so great a proportion of
urban taxes was going to pay off interest (usury) on debts. And so they
intervened in 1262 with a set of regulations that imposed a new set of
standards on administrative behavior in the towns. These standards largely
mimicked those the king had imposed earlier in December 1254 on the
royal administration in the Great Reform Ordinance, except where mim-
icking them was absurd: no restrictions, for example, were put on municipal officials preventing them from holding property in the towns where
they lived.

---

[32] This and the following two paragraphs summarize Jordan, "Communal Administration
in France," pp. 292–313.
[33] Cf. Bove, *Dominer la ville*, pp. 189–200.

Nonetheless, like royal councilors and administrators, municipal officials, in order to avoid the accusation of bribery, were not to accept anything more than token presents. Nor were they to offer dignitaries anything more than single servings of wine. The king himself adhered to a self-imposed regime of restraint in these years when it came to demanding hospitality during his own visits, both to towns and to ecclesiastical establishments. On this matter his relief of hospitality payments, *gîte*, from Saint-Denis in 1259 foreshadowed the more comprehensive reform.[34] The regulations of 1262 also stipulated that delegations sent out on municipal business were to be restricted in size to reduce expenses. They curtailed debt financing and put strict controls over the care and disbursement of municipal revenue. The mayors as the heads of municipal governments, like *baillis* and *sénéchaux* as provincial captains in royal service, were put on notice that they would be held accountable for any failure to live up to the spirit of the reforms. The information to determine their success or failure was to be made available to the Norman Exchequer and the court at Paris through the annual submission and subsequent auditing of the accounts of every town affected by the regulations, in obvious imitation of the twice-yearly Norman and thrice-yearly Parisian auditing of *baillis'* and *sénéchaux's* accounts.

There was very little the king did not want to or try to reform.[35] He established sound standard coinage at agreed-upon exchange rates with England and regulated the operation of baronial coinages in his own kingdom, forcing seigneurial minters to adhere to high standards or face loss of their rights. He introduced the gold *écu* coin, which had less fiscal use than prestige value, with its impressive motto "Christ conquers, Christ reigns, Christ rules" (*Christus vincit, Christus regnat, Christus imperat*). Louis's striking of these coins was in a sense a parallel to Henry III's introduction of gold coinage, with a representation of himself as a kind of latter-day Edward the Confessor, a few years earlier (1257), but that had been a failure in every way.[36] Most unfortunately, in Henry's project, the intrinsic value of the metal was superior to the extrinsic or denominational value of the coins. Hence shrewd people withdrew them from circulation. Louis never intended the *écu* to be anything but a European standard coinage of high denominational value. This did not happen, but it failed for political reasons, not because he bought the gold high and sold it cheap as Henry did—indeed, as Henry did against his counselors' advice.

---

[34] Above, p. 33.

[35] Besides the references above, pp. 73–74, see Jordan, *French Monarchy and the Jews*, pp. 148–50, 155–76, and Wakefield, "Heretics, pp. 209–226.

[36] Carpenter, "Gold and Gold Coins," pp. 106–7, 110–12; idem, "Gold Treasure," p. 126.

The French king also nudged the judicial system toward repudiation of trial by battle as a mode of proof. He tried to eliminate swearing, taking the Lord's or the Virgin's name in vain, eventually decreeing draconian punishments, like branding on the lips and having the tongue bored through, for infractions. He attempted to suppress gambling and prostitution. He fully supported the repression of religious heterodoxy through inquisitions of heretical depravity. He wanted the Jews to abandon usury and to convert. So he made economic life dreadful for them by limiting the access of their businesses to Christian consumers in order to encourage conversion. He promised pensions and offered royal sponsorship at the baptismal font for those who did accept the Catholic faith. For those who did not, he refused to give up. Ultimately, he would issue an order compelling them to listen to sermons that exposed the tragic fallacies of their religion, as the Christian evangelizers of the time understood the matter.

None of Louis IX's measures was without opposition. The evangelical (mendicant-friar) severity of the whole enterprise seemed a bit much to a few critics.[37] Jews vented to one another about the limited understanding the king had of the need of his own people for consumption loans.[38] There is evidence that his coinage policies were occasionally regarded as acts of usurpation or unnecessary interference, even if their moral earnestness might be recognized.[39] Open defiance of the king, however, was rare in the extreme, with regard either to the reforms or to any other aspect of his governance. Nobles, like the seigneur of Coucy, who violated what Louis imagined were binding moral norms—in the seigneur's case by exercising his right of high justice and executing three boys on the threshold of adulthood on inadequately substantiated charges of poaching—were humiliated.[40]

His crowning achievement after his return from Crusade (God's holy war) was peace among Christian powers: peace with Aragon, peace with England, arbitrated peaces, brokered by him, among other Christian potentates, and, though most problematically, peace for the papacy.[41] The last meant accepting the view of a succession of popes, the view he had long resisted, that the sole way the empire and peninsular Italy and Sicily could achieve stability and the status of righteous partners among the kingdoms of Christendom and that the papacy could achieve security was

---

[37] Jordan, *Louis IX*, pp. 129, 201; Menache and Horowitz, "Quand le rire devient grinçant," pp. 444–45.

[38] Jordan, *French Monarchy and the Jews*, p. 149.

[39] Jordan, *Louis IX*, p. 208.

[40] Jordan, "Representation of Monastic-Lay Relations," pp. 227–29. Barthélemy's effort (*Deux âges de la seigneurie banale*, pp. 482–86) to soften the importance of this confrontation is not persuasive.

[41] Jordan, *Louis IX*, pp. 194–206; Berg, "Manfred of Sicily and Urban IV," pp. 119–23.

the permanent transfer of suzerainty away from the Hohenstaufen claimants to rule in these regions.[42] Despite the Treaty of Paris of 1259 and his submission to baronial rule, Henry III was never in a position to fulfill his vow to conquer Sicily. The promised subsidy with which his barons tantalized him for letting them reform government never materialized. Other candidates for the Sicilian crown thus put themselves forward or were solicited. With Louis IX's permission, Charles of Anjou accepted the call. He commanded vast resources as count of Anjou and Maine and also as count of Provence through his marriage to Béatrice, technically only the coheiress with her other sisters of that fief, but who had full overlordship as long as she lived (she died in 1267). Charles achieved the conquest of southern Italy and Sicily in a series of campaigns against the last of the male Hohenstaufen in 1264–1268. With their successful completion began a short era of more or less general European peace, the crown and glory of Louis IX's magisterial reforms and the culmination of his new moral order. For the king's admirers, it was the best of times.

There were major political and administrative reforms in England as well. They were generated, however, not by a self-motivated *magister* like Louis IX but from below.[43] They were imposed, ultimately rather brutally imposed, on a reluctant king. The new regime had commenced with the Oxford Parliament of 1258 and the publication of the Provisions of Oxford. The barons supported, even pushed, the settlement with France in the Treaty of Paris of 1259. Henry III, although he showed some spunk when he was in France and not directly under the barons' thumbs from early November 1259 until April 1260 (he was incensed, for example, when they tried to hold a parliament without him in February), was in no position to pressure them to come through with the subsidy for the Sicilian business upon his return home.

Henry never got his subsidy, but the political configuration he perceived on his return from France was more positive for him than he could have reasonably expected. It was not the well-unified party that had opposed him in parliaments at Oxford in June 1258 and Westminster in October 1259 that confronted him in April 1260.[44] A few barons distanced themselves from the earlier humiliation of God's anointed. Others were concerned about further alienating some of the weightiest churchmen in the realm. The church itself was divided, with many churchmen willing to

[42] Berg, "Manfred of Sicily and Urban IV," pp. 111–36.

[43] Carpenter, "Meetings of Kings Henry III and Louis IX," p. 6.

[44] Valente, *Theory and Practice of Revolt*, pp. 68–107, sums up recent research and offers a richly contextualized narration of events, laying emphasis on the contested notion of the "community of the realm."

bridle the king. By one estimate, half of England's eighteen bishops and many of the most eminent abbots, those of Peterborough, Ramsey, Bury-Saint-Edmunds, Saint-Albans, and possibly Gloucester, but not Westminster, assailed the king in rebellious words or deeds or both.[45] Others were far more circumspect, partly because information filtering back from the Continent made it seem increasingly probable that the pope would intervene on the king's behalf. Richard de Ware, who was one of the king's liaisons with the pope in 1260, appears to have done his work well, and his never-wavering loyalty to Henry III, after his return from Rome, meant a great deal to the weary king in the circumstances. The king felt confident enough to go after Simon de Montfort, even before the royal party had fully retaken command of the government.

To the extent that he could, while these events were taking place Henry also saw to the abbot's and his monastery's needs. Sometimes the matters were mundane, like the order to the foresters dated 17 July 1260 to take eight deer from one or two of the royal forests to fulfill a regularly scheduled render to the monks.[46] Six oaks were found in royal woodlands at about the same time for delivery at the king's command to the abbot and convent for roofing their grange at Oakham (Rutland).[47] Sometimes the king's intervention was delayed. In early 1260 the abbot and convent asserted their claim to eight pounds annually, payable at Easter, from the bailiffs of Droitwich in Worcestershire, a county where a great many of their financial rights were concentrated. Yet Easter, the 4th of April, came and went that year with no payment—to the monastery's prejudice and injury (*in dispendium ipsorum abbatis et conventus et gravamen*). On 18 June, with the king returned from France after the solemn ratification of the Peace of Paris, this claim, first rejected by the Exchequer, was vindicated. The barons of that institution had completed a scrutiny of the rolls intended to establish or deny the veracity of the monastery's case. The records agreed with the petitioners, and as a result Henry III was able to direct that thereafter the eight pounds should be remitted to the monks as they specified in their complaint.

One day the mundane (venison, lumber, a claim for eight pounds), a few days later a high matter of state: the Welsh borderlands had been disturbed by military unrest since before the Provisions of Oxford, and no measures had been effective in bringing peace and order. In letters from France, the king gave instructions to assemble troops, ostensibly to thwart ever more daring Welsh incursions into the realm. At the back of his mind

---

[45] Ibid., p. 98; Ridgeway, "Ecclesiastical Career of Aymer de Lusignan," pp. 149–50, 172–73.

[46] *Close Rolls, 1259–1261*, p. 75.

[47] Ibid., p. 81.

may also have been the utility of having such a contingent available in a potential but rather different military contest, one with his disaffected barons, if it should come to a matter of meeting force with force. In a letter of 1 August 1260, Henry demanded the knights' service owed by those he felt were loyal, including the abbot of Westminster.[48]

In fact, a preemptive and very selective military strike against the baronial opposition might have been strategically wise, for consensus was continuing ever more decisively to break down among the magnates. Not all of them were happy, for example, with the results of the investigations proceeding under judicial mask in the eyre authorized under the Provisions of Westminster of October 1259. Often enough, the justice administered in the eyre inflicted financial injury on them. Resentments ran high. And many lords tried to get excused from answering claims against their properties. The royal party saw the king's grant of excuses as a way to encourage loyalty and to draw active support to him. On 22 December 1260, many great men and institutions, lay and ecclesiastical, received official excuses from having to appear before the circuit judges. Westminster Abbey received them for suits against it with regard to its property in Worcestershire, Oxfordshire, and Gloucestershire.[49] The ostensible justification for granting the excuses for the abbey was the king's decision to send its abbot back to Rome in January 1261. It could be argued that planning his trip and consulting with the king in anticipation of the journey prevented Richard de Ware from appearing before the judges himself or sending adequately prepared proctors to answer any legal complaints (*querele*). Certainly, many such exemptions were customarily granted to men because of their going about on the king's business.

Royal protection for Abbot Richard until his return was issued on 11 January 1261. He was, the order of protection states, going to the court of Rome on both his own and the king's business.[50] The king's business was pretty obvious. The supreme pontiff, upon being brought up to date on conditions in England, especially the breakdown of consensus in the baronial party, would be urged to allow Henry III to forswear his oath to uphold the Provisions of Oxford. The oath was coerced and thus revocable, and, even if it had been voluntary, the restrictions imposed on Henry were illegal; they effectively un-kinged him, which was also an injury to the English monarch's overlord, the pope, a status all popes had enjoyed since the time of King John. Treharne attributed the pope's quashing of the Provisions of Oxford on 14 April 1261 to the influence of John

---

[48] Ibid., pp. 191–94; the entry for Westminster appears on p. 194.

[49] Ibid., pp. 453–55.

[50] *Patent Rolls, Henry III, 1258–1266*, p. 118. Carpenter, "King Henry III and the Cosmati Work," p. 191.

Mansel, one of Henry III's most loyal partisans, but he did so on little more evidence than the phrase also used to describe Abbot Richard de Ware's contemporaneous mission to Rome, that is to say, that another among the king's agents went there on royal business and his own.[51]

The abbot's personal business had various aspects and was not trivial. It was clear that, for a partisan of the king, the situation in an England under hostile baronial control had made the exercise of some of his powers precarious, and that he had therefore refrained from certain actions and making certain claims that were granted him by papal authorization. In a few cases, the authorizations were circumscribed as to time, by their drafting, and had lapsed by 1261. Abbot Richard sought and succeeded in obtaining the pope's permission to use the lapsed bulls, that is, to reactivate them and exercise the privileges they bestowed. He also obtained a more general papal confirmation of Westminster Abbey's privileges in this trying time.[52] Finally, he used his visit to Italy to deal with the problem of unpaid debts owed to Italian merchants and bankers.[53]

Pressures on the abbey did not abate in England merely because of the formal protection its head received for his interests while abroad. In March 1261 the monks were back in court trying to overturn a distraint of property that the sheriff of Essex had carried out in Feering against them.[54] Westminster had a manor in Feering, and the church there had been appropriated to the abbey since 1249. Income from its holdings was earmarked for the future celebration of masses for Henry III and his wife after their deaths.[55] This was obviously a situation that the devout king would have prevented or would swiftly have reversed, if he had been in firm control of the provincial administration or had not had other pressing matters on his mind, like the continuing Welsh insurgency.

The works at the shrine of the Confessor were a different story. Pressed or not with other concerns, Henry tried to keep operations going. It was in 1261, probably May, that he imposed a series of potential penalties on a landholder, a woman—penalties that are indicative of the creative approaches he (or rather his advisers) employed to keep the work at the abbey proceeding. Monies that were directly assigned to the works might escape the control of the barons' auditors. One of the clauses in the

[51] Treharne, *Baronial Plan of Reform*, p. 260, identifies this agent as John Mansel, and I at first took him for the great royal councilor, but it appears to have been John Mansel, Jr. (my thanks to David Carpenter for this information). The two men have been conflated before; cf. Elwes, *History of the Castles . . . of Western Sussex*, p. 54.

[52] These matters are referenced in WD, fol. 21b.

[53] Below, pp. 84–85.

[54] *Close Rolls, 1259–1261*, p. 461. The distraint is implied in the abbey's seeking releases for its draft animals (*replegiandis averiis*).

[55] *Documents Illustrating the Rule of Walter de Wenlok*, p. 229 n. 2.

agreement the king had made with the woman in question vested in him the right to take a penalty payment if she defaulted on the variety of promises she had made in order to secure her estate. In this case, the king assigned the potential penalty payment of one hundred pounds (*pene C. libras*) from the produce or issues (*de exitibus*) of her property directly to the fabric of the abbey church.[56]

Yet no king could be perfectly attentive to the needs of the monastery. The fact is the abbey needed its abbot if it was to flourish, and in the years to come Richard de Ware's frequent and unusually long absences on royal business were to have deleterious consequences for Westminster. In one early instance it was the enfeoffment of the bishop of Coventry and Lichfield with the manor of Oddington that was the issue. The conveyance appears to have escaped the king's notice or not to have been brought to his attention as a potential problem. In 1261, after Abbot Richard had returned from abroad, he learned about the transfer and found himself having to assert that the enfeoffment was undertaken to Westminster's prejudice. His case may not have been airtight, but it was sufficiently strong that he succeeded in reaching a compromise settlement with the donor.[57]

The way for the king to protect Westminster and exercise all other traditional powers of his dignity was, of course, defeat of the baronial reform party. There was some hope of this. Cohesiveness among the barons continued to weaken through 1261 and periodically thereafter, partly because the crown chose to champion some of the barons' less threatening causes (less threatening to the royal majesty), like the virulent anti-Judaism the upper class felt over its indebtedness to Jews.[58] By May of 1261 the royalists can be said to have engineered one of their periodic turnings of the tables on the baronial opposition, at least with regard to the formulation of policy. More needed to be accomplished, though, and this took time. It was not until July that the king's men were firmly in command of the provincial administration and had ousted several of the sheriffs appointed by the barons. This was followed by a more graduated set of actions that took months—the patient reconstruction of government at all levels through the appointment of men loyal to Henry. Yet success was only partial; resentments, indeed opposition, remained vigorous.

Perhaps the death of the king's sister-in-law, Sanchia of Provence, on 9 November 1261 was another factor in the crown's surprising string of turnabouts. Her death would have elicited sympathy from many for her

---

[56] *Close Rolls, 1259–1261*, p. 475.

[57] WD, fols. 271–271b; the dispute and compromise probably date from 1261–1263.

[58] Coss, "Sir Geoffrey de Langley," pp. 186–87, 192–97; Stacey, "Anti-Semitism and the Medieval English State," pp. 163–77.

husband, the king's brother, Richard of Cornwall, whose well-meaning attempts to avert civil war had raised his stature.[59] Perhaps the sympathy extended to other members of Richard's family, such as the king's wife, Eleanor (Sanchia's sister), and even to Henry III himself, who made it clear that he mourned her loss. On 11 December the king granted five marks a year to Abbot Richard and the convent of Westminster to be drawn every All Saints from the Exchequer to support the celebration of Sanchia's anniversary mass at the abbey church.[60] However much or little the royal family's personal loss affected the political atmosphere and political tactics as 1262 opened, almost any neutral observer would have concluded that the royal party, indeed the king himself, had done remarkably well and might have been on the verge of fully regaining the ascendancy in England.[61]

In part it was the material and military support of institutions like Westminster Abbey that made this possible. As with many other ecclesiastical institutions and lay aristocrats, the abbey owed a great deal of service, military and otherwise, to the crown, and Henry's partisans were careful to make sure that oaths of fealty were extracted when necessary from these dependents and their tenants.[62] Partly with the military aid they supplied, the king's forces appeared temporarily to gain the upper hand in the Welsh insurgency, a fact that in a snowball effect further increased the royal party's and his own prestige.[63] There were even rumors of the death of the Welsh archrebel, Llewellyn. These turned out to be inaccurate, but before the facts were fully known, the misinformation was widely distributed by the crown to its supporters, including the monastic community at Westminster.[64]

Support for the crown led to benefits for the supporters. One measure of the king's newfound, if tenuous, power, perhaps, is the series of releases from having to come to the eyre delivered to potential litigants in 1262. It is possible that these were routine, of course, and had little to do with the reality of the king's personal authority. At any rate, Westminster Abbey was released with regard to cases touching its property in Buckinghamshire, Bedfordshire, Essex, Hertfordshire, Sussex, and Surrey.[65] Indeed on 12 July 1262 a general release was issued to the abbot for three years

[59] Cf. Treharne, *Baronial Plan of Reform*, p. 230.

[60] *Patent Rolls, Henry III, 1258–1266*, p. 195; WD, fol. 341b.

[61] Carpenter, "Westminster Abbey in Politics," p. 51.

[62] Cf. *Patent Rolls, Henry III, 1258–1266*, p. 186.

[63] Treharne, *Baronial Plan of Reform*, p. 284. For Westminster's aid (it had been ordered to be delivered by 12 November, the morrow of Saint Martin's day, 1261), see *Close Rolls, 1259–1261*, p. 498.

[64] *Close Rolls, 1261–1264*, p. 144.

[65] Ibid., pp. 101, 108–9, 135, 268.

commencing at Michaelmas, 29 September 1262, from all common eyres and forest eyres. The prior of the Hospitallers of London received a welcome similar release by the same instrument for two years.[66] Routine or not, it was a valuable gesture to the prior who had suffered the occupation of his properties by baronial rivals while the king was still abroad in France in 1260.[67]

All the relief was a delight, but whether it was sufficient is another question. Abbot Richard, like the prior of the Hospitallers of London, endured pressure of course from the still not fully resolved political tensions in England and the maddening vacillations in power (an upswing in royal authority, a downswing, an upswing, and so forth). He sometimes found it hard even to procure the most traditional oblations to which his abbey was entitled. The crown's annual render of eight deer, for instance, which had been paid regularly and with few glitches despite the political disruptions down through 1261, ran into trouble in 1262.[68] True, an order went out on 27 June 1262 to deliver the deer, but conditions in and around Windsor forest, from which the animals were usually culled, forced the foresters to find them elsewhere.[69] What must have appeared to be an anomaly in an otherwise more or less smooth series of annual renders would prove to be not an anomaly at all but symptomatic of the continuing fragility of normalcy until the definitive defeat of the baronial opposition several years later.[70]

Yet specific concerns about matters like the annual render of venison were trivial and infinitely less fraught than the general fiscal weakness that was beginning to affect Westminster Abbey. One way to appreciate this situation is to consider the monastery's relations with its Italian bankers and the debts the abbot, the prior, and the convent in their various capacities owed them. As I have shown in detail elsewhere, from the time of his election in 1258 (and the taking out of loans for the delegations sent to Rome for his and his predecessor's confirmation) until the close of 1267, Richard was caught in a web of financial transactions with Italian interests that spiraled almost out of control.[71] The problem was that the political troubles in England undercut the abbot's and monastic revenues both by making collection difficult and, equally important, by requiring the monks to contribute to the king's efforts to regain his authority. What revenues remained went to the needs of the community for sustenance.

---

[66] *Patent Rolls, Henry III, 1258–1266*, p. 226.

[67] Treharne, *Baronial Plan of Reform*, p. 230.

[68] For the 1261 render, see *Close Rolls, 1259–1261*, p. 409.

[69] *Close Rolls, 1261–1264*, pp. 62, 68.

[70] Ibid., pp. 344–45; *Close Rolls, 1264–1268*, p. 69.

[71] Jordan, "Westminster Abbey and Its Italian Bankers," pp. 334–47.

Paying down debts was therefore slow and painful, painful because the easiest way to pay down debts and make up for dips in expected revenues or provide money to the king was by contracting new debts.

Italian merchant bankers, either in Italy itself or with branch offices in London, with whom Westminster contracted, did not offer loans gratis. Service (interest of 10 percent) and penalty payments were charged. Penalty payments were, indeed, open-ended. Every missed deadline for the payment of an installment on a loan automatically provoked an additional penalty. The papacy as the immediate superior of the abbey was in a unique position to protect Westminster, to insulate it from the most aggressive treatment by Italian businessmen, but the papacy was fighting its own costly battles against the Hohenstaufen and needed access to funds that only merchant bankers could provide through loans. The popes walked a very thin line between trying to soften Westminster's relations with the Italians and not alienating the Italians. These facts help explain the tortured and lingering nature of legal disputes between the abbey and its creditors, disputes that fell under the judicial authority of the pope because of the monastery's exemption. To read through the records of these disputes and Abbot Richard's elaborate attempts to buy more time through cajoling, technicalities, and sheer stubbornness is to wonder whether he ever had time to pray—or maybe his prayer was the continuous one, "Forgive us our debts." Only when the baronial rebellion and guerrilla warfare were fully over and the situation in Italy had been resolved by Charles of Anjou's victories was Richard able to extricate himself and his abbey from the burden of Italian debt. The year 1268 was the first year since his election that the archive mercifully reveals the abbot's freedom from the Italian financial yoke.

This, however, gets us ahead of our story or that part of it that has King Henry III as its focus. In the year 1262, neither Abbot Richard nor the monarch could have guessed that the positive signs of the preceding months of a recovery of royal authority were to be reversed, or that, in the abbot's case, the need to curry loans from the Italians would continue. Henry made preparations early in the year for his annual ceremonial sojourn at Westminster Abbey for 13 October 1262, the Confessor's feast day. He ordered more than seventy units of gold as an offering at the Confessor's shrine and three hundred wax candles for setting up around it. He also ordered a repast with wine to be prepared that was to feed the king and the entire convent on the feast day.[72] He wanted his younger

---

[72] *Close Rolls, 1261–1264*, p. 151. The phrase that I have rendered as "units of gold" (*ob' de murc'* or *murc'a* elsewhere; *Calendar of the Liberate Rolls*, 5:147) means, more technically, "gold obols." At this date the gold *obolus* should probably be understood as a unit of weight equal to that of the standard *obolus* of France.

son Edmund to take an offering of a large and beautiful cloth covering, embellished with decorative roundels (*roatum*), for the shrine.[73] And he directed that his queen should offer what was at a price of one hundred shillings a precious clasp (*firmaculum*), certainly of broochlike quality, presumably to accompany the proffered cloth.[74] He obviously thought the crisis was over.

He was in such a good mood that he decided to squeeze in a trip to France before the autumn. It would be agreeable to see his brother-in-law, Louis IX, and his sister-in-law, Marguerite of Provence, again. And it would be a pleasure to enjoy the hospitality of the abbot of Saint-Denis, Mathieu de Vendôme, at the French royal monastery. At first he was not disappointed. He spent the last few days of July and early August as Abbot Mathieu's guest at the ancient martyr's abbey.[75] Unfortunately, he was unable to keep the Confessor's feast day at Westminster, though, for he fell dreadfully sick during his stay in France.[76] The king could not seem to shake the illness. Yet feeling just a little better in November, but hardly hale, he requested Richard de Ware and Peter de Aquablanca (from Aigueblanche in Savoy), the bishop of Hereford, to come to Paris to meet with him on 25 November.[77] (A writ of protection for Richard was issued a week before, on 18 November, in anticipation of the abbot's departure.)[78] Bishop Peter was one of Henry's steadfast supporters, and the king had repeatedly sent him on diplomatic missions, including the most important, such as the embassy to accept the Sicilian crown for Prince Edmund. Abbot Richard de Ware's intended accompaniment of the Savoyard on the visit to the king in France strongly testifies to his steadily increasing stature in the English ruler's sight, even though Henry's debilitating illness, or, rather, his painfully slow recuperation, induced him to write to the two prelates to postpone the meeting until 16 February 1263.[79] The pattern would soon become familiar: a royal request for Richard de Ware's service, the abbot's rapid arrangements for his absence, including the appointment of attorneys (with royal license, in this instance, provided on 20 November) to protect his legal interests, safe-conducts for the travel to Dover and for passage across the Channel (*ad partes transmarinas*).[80]

---

[73] *Close Rolls, 1261–1264*, p. 161.

[74] Ibid., p. 177. She was to offer a similar clasp at the shrine of Saint Thomas at Canterbury.

[75] See, for example, an order issued by Henry III and dated at the French royal abbey in ibid., pp. 145. Treharne, *Baronial Plan of Reform*, p. 386.

[76] *De antiquis legibus liber*, p. 50.

[77] *Close Rolls, 1261–1264*, p. 177.

[78] *Patent Rolls, Henry III, 1258–1266*, p. 237.

[79] *Close Rolls, 1261–1264*, p. 177.

[80] Ibid., pp. 268–69.

Although in the end he was in no condition to welcome Richard de Ware to France in November 1262, Henry did not forget to provide for the great Christmas feast that he usually attended and was still hoping to attend at the monastery with the abbot and monks of Westminster. On the 6th of November he instructed his agents to provide venison and rabbit for the occasion, five marks of gold as an offering, the *firmaculum* that would have fastened the cloth covering of the Confessor's shrine, and many other payments for which he was in arrears.[81] He confirmed these orders in a separate instrument sent to the treasurer on 15 November.[82] Prior to this, longing to get well before returning to his realm, he had set out on a pilgrimage to Burgundy, where Saint Edmund of Canterbury's shrine was.[83] The journey took him from Saint-Germain-en-Laye, a royal palace town near Paris, and up the Marne River. He passed through Gournay and Lagny, but at Meaux or Château-Thierry judging from his itinerary must have changed his mind about going on to Burgundy. Instead, he turned north toward Reims, passing on the way through Fère-en-Tardenois, a castle town whose deliciously creamy-white château—a possession of the family of Dreux, a cadet branch of the French royal family—perched magnificently on an overlooking hill. Reims, the French coronation city with its even more breathtaking cathedral church, was full of healing shrines, including that of Saint Remigius, the baptizer of the first Christian king of the Franks, Clovis. No miraculous healing came Henry's way, though, and on 21 November, under the additional weight of unexpectedly bad news from England about the political situation, he abandoned the pilgrimage altogether to begin his return to his own realm, stopping along the way for a conference in Compiègne with his royal brother-in-law.

In late December, still not fully recovered, he crossed the Channel. A report circulated that he had expired from his lingering illness, and a monk wrote a flattering obituary praising him as a lover and sustainer of the church, a friend of monks, a fit ruler, a peacemaker, and the solace of widows, orphans, and the poor. The embarrassed monk, on learning that the king still lived, "vacated" the obituary.[84] Yet the year 1263 saw the king almost as good as dead, metaphorically speaking. The year was the negative counterpart of the relatively successful months before the ill-fated trip to France. The Welsh rebellion had resurged and appeared to be on the verge of success. Henry was persuaded that only endorsements of

---

[81] Ibid., p. 179.

[82] Ibid., p. 180.

[83] Treharne, *Baronial Plan of Reform*, pp. 289–90, 387, and Jordan, "English Holy Men of Pontigny," p. 73.

[84] Carpenter, "Unknown Obituary," pp. 253–60.

his barons' reforms would rally them to help royal forces meet the rebellion and the other problems of governance effectively. Even the active engagement of his heir, Prince Edward, a good general, in the fighting against the Welsh failed to achieve the desired objective by summer. And, more troubling still, the king could not settle on a way to mollify Simon de Montfort, who had unsatisfied monetary claims against the treasury. The outcome of the only alternative, direct military confrontation, would be uncertain, if it came to that. Prudence perhaps dictated royal gestures of conciliation toward the earl, but the muster of forces against the Welsh (summonses to military service went out to vassals, including the abbot of Westminster, at various times until early 1264) did not preclude their preemptive or eventual use against the barons.[85] Suspicions of the king's intentions were rife.

From the end of July Simon de Montfort regained the ascendancy and emerged as the effective governor of the realm; these developments were marked in part by Henry's "Statute against Aliens" that was forced on him that month.[86] Henry found modest solace in managing to make some donations to and raise his voice in favor of the Confessor's shrine.[87] Yet, despite all his efforts, Westminster began to weaken before the onslaught of its rivals. Customary privileges were curtailed. Thus, for example, on 28 July 1263 a papal order of Urban IV to the prior and convent of Great Malvern confirmed that they did not have to expend more than four marks on the occasion of the abbot of Westminster's visitation of their priory, in accord with a statute of Pope Innocent, but presumably contrary to customs that had grown up since then.[88] A papal order of 31 May 1264 reveals another (this time near) slippage. Urban IV compelled the admission of one Adam de Fileby to the vicarage of Stanes. He had been presented by Abbot Richard and the convent of Westminster, to whom the presentation of a perpetual vicar there belonged. The potential slippage alluded to was the effort of the bishop of London to make an appointment.[89]

Infinitely more important than individual headaches of this sort was the baronially dominated government's setting in motion of a general inquiry

---

[85] *Close Rolls, 1261–1264*, pp. 305 and 379.

[86] Carpenter, "King Henry III's 'Statute against Aliens,'" pp. 261–80, and in general on Simon de Montfort's leadership, Maddicott, *Simon de Montfort*, pp. 228–38. (The older biography, Bémont, *Simon de Montfort*, still makes interesting reading, even though on most points relevant to this chapter it has been superseded by Maddicott's.)

[87] He excused the abbot from pleas of the forest of Essex, tried to protect the rights of the abbey fair, and attempted to assure the supply of grain and the restocking of the abbey park with deer in various orders (*Close Rolls, 1261–1264*, pp. 208, 299 and 316; *Patent Rolls, Henry III, 1258–1266*, p. 278). In general, cf. Carpenter, "Westminster Abbey in Politics," p. 51.

[88] *Calendar of Entries in the Papal Registers*, 1:379.

[89] Ibid., p. 406.

on 26 August 1263 into the liberties of Westminster because of contentions that had arisen between the abbot and convent, on the one hand, and London, on the other, with respect to the privileges alleged to pertain to the abbey's franchises, demesne lands, and fees throughout Middlesex.[90] The sheriffs of London and the keeper of the peace in Middlesex were to name jurors for the inquest.[91] The potential loss to the abbey from the inquest's unfavorable conclusion two months later in October, if it had remained in force and never been reversed, would have been enormous.[92]

Even King Henry's efforts to help the monastery in this grave period occasionally had negative consequences. He tried to force the earl and great marcher lord Gilbert de Clare by distraint of some of his property to pay five hundred marks that he owed for the abbey works. Gilbert de Clare was a terribly important man, whose loyalty was desperately needed at this time. The king's high-handedness, as the earl regarded it, may actually have pushed Gilbert definitively into Simon de Montfort's camp and hastened the collapse of Henry's rule and, thus, the worsening of conditions for Westminster.[93]

The situation in England in 1263 reached the sympathetic ears of Henry's royal brother-in-law in Paris. Louis IX had compassion, as Nicholas Trivet so nicely put it, on the desolation of the English kingdom (*Anglicani Regni desolationi compatiens*).[94] The French king invited Henry—summoned is a less nice word—for a visit to the Continent. In mid-September, just before the king left, Abbot Richard de Ware obtained a writ of protection, an act for which Richard wisely sought and obtained confirmation from the justiciar immediately after the king's departure for France.[95] Henry's short visit, about a week, managed to reinvigorate him, and the day after his return, he showed it. On 9 October 1263 while still in Dover, hardly having set foot in England, Henry ordered the suspension or, rather, postponement of the potentially damaging inquest on the liberties of Westminster Abbey.[96] He needed his abbot—and his saint—on his side, as he came closer and closer to a showdown with the barons.

Could civil war be averted? Simon de Montfort and the reformers around him admired Louis IX and adapted some of his measures to their

[90] For the deep background and context for these developments, see Williams, *Medieval London*, pp. 196–242.

[91] *Patent Rolls, Henry III, 1258–1266*, p. 288.

[92] *De antiquis legibus liber*, pp. 57–58. Williams, *Medieval London*, p. 222.

[93] Carpenter, "Westminster Abbey in Politics," p. 54; idem, "Westminster Abbey and the Cosmati Pavements," p. 42.

[94] *Nicolai Triveti, Dominicani, Annales*, p. 214.

[95] The writ of protection was issued 18 September 1263; the confirmation, ten days later on the 28th (*Patent Rolls, Henry III, 1258–1266*, pp. 278 and 280).

[96] Ibid., p. 283.

own reforms.[97] The earl respected Christian kingship, properly exercised, according to his and his supporters' definition of proper, although they were willing to be flexible.[98] Louis IX had been circumspect in all his relations with the earl. Had Simon thought about the nearly parallel case of Louis's studied "refus[al] to have anything to do with" Henry of Castile, who revolted against Alphonso X in 1256, he might have guessed that the French king's circumspection was not the same as tolerance of rebel ideology.[99] Even if he had thought about it, the case might still have seemed to point to Louis as the necessary choice as arbiter, the only one who would be wholly acceptable to the English king and the political community at large. Both Henry and Simon and both parties surrounding them must have expected that they would have to yield on some demands, but modest, even more than modest, concessions were worth making to avoid bloodshed. Louis agreed to their request to arbitrate, even as temporary truces between royalist and baronial forces periodically broke down and led to nasty fighting.

In the midst of the confusion and the barons' growing tactical advantage on the ground, but fortified by another temporary truce, representatives of the parties met before Louis IX at Amiens in northern France on 8 January 1264. The French king's decision, the Mise of Amiens, was formally published two weeks later on the 23rd.[100] It certainly pleased Henry III but must have shocked Simon de Montfort, because he could not accept that an arbitration, by its nature, could be so unbalanced. The French king, having at last fully studied the Provisions of Oxford and companion documents, whose limitations on kingship he had probably underestimated or at least earlier thought were being exaggerated by the English royalist party, was completely disgusted with the impositions of the baronial party. He simply annulled all the restrictions that had been inflicted on his brother-in-law. They were contrary to the very essence of kingship and were intolerable.[101] He wished never again even to hear barons make such claims against regality (*imponens aliis* [*baronibus*] *silentium quantum ad jura regalia ordinanda*).[102] The last few sentences of the Mise could be interpreted as implying that really old customs, like those embod-

[97] Maddicott, *Simon de Montfort*, pp. 90–93; Hershey, "Justice and Bureaucracy," pp. 848–49.

[98] On the (feigned?) willingness to be flexible and revise the Provisions of Oxford, cf. Carpenter, "Simon de Montfort and the Mise of Lewes," pp. 1–11.

[99] Parsons, *Eleanor of Castile*, p. 19.

[100] *Documents of the Baronial Movement*, pp. 280–91.

[101] The fundamental study of the Mise as an expression of Louis IX's views of kingship is Charles Wood's, "Mise of Amiens," pp. 300–310. See also Valente, "Provisions of Oxford," pp. 38–39.

[102] *Chronicon domini Walteri de Heminburgh*, 1:309.

ied in Magna Carta and the Charter of the Forest or the various coronation charters before them, remained in force, but the barons' fetters on
English kingship from the time of the Provisions of Oxford on were null
and void. When he received the news, the pope, Urban IV, issued a series
of orders dated at Viterbo the 17th, 21st, and 24th of March 1264 to the
archbishop of Canterbury, as primate of the English church, and to the
abbot of Saint-Denis, presumably as a stand-in for all the metropolitans
of France taken together, to inform prelates and lay elites alike of the
French king's decision and to do their best to enforce it.[103]

I do not believe that the baronial party fully accepted *ante quem* that the
French king's power extended to the annulment of their work.[104] Stacey is
almost certainly correct when he argues that the barons originally asked
the French king to arbitrate all matters, but that is not the same as saying
that they vested in him the plenitude of authority he exercised. Still, they
may have been wary, and this may explain why they later added a *gravamen*
on Henry III's failure to go on Crusade to their grievances. They thought
it would be received sympathetically by the Frenchman and would restrain
him a little if he decided in general against them.[105] Yet Louis acted as if
his charge were and remained general on all matters, and, even if he was
sympathetic about the *gravamen* on Henry's failure to fulfill his crusader's
vow, he did not let it moderate his decision. Efforts to resurrect the arbitration on altered understandings failed because Louis IX would not agree
to limitations on his charge.

Civil war erupted in England in earnest in April and with it a period
when Henry III scarcely ceased to hear masses in Edward the Confessor's
honor, behavior meant to enlist the saint for his own relief.[106] Henry also
campaigned with the dragon ensign, a less historic banner than Saint-
Denis and France's *oriflamme*, but a marvelously wrought battle standard,
which on its creation in 1244 at the English king's order had been received
into solemn custody at Westminster Abbey.[107] These symbolic efforts notwithstanding, relief failed to materialize. The battle of Lewes, 14 May
1264, which included an uncharacteristically bad day of generalship by
the king's son, was the nadir. The king and Prince Edward became prisoners. Simon de Montfort ruled now in the monarch's name, although he
seems to have desired to revive a more limited arbitration, again with
Louis IX as judge, rather than govern without a mandate. Louis would
not agree to be complicit in this.[108]

---

[103] *Original Papal Documents*, nos. 695–96, 698.
[104] This is a contentious matter; see Maddicott, *Simon de Montfort*, p. 258.
[105] Stacey, "Crusades, Crusaders, and the Baronial *Gravamina*," pp. 142–43.
[106] Carpenter, "Westminster Abbey in Politics," p. 56.
[107] Tatlock, "Dragons of Wessex and Wales," p. 226.
[108] Maddicott, "Mise of Lewes," pp. 588–603.

It was a parliament scheduled for midsummer that had to ratify the baronial regime and its directives; another would meet in January of the following year to sanction baronial rule as it continued. Richard, as abbot of Westminster, whose monastery's properties suffered in the depredations of 1263 and 1264, got a formal summons, but he did not alter his loyalty, which remained firmly attached to King Henry.[109] It is no accident that he emerged as a go-between for the brokenhearted monarch and his royal brother-in-law in France. On 8 April 1265 the English king succeeded in persuading the government to issue letters of credence for him, that is, for Abbot Richard de Ware, and for Henry, the son of Richard of Cornwall, otherwise known as Henry Almain. They were to visit Louis IX on matters of state and undoubtedly to reassure him on the English king's and his family's treatment.[110] A week later, 15 April 1265, came the expected issuance of protection for the men, lands, rents, and possessions of the abbot of Westminster for the period he was abroad.[111]

Baronial factions hung together precariously whenever there was political strife in England. Fissures developed especially when the enemy, the royalist party, was quiescent. It was always easier to remain united if there was an enemy to focus on. Simon de Montfort's government almost certainly would have cracked in time in the same way. Prince Edward's escape from captivity and his rallying of royalist sympathizers thereafter offered the opportunity to hasten that cracking. And Edward, who had always shown signs of being a fairly good commander of troops, had learned from his earlier defeat at Lewes and the rout of his ill-coordinated royal cavalry and foot soldiers. At Evesham, 4 August 1265, he had the opportunity to show his progress and destroyed the baronial forces that Simon de Montfort had mustered. His people humiliated the archrebel's corpse savagely (*more seculis inaudito*), his head and testicles being sent to the wife of one of his enemies—acts that fed Simon's representation as a martyr.[112]

On the day the battle of Evesham was fought "roughly a hundred masons, marblers, carpenters, polishers and labourers were working on the

---

[109] The summons is noted in *Close Rolls, 1264–1268*, pp. 84–87 (dated 24 December 1264). The depredations are discussed in the context of the violence against a number of institutions in Williams, *Medieval London*, p. 226.

[110] *Patent Rolls, Henry III, 1258–1266*, p. 418.

[111] Ibid.

[112] Maddicott, *Simon de Montfort*, p. 342; Valente, "Simon de Montfort," pp. 27–49. Many texts, like William of Newburgh's chronicle, associate the miracles attributed to Simon with the desecration of his corpse and freely use forms of the verb "to martyr" to describe the perpetrator's actions; see, for example, *Chronicles of the Reigns of Stephen, Henry II . . .*, 2:548. Bémont, *Simon de Montfort*, p. 380 (Evesham Chronicle): ". . . capitur, exarmatur, et, more seculis inaudito, membris propriis mutilatur et christianus a christianis tandem decapitur. Atque sic cilicio proprio carnem artius domuerat contectus, [*marginal*, ut dictum est,] martyrizatur. [*Later hand*, Dominus, defensus meus.]"

Abbey."[113] Victory for Simon would have transformed the abbey into a monument for the new regime. His defeat ensured its continued role as the royal abbey par excellence. True, loyal churchmen in general looked to relief and reaffirmation of their status in the aftermath of Evesham, using their disciplinary powers of excommunication to help secure them and counting on the king's help to recover.[114] Yet the royal abbey was special. It was there, on 13 October 1265, the feast of Edward the Confessor, that Henry wore his crown, thus signifying his recovery of royal authority and, one might conjecture, the saint's and the abbey's and even the abbot's role in the recovery.[115]

For Westminster Abbey or, rather, for God, Saint Peter of Westminster, Saint Edward the Confessor, Abbot Richard, and his monks, the crushing of the rebellion was manifested in a royal grant of about the same time.[116] It stipulated that lands and tenements scattered through three counties (Northamptonshire, Berkshire, and Essex) and worth one hundred pounds annually were to be conveyed to them, saving only the homage and service due to capital lords. These lands and tenements belonged to Richard de Culworth, denounced by the crown as an enemy and rebel and an adherent of Simon de Montfort, now vilified as the man who wished to disinherit and destroy Henry's crown. God, Saint Peter, Saint Edward, and their earthly representatives received the lands as an endowment for anniversary masses for King Henry and Queen Eleanor, with the stipulation that if the issues from the lands did not produce one hundred pounds of income, the king and his successors would routinely make up the difference. It was an impressively drafted document and still impresses (see fig. 6).[117]

The royal victory in the war also indirectly brought the monastery the most spectacular and uniquely valuable acquisition of Richard's abbacy, (Great) Amwell, Hertfordshire, one of the few major pieces of real estate and rights added to the Westminster holdings in the thirteenth century.[118] In 1263 Ralph de Limesey, the lord of Amwell, leased the manor to Abbot Richard for £10 per year, an amount the parties intended to let rise to £40 after twelve years. Barbara Harvey convincingly argues that these were good terms, offered to the abbot or demanded by him, in return for a loan of money, ready cash, to Ralph, money that otherwise could have helped

---

[113] Carpenter, "Westminster Abbey in Politics," p. 51.

[114] Cf. Maddicott, "Mise of Lewes," p. 599.

[115] Cf. Weiler, "Symbolism and Politics," p. 23.

[116] WAM, no. 1692; WD, fols. 61b–62.

[117] The grant, with royal seal intact, was on display at the time I requested it, and was temporarily removed for my consultation.

[118] Cf. Stern, *Hertfordshire Demesne of Westminster Abbey*, p. 48.

pay down the abbot's and the monastery's Italian debts. There is evidence, too, of other small loans to Amwell's lord. But unlike Richard de Ware, Ralph de Limesey supported Simon de Montfort in the later phases of the dispute with Henry III, and he is presumed to have paid a huge redemption fee to secure his diverse properties after the collapse of the baronial party. Thus, in need of money once more, he opted in 1269 to sell the manor of Amwell outright to Abbot Richard at the price of 850 marks (£566 13s. 4d.), to be paid in installments, the first of which, 200 marks, was scheduled for January 1270.[119] The transfer of lordship was symbolized by the yearly render of a clove-gillyflower (a single dried bud of the clove).[120]

Guerrilla warfare, possibly sustained by the nascent cult of Simon de Montfort, along with lethal anti-Jewish violence in Lincoln, Cambridge, Norwich, and London, marked the period after the battle of Evesham.[121] In the circumstances, and despite the evidence of some rebels' property coming into the abbey's hands, the full or nearly full reconstitution of the old order was slow. All aggrieved parties, particularly those like the abbot and monastery of Westminster, who had suffered at the hands of the barons' supporters, were insistent on being recompensed for their losses but, beginning in 1265, had to work through the reconstituted legal system.[122] Prince Edward was the most potent force in government now. The death of Joan, his infant daughter, also in 1265, the very year of her birth, did not impede his efforts at pacification, which included mollifying the former rebels by allowing them in many cases to repurchase their confiscated lands, but it seems to have hurt him. It was perhaps a measure of his and possibly his father's continuing gratitude to the loyal monastery that Westminster was chosen for little Joan's interment. On the 7th of September 1265 Edward authorized the purchase of a cloth with gold filigree (*ad aurum*) to cover her tomb.[123] The name Joan would be reused for a later daughter fathered by him.

A more explicit sign of gratitude to the abbey was King Henry's confirmation, one right after another, on the 17th of November 1265 of the charters of liberties the citizens of London had taken away (*ablata*) from

---

[119] These and related transactions are documented abundantly in WAM but are conveniently assembled in WD, fols. 232b–233, 234–234b, 239. See also Harvey, *Westminster Abbey and Its Estates*, pp. 191, 194, 196, 415.

[120] *Patent Rolls, Henry III, 1266–1272*, p. 473.

[121] Valente, "Simon de Montfort," pp. 27–49; Carpenter, "Westminster Abbey in Politics," p. 49; De Ville, "John Deyville," pp. 30–31; Mundill, *England's Jewish Solution*, p. 41; Stacey, "Conversion of Jews," p. 272; Nisse, "'Your Name Will No Longer Be Aseneth,'" pp. 742–43.

[122] Williams, *Medieval London*, p. 238.

[123] *Close Rolls, 1264–1268*, pp. 70–71.

Westminster Abbey literally and figuratively during the troubles.[124] When the king, on 30 April 1266, permitted Londoners to nominate a sheriff, stipulating that he had to be a man who had been faithful during the late troubles, he also specified that whoever they chose should not intrude upon the liberties of Westminster Abbey.[125] Abbot Richard, on his part, made sure to parallel royal confirmations with papal confirmations of his and the abbey's ecclesiastical liberties, for these, too, had been encroached upon during the period of baronial rule.[126] Indeed he took every opportunity to restate claims to property and power, such as during so-called inquisitions post mortem, involving transfers of estates.[127]

As one might expect, the troubles of the late 1250s and 1260s also generated a backlog of disputes about money, in particular whether the abbey had fulfilled its obligations to donors or had siphoned off resources for what were regarded as more pressing matters. (Think of the loans to Ralph de Limesy while Italian creditors went wanting.) A particularly fraught dispute concerned Abbot Richard de Crokesley's anniversary requiem masses. Crokesley, to recall, had died, allegedly by poison, following the momentous Oxford Parliament of 1258, but in 1267 it was acknowledged that services in remembrance of him and for his soul had not been attended to properly at Westminster, where he was buried, because of money woes and the civil war (*tam per debitorum onera . . . et propter guerrarum dispendia*).[128] A great deal of animosity arose from this failure, presumably fueled by the deceased abbot's family. The scandal culminated in intensity with the excommunication of the monks of Westminster on the basis that they had breached the Rule of Saint Benedict.[129] One knows, in part from a letter which Adam, papal judge delegate and prior of the exempt monastery of Waltham, wrote to Richard de Ware in December 1267, that arrangements were in place by the end of the year to provide

[124] WD, fols. 60b–61. The original charters had been physically restored to the abbey in October; Williams, *Medieval London*, p. 234.

[125] *Patent Rolls, Henry III, 1258–1266*, p. 588. Also, in 1266 the abbot granted related liberties to his manorial tenants, both free men and others (*hominibus liberis et aliis*), including freedom from the sheriff's tourn, that is, from serving as presentment jurors during the sheriff's twice-yearly judicial visitations of the district, from being subject to the tourn's jurisdiction, and from contributing to the sheriff's aid in Hertfordshire; WAM, no. 4269 (the document is badly damaged, but I have been able to make out enough to feel confident to fill out my reading with suggestions from the catalog entry).

[126] WD, fols. 22b–25.

[127] *Calendar of Inquisitions Post Mortem*, 1:274 no. 808, 285 no. 822, 304 no. 900. See also Pearce, *Walter de Wenlock*, p. 27.

[128] WAM, no. 5400.

[129] WD, fol. 118b. The excommunication could have had force only because a papal judge delegate or other papal official or delegate could exercise the power against otherwise exempt monks.

the revenue to celebrate the anniversary regularly, and that these arrangements had received papal approval.[130] Adam was a convenient and appropriate external party to serve as a papal monitor of the arrangements and to report on their successful execution. His commission as papal judge delegate authorized him to exercise pontifical authority in the cases in which Abbot Richard was a litigant with his Italian creditors, and which he orchestrated toward a compromise solution in 1268.[131] In 1268, too, the settlement of Abbot Richard de Crokesley's anniversary having been attained, the monks' excommunication was lifted.[132]

Twelve sixty-eight was a banner year for settlements, including one between Westminster and Pershore Abbey. The anomaly of the royal abbey's having, as a consequence of Edward the Confessor's original endowment, a cluster of important rights in what would otherwise be the heart of Pershore Abbey's lordship led to repeated controversies. Pershore's archives, secured in a strongbox at the abbey (*in cophino cartarum de Pershore*), would have been replete with the evidence of these disputes with Westminster.[133] Animosity and contention did not mean that solutions were out of the question, or that one side or the other inevitably felt that compromise was impossible. A record from 1268 provides evidence that Abbot Henry de Bideford of Pershore reached agreement with Richard de Ware through what is pleasingly called the mediation of mutual friends, thus terminating still another bundle of nasty disputes, undoubtedly exacerbated by the baronial troubles (*intervenientibus amicis communibus fuissent per concordiam terminate*).[134]

Abbot Richard worked hard in other ways to fortify the monastery's position. In the long history of the monastery, what Barbara Harvey has called "the fear of unfettered alienation," particularly to other religious and Jews, motivated the abbots, albeit rather inconsistently, to restrict their tenants' free access to the land market.[135] The inconsistencies, easily documented in Abbot Richard de Ware's practices, owed a great deal to the contingencies of the moment, and there is evidence that, whenever circumstances permitted, the abbots, again including Richard, tried by a policy of repurchase to reverse alienations that adversely affected them.[136] We have already seen that he was spending a great deal of time trying to

---

[130] *Fourth Report of the Royal Commission on Historical Manuscripts*, pt. 1, p. 172.
[131] Jordan, "Westminster Abbey and Its Italian Bankers," p. 346.
[132] WD, fol. 118b; *Monasticon Anglicanum*, vol. 1, A, pp. 272–73.
[133] Cf. WD, fol. 295b.
[134] Ibid., fol. 285b.
[135] Harvey, *Westminster Abbey and Its Estates*, p. 119.
[136] Ibid.

reach some sort of financial settlement with the Italians, a process that also achieved success under the mediation of Prior Adam of Waltham by the end of 1267.[137] There was not much the abbot did or perhaps could do to drum up sustained support from local donors for endowing the monastery with substantial additional properties that would secure its future fiscal health or its rapid return to solvency. Everyone expected the wearer of the crown to act as the principal financial patron of the abbey.

Nonetheless, there were occasions when the property base of the abbey and the abbatial office expanded by means of small endowments of property and people (serfs).[138] Monks of Westminster, ordinary laypeople, and special laymen (*confratres*) who shared in the spiritual benefits offered by the community made oblations to secure prayers in their name. When a *confrater* died, all the ordained members of the community participated in the celebration of his requiem mass; his name was entered on the monastery's mortuary roll; and the messenger who went on circuit to solemnly inform other ecclesiastical institutions of deaths at Westminster included the name of the *confrater* along with the names of deceased choir monks.[139] Larger oblations or endowments, though still a very small part of the abbey's entire revenue stream, purchased perpetual annual requiem masses. Barbara Harvey's work shows that the purchasers, in addition to the families and friends of the monks, were, excepting the crown, rather middling individuals.[140] Abbot Richard de Ware himself in 1265 and 1271 made arrangements to have land in Kelvedon (Essex) and eight pounds

---

[137] Jordan, "Westminster Abbey and Its Italian Bankers," pp. 346–48.

[138] See, for example, WAM, no. 1667: an undated gift from Roger Bolloc (pronounced like the farm animal, if the bullock on his seal is determinative) included two yearly rents and a serf. The serf's name was William de la Wode, and Abbot Richard accepted him, his offspring, and his tenement and chattels in Sidwood (Pyrford manor, Surrey).

[139] Harvey, *Westminster Abbey and Its Estates*, pp. 39, 371.

[140] Ibid., pp. 39, 347, 392. A few examples follow: Henry III honored Sanchia, his sister-in-law and his own wife's sister, with the promise of an annual offering of £3 6s. 8d. when she died in 1261. The executors of the will of one Haymo de Wroxhille endowed, from rents in the estate he left behind, a yearly commemoration of his death at the altar of Saint Nicholas in the abbey church. A certain Thomas, a brewer from Stratford in Essex, gave the monastery a small arable field in Feering, also in Essex, and £10 (for the purchase of rents), in order to endow both his anniversary requiem and that of Brother John le Fundur, a monk of the Westminster community, whom he regarded as his special friend. Brother Robert de Tayleboys supported his anniversary requiem from the funds generated by a tenement he left the abbey in the village of Aldenham (Hertfordshire) and with additional revenue from rents in Aldenham and in Westminster itself. Brother Gregory de Stanes provided his former community with fifteen acres of arable, one acre of meadow, 15s. 8d. in yearly rents, and six tenements in Aldenham for the annual commemoration of his death. He added to this the homage—that is, the pecuniary rights associated with the homage—of six free tenants and their heirs in the village and rents amounting to 6d. in Westminster.

per year from lands and revenues in Combe (Kent) go to the endowment of his anniversary mass, although these dispositions were in fact modified after his death.[141]

Nevertheless, in the closing years of the decade of the 1260s, the burden was squarely on Henry III to sustain and improve the prospects of the abbey. With almost feverish enthusiasm he tried to fulfill this role, which had been necessarily muted during the troubles. He quitted some goods coming to the monastery from overseas of special duties, confirmed or gave supplementary grants for the future celebration of annual requiem masses in his and his family's honor, often without commanding any other service for the property in return, and showered small gifts on the abbey or redirected income to it—for example, from Jewish debts.[142] Yet, as we shall see, the king was unable to turn his own financial situation around as quickly as he wished, despite his avid desire to enhance the cult of Saint Edward at Westminster.[143]

The period of the baronial troubles had highlighted the vastness and variety of Westminster Abbey's holdings and rights, for wherever there were monastic franchises, they came under threat. The abbey's superb record keeping was a powerful tool in protecting its properties and in recovering them when they suffered unjust confiscation. It seems to have been felt that another tool would be useful in this regard, one that provided firm evidence of the internal and external relations of the abbot and monks, and it is significant in this regard that this sentiment expressed itself most insistently in the immediate aftermath of Evesham and coincidental with the effort to reclaim normalcy. The result was the *Consuetudinary* or customary of the abbey, a large manuscript book produced during Richard de Ware's abbacy, sometime between 1266 and 1270, although internal evidence suggests that additions were being made after Henry III's death in 1272.[144] It survives in a badly fire-damaged state as Cotton MS Otho C. XI in the British Library.[145]

The compiler of the *Consuetudinary* was Brother William de Hasele, Westminster's subprior and the master of the novitiate.[146] He collected

[141] WD, fols. 591b–592. For the modification, see Harvey, *Westminster Abbey and Its Estates*, p. 347.

[142] Acquitting of special duties: *Patent Rolls, Henry III, 1258–1266*, p. 502. Endowments and unencumbered confirmations *pro anima*: *Patent Rolls, Henry III, 1258–1266*, p. 540; *Calendar of the Charter Rolls*, 2:146. Gifts: *Close Rolls, 1264–1268*, pp. 205–6, 213. Jewish debts: Rokéah, *Medieval English Jews*, pp. 1 no. 2, 75 no. 308 (items 18 and 19 and n. 50), 82 no. 323, and 88 no. 363; WD, fol. 591b, 593; *Close Rolls, 1264–1268*, p. 261

[143] Below, pp. 104–7.

[144] Harvey, *Obedientiaries of Westminster Abbey*, p. xix; Robinson and James, *Manuscripts of Westminster Abbey*, p. 2; Pearce, *Walter de Wenlock*, p. 51.

[145] Robinson and James, *Manuscripts of Westminster Abbey*, pp. 2 (n. 1) and 24.

[146] Harvey, *Obedientiaries of Westminster Abbey*, p. xxvii.

books for the abbey, including a manual on how to write letters, which, of course, was a teaching text appropriate for the novices.[147] He is also "mentioned in Bodl. Ashm. MS. 842, f. 86*b*, as attesting the miracle of the resuscitation of a boy drowned at Paddington *temp.* Hen. III."[148] Much later Hugh of Balsham, the bishop of Ely (1257–1286), would grant an indulgence of twenty days for those visiting and praying at William de Hasele's tomb at Westminster.[149] Was it the subprior in 1265 who, perhaps at the instruction of Abbot Richard, received from Saint-Albans and also lightly edited the chronicle compilation known as the *Flores histori-arum*?[150] The few erasures and additions speak to a desire to include West-minster-related events in the narrative, but they are insufficient to warrant further speculation.[151]

Whatever the answer to the questions surrounding the *Flores histori-arum* and that text's migration to, its slight revision in, and its continua-tion at Westminster's scriptorium, William de Hasele's *Consuetudinary* alone makes his contribution to the abbey's book collection significant. In it he dealt with the abbot's and monks' duties and protocols—and all manner of statuses and dignities—from garden servants and their food allotment to corrodarians (lay retirees and converted Jews housed and hospiced at the abbey) and their privileges.[152] Even in its present damaged state the great book is a textual monument of sorts, parallel to the impres-sive shrine on which the abbot and king were now lavishing more and more of their time and resources, as the worst of times finally waned.

[147] Carlin, "Shops and Shopping," pp. 492, 498–501, with a transcription and translation of the manual at pp. 517–30.

[148] Robinson and James, *Manuscripts of Westminster Abbey*, p. 25.

[149] *Fourth Report of the Royal Commission on Historical Manuscripts*, pt. 1, p. 183 (3 May 1283). Flete, *History of Westminster Abbey*, p. 75.

[150] On the manuscript's migration, see the editor's remarks in *Flores historiarum*, 1:xiii–xiv.

[151] Ibid., pp. xiii–xiv, and 2:418, 439, and 443.

[152] On the gardeners, see Harvey, *Living and Dying*, p. 219. For a full list of all known corrodarians in the abbey's history, see, pp. 239–51; for several of those most likely of Abbot Richard's time, pp. 240–42. The *Fourth Report of the Royal Commission on Historical Manu-scripts*, pt. 1, mentions two corrodarians that it assigns to Abbot Richard's time, but Barbara Harvey has redated the records on them (nos. 28 and 45 in her list) to the reigns of Edward II and Edward III. Whether any of Abbot Richard's corrodarians were converts from Juda-ism is unknown to me; on the conflicted response of the abbeys to accepting Jewish apos-tates, see Greatrex, "Monastic Charity for Jewish Converts," pp. 133–43.

V

A MONUMENTAL RIVALRY

IN THE ABSENCE OF WAR between France and England after 1259, the continuation of politics by other means took the form in part of a contest between crown-sponsored building projects in the two realms. For Henry III, hampered by the uncertainties and penuries accompanying his decade-long confrontation with his barons, it was a game of catch-up. One scholar, not surprisingly an urban historian, sees the focus of the rivalry in the fabric of the capital cities. Henry's goal, according to Derek Keene, was to make urban London as impressive as urban Paris, or, to use Keene's own words, Henry "saw London and Westminster with the Paris of Louis IX in mind."[1] Westminster—the entire suburb—is implied here, and there is obviously truth in the observation, for it was not just the abbey that challenged the preeminence of the religious monuments of Paris and its environs. Among secular buildings, the royal palace stood comparison with French palatial residences. This being granted, the "notion of Westminster Abbey" per se as the principal "ideologically charged image created to rival the powerful monarchical structures associated with the Capetian kings of France" has been seen by many scholars as "both plausible and compelling."[2]

The plural, structures, in the last sentence is necessary, because English scholars have regarded the abbey as a competitor with many French buildings, particularly the abbey of Saint-Denis, the cathedral of Reims, and the Sainte-Chapelle of Paris.[3] Even if some scholars dissent from this particular grouping, no one would rank any complex of edifices except those that made up the precincts of Saint-Denis as Westminster's principal rival. No one, perhaps, except Paul Binski. For Binski, Saint-Denis is

---

[1] *Cambridge Urban History of Britain*, 1:214.

[2] The quotation is from Lewis, "Henry III and the Gothic Rebuilding of Westminster Abbey," pp. 130–31. For examples of the reception of views like this, see Leyser, "Cultural Affinities," p. 189; Vincent, "Pilgrimages of the Angevin Kings," p. 36; Clanchy, *England and Its Rulers*, p. 163; Foster, *Patterns of Thought*, p. 14, Wilson, "English Response," p. 77; Matthew, *English and the Community of Europe*, p. 37; and Prestwich, *Plantagenet England*, p. 44, and Vale, *Princely Court*, p. 167 (though Prestwich and Vale have explicit reservations about the potential reductionism of exclusively emphasizing the abbey as the material manifestation of royalist propaganda).

[3] At one point, Foster, who elsewhere endorses the conventional view, suggests the cathedrals of Reims and Amiens and the Sainte-Chapelle as the model churches; *Patterns of Thought*, p. 12. Vale, *Princely Court*, pp. 167, 251, 256, also endorses the consensus opinion, while adding Amiens's cathedral to the list.

important, but he argues vigorously against what he regards as the overemphasis on Saint-Denis, a "mausoleum for anointed sovereigns," as the unique and perfect counterpart for Westminster, which was rather a "family mausoleum in the spirit of the Castilian Las Huelgas, or the Capetian Royaumont."[4]

Still, the comparison with Saint-Denis is meaningful when one considers that the closest institutions to a Plantagenet "mausoleum for anointed sovereigns" *and* "family mausoleum" combined were the cathedral of Our Lady of Rouen and the cathedral of Saint-Etienne of Caen, both in Normandy, and the Loire Valley abbey of Fontevraud. Rouen, the capital of the duchy of Normandy, was the site of the ceremonial investment (virtually, coronation) of Richard the Lionhearted as duke and a decade later of that of his brother, John. Along with Richard's heart, the bodies of a number of members of the ducal family were also entombed there. Caen was like a second capital of the duchy before the French conquest of 1204. The treasure was housed in the city. The chief financial department of provincial government, the Exchequer of Normandy, met in Caen until Philip II Augustus moved it to Falaise, nearer Paris, following his seizure of the duchy. William the Conqueror was buried in Saint-Etienne, and the cathedral chapter had charge of the ducal regalia for safekeeping.[5]

Fontevraud possessed the bodies of Henry II, his queen Eleanor of Aquitaine, and his daughter-in-law Isabelle of Angoulême (John's wife and Henry III's mother); it also possessed most of the body of Henry and Eleanor's son Richard the Lionhearted.[6] Unfortunately, Fontevraud, like Rouen and Caen, was located in lands that for two generations were under the de facto control of the Capetians and remained under their de jure authority after the Treaty of Paris of 1259. When Henry III decided in 1246 that he would be buried in Westminster, and when he chose to lavish his attention on the shrine of his kingly predecessor the Confessor, he was in essence inaugurating the insular abbey as the displaced Plantagenet Rouen, Caen, and Fontevraud and inevitably also as a kind of Saint-Denis counterpart.[7] The sentimental pull of Fontevraud, however, after his mother died and was buried there, continued strong on Henry. His heart was to be translated to the Loire Valley abbey in 1291.[8]

Despite an architectural style and monastic character that distinguished Westminster from the Sainte-Chapelle of Paris, Henry's abbey was in part

---

[4] Binski, "Cosmati at Westminster," p. 6, including n. 5. The view, specifically with regard to the burial character of the church, is endorsed by Vale, *Princely Court*, p. 224.

[5] On Rouen and Caen, see Grant, *Architecture and Society*, pp. 8, 11–12, 122.

[6] Carpenter, "Meetings of Kings Henry III and Louis IX," p. 14; Foster, *Patterns of Thought*, p. 13.

[7] For Henry's and his wife's burial arrangements, see WD, fols. 62–62b (dated 1246).

[8] WD, fol. 71b. Foster, *Patterns of Thought*, p. 13.

his Sainte-Chapelle, a monumental Christ-reliquary, as well.[9] One contemporary writer considered the whole collection of relics to be the abbey's defining characteristic: to think Westminster was to conjure relics.[10] More specifically, it was the counterpart to the Parisian repository as a memorial of the Incarnation. From the late 1240s the Sainte-Chapelle housed the relics of the Passion, most notably the Crown of Thorns and a piece of the True Cross. Westminster claimed to have a semi-Passion relic, a piece of bread from the Last Supper (*quadam particula panis cene domini*). After Bishop William of Llandaff visited the abbey and venerated the morsel, he issued an indulgence (6 April 1262) stipulating that penitent pilgrims undertaking similar journeys in contrition and confession would be released from forty days penance "by the mercy of God, the Virgin Mary, the apostles Peter and Paul, [and] the confessors, King Edward and Teilo," the last being the sixth-century Welsh saint who gave pastoral care to the Christians of Llandaff.[11]

A vial of Christ's Blood also reposed at Westminster Abbey. Potentially a greater relic than the Sainte-Chapelle's Crown of Thorns and True Cross and the abbey's own Last Supper bread, this particular vial of Holy Blood nonetheless seems to have had far less importance in the wider economy of Catholic devotion than did the French relics. Compare, for example, the case of the Crown of Thorns. Even though it was no more than a circlet of wood by the thirteenth century, with all its thorns having long since been appropriated as individual relics, other thorns properly blessed in its proximity became devotional objects and proper Christ-relics themselves. They also became tokens in promoting and sealing friendships between Louis IX and other great men, including bishops, abbots, priors, and secular powers.[12]

Westminster's Holy Blood, solemnly received from the king on the Confessor's feast day, 13 October 1247, was quite another story. It may not have been used to seal a wide network of friendships and alliances, but Henry III thought the world of it and made his devotion manifest at the time of the one alleged miracle it performed, probably in the last decade of his reign. It was an excellent miracle. A two-year-old child, William le Brown, drowned in his father Thomas's fishpond. A traditional form of votive offering—a taper measured to the length of the victim's body and placed before the relic—evoked the desired response. The boy,

---

[9] Foster, "Context and Fabric," p. 51; Coldstream, *Medieval Architecture*, p. 87; Carpenter, "Meetings of Kings Henry III and Louis IX," pp. 7, 28; Binski, *Westminster Abbey and the Plantagenets*, pp. 141–45.

[10] See the fragmentary ditty, mid-thirteenth-century, on English places and their distinctive characteristics published in *English Historical Documents*, 3:881.

[11] Crouch, *Llandaff Episcopal Acta*, p. 92 no. 101; WD, fol. 392.

[12] Jordan, *Louis IX*, pp. 192–95.

dead, rose again. Speechless his whole short life before his death, he straightaway began to talk after his resurrection. Now, fifteen or twenty years after the king had processed barefoot with the blood at the time of his gift, Henry processed, once again barefoot, to the abbey in celebration of the new miracle. Abbot Richard had all Westminster's bells, great and small, pealed in joy; indulgences were offered pilgrims; and the ebullient king commissioned a liturgical vessel, probably a cup, golden and encrusted with costly gemstones, for the abbey as a thank offering.[13] Yet there were no more miracles.

The edifice that was home for the Holy Blood at its reception in 1247 had been transformed gradually but to a very large extent by the time of the unique resurrection miracle two decades later (see fig. 5).[14] The stages of transformation drew fruitfully for inspiration on styles in France. Indeed, it has been argued that Westminster Abbey was based on French models to a greater degree than other English monumental buildings of the period, although every borrowing underwent characteristically insular adaptations.[15] Westminster's sculpture, in the same way, was often based on French models but carried with it touches that were (and are) "so very English."[16]

The heart and soul of Henry III's effort to make Westminster Abbey both the most stunning and the most holy royal site in the realm was the creation of the shrine of Saint Edward king and confessor. It was less French influence than Italian that allowed him to do the first, insofar as the evocation of a distinct sort of beauty at the shrine would set the tomb of the royal saint apart from all others in England and northern France. The key figure in the scenario, after the king himself, was Abbot Richard de Ware. When Richard visited Italy for the first time in late 1258 and early 1259 to procure papal confirmation of himself as abbot, he found it necessary to spend March in Anagni where the pope was in residence. Anagni boasted some very impressive decorative pieces, now known as Cosmati work, produced in a then newish style (on which more later). Richard must have been impressed and on his return to England shared

---

[13] The fullest study is now Vincent, *Holy Blood*; the text describing the events narrated above is published in Vincent's appendix 2, p. 205. See also idem, "Pilgrimages of the Angevin Kings," pp. 12–45, and Sumption, *Pilgrimage*, pp. 30–31. For a 1267 indulgence text issued by the bishop of Worcester to coincide with the feast of Saint Edward (13 October), see *English Episcopal Acta*, vol. 13, no. 180.

[14] For a good description of the phases of building in the 1260s and until the death of Henry III, see Binski, *Westminster Abbey and the Plantagenets*, pp. 29–33.

[15] Wilson, "English Response," pp. 74–82, on the general reluctance to imitate French Gothic forms, and on the special nature of Westminster Abbey (p. 77). See also Mortimer, *Angevin England*, pp. 221, 228; Vale, *Princely Court*, p. 167; Stone, *Sculpture in Britain*, p. 121.

[16] Stone, *Sculpture in Britain*, pp. 123–24, 130.

his zeal for the workmanship with the king. Throughout the 1260s, perhaps as early as 1260 itself, work began on the shrine. During a visit to Rome in March of 1267 Pope Clement IV gave permission to Richard, who received it in his and the abbey's name, to arrange for the translation of the Confessor's body from his old tomb in the abbey to a new one.[17] In the same year the cardinal legate in England, Ottobuono Fieschi, offered indulgences to everyone who helped the abbot complete the works associated with the new tomb.[18]

So far, so good. It almost seems as if the end of the baronial troubles finally liberated the funds to complete the shrine. In fact, this was not the case. Debts and arrears still lay on the government's weary shoulders, as did the need to suppress the guerrilla warfare after the battle of Evesham. It is a mark of Henry's determination and his abbot's complicity that despite these burdens the shrine work continued to be carried on at all. In Rome Abbot Richard and two other English prelates, the bishops of Rochester and Bath, who were accompanying him in 1267 obtained a loan of nine thousand marks in the king's name in order to facilitate his interests at the papal court, as they had been instructed. The king was not soon in any financial condition to make payment on this loan. At a parliament held at Bury in February 1267, still largely devoted to issues related to suppressing the guerrillas who remained loyal to the cause of their fallen leader, Simon de Montfort, and to establishing a lasting peace, Henry's representatives also implored the assembled clergy to pledge themselves to pay off this nine-thousand-mark debt. According to a near contemporary source, they indignantly refused, on the basis that, although clerics like Richard de Ware had been engaged to borrow the money for him, the clergy as a corporate group had not consented to their doing so (*nunquam consentiebant*), and thus the clergy as a whole incurred no obligation to repay (*unde in nullo tenentur illud adquietare*).[19] As a consequence, a few months after Henry had promised to repay a relatively small loan that the prior and convent of Westminster had secured to pay for Abbot Richard's trip to Rome, the king's financial situation was dire and he was thousands of marks deeper in debt, with no likelihood of having regular revenues available to fulfill his ordinary and customary obligations or to discharge his debts.

After consultation with his advisers (*inito quoque consilio*) and in desperation, Henry decided to turn once more to Westminster for help. On March 8th, a Tuesday and a week into Lent, an appropriately somber sea-

---

[17] Carpenter, "King Henry III and the Cosmati Work," p. 182.

[18] WD, fol. 389.

[19] *Willelmi Rishanger . . . Chronica*, p. 52. The chronicler, a monk of Saint-Albans, wrote relatively soon after 1290, perhaps in the early fourteenth century (p. xxiii).

son, Henry took a drastic and dramatic step, though not one without precedent or parallel. Contemporary French aristocrats ruling Byzantium found it expedient to pawn the Crown of Thorns to obtain the money to govern the empire, the act that gave Louis IX the opportunity to redeem the Crown for France.[20] King Alfonso X of Castile (1252–1284), also a contemporary, raised money by pawning one of his crowns in order to cement an alliance with the Merinid sultan.[21] So Henry III, reserving only the regalia, pledged the royal jewels and other precious objects kept at Westminster and at the Tower of London to raise money.[22] Because Abbot Richard had not yet returned from his altogether leisurely trip to Rome at the time this decision was made, the king instructed the prior, subprior, precentor, and sacristan of Westminster to give up the treasure to the legate so he could carry out his wishes. It was delivered to Cardinal Ottobuono on the 28th of March, three weeks before the Easter session of the Exchequer, at which the Italians were scheduled to be repaid for the small loan that was underwriting Abbot Richard's travels, an obligation that was, of course, trivial in relation to the total financial burdens now facing the crown.[23]

Were the king's actions sufficient for his needs? The answer, an infinitely depressing one, came on April 4th. The abbey was asked to turn over precious items and materials assigned for the refurbishing of the shrine of Edward the Confessor (*jocalia ecclesiae Westmonasterii, imagines feretri aureas, et lapides preciosos*), in addition to the treasure already rendered, for disposal. Henry still protected the coronation regalia, but the necessity to put the shrine of Saint Edward in jeopardy cut him deeply. The king's son, Prince Edward, was instrumental in getting him to see just how bad the financial situation had become and how radical a means was necessary to rectify it.[24]

Disposing of the treasure proceeded steadily. By 28 May 1267 the king acknowledged that some of the treasure had been sold and some pawned, and that his men were negotiating to pawn other parts of it. He informed Richard de Ware of this when the abbot returned from Italy. Not knowing of the situation in England before then, Richard had innocently engaged Cosmati craftsmen for work on the Confessor's shrine.[25] Now the abbot

---

[20] Above, p. 15.

[21] Stearns, "Exceptional Footnotes," p. 18.

[22] A comprehensive study is Wayno's *Instance of Pawning*.

[23] *Patent Rolls, Henry III, 1266–1272*, pp. 50, 133.

[24] Ibid., p. 52; the prince's role in the earlier decisions may be inferred from the documents cited in the preceding note. The quoted phrase is from *Flores historiarum*, 3:14–15. A synopsis of the records regarding these events is provided in the *Fourth Report of the Royal Commission on Historical Manuscripts*, pt. 1, p. 191.

[25] Or so it is presumed: Carpenter, "King Henry III and the Cosmati Work," p. 191. See also *History of the King's Works*, 1:147 n. 1.

chafed from criticism from his monks for not protesting the alienation, even though King Henry insisted that the prelate should regard himself as blameless. Henry also made clear to the abbot and the other high dignitaries of the monastery that he intended to compensate them, one way or another, by the end of September 1268, not quite a year and a half in the future. He allowed his own movable property to stand as surety for fulfilling the promise, and he swore that he would accept the judgment against him of the pope or the legate, Cardinal Ottobuono, if he failed to fulfill his oath, even to the laying of an interdict on the royal chapel. Prince Edward sealed these letters too.[26] The itemized list of the treasure is almost incredible in its length and variety.[27] Its disposition brought in substantial sums, perhaps as much as the equivalent of a tenth of ordinary annual royal revenue, from the merchant moneylenders (*in manibus tradidit mercatorum, non modicam pecuniam mutuo recipiens pro eisdem*).[28] Yet the question of the redemption of the treasure remained.

This time it was the church, under the cardinal-legate's immense pressure, that saved the king by levying a 10 percent income tax on itself, which went largely to royal use. On 8 April 1268 an order went out to two recently commissioned collectors of this tenth, one of whom was a Westminster monk, Walter of London, to transfer two hundred marks of the first returns from the archbishopric of Canterbury and the bishopric of Worcester to Richard de Ware so he could begin the process of redeeming the royal and abbatial treasures.[29] This transfer was repeated as more revenue from the tax became available.[30] Not everything went smoothly, of course, and the king did not fully make the September 1268 deadline.[31] Collection of the tax was plagued, or so it was intimated by royal officials, by the fact that the clerical commissioners were too indulgent to their clerical brethren. Even commissioners who were Westminster monks—and who might be expected to have a vested interest in making sure the government was paid so that their abbot could redeem the jewels—were sacked for perceived leniency in making assessments.[32] More-

---

[26] *Patent Rolls, Henry III, 1266–1272*, pp. 64–65. See also the *Syllabus* (p. 76) to Rymer's *Foedera* and *Monasticon Anglicanum*, 1:311.

[27] *Patent Rolls, Henry III, 1266–1272*, pp.135–40 (this list is dated 1 June 1267).

[28] *Flores historiarum*, 3:15.

[29] On the transfer, *Patent Rolls, Henry III, 1266–1272*, p. 217; for the initial commission, 20 March 1268, p. 210. See also Lunt, *Financial Relations*, pp. 626, 628–29.

[30] *Patent Rolls, Henry III, 1266–1272*, p. 252 (18 August 1268).

[31] A brief summary of the records with regard to the collection of the tenths is provided in the *Fourth Report of the Royal Commission on Historical Manuscripts*, pt. 1, p. 196.

[32] *Patent Rolls, Henry III, 1266–1272*, pp. 332, 352–53 (examples of these troubles from 14 April and 13 July 1269).

over, only part of the revenue from the tax went toward the redemption. Some was diverted to pay the king's household expenses.[33]

Nevertheless, Henry acted in good faith. He ultimately succeeded in providing the funds to redeem the pledges and in restoring the treasure to Westminster (*quae tamen tranquillitatis tempore restituit ecclesiae*), indeed, not too long after the September goal.[34] And whenever he could, the king shuffled additional funds for the shrine to the abbot.[35] One gift in 1267 permitted the purchase of three hundred pounds of wax. The intent was to measure candles to the king's height (*pro mensuris regis*) and to set them about Saint Edward's shrine.[36]

The abbot's support for Henry, though it put him in conflict with those who wanted him to fight the pawning of the jewels, did secure certain advantages for the abbey. In Sept 1267 the crown temporarily remitted the military service Richard owed and forbade royal officers to use distraint to force his military tenants to do service.[37] On 17 January 1268 a royal license was issued to the abbot and convent to have firewood, corn, and other victuals brought by land or water to the abbey without prises on the goods; the order was to be effectuated by the constable of Windsor Castle and all royal bailiffs.[38] The crown also excused the abbot from common summons of pleas in various counties.[39] Finally, Henry was scrupulous in reimbursing every last farthing he owed Richard for tasks he had carried out on royal commission. The assessment of the abbot's tenth on properties in the diocese of Worcester in 1269, for instance, was reduced by fifty pounds because the king still owed the abbot money for services his men had rendered during the baronial troubles at the siege of Kenilworth Castle, for a loan to the Wardrobe at a particularly needy time, and for monies Richard had expended in Italy for the (probably largest part of the) pavement set before the high altar.[40]

The new and lustrous-hued pavement employed geometrical patterns, whose materials included red and green porphyry obtained in Italy, col-

---

[33] Ibid., p. 318 (this example is dated 13 February 1269).

[34] The quotation is from *Flores historiarum*, 3:15.

[35] *Close Rolls, 1264–1268*, p. 549; *Patent Rolls, Henry III, 1266–1272*, pp. 293–94.

[36] *Close Rolls, 1264–1268*, p. 288; *Calendar of the Liberate Rolls*, 5:292.

[37] *Close Rolls, 1264–1268*, p. 332.

[38] *Patent Rolls, Henry III, 1266–1272*, p. 181.

[39] *Close Rolls, 1264–1268*, p. 552; *Close Rolls, 1268–1272*, p. 109.

[40] For the assessment, see *Patent Rolls, Henry III, 1266–1272*, p. 380; for the reduction and the debts, see , p. 338. On the pavement, *Flores historiarum*, 3:17 n. 4. See also Carpenter, "King Henry III and the Cosmati Work," pp. 192–93, and Lunt, *Financial Relations*, p. 299 n. 6. Bradley's supposition (*Annals of Westminster Abbey*, p. 63) that the tiled floor of the chapter house was also included in this project is highly unlikely. The chapter house pavement is more likely fourteenth-century.

ored glass, alabaster, and, when the alabaster ran out, Purbeck marble.[41] Reference to the purchase of the alabaster ("almost certainly of English origin") for the pavement appears in the Pipe Roll of 53 Henry III (1269).[42] In general there was a preference for alabaster over the less expensive Purbeck marble, a "grey-green limestone" laced "with the fossilised shells of freshwater pond snails." Purbeck marble, quarried in the shadow of Corfe Castle on the Isle (or more properly *presqu'île*) of Purbeck in Dorsetshire, was as beautiful as green porphyry and alabaster in some estimations and could be burnished to as satiny a luster, but it was less durable.[43]

The inscription that came to accompany the geometric inlays lists the men responsible for the pavement: Henry III; the chief craftsman, Odoricus of Rome (possibly the Italian otherwise known as Pietro di Oderisio, although this has been hotly denied); and Abbot Richard. It also ascribes a meaning to the pattern.[44] The reasonably well-attested original form of the inscription, provided here with the abbreviations extended and ornamental points suppressed, would have read as follows:[45]

CHRISTI MILLENO BIS CENTENO DUODENO

CUM SEXAGENO SUBDUCTIS QUATUOR ANNO

TERTIUS HENRICUS REX URB[I]S ODORICUS ET ABBAS

HOS COMPEGERE PORPHYREOS LAPIDES

[41] *History of the King's Works*, 1:146–47. True purple-colored porphyry (the Greek word, of course, means purple) was available only from classical ruins, since the location of the ancient imperial Roman mines in Egypt from which it was quarried was unknown in the Middle Ages; Foster, *Patterns of Thought*, p. 35.

[42] *History of the King's Works*, 1:147 n. 2; the quotation is from Foster, *Patterns of Thought*, p. 39. On English alabaster, as opposed to that used in ancient Continental monuments, see Ramsay, "Alabaster," pp. 29–40.

[43] Stone, *Sculpture in Britain*, p. 148; Mortimer, *Angevin England*, p. 185; and for the quotations, Foster, *Patterns of Thought*, p. 34. Blair, "Purbeck Marble," pp. 41–56, provides additional material on the mining and use of this material.

[44] In general, see *History of the King's Works*, 1:147. On the debate over the identification of Odericus, see Foster, *Patterns of Thought*, p. 22, 26–27; idem, "Context and Fabric," pp. 52–53; Binski, "Cosmati at Westminster," pp. 18–19; Claussen, *Magistri Doctissimi Romani*, pp. 176–85 (and more generally on Pietro and other works known to be his or ascribed to him, pp. 174–76, 185–205).

[45] Foster, *Patterns of Thought*, p. 80. On only one matter do I differ with Foster, who otherwise reviews the evidence competently. He and many other commentators prefer *urbs* (attested by Flete) to *urbis* (p. 93). He has good, but not in my view conclusive, arguments, as is suggested by phrases like "is almost certainly confirmed," which means "is not actually confirmed." Preservation of scansion, in this case to a hexameter line (with *urbs* rather than *urbis*), is rarely a decisive argument for adopting a particular verbal form in inscriptions. It is a substantive consideration that inclines me to *urbis*. The reading *urbis* would mean that the line in which it appears emphasizes a triad—three men, not three men and a place. Given the prominence of three-ness throughout the inscription and the fact that the line itself begins with *tertius*, this makes a great deal of sense.

SI LECTOR POSITA PRUDENTER CUNCTA REVOLVAT

HIC FINEM PRIMI MOBILIS INVENIET

SEPES TRIMA CANES ET EQUOS HOMINESQUE SUBADDAS

CERVOS ET CORVOS AQUILAS IMMANIA CETE

MUNDUM QUODQUE SEQUENS PREEUNTIS TRIPLICAT ANNOS

SPERICUS ARCHETIPUM GLOBUS HIC MONSTRAT

MACROCOSMUM

I largely follow Richard Foster's various suggestions for translation as a guide, although I have occasionally departed from them.[46]

In the year of Christ one thousand, two hundred, twelve, plus sixty, minus four [1272 – 4 = 1268], King Henry III, Odoricus of Rome ["the City"], and the Abbot set in place these porphyry stones.

If the reader intelligently moves around all that is laid down, he will discover here the measure of the prime mover: the hedge three years, add in turn dogs, and horses and men, stags and ravens, eagles, huge sea monsters, the world: each that follows triples the years of the one before.

Here is the perfectly rounded sphere which reveals the eternal pattern of the universe.

This inscription has been said by commentators to reveal the "esoteric significance of the circular figure in the centre as a microcosm of the universe," "if the reader intelligently moves around [that is, reads and walks around] all that is laid down."[47] Another impression, recorded as early as 1636, is similar: the pavement contains "the discourse of the whole world, which is at this day most beautiful; a thing of that singularity, curiousness, and rareness, that England hath not the like again."[48] Such over-the-top sentiments have not been universal.[49] Fuller, also writing in the seventeenth century and reacting to the words just quoted, was a bit embarrassed that he found the pavement dull and uninspiring, although he excused himself by invoking his own aesthetic infirmity.

See, readers, what an enemy ignorance is to art. How often have I trampled on that pavement, so far from admiring, as not observing

---

[46] Foster, *Patterns of Thought*, pp. 3, 91, 109–10.

[47] *History of the King's Works*, 1:147. The phrase "moves around" for the Latin *revolvat* captures the importance of the circle better than Foster's preferred "reflects upon" or Wander's "considers" ("Westminster Abbey Sanctuary Pavement," p. 141).

[48] John Philipot, cited in Fuller, *History of the Worthies of England*, 2:43.

[49] Cf. Norton's review of the varied reactions to the pavements, "Luxury Pavement," p. 7.

it; and since upon serious survey, it will not, in my eyes, answer this character of curiosity. However, I will not add malice to my ignorance (qualities which too often are companions) to disparage what I do not understand: but I take it, on the trust of others more skillful, for a master-piece of art.[50]

The present designs, though somewhat restored, are basically original or faithful to the original (see fig. 7).[51] And there is nothing wrong, as far as I can tell, with serious scholars' general conclusions.[52] Occasionally, it may, perhaps unjustly, strike one that the esoteric becomes more mysterious under certain scholars' gaze than it was at the time of the pavement's creation.[53] Foster's otherwise useful and interesting *Patterns of Thought* invokes such an extraordinarily rich and arcane body of influences on the inscription and the design that his argument almost begs to be characterized as overdetermined. But there is enough contemporary corroborating evidence of ditties based on the years lived by various plants and animals, ditties similar to the midsection of the inscription, to establish that the words and design were intended to look forward and predict the date of the apocalypse: the hedgehog lives three years, dogs three squared years (nine), horses three cubed (twenty-seven), men, three to the fourth power (eighty-one), and so on. The last element in the series, the world, at the time of the end will therefore be three to the ninth power ($3^3 \times 3^3 \times 3^3$) years old or 19,683. In point of fact, this would rather intrigue than help the medieval audience: did the figure 19,683 refer to years since Creation (and, if so, how many years had already gone by, for computists differed)? Did it refer to the years since the new birth of the world, variously considered the Incarnation or the Crucifixion?

In any case, why do all this? One suggestion is that Henry or Abbot Richard wished to go "one better than the labyrinths of the French cathedrals, which it [the geometrical design of the pavement] was perhaps intended to emulate."[54] For Michael Clanchy the motivation was wholly that of the king, who, through the cryptic inscription, "placed himself symbolically at the centre of Europe (in Rome), chronologically in Christian time (AD 1268) and in the space-time of the *primum mobile*."[55]

[50] Fuller, *History of the Worthies of England*, 2:43.

[51] Foster, *Patterns of Thought*, pp. 78–79.

[52] Cf., for example, Wander, "Westminster Abbey Sanctuary Pavement," pp. 137–56.

[53] Cf. Howlett, "Inscriptions in the Sanctuary Pavement," pp. 100–110, for some fascinating possibilities. See also Binski, *Westminster Abbey and the Plantagenets*, pp. 97–100; and idem, "Cosmati and *Romanitas*," pp. 123–26.

[54] *History of the King's Works*, 1:147. This is not to say that the pavement is a "true labyrinth"; see Binski's cautionary remarks in "Cosmati at Westminster," p. 31.

[55] Clanchy, *England and Its Rulers*, p. 204.

Possibly. But this motivation could just as easily fit Abbot Richard de Ware, who had spent time genuinely, not virtually, in Rome (presuming *urbs* was the original form), and who may have had what Foster calls an "esoteric eye," even if he had never chatted in Italy about the spiritual meaning of Cosmati work with Thomas Aquinas and was not quite so familiar, as Foster suggests, with Robert Grosseteste's recondite Neoplatonic musings on the necessary geometric perfection of the universe.[56] Indeed, it may be fairest to say that both king and abbot are mutually presented through the inscription, especially if the inscription was added, as Binski has argued, after Henry III's death as a remembrance from the abbot. (How else ought one to explain the strange dating formula: 1272, the year of Henry's death, minus four, to give the year of the pavement's installation, 1268?)[57] The abbot's coming last in the list of men (Henry III, Odoricus, Abbot) in the relevant line in the inscription conforms to the rhetorical convention of emphasizing the first (the king) and the last (himself) in a series: Odoricus, the mere craftsman, in the middle is, in fact, backstage.

Even without the inscription laid, Henry III, who spent Christmas at Westminster in 1268 as a kind of thank offering to the Confessor, was "pleased with the result. . . . [I]n the course of time his own tomb was to be ornamented in the same manner."[58] Indeed for Henry there was a sense that time was running out. Since his terrible illness in France in 1262, the king's health had been uneven. On 21 June 1269 he was delayed in coming to Parliament owing to another bout of sickness, and he delegated an embassy of three to represent his views to the assembled multitude until he could come himself. Abbot Richard, now one of the king's closest counselors and an always loyal supporter, was selected as one member of this troika.[59] Every effort was put into securing the necessary funds to accomplish as much as possible for, and indeed perhaps to completely finish, the Confessor's works at Westminster.[60]

The culmination of all this effort was the thrilling translation of the earthly remains of Saint Edward from their modest coffret to a new or, perhaps more accurately stated, a refurbished reliquary (see fig. 8).[61] Papal

---

[56] Foster, *Patterns of Thought*, pp. 129–30, 149, 162–65.

[57] Binski, "Cosmati at Westminster," pp. 10–11, 28–29; Carpenter, "Westminster Abbey in Politics," p. 57.

[58] The quotation is from the *History of the King's Works*, 1:147, though the installation sequence suggested in a (nonquoted) part of the text is dubious. On the nature of Henry's Christmas sojourn at the abbey, see *Flores historiarum*, 3:17.

[59] *Patent Rolls, Henry III, 1266–1272*, p. 384.

[60] Carpenter, "Westminster Abbey in Politics," p. 55; idem, "King Henry III and the Cosmati Work," p. 182 n. 17.

[61] Carpenter, "Westminster Abbey in Politics," p. 58.

permission had been sought and obtained for the translation and the indulgences to go along with it in anticipation two years before.[62] Even unfinished, the shrine was a marvel, gem-encrusted and lavishly gilded (Henry III's gift), revealed to all on the feast day, 13 October 1269.[63] The year, according to Carpenter's quite clever argument, was chosen because it was the only time between 1258 and 1353 when the year lined up, movable feast by movable feast with 1163, the year of Edward the Confessor's original translation. This symmetry was not, as Carpenter shows, lost on contemporaries.[64]

Indulgences of forty days' release from purgatory were being granted to pilgrims—perhaps significantly, Welsh pilgrims—visiting the mostly finished shrine even before this ceremony. At least, it was the bishop of Saint David's, by the reckoning of many the ruler of Wales' most prestigious see, who granted the indulgence while at court on 4 May 1269, and who did so, as Carpenter notes, both for the king and for peace.[65] The king's eye, of course, was still primarily focused on the translation, and he crowed ecstatically about the coming festival in a letter to his erstwhile Welsh enemy Llewellyn, reconciled and recognized as Prince of Wales since 1267, who was invited. He would be celebrating the feast as solemnly as possible, he told the Welshman, in the newly refurbished abbey church, with his son, recently vowed in Paris as a crusader, in attendance.[66]

The banquet was intended to be, in Weiler's words, "a truly festive occasion." The quantity of venison, meat from 125 deer, was staggering (pun intended).[67] The occasion was marked by the presence of dignitaries from all over the kingdom, good cheer, the investiture of more knights than ever before at a single time, and an extraordinary level of royal largesse—not exactly unrelated phenomena.[68] There was also a great deal of postur-

---

[62] WD, fols. 386–386b.

[63] I follow Carpenter, "King Henry III and the Cosmati Work," p. 183, and idem, "Westminster Abbey in Politics," p. 58, as to the largely, if not entirely, finished character of the shrine, but cf. Binski, "Cosmati at Westminster," pp. 14–17. On the spectacular nature of the shrine, see *Willelmi Rishanger . . . Chronica*, pp. 56, 429, and the "Annals" of Winchester and Oseney in *Annales Monastici*, 2:108, and 4:226–27. The splendor of the shrine in one way or another, but especially its use of gold, would be remarked for generations; see, for example, the late fourteenth-century *Ypodigma Neustriae*, p. 168 (and p. viii on the date).

[64] Carpenter, "Westminster Abbey in Politics," pp. 54–55; idem, "Westminster Abbey and the Cosmati Pavements," pp. 42–43.

[65] *Fourth Report of the Royal Commission on Historical Manuscripts*, pt. 1, p. 183. Carpenter, "Westminster Abbey in Politics," pp. 57–58.

[66] *Close Rolls, 1268–1272*, p. 71.

[67] Weiler, "Symbolism and Politics," p. 34.

[68] See the various reports in the "Annals" of Winchester, Waverley, Dunstable, and Worcester in *Annales Monastici*, 2:108, 378; 3:252, and 4:458. Weiler, "Symbolism and Politics," pp. 20, 34–36.

ing and jockeying among attendees. The thirteen bishops refused to process behind the archbishop of York who, by carrying his cross, appeared to be usurping the prerogatives of Boniface of Savoy, the archbishop of Canterbury, who was in Savoy preparing to go on Crusade with Prince Edward at the time and could not be present at the festivities.[69] Representatives of the cities of Winchester and London, who were suspicious of their rivals' efforts to obtain preferential treatment in doing food service at the formal ceremonies, displayed open contempt for each other.[70] The old king, who had intended to wear his crown, decided against doing so to try to prevent or soften antagonisms among attendees, for the wearing of the crown implied specific ceremonial roles for specific attendees to play, and there were often, as in the case of the argument of the Winchester men and the Londoners as to the butlership for the feast, conflicting claims over who should play these roles.[71]

More happily, the occasion was celebrated on account of the miraculous healing of two men possessed of demons—a cleric from Winchester and a layman from Ireland—through the intercession of the saint (*per Sancti Regis merita*).[72] They were said to be fully restored to health (*receperunt pristinam sanitatem*).[73] Miracles of this sort were added enthusiastically to the existing record of the Confessor's wonder working.[74] Perhaps David Carpenter is correct that the king's evident emphasis on the sacrality of his rule, instantiated in the splendor of the church and the shrine, "may well have saved" Henry's throne.[75] Indeed, the air of devotion the king's single-mindedness imparted to the making of the great edifice and shrine must have led even some critics of his rule to believe that God would welcome their sometimes foolish but often well-meaning monarch with tender compassion to the Heavenly Court. This did not mean that they would lavish money on him in the here and now. As Carpenter also points out, the day after the translation, the clergy, less the bishops, refused in formal assembly to grant a desired tax to the king and instead used the forum as an occasion to criticize his efforts to take their money in the past.[76] And yet, and yet—just maybe the more than forty thousand pounds

---

[69] *De antiquis legibus liber*, p. 117. Carpenter, "Westminster Abbey in Politics," p. 58.

[70] Carpenter, "Westminster Abbey in Politics," p. 58.

[71] *De antiquis legibus liber*, pp. 116–17. Weiler, "Symbolism and Politics," pp. 35–37, is excellent in general on the events and in particular unpacks the crown-wearing fiasco nicely.

[72] *Willelmi Rishanger . . . Chronica*, p. 56.

[73] Ibid.

[74] London: Lambeth Palace Library, MS 761, a thirteenth-century Life of Saint Edward owned by Westminster shows some evidence, in its few near contemporary glosses, of drawing attention to the Confessor's miracles.

[75] Carpenter, *Struggle for Mastery*, p. 382.

[76] Carpenter, "Westminster Abbey in Politics," p. 58.

Henry is estimated to have spent on Westminster, as much as the cost of building three or four castles, was worth it.[77]

As the great works at the edifice were reaching conclusion and soon after the consecration, the abbey church became the locus for many besides the merely routine ceremonies necessary for the celebration of the Christian cult.[78] Some were happy affairs, such as the festive marriage of Edmund, Henry III's younger son, and the countess of Albemarle in 1269, a ceremony attended by the king and by many of the noblest born in England.[79] Others were somber. Solemn obsequies attended both the interment of the heart of Henry of Almaine, the king's nephew (his brother Richard of Cornwall's son), in 1271 and the burial, with appropriate honors, of John the son of Prince Edward in the same year in a Purbeck marble tomb partly in the Cosmati style and on which work continued into 1272.[80] Every such ceremony—partly because later tombs, like that of Henry III's nephew, John of Valence (d. 1277), recalled the same royal Italianate forms and materials—confirmed Westminster Abbey as the preeminent royal and family cult center, and its abbot as the high priest of the religion of English monarchy.[81]

The peace that blessed France during Abbot Mathieu de Vendôme's abbacy at Saint-Denis makes the story of his monastery's physical enhancement less fitful than Westminster's. In Louis IX's day there was no need for

---

[77] Carpenter, *Struggle for Mastery*, p. 382. The estimate of about forty thousand pounds is widely accepted: Summerson, "Kingship, Government, and Political Life," p. 227; Foster, *Patterns of Thought*, p. 12. An estimate of about thirty thousand pounds was made on 1 October 1261 (Colvin, *Building Accounts*, p. 415; cf. Mortimer, *Angevin England*, p. 38), but this was before many of the expenditures described above took place. See also Carpenter, "Westminster Abbey in Politics," p. 49.

[78] Which is not to say that routine services lacked the kind of crown support, like gifts, that emphasized the royal nature of the building and shrine; cf. *Close Rolls, 1264–1268*, p. 442.

[79] "Annals of Winchester," in *Annales Monastici*, 2:107; *Historical Works of Gervaise of Canterbury*, 2:248.

[80] The "Annals" of Winchester and those of Oseney and the "Chronicon Thomae Wykes" in *Annales Monastici*, 2:111 and 4:244–45 (the Oseney annalist, to cite just one example, described John's burial as *honorifice*). Carpenter, "King Henry III and the Cosmati Work," p. 193.

[81] The case for John's tomb in this evocation of the royal style, based on a slab from it uncovered in excavations in the mid-nineteenth century, seems compelling to me, but Barney Sloane humorously hedges his bets: the "really quite beautiful" slab "was (so it is believed)" part of John's memorial and "was inlaid with an extraordinarily rich glass mosaic. Whether this can in any way be tied to the fabulous Cosmati pavement not a million miles distant from the slab's location is something I am not able to tell, although the dates of the completion of the pavement (finished 1268) and John of Valence's death (January 1277) are suggestive." See Sloane, "Archaeology in London," pp. 12–13 and 14 figure 3.

an abbot of Saint-Denis to contract huge debts, to squirrel away revenues desperately needed for other pressing and depressing tasks, to defend properties from the violence of belligerent barons, or to rescue a penurious king repeatedly from the pathetic consequences of his own follies. Saint Denis, the martyr, and his cult were precious to Louis IX, perhaps not so singularly precious as Edward the Confessor and his cult were to Henry III, but very special indeed, and peace and great wealth allowed him to show it as much and as often as he wished.[82] Yet the Capetians and by inference the abbey that so relentlessly celebrated their lineage and the patron-martyr's cult were marred by one fact, the memory, even more than 250 years after they achieved the kingship, that the ruling dynasts were usurpers.

To defang this memory, publicists invoked the concept of the *reditus ad stirpem*, the "return to the root stock," a way of saying that no matter how the third dynasty acquired the crown, continuity with the ancient Frankish rulers had been reestablished according to God's eternal plan. That is to say, through a series of opportune marriages the earlier royal lineages came to be blended with what scholars since the late eighteenth century have called the Capetian. New generations of Capetians could therefore trace their origins back to the root stock of the early dynasts. The verbal expression of this propaganda, articulated in large part but not uniquely at Saint-Denis, received lapidary confirmation in a project that rearranged the royal tombs so as to emphasize this return to the root stock.

Plans for the rearrangement had been incubating a long while, indeed since before Mathieu de Vendôme's abbacy. The tombs themselves may have been sculpted also considerably before the date of their installation, which was delayed for years.[83] According to Caroline Bruzelius, the original work of thirteenth-century reconstruction of the sanctuary proceeded reasonably steadily from the 1230s until the abbacy of Henri Mallet, Mathieu's predecessor. There was then a lengthy hiatus in the building campaigns. There is no mention in the sources of the availability of tithes *ad opus dei*, that is to say, for the church fabric, between 1250 and November 1261.[84] The completion of the five western bays of the thirteenth-century church along with changes in the styles of the capitals and the upper run of the pillars and plinths or pedestals in the arcade testifies to Mathieu's activity and bespeaks the recommencement of the building campaign under his aegis.[85] It was Mathieu, too, who finished buttressing the church

---

[82] So says Guillaume de Chartres in his *vita* of the king; HF, 20:33. Spiegel, "Cult of Saint Denis," pp. 62–65.

[83] Bruzelius, *13th-Century Church*, p. 134.

[84] Ibid., p. 135.

[85] Ibid., p. 133.

to the west of the tower and along the nave. The style and technique, rayonnant, represented the latest in innovation that the architect could have indulged.[86] The chroniclers' chorus is simple: Mathieu built the basilica of Saint-Denis.[87]

When the interior space became sufficiently advanced toward completion to receive the new tombs, it was up to the abbot and the king to agree on the arrangement. It may be the case that the guiding principles of the arrangements were originally intended, like the thirteenth-century fabric of the church itself, to conform to pseudo-Dionysian mystical ideas of light and darkness and number symbolism that had influenced Suger in the twelfth century.[88] Yet, even if so, this conceptual overlay in the thirteenth century church is very thin. There neither is nor was anything in the church to compare to the strange inlaid dating inscription on Westminster's Cosmati floor.

The mutual enthusiasm, it is presumed, of Louis IX and Abbot Mathieu for the rearrangement of the tombs has been tied neatly and simply to the overriding desire to link dynasty and necropolis. The agreement they came to that issued in the installation has been variously dated within the decade of the 1260s. The most persuasive discussions see the installation commencing in earnest in 1263–1264 and completed in 1267, the date assigned to the undertaking by the chronicler-monk of the abbey, Guillaume de Nangis.[89] Le Goff may be correct that the principal agent in bringing about the rearrangement was the king rather than Abbot Mathieu.[90] Yet the abbot had already shown his concern for the dead interred at the monastery by translating the bodies of his predecessors early in his headship. Moreover, as Carolus-Barré insisted, the collapse of the abbey scaffolding and wall in January 1259 would have immediately initiated a more radical rethinking about the future of the church fabric, setting in motion a chain of events resulting in modifications of the building, a symbolic *renovatio* that produced the thirteenth-century church as we now know it.[91] In this process, the rearrangement of the tombs was only one part, although a key part, of the overall renewal of the abbey fabric and the monastic precincts.[92]

The reference to the monastic precincts brings up another issue. Work was not going on merely at the basilica. On 23 July 1268 a lease was

---

[86] Ibid., pp. 54—55.

[87] *HF*, 20:571, 654; 21:8.

[88] Bruzelius, *13th-Century Church*, p. 4.

[89] Cf. Le Goff, *Saint Louis*, p. 280. See also *GC*, vol. 7, col. 392.

[90] Le Goff, *Saint Louis*, p. 280. Cf. Brown, *Saint-Denis*, pp. 385–88.

[91] Carolus-Barré, *Procès de canonisation*, p. 224.

[92] Ibid.

extended to Jean Porcheron, castellan of Breteuil, for a house abutting the wall of the abbey precincts and other holdings along the fosses, with the proviso that the abbey could cancel the lease if it should need to reclaim the property.[93] This provision was obviously related to expected needs with regard to exterior walls, the rampart. For the fine strong rampart enclosing the entire abbey complex and surmounted by turrets was also owed to Mathieu de Vendôme's inspiration and commission.[94] Saint-Denis's chroniclers, judging from their notice of the fact, thought that the quality of the walls the abbot ordered constructed was well worth remarking (see fig. 9).[95]

Nevertheless, if the church per se, leaving aside the rampart and turrets, was sufficiently advanced in its *renovatio* to permit the installation of the new and rearranged tombs by 1267, why date the completion of the building only in 1281, fourteen years later? Since the text providing the dating is reliable, what explains the delay?[96] It is possible that additional work still needed to be done to the nave in 1267, but even if this is true, fourteen years is a long time.[97] Bruzelius is again very helpful on this point. Yes, Saint-Denis was wealthy, and yes, even apart from direct royal contributions to the rebuilding, the abbey had sufficient funds to complete the fabric of the church.[98] Yet even Saint-Denis was hit hard by papal taxes to which the abbey contributed during the 1260s and 1270s, cutting the amount of money available to finish the building. Crusading taxes, as she points out, were levied in 1263 to aid in restoring the Latin Empire (Constantinople), in 1267 for Louis IX's planned second Crusade, and in the mid-1270s for the new Crusade authorized at the Second Council of Lyons.[99] Under these circumstances it might have been judicious to stretch out the building project, since the sanctuaries—the essential cultic parts of the building—were operating quite well even without every single feature of the building completed.

If this scenario is convincing, it remains to explain why the year 1281 was specifically chosen as a target date for ceremonies celebrating the church's completion. Is it a fortuitous date or not? Perhaps not. The canonization hearings for Louis IX were planned to take place at Saint-Denis in 1282, and a quick and positive response to those hearings

---

[93] *Atlas historique de Saint-Denis*, p. 236.

[94] Ibid., p. 237 (citing Félibien).

[95] *HF*, 20:571, 654.

[96] *GC*, vol. 7, col. 393; Carolus-Barré, *Procès de canonisation*, p. 225; *Atlas historique de Saint-Denis*, p. 76.

[97] Bruzelius, *13th-Century Church*, p. 136.

[98] Ibid., p. 128. This was true despite the possibility that the abbacies of two of Mathieu's immediate predecessors were fiscally less successful (cf. pp. 129–34)

[99] Ibid., p. 136.

was expected. The abbey church needed to be readied for the magnificent ceremony that would inevitably take place, when Abbot Mathieu de Ven-dôme honored his old friend, the new saint, and the redone tomb (see fig. 11). Even if the building was essentially complete a year or two before, celebration of its completion immediately before the commissioners sat might have seemed auspicious.[100] The plan, one now knows, was unnecessary, since Louis IX's formal canonization was, rather surprisingly, delayed until 1297.

Mathieu did not merely carry out the rearrangements of the abbots' and royal tombs, build the rampart and turrets, and finish the fabric of the abbey church in the years of his headship of Saint-Denis. Another key part of his enhancement of his monastery, one that compares in a modest but meaningful way to Henry III's enhancement of Saint Edward's shrine, was the creation of a new repository for the most important relic of the martyred Saint Denis, namely, the head that had been severed from his body, retrieved by the walking corpse, and taken to the spot where the abbey would later be built. It was a marvelously decorated reliquary; the principal metals used in its fabrication, as one might guess, were gold and silver, the silver being largely gilded. The whole was encrusted with precious gemstones worthy of the patron of the realm.[101] Mathieu celebrated the translation of the head to the new reliquary under the solemn aegis of the cardinal-priest of Saint-Cecilia, the future Pope Martin V, and in the presence of King Philip III.[102] Undoubtedly the festivities were concluded by a convivial feast worthy of the hospitality for which the great abbey and its abbot were famous.

---

[100] Ibid., pp. 136–37.
[101] *GC*, vol. 7, col. 393.
[102] *Chronicon* of Guillaume de Nangis, *HF*, 20:746.

1. A page with the record of a charter from Mathieu de Vendôme's abbacy, with his name visible, from the *Cartulaire blanc de Saint-Denis*, AN, LL 1157, fol. 487. "Document conservé aux Archives nationales, Paris. Cliché Atelier photographique des Archives nationales."

2. Original charter, AN L 589, no. 51, represented in the *Cartulaire blanc de Saint-Denis*, AN, LL 1157, fol. 487. "Document conservé aux Archives nationales, Paris. Cliché Atelier photographique des Archives nationales."

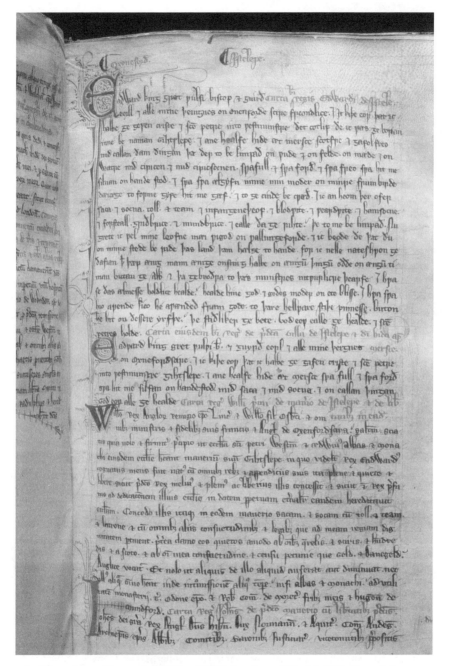

3. Westminster Domesday (WD = WAM, book no. 11), fol. 270. Copyright,
Dean and Chapter of Westminster.

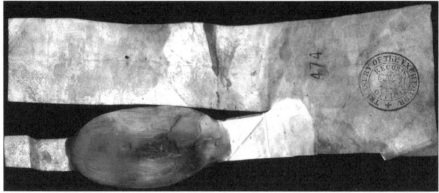

4. Seal of Richard de Ware. National Archives (formerly the Public Record Office) of the United Kingdom E 42/474; copyright National Archives, UK.

5. Exterior of Westminster Abbey (before the addition of the eighteenth-century towers), after a drawing by Wenceslaus Hollar, 1654. Copyright, Dean and Chapter of Westminster.

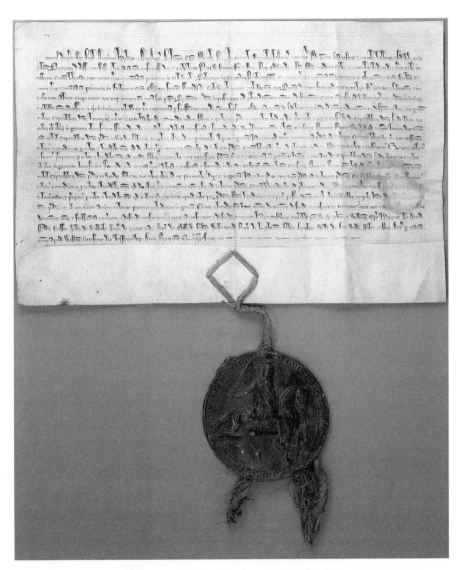

6. Royal grant of the Culworth properties to Westminster Abbey, 1265; WAM, no. 1692. Copyright, Dean and Chapter of Westminster.

7. Cosmati pavement at Westminster Abbey. Copyright, Dean and Chapter of Westminster.

8. Tomb of Edward the Confessor at Westminster Abbey (image from the north-west). Copyright, Dean and Chapter of Westminster.

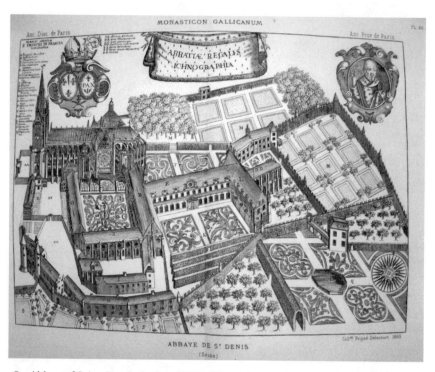

9. Abbey of Saint-Denis, before 1789. *Monasticon Gallicanum* (Paris, 1871), plate 66.

10. Mathieu de Vendôme. Les Grandes chroniques de France. Miniature de frontispiece représentant le sacre d'un roi. Reims. Bibliothèque municipale. Ms 1469, folio 1.

12a. Tomb of Henry III at Westminster Abbey (image from the northeast). Copyright, Dean and Chapter of Westminster.

12b. Tomb of Henry III at Westminster Abbey (image from the north).

VI

TWO ROYAL SUCCESSIONS

URING THE LAST TWELVE YEARS of Louis IX's reign Abbot Mathieu de Vendôme sat as a judge in Parlement, the High Court of France. He is specifically named in the *Olim*, the records of Parlement, for example, as attending sessions in this capacity in September 1258, on the octaves of Candlemas 1261, and on the Thursday after Trinity (7 June) 1268. His name follows first after those of the archbishops and bishops present, indicating his prestige within the monastic establishment.[1] The French Parlement was not a frozen, unchanging institution. It had some similarities with the English Parliament (also a High Court), but although its nature changed over time, it did not have in the mid-thirteenth century nor did it ever fully take on the representative character of the English institution. Representative assemblies in France emerged separately in the thirteenth and early fourteenth centuries in meetings later known and institutionalized as Estates Provincial and Estates General. Yet although Mathieu was not a proctor for the church when he sat in Parlement, he must occasionally have expressed opinions that mirrored or emphasized the special interests of ecclesiastics. His counterpart, Richard de Ware, sat in the English Parliament, however, explicitly because abbots of great monasteries were invited to do so to speak for the monastic or clerical estate.

Abbot Mathieu sat in Parlement according to the traditional subordination of abbots to bishops, but his real heft was never in doubt either within the church or with regard to important laymen. It was not at all surprising that he should preside at an ecclesiastical synod, for example, on 8 October 1269, even if it was more common for bishops to preside at such assemblies.[2] Had he chosen to do so, Mathieu could have moved up the traditional ecclesiastical hierarchy and thus the pecking (or at least seating) order in Parlement by actually becoming a bishop, but when offered the Norman see of Evreux in 1269, he declined.[3] He experienced fulfillment as an abbot, a monk, who served God and the realm as a provider of pastoral care within the monastery he ran and for the dependent houses he

---

[1] See, for example, *Layettes*, 4:276 no. 5393. Carolus-Barré, *Procès de canonisation*, pp. 225–26.

[2] Carolus-Barré, *Procès de canonisation*, p. 226.

[3] *GC*, vol. 7, col. 392; Richard, *Saint Louis*, p. 553; Sivéry, *Philippe III*, p. 92.

oversaw, but not elsewhere. Briefly, and under extraordinary circumstances, it was duty to the realm, however, that took precedence.

In 1267 Louis IX again assumed the cross. It is not known when he first came up with or broached the idea of a double regency to his closest confidants or to the abbot of Saint-Denis in particular, but in March 1270 he formally appointed two regents to rule during his absence on Crusade. Abbot Mathieu de Vendôme was one of these men (he would soon, in May, along with the bishop of Bayeux, also be authorized by the pope to excommunicate anyone who violated the new royal crusader's rights); the coregent was a lay aristocrat, Simon de Clermont, lord of Nesle.[4] Most of the royal powers—the guard, defense, and administration of the kingdom under the royal seal—were vested mutually in the coregents, but the king reserved one power, the collation of benefices, for the bishop of Paris, Etienne Tempier. This reservation was a sop, if Gérard Sivéry is to be believed, offered to conciliate the distinguished prelate for his having been denied the regency and thus enduring the indignity of being subjected, though he was a bishop, to an abbot. Perhaps this explanation works, but an abbot of Saint-Denis, Suger, had set a precedent when he served as regent during the absence of Louis VII on Crusade. More persuasive is the fact that Louis IX stipulated that if Bishop Etienne died before his return, the power of collation was to migrate to the abbot.[5] When the king made contingency plans in case of either regent's death, he designated Philippe de Chaource, the bishop of Evreux (the see that Mathieu had declined), as the abbot's successor and Jean de Nesle, count of Ponthieu, as Simon's.[6] It seems from these choices that King Louis probably did prefer bishops and lay aristocrats to exercise delegated temporal power in general, but the abbot of Saint-Denis was an exceptional man.[7]

In the interval between taking the vow to go on Crusade and departing in 1270, Louis IX still had a country to govern and ceremonial or, rather, ritual duties to perform; he also had to make preparations for the Crusade. Governing from Saint-Denis was not unusual. When one sees him at the abbey of Saint-Denis in October of 1268, one gets a sense of just how crowded his schedule was. He was there on the vigil of the martyr's feast day, which implied his participation in all the devotional activities required

---

[4] Carolus-Barré, "Recueil épistolaire," p. 561; *Layettes*, 4:220 no. 5283. *GC*, vol. 7, col. 392; Richard, *Saint Louis*, p. 446; Sivéry, *Philippe III*, p. 41; Carolus-Barré, *Procès de canonisation*, p. 226.

[5] *Layettes*, 4:430 no. 5664. Richard, *Saint Louis*, p. 554; Le Goff, *Saint Louis*, p. 294; Sivéry, *Philippe III*, p. 80.

[6] *Layettes*, 4:429–30 nos. 5662–63.

[7] On Mathieu's character, see Sivéry, *Philippe III*, p. 93.

of the royal visitor, but while in residence he also put the finishing touches on a series of contracts by which he secured a navy in the form of Genoese ships for the future Crusade army.[8]

Louis Carolus-Barré showed with great probability—and his views were strongly endorsed by the great diplomatics expert and paleographer Georges Tessier—that Mathieu de Vendôme grouped copies of the correspondence relative to his regency during Louis IX's last Crusade in a very selective collection intended to provide source material for the official histories to be written at the abbey of Saint-Denis. And there is evidence that the collection was later used in this way as well as copied once more in the early fourteenth century possibly when plans were afoot to mount a new Crusade. Mathieu's decision to collect the correspondence followed in the footsteps of the twelfth-century Abbot Suger, who had done so when he was regent under Louis VII.[9]

The king departed Paris on 15 March after having made ritual visits in the days before to the abbey of Saint-Denis and the cathedral of Notre-Dame, just as he had done in 1248. At Saint-Denis he prayed before the high altar and the body of the martyr and his companions; either before or right afterward, at Vincennes, he confirmed the famous privilege that Charles the Bald had granted to Saint-Denis.[10] At the abbey he received the purse and staff directly from Mathieu de Vendôme's hands and then took the *oriflamme* down from the altar table. These gestures completed, he proceeded to the chapter, commending himself and his children to the prayers of Saint-Denis's monks, and he humbled himself before the assembled community and the abbot.[11] Thereafter, as Louis traveled south, he received messages from several quarters asking for his intervention in various cases and disputes, but increasingly he referred these requests to the regents. On 19 May 1270 from Nîmes, for example, the king ordered the regents to take care of a messy dispute in Lyon.[12] Among the last orders Louis issued to the regents from French territory was a missive dated at Aigues-Mortes on 25 June 1270, instructing them to repress blasphemy, prostitution, and other crimes.[13] In a separate instrument addressed to

---

[8] *Layettes*, 4:285 no. 5418, with additional allusions at pp. 296, 300, 311.

[9] For a full treatment of the collection and the manuscripts and for Carolus-Barré's argument in its entirety, see Carolus-Barré, "Recueil épistolaire," pp. 555–68, where Tessier's endorsement is reported at pp. 567–68. On the selectivity and therefore very incomplete character of the collection, see Carolus-Barré, *Procès de canonisation*, p. 229.

[10] *Layettes*, 4:428 no. 5655.

[11] Guillaume de Nangis (*vita* of Saint Louis), *HF*, 20:440–41.

[12] Carolus-Barré, *Procès de canonisation*, p. 227.

[13] Carolus-Barré, "Recueil épistolaire," p. 558 no. 10 and p. 561. Richard, *Saint Louis*, p. 557; Le Goff, *Saint Louis*, p. 292 (the date 1269 given on this page is in error but rendered correctly as 1270 on p. 684). Carolus-Barré, *Procès de canonisation*, p. 227 (a truncated French translation is provided at pp. 119–21).

Mathieu and a number of other churchmen, he reminded the recipients of the letter to make sure that the chaplains of the Sainte-Chapelle obtained the income from the rents he had assigned them.[14] Thereafter it was the regents who bore the full responsibility of domestic governance, exercising it mostly from Paris, but often from Saint-Denis, and occasionally on the road, as from the Exchequer of Normandy in Rouen.[15]

It was in a letter of 25 July 1270 addressed solely to Mathieu that Louis reported the decision, taken after counsel in Sardinia, to strike at Tunis, and he described the initial successes of the consequent assault.[16] Less than a month later, however, and despite some lingering hopes for a sweeping victory once the besieged city fell, a royal clerk, Pierre de Condé, wrote to the abbot that the king and numerous other personages were ill and that the king's son Jean was dead. Pierre was still unwilling to give up hope on 21 August, the date of this letter.[17] Four days later, however, the king was dead, having succumbed with an invocation of Saint Denis on his lips.[18] Pierre de Condé took up his pen on 4 September to inform a friend, who was to convey the news to the abbot of Saint-Denis, that Charles of Anjou and his complement of troops had finally arrived. He also reported on the progress of the siege, on other military matters, and on the precarious condition of the new king, Philip III, who had fallen ill but was recovering. He would have written personally to the abbot, but the letter bearers were ready to depart for France before he had time to do so.[19] In a subsequent personal letter, however, dated 18 November he was able to report that a truce, whose details he provided, had been negotiated, and that the siege army was preparing to embark and leave the "accursed land" of North Africa behind.[20]

Louis IX's death imposed a new though not particularly pressing task on Mathieu de Vendôme, for he was one of the executors of the king's last will and testament.[21] The really imperative matter involved arrangements surrounding the transfer of power to the absent new king. From Tunisia, soon after his father's death (25 August) and his own recovery from illness, Philip III confirmed Abbot Mathieu and Lord Simon in their authority

[14] *Layettes*, 4:451–52 no. 5710.

[15] *GC*, vol. 7, col. 392; Carolus-Barré, *Procès de canonisation*, p. 229.

[16] Carolus-Barré, "Recueil épistolaire," pp. 557–58 no. 4.

[17] Ibid., p. 558 no. 9. On Pierre de Condé and his career, see Sivéry, *Philippe III*, pp. 51–53, 58, 66, 197, 216, 218–19, 226, 233, 244, 246, 305.

[18] Anonymous of Saint-Denis, *HF*, 20:56.

[19] Carolus-Barré, "Recueil épistolaire," p. 558 no. 6 and pp. 562 and 565.

[20] Ibid., p. 558 no. 13 and p. 561.

[21] The king had named several executors besides Mathieu, including Bishop Etienne Tempier of Paris; *Layettes*, 4:419–21 no. 5638. *GC*, vol. 7, col. 392; Richard, *Saint Louis*, p. 446; Carolus-Barré, *Procès de canonisation*, p. 226.

as regents and in a separate instrument informed the nobility and the prelates in the kingdom of this decision; these missives are dated 12 September.[22] To make sure this important information reached France, Philip III entrusted a second copy of the confirmation, dated 4 October, to a mission that departed three weeks later for Paris.[23] Incidentally, this was the first time that a man styled himself officially king of France, a usage that seems to have been paralleled by his wife's recognition as queen, before his anointing, and the first time that scribes dated regnal years from the death and burial of the old monarch rather than from the coronation of the new.[24] The formal rituals of consecration were postponed until Philip's return to France and the coronation ceremony at Reims on 30 August 1271, more than a year after his father's death.

The new king while yet in Tunisia was already concerned with a shortage of funds to bring the Crusade to closure, and on the same day as he sent out his original confirmation of the regents' authority, 12 September 1270, he commanded them to make as much money as possible available to him as soon as they could.[25] It was requests like this that induced the regents to seek loans from the great towns of northern France which had occasionally aided the monarchy and the interests of the royal family in times of financial stress as well as from the fabulously wealthy Flemish cloth towns. One such loan, from the burghers of Ghent, amounted to the colossal sum of 7,500 l.[26] In a tone that Sivéry regards as paternal, but that may only have been intended to convey their displeasure at having to solicit loans, the regents asked the new king to hasten back.[27] Each of them had plenty of other routine administrative work, such as, for example, the abbot's issuance of a license to a knight, Humbaud Gaubert, lord of La-

---

[22] Carolus-Barré, "Recueil épistolaire," pp. 557 nos. 1 and 2, and p. 561. *GC*, vol. 7, col. 392; Richard, *Saint Louis*, p. 571; Le Goff, *Saint Louis*, p. 298; Sivéry, *Philippe III*, p. 64.

[23] Carolus-Barré, "Recueil épistolaire," p. 558 no. 5. *GC*, vol. 7, cols. 392–93; Sivéry, *Philippe III*, p. 64.

[24] On the innovative dating of regnal years, see Kantorowicz, *King's Two Bodies*, p. 330. On the recognition of Philip's queen's title (though it would soon die with her), see *Chronik des Malaspina*, p. 231, "licet vir suus non esset inunctus, regina tamen Francie dicitur poterat."

[25] Carolus-Barré, "Recueil épistolaire," p. 558 no. 11 and p. 561.

[26] The royal—or, rather, regents'—charter recording the loan (possibly in money *tournois*) is referred to in a judgment of Parlement of 24 May 1304 which notes that the goods and archives of Ghent had been seized during the recent rebellion against Philip IV the Fair (1285–1314), and that this document was among the records taken; *Actes du Parlement de Paris*, 2:23 no. 3218. For the tradition of turning to the northern French towns for help in times of royal and familial financial need, see above, p. 75, on their gifts for Louis IX's first Crusade, for Charles of Anjou's intervention in the war of the Flemish succession, and for their contribution to the fiscal settlement included in the Treaty of Paris.

[27] Carolus-Barré, "Recueil épistolaire," p. 559 no. 17; Guillaume de Nangis (*vita* of Philip III), *HF*, 20:478–79. Sivéry, *Philippe III*, p. 65.

zenay in the *bailliage* of Bourges, to resign his fief and have his son invested with it by the *bailli* in late 1270.[28] The return from their absence abroad of men like Pierre de Condé who were administrative and financial experts was much to be desired to help with the administrative burdens, especially with the demands now on the regents to raise substantial sums of money for King Philip.[29]

For both Mathieu and Simon also had their own personal business to attend to. The abbot had to work out or at least approve and monitor the property transactions that his monastery entered into, to give one category of activity that drew his attention. In November 1270 he received notification from Thomas Hueline, *prévôt* of Meulan, of the sale made to Saint-Denis, for 60 l. p., of the revenues of the fief that a knight by the name of Henri d'Auteil and his wife possessed in Arthies and Génainville (both in the department of Val d'Oise), and which the squire Jean d'Anfreville held of Henri in liege homage.[30] Also in November Jean de Tremblay, a squire, sold Saint-Denis thirty-five arpents of arable land in Tremblay (department, Seine-Saint-Denis) for 52 l. 10 s. p.[31] His wife made formal consent to the sale in a separate instrument dated 9 December 1270.[32]

Disputes involving the monastery and resolved in Parlement, the abbot recusing himself as a judge, also took up Mathieu's time. Whether recusal really assured a fair decision or even the perception of one is moot. Nonetheless, it was at Pentecost 1270, before the events of the end of the year (Louis IX's death and the winding down of the Crusade in Tunisia), that the abbot turned his mind to an incident that upset him concerning the monastery's Jews. He discovered that Hubert de Laon, a goldsmith of Paris, had taken 150 l. p. from capitalizing the goods of certain of Saint-Denis's Jews and had claimed to do so by the absent king's favor. Mathieu challenged him and demanded return of the money. Although Hubert denied that he should be compelled to repay the money, he could not prove that he had acted under the king's license and had to pay up.[33] A second dispute turned on the existence of two badly drafted charters, one in the possession of Saint-Denis and the other in that of the lord of Marly, about the justice of Rueil (department, Hauts de Seine). The charters were

---

[28] *Olim*, 1:828 no. XXXI; *Actes du Parlement de Paris*, 1:151 no. 1609 (dated Saint-Martin in the Winter). Carolus-Barré, *Procès de canonisation*, p. 229, summarizes the work that is documented in the collection, but by the very nature of the collection, this work was not principally routine. Moreover, some of Carolus-Barré's interpretations feel forced (he did not have the opportunity to revise and correct his draft before he died).

[29] On the bureaucratic expertise of Pierre de Condé, Sivéry, *Philippe III*, p. 246.

[30] *Série L . . . L829 à L839B*, pp. 66–67, L837 no. 82.

[31] *Cartulaire blanc de Saint-Denis*, Tremblay no. 33.

[32] Ibid., Tremblay no. 34.

[33] *Olim*, 1:807–8 no. XXIII; *Actes du Parlement de Paris*, 1:135 no. 1522.

very similarly worded and had to be parsed carefully because of two vague clauses. In the event both charters were validated. One was said to imply reference to the justice as it pertained to the lands and men of Saint-Denis for Saint-Denis; the other, to the lands and men of the lord of Rueil for the lord.[34] A third dispute resolved at this session pitted the monastery against the mayor and peers of Pontoise. It was a very complicated jurisdictional dispute as well, one part of which involved the abbot's querying of the commune's erection of a gallows in Osny and in Cergy (department, Val d'Oise). Investigation showed that the gallows was erected unlawfully and to the prejudice of Saint-Denis's justice in the villages; it had to be taken down.[35]

Matters of this sort arose repeatedly in Parlement. At Purification 1271 there were a number of arguments over the territorial limits of the rights and jurisdiction of the abbey. What were the precise delimitations of the rights of the hunt between Saint-Denis and the count of Roucy? Arbiters were assigned, and the case was proved largely to Saint-Denis's advantage on the showing of a very old letter (*visa eciam quadam littera, diu est facta, super dictis territoriis*).[36] Another inquest led to the definition of the limits of high justice (*viaria*) in Charlevanne (now Bougival, department Yvelines), with regard both to the times it might be exercised and to the precise locations. Authority was apportioned among the family involved, the abbey of Saint-Germain des Prés, and the abbey of Saint-Denis.[37] On the octave of All Saints 1271 the mayor and peers of Beaumont (department, Val d'Oise) were rebuffed—they had proved nothing—for transgressing the monopoly of justice of Saint-Denis in certain disputed terrains near the town.[38]

Pierre de Condé had called North Africa an accursed land. In part he was mourning the death of Louis IX as well as lamenting his heir's sickness. Other friends of the clerk and members of the royal family died on the way to Tunisia, on the spot, or coming back. All of this meant that Saint-Denis, the royal necropolis, would receive the remains of his and many of Abbot Mathieu's intimate associates and their children. Interments at Saint-Denis took place for Louis IX's brother Alphonse of Poitiers, who

---

[34] *Olim*, 1:812 no. XXXIII; *Actes du Parlement de Paris*, 1:136 no. 1532.

[35] *Olim*, 1:812 no. XXXIV; *Actes du Parlement de Paris*, 1:136 no. 1533. For further clarifications on the justice of these villages, some of the low justice of which was conceded in 1276 to be in the hands of the mayor and peers, see *Actes du Parlement de Paris*, 1:340 no. 257.

[36] *Olim*, 1:362–63 no. III; *Actes du Parlement de Paris*, 1:156 no. 1666. Cf. *Actes du Parlement de Paris*, 1:321 no. 80 (year 1280), for further specifications of the rights of the two parties.

[37] *Olim*, 1:363–64 no. V; *Actes du Parlement de Paris*, 1:156 no. 1668, 321 no. 79.

[38] *Olim*, 1:405 no. XIII; *Actes du Parlement de Paris*, 1:173 no. 1889.

had left a small testamentary bequest to Saint-Denis, and Louis's son Jean-Tristan in 1271 and for his daughter Marguerite in 1271 or 1272.[39] Much later, in 1285, the tombs of the two royal children were resituated at the foot of their father's tomb.[40]

The burden on the abbot must have been great at the king's funeral. Dignity, however, was required more than public sentiment. Obsequies were arranged as soon as Louis's "body" arrived in Paris. His flesh already lay in the Tunisian sands, boiled from his corpse in wine and spices. His heart and entrails traveled with his brother Charles of Anjou to Monreale in Sicily for honorable interment. Philip III in accompanying his father's remains had commemorative stone crosses erected at various places along the way in France with royal insignia and likenesses.[41] Whenever and wherever the royal remains rested en route while the retinue refreshed itself, prelates took precautions to sanctify the sites, going so far as to lift (temporarily) regional interdicts that had been otherwise imposed for some grievous offense. The bishop of Autun, for example, suspended on 30 April 1271 the interdict he himself had levied on Lyon's cathedral church, because Louis reposed there overnight.[42]

The final solemn procession for the king's earthly body, the creamy white and brown-streaked bones nestled in aromatic spices and enfolded in rich silks, began soon after the cortege reached the abbey church of Saint-Denis.[43] In front of the sanctuary stood the assembled Benedictine monks. Holding candles in their hands and arrayed in their long silken night copes, they waited to receive the old king. The still unconsecrated Philip III was accompanied by a coterie of relatives in mourning. Also present were the archbishop of Sens, Pierre de Charny, and his suffragan, the bishop of Paris, Etienne Tempier, who might have expected two years before to have been appointed to the regency.

Perhaps the bishop was resentful at being passed over for the regency and blamed Abbot Mathieu. In this scenario, it would be the abbot's prominent role in the obsequies that resparked Etienne's animosity, for although a deeply learned man, the bishop made an embarrassing error or decided

---

[39] Brown, *Saint-Denis*, p. 395 (Marguerite's interment may have been just a little later, in 1272). On Alphonse's seemingly pro forma bequest to Saint-Denis (it was one of scores to ecclesiastical institutions), see *Layettes*, 4:453–62 no. 5712 (p. 455, for the specific mention).

[40] Brown, *Saint-Denis*, p. 395.

[41] Boullé, "Maison de Saint-Lazare de Paris," pp. 180–81. These crosses were destroyed by Huguenots during the Wars of Religion. As others have done, Prestwich (*Plantagenet England*, p. 45) suggests that the erection of these monuments may have inspired the future Edward I to erect monumental crosses along the cortege route of his queen Eleanor of Castile (d. 1290).

[42] Charmasse, *Cartulaire de l'évêché d'Autun*, p. 292 no. xlvi.

[43] Guillaume de Nangis (*vita* of Philip III); *HF*, 20:468–69. Langlois, *Règne de Philippe III*, pp. 54–5.

deliberately to provoke the community at Saint-Denis on what should otherwise have been a singularly serene occasion.[44] He and the archbishop attempted to process with the others in the royal retinue while dressed in their pontifical vestments. The pontificals represented in part their episcopal jurisdiction; it was inappropriate (and indeed forbidden) for them to wear these vestments when entering an exempt monastery, like Saint-Denis. Westminster Abbey also diligently resisted the archbishop of Canterbury's attempts to enter its precincts in his pontificals.[45] There may have been a more delicate way to forestall the transgression of Archbishop Pierre of Sens and Bishop Etienne of Paris, but Abbot Mathieu chose to stand on his and Saint-Denis's rights and dignity by physically barring entry to the cortege—literally closing the doors in front of them—until the bishops unvested. And, though most scholars acknowledge Mathieu's right to do this, they have been puzzled by the aggressiveness of the action in such sad circumstances as the new king's burial of his father. Was the abbot warning the new king that he and his familiars would not be allowed to ruin the delicate balance of powers that his father had arranged for the good governance of the realm? Something like this has been argued by Gérard Sivéry, and the possibility will have to be assessed more fully momentarily.[46]

The interruption was only temporary, though, and the funeral resumed. Louis IX's bones were placed in an unadorned tomb located behind the altar dedicated to the Holy and Undivided Trinity, as he had instructed. Already, however, simplicity seemed inappropriate for a man who was a saint. A saint's body needed the sort of tomb and shrine that could focus the devotion of the faithful, and that showed their respect—or, at least, this was often argued and certainly was the motive across the Channel for Henry III's lavish decoration of the shrine of Edward the Confessor. Yet how did the assembled guests at Saint-Denis really know that their dead king was a saint? The answer: reports were already circulating about miracles. As the bones were being transported up the Italian peninsula, there were healing miracles. In time the tomb at Saint-Denis would have to be enhanced. For now, it was Abbot Mathieu's happy duty to arrange for the recording of testimony concerning miracles already alleged as well as the new ones he expected the dead king to perform.[47]

On 30 August 1271 Milon de Bazoches, the bishop of Soissons, presided at the coronation of Philip III at the magnificent cathedral of Reims. The prerogative of crowning the king lay with the archbishop of Reims, but

---

[44] Sivéry, *Philippe III*, p. 80–81.

[45] WD, fol. 643.

[46] Sivéry, *Philippe III*, p. 81.

[47] Richard, *Saint Louis*, p. 576. See also *Atlas historique de Saint-Denis*, p. 124. On the original simplicity of the tomb, see Brown, *Saint-Denis*, p. 396.

the see was vacant, and thus the duty devolved onto the archbishop's suffragan, as it had done for Philip III's father's consecration in 1226. The abbot of Saint-Denis was, after the bishop of Soissons, the principal religious figure at the ceremony. Mathieu de Vendôme gave spiritual protection and blessing to the coronation regalia and positioned himself at Reims cathedral's high altar. A famous miniature in the *Grandes Chroniques de France*, written and illuminated at Saint-Denis, depicts this scene with the abbot at the right hand of the seated king and the bishop at the left hand both blessing the crown with their left hands. Yet it is the abbot whose other hand is affixing the crown to Philip's head, not the bishop's. And it is toward the abbot that the king addresses all his attention, his eyes focused on his father's friend (see fig. 10).[48] There is no doubt who is in charge—or who the viewer is meant to think is in charge—at least according to the representation of the monks of Saint-Denis. And this is true of other scenes depicted in the manuscript as well.[49]

Did this representation reflect reality? One of the most perplexing aspects of Abbot Mathieu's relationship with the new king after the latter's return from North Africa touches upon the conduct and influence of a royal chamberlain by the name of Pierre de la Broce, who had emerged in the difficult days following Louis IX's death as Philip III's close companion and trusted adviser. Many scholars have tried to explain the bond between Pierre and Philip.[50] One basis was simply their previous acquaintanceship. Pierre, of an administrative family from Touraine, had served in various capacities in the provinces and in the royal household since at least 1256. He and his brother, Guillaume de la Broce, accompanied Louis IX to Tunisia, the latter serving as Prince Philip's *panetier* or provisioner. But neither of the brothers was a great official, and their family, though of knightly origin, was not aristocratic in the elevated sense of that term.

Nevertheless, familiarity counted for a great deal amid the distress following Louis IX's death and the deaths of so many other members of the royal family and close friends, or as one chronicler would put it in a poignant Latin play on words, Philip III succeeded his father under a heavy burden yet in honor (*in onere et honore*).[51] It was not surprising that the new king turned to a familiar face and a familiar voice for support. Moreover, Philip was ill when his father died, and Pierre de la Broce, even if he was not professionally a doctor, is known to have possessed some medical

---

[48] The miniature is used as the cover art of Sivéry, *Philippe III*.

[49] Hedeman, *Royal Image*, p. 15 and 17 (figure 4).

[50] I have treated *l'affaire de la Broce* at length in "Struggle for Influence at the Court of Philip III," pp. 439–68. Full discussion of all the points made in the next several paragraphs and copious references to the original sources and the older literature are available there. Now, see also Hélary, "Pierre de la Broce," pp. 275–305.

[51] *Chronik des Malaspina*, p. 230.

knowledge. His good services to the new king and perhaps to a number of other aristocrats brought low by sickness during the siege may also help explain his initial influence in royal circles. Was there more? Did Pierre exercise a Svengali-like control over the new king, as some chroniclers maintain? He certainly enjoyed privileged access to Philip and began to receive very significant gifts from the king. This, in turn, convinced aristocratic opportunists to seek out the chamberlain's aid on matters that affected them, and they did so with gifts. Within a very short space of time, the accumulation of properties by gifts (or bribes) began to transform the chamberlain into one of the richest men and greatest landholders in the kingdom of France and incited profound aristocratic resentment against him, which Philip III evidently put down to simple envy.

A chamberlain had real tasks to perform in royal government with regard to keeping accounts, arranging for disbursements of revenue, and giving advice on fiscal and related matters.[52] Pierre's influence extended beyond this, to the point that chroniclers (hostile ones, to be sure) represented him as a parvenu who achieved the role of most intimate of all royal counselors. They also represent this influence or power as having gone to his head. He began to arrange "inappropriate" marriages for his children, buying into aristocratic lineages, as it were, with grandiose dowries, and even to imitate royal styles of dress. Every possible aristocratic trapping that he could afford in the first few years of Philip III's reign—and Pierre could afford them all: private chapels and chaplains, incredible numbers of monastic prayers, a large gracious gift for a new Crusade—he indulged. And he passed on some of the wealth he received as gifts and bribes to a small set of minions, among them some kinsmen, who managed to get good positions in the church and the administration. The bishop of Bayeux became his "creature," as did a number of *baillis*, the highest-ranking regional governors, who owed their appointments to his good offices.

In the end he fell from grace. Philip III, who had lost his wife, Isabelle d'Aragon, on Crusade (Pierre was one of the executors of her will), remarried in August 1274. At about the same time Philip commissioned an elaborate monument to the late queen at Saint-Denis, installed in 1275.[53] Elizabeth Brown conjectures that he did so as a kind of penance or apology to the deceased queen for remarrying and not remaining in (chaste) widowerhood.[54] His new wife, Marie de Brabant, had not only to contend with the king's fond or fretful memory of his first spouse, but she and her Brabantine and Burgundian kinsmen also detested Pierre de la Broce,

---

[52] See Hélary's cautious assessment of the extent of the chamberlain's authority, "Pierre de la Broce," pp. 283–90.

[53] Erlande-Brandenburg et al., *Gisants et tombeaux*, pp. 16–17.

[54] Brown, *Saint-Denis*, p. 396.

Pierre's (allegedly) pretentious spouse, and the chamberlain's untoward influence over the monarch. As far as can be determined, Pierre did not yield to their pressures easily. A number of rumors began to circulate that Philip III was a sodomite, and that the death of his eldest son was a consequence of his refusal to refrain from sodomy. Philip learned of the rumors and decided to launch a thorough investigation. The investigation, led— perhaps unsurprisingly—by Pierre de la Broce (who else would the king turn to but the man who had helped sustain him at the first crucial juncture of his reign in the battle camp of Tunis?), found the alleged source of the rumors in two Flemish-speaking Liègoise prophetesses, but when questioned closely, or so it was reported, these women placed responsibility for the death of the king's eldest son not on Philip's reputed sodomy but on a plot laid by the new queen, Marie de Brabant, who, it was said, planned to kill all of the king's other children from his first marriage to make room for her own in the royal succession.

Briefly Philip III came to countenance these rumors, although other developments, particularly a failed attempt to invade Castile following a diplomatic standoff, made him suspicious of Pierre de la Broce, whom many barons, especially Burgundians, accused of treachery in preparing for the invasion.[55] Either Pierre neglected to prepare effectively for the war effort, or he was taking bribes to let people avoid their obligations to contribute men or money, or he was involved in negotiations with the Castilian enemy for some sort of unsavory gain. None of these charges was capable of absolute proof.[56] Yet they all upset the king, who ordered still another and even more comprehensive investigation. The prophetesses were reexamined, but of course this time without Pierre de la Broce or his associates mediating their testimony with the king. Indeed, it was Abbot Mathieu de Vendôme who was called on to help head up the new inquiry.[57] The result was—or the report that came in asserted—that the prophetesses denied everything. Through their interpreter they expressed utter disbelief at the original report of their words. They had never said anything about Marie de Brabant or her alleged crime or future criminal

[55] On relations with Castile, see Langlois, *Règne de Philippe III*, pp. 96–108, who notes that the invasion was preceded by Abbot Mathieu's investiture of Philippe with the *oriflamme*.

[56] Sivéry has a theory—"proved" by its being stated as a rhetorical question—that Pierre, a victim of the charge of treason, was opposed to the war because he was a true child of Louis IX's foreign policy aims; *Philippe III*, pp. 167, 171. This is part of a broader set of implausible theories about Pierre (and about Mathieu de Vendôme) that I critically examine below.

[57] Carolus-Barré, *Procès de canonisation*, p. 230. Sivéry's interpretation of Mathieu's role in this inquiry (*Philippe III*, pp. 159–60) is forced, in line with some other indefensible views described below.

intentions. Yet if this new report was credible, it pointed an accusing finger at Pierre de la Broce for misrepresenting the earlier investigation.

Then word reached the king that a box had been recovered with incriminating letters of some sort attributed to Pierre. Read aloud to the king before a group of barons hostile to the chamberlain and with the chamberlain absent on his own personal business, in which he was trying to accumulate still more property, the stunning revelations, which were never made public, induced the king to order his friend's arrest. Philip III may not have wanted to see the chamberlain executed, but his barons chafed at his delay after the arrest in dispatching this man whom they so thoroughly hated. They pressured him to give Pierre de la Broce over to them. Philip finally capitulated, and without a trial, some of the greatest aristocrats in the kingdom—the duke of Burgundy, the duke of Brabant, and the count of Artois—personally led the disgraced chamberlain to the gibbet to be hanged in 1278.

One of the great scholarly experts on *l'affaire de la Broce* was Louis Carolus-Barré.[58] He detested the chamberlain, and he admired the great abbot of Saint-Denis, Mathieu de Vendôme.[59] He was therefore troubled by the fact that Abbot Mathieu, who clearly knew Pierre before his prominence, continued to be active in government in the early 1270s, during the years of the chamberlain's ascendancy.[60] Carolus-Barré did not want his hero, Mathieu, tainted by any implied complicity in Pierre de la Broce's machinations. The result was that in his last work, unrevised and published posthumously, Carolus-Barré made a very strong division between what he regarded as the chamberlain's successful encouragement of Philip's bad habits of rulership, especially his neglect of administrative supervision, and the wider vigor of royal government, as he saw it, as if the only consequences of the chamberlain's actions were Pierre's own personal gain and Philip's lack of self-discipline. For Carolus-Barré, serious governors of the kingdom, like Abbot Mathieu de Vendôme, naturally despised Pierre, but the king could have whatever friends he liked. Real administrators sucked their teeth bitterly at Pierre's flamboyance and Philip's ethical flaccidity but they focused on genuinely important matters, running the kingdom as the king's father, the holy Louis IX, would have wanted them to run it.

Gérard Sivéry took this theory many steps further. In his telling, Abbot Mathieu de Vendôme was so suspicious of Pierre de la Broce, almost from the moment of the return of the royal entourage to Paris from Tunisia in 1271, that he used the occasion of Louis IX's funeral to discipline Philip

---

[58] Besides the references in subsequent notes, see, most especially, Carolus-Barré's "Baillis de Philippe III," pp. 109–234, and his "Service militaire," pp. 88–93.

[59] Carolus-Barré, *Procès de canonisation*, pp. 229–30.

[60] On Mathieu's recognition as coregent of some of Pierre's business transactions before Louis IX's death, see *Layettes*, 4:437–38 nos. 5686–87.

III. The whole incident when Abbot Mathieu barred the funeral procession from entering the monastery as long as the bishop of Paris was
wearing his pontificals was meant to convey a message to the new king—
to humble him and warn him off from corrupting the administration of
the kingdom. Indeed, like Carolus-Barré, Sivéry saw the new king thereafter deliberately confiding governance to Abbot Mathieu and his former
coregent, Simon de Nesle, in return for their otherwise silent toleration
of his friendship with Pierre de la Broce.[61]

Furthermore, according to Sivéry, the decision to bury Louis IX's son
Jean-Tristan at Saint-Denis, contrary to the general principle favored by
the dead king that princes who had not reigned as kings should be interred
honorably elsewhere, was another deliberate gesture on Abbot Mathieu's
part to indicate to Philip III that he could exercise—and would continue
to exercise—governmental powers, notwithstanding Pierre de la Broce or
any other royal favorite. No one, not even the new king, was going to
tarnish the old king's government.[62] This seems, however, to be a pretty
far-fetched position, since the evidence is quite substantial that the despised chamberlain came to have tremendous influence in governmental
appointments in those regions where he accumulated property.[63] The
abbot could not or did not restrain him, or if he did, the restraints only
slightly tempered his meteoric rise.

This fact undermines another of Sivéry's assertions, regarding a dispute
over the extent of the dower property to be assigned to the queen dowager,
Marguerite of Provence.[64] It was the regency government that had assigned the dower lands, but it differed with Marguerite's representatives
about what actually pertained to the castellanies Louis IX had assigned to
her. Marguerite complained to her son when he returned, and indeed he
decided to yield to her or her advisers' more expansive definition of her
properties. Sivéry has claimed that the regents were unscrupulous, though
the evidence suggests that they were in fact overscrupulous in trying to
fulfill Louis IX's wishes by not conceding more than legally had to be
conceded. Sivéry also averred in his biography of Philip III that Pierre de
la Broce intervened on the queen dowager's behalf and had the new king
overturn the regents' decisions. The king and chamberlain with no power
vis-à-vis the regents in other parts of Sivéry's scenario are at the same time
full of power, to the point (Sivéry's words) of cowering them into silence.
His evidence—if there really can be evidence of such a contradictory picture: Sivéry referred the reader of his biography of Philip III, where he

---

[61] Sivéry, *Philippe III*, p. 81.

[62] Ibid., p. 82.

[63] Even Sivéry, elsewhere in his biography of the king, admits Pierre's successful implanta-
tion of his creatures in the administration; ibid., p. 204.

[64] Ibid., pp. 103–4

made these claims, to his earlier biography of Marguerite of Provence for support.[65] There the evidence turns out to be nothing more than a "no doubt" and a rhetorical question, meaning there is no evidence at all.[66] What is certain is that there had been concern that the chamberlain might get a toehold in the queen's property. To ensure against the possibility of a new favorite's achieving anything similar, Abbot Mathieu and the convent of Saint-Denis in 1279, soon after Pierre's execution, secured assurance in Parlement that their lands and the lands of their dependent priories in the *dos* of the queen mother would never enter into anyone's hands but the king's.[67]

Carolus-Barré's assessments, however, which belittled the chamberlain's governmental powers, naturally led him to see all the legislation and ordinances of the early years of Philip III's reign as consistent with the outlook of Louis IX and of the councilors whom the new king inherited from his father.[68] And it also caused him to accept uncritically later monastic encomia to the abbot, the man "by whom the whole kingdom of France was governed, at whose will everything happened, and whom he wished he raised, and vice versa."[69] Carolus-Barré thus saw Mathieu de Vendôme, the man he came to idolize, as the most faithful heir of Louis IX's vision and the principal authority in government, the *premier ministre*, after the old king's death.[70] If there was consistency and honesty in royal governance after 1270 and indeed throughout Philip III's reign, it was because Abbot Mathieu was consistent and honest—and ever present, with Simon de Nesle as well, to run the government.[71]

---

[65] Ibid., p. 323 n.16 (he cites "p. 266 sq." of the queen's biography; the correct citation is pp. 226 ff.).

[66] Sivéry, *Marguerite de Provence*, p. 228: "Marguerite de Provence obtient gain de cause. Philippe III, sans nul doute en accord avec Pierre de Brosse, le véritable maître du royaume sans lequel il ne décide rien, lui accorde la réparation des torts que lui avaient causés les membres du Conseil de régence. Ne découvre-t-on pas là une nouvelle raison de son silence face à l'usurpation du pouvoir de l'ancien chambellan de Louis IX?"

[67] *Olim*, 2:140 no. XXIV; *Actes du Parlement de Paris*, 1:207 no. 2217.

[68] "Et c'est bien grâce à lui, à son entourage actif et dévoué et à sa sage administration que le règne de Philippe le Hardi peut être considéré comme le prolongement de celui de saint Louis"; Carolus-Barré, *Procès de canonisation*, p. 229. Carolus-Barré was following but pushing further the views of Langlois, *Règne de Philippe III*, p. 41.

[69] *HF*, 20:490–91. The quotation is from a Rouennais chronicle, *HF*, 23:345, "per quem totum regnum Franciae regebatur, et ad nutum ejus omnia fiebant, et quem volebat, exaltabat, et contra."

[70] Carolus-Barré, *Procès de canonisation*, p. 230.

[71] "A la vérité, depuis quinze années [1270–1285], Mathieu et Simon [de Nesle] appelés au pouvoir par le saint roi, n'avaient cessé de tenir les rênes de l'Etat, malgré les obstacles suscités par Pierre de la Brosse, par Charles d'Anjou et . . . par le roi [Philippe III] lui-même"; Carolus-Barré, *Procès de canonisation*, p. 235.

Sivéry, however, again went even further, ending up by turning Carolus-Barré's proposition on its head. He conjured a Louis IX who was something of a seer: the old king, in his opinion, deliberately chose Pierre de la Broce to counsel his heir, knowing full well that only a strong-minded individual could make his son persevere in his foreign policy, though elsewhere he speaks of Pierre as a usurper![72] In the event, Pierre went too far in his *personal* domination of Philip III, but Louis envisaged the domestic administration under the control of Mathieu de Vendôme and Simon de Nesle with only a few aspects of governance after his death in Pierre's control. None of the innuendo surrounding the new royal court or Pierre's arrogance and peccadilloes or even aristocratic resentments were sufficient to compromise the success of Louis's plans. In a sense, through his arrangements, he (or his ideal of rule) continued to direct the realm from his tomb at Saint-Denis.[73] Unfortunately, this scenario is more appropriate to a work of fiction or fantasy than to a scholarly history of French politics and government during the 1270s.

It may very well be the case that eminent royal councilors desired, endeavored, and managed by and large to preserve governance in consonance with the guidelines Louis IX had established. It may also have been the case that these same councilors, despite their distaste for Pierre de la Broce, largely ignored the entanglements of favoritism affecting the court out of their disdain for getting involved in something beneath them. Or perhaps they persuaded themselves that their contempt for Pierre rather than their fear of the king's response kept them from openly censuring the chamberlain. It is possible, however, that these impulses worked together: to challenge the king's dependence on his favorite was to invite dismissal and risk the survival of "good governance." Particularly compelling in this regard is that in the battle camp at Tunis, Philip, lying ill, provided for the establishment of an on-site council of regency if he died before returning to France. This regency council was supposed to have included Pierre de la Broce.[74] Of course, Philip recovered and made Pierre his intimate friend rather than regent of his realm, but even councilors as venerable as Abbot Mathieu de Vendôme and Simon de Nesle must have wondered, given this history, who their replacement might be if they fell afoul of the chamberlain and directly affronted the new king.

In fact, Mathieu, despite Carolus-Barré's and Sivéry's assertions, was not all that prominent in government in the high days of Pierre de la Broce's ascendancy. They presumed that he was, but even Carolus-Barré

---

[72] For Sivéry's assertion of the prophetic choice of Pierre and the chamberlain's deliberate investiture with power, see his *Philippe III*, p. 107.

[73] Cf. ibid., pp. 90–94, 102.

[74] Langlois, *Règne de Philippe III*, p. 15.

acknowledged that he could not directly associate the abbot with the few pieces of legislation scholars know about from the first several years of the reign.[75] In fact, when one examines texts that show the abbot active in or on the edges of government in these years, one discovers that the issues are minor or that his role, insofar as it can be reconstructed, is merely formal.[76] Moreover, it was in precisely this period that Mathieu had one of the Saint-Denis monks, known as Primat, begin the redaction and illustration of the *Grandes Chroniques*, the official history of the realm.[77] The task required, of course, systematic work in identifying and assembling relevant documents.[78] Among these was the collection concerning the regency of 1270 and 1271 that Mathieu himself put together.[79] Many of the documents in this collection, as remarked earlier, were directly relevant to Mathieu's role as regent, detailing his and Simon de Nesle's joint appointment to the office and the powers designated to them. Others included personal letters that Mathieu received in his own name, official letters he jointly received with his coregent, and letters that he and Simon jointly sent out.

Mathieu intended the collection to provide more than the lean details of administration, as a consequence of which he also included a number of letters that furnish the kind of information that would enrich an intimate yet still official history of the crown and the kingdom. And the dossier would prove that governance was honest and that it faithfully served the late king's intentions during the regency. Indeed, putting it together was a kind of acknowledgment that pollution had lately entered the system with the ascendancy of Pierre de la Broce. It was not a challenge so much as a retreat. To acquire some of the personal letters for the dossier, the abbot probably had to contact their recipients and persuade them to let him have access to them, and this took time—and perhaps the recipients wished them to be edited as well. Who knows how much time the abbot devoted to this effort of soliciting and editing these letters? But the fundamental point is that he had the time because of his now muted role in governance.

In the end, he received a small treasure trove of material that offered him, Primat, and other historiographers at Saint-Denis vivid descriptions of Louis IX's Crusade: the stopover in Sardinia en route to Tunisia; the

---

[75] "On ne saurait certes attribuer personellement à Mathieu de Vendôme chacune de ses décisions ou ordonnances, mais . . ."; Carolus-Barré, *Procès de canonisation*, p. 232.

[76] This, despite Carolus-Barré's intimation; for the list, however, ibid., pp. 232–33.

[77] Spiegel, *Chronicle Tradition of Saint-Denis*, pp. 72–96; Nebbiai-Dalla Guarda, *Bibliothèque de l'abbaye de Saint-Denis*, pp. 48–49: Hedeman, *Royal Image*, pp. 9–11.

[78] Richard, *Saint Louis*, p. 432; Le Goff, *Saint Louis*, p. 347.

[79] Carolus-Barré, "Recueil épistolaire," p. 564.

king's death, the deaths of numerous other noble crusaders, and the transfer of power to Philip III; the depth of the new king's grief and his desire
to have his father's memory, and the memory of other loved ones who
had perished, treasured widely; the concern of the leadership, especially
Charles of Anjou and Philip III, with the cardinals' failure to elect a new
pope (it was the longest papal interregnum, thirty-nine months, in
history).[80] One letter in particular, although addressed by Philip III to
the abbot from Italy, *while* the latter was still regent (11 February 1271),
was not addressed to him *as* regent, yet Mathieu placed it in the collection. It was Philip's particular request to the abbot and convent of
Saint-Denis for prayers. The king again described the grief at the loss of
his brother, father, brother-in-law, and wife that occasioned his request.
The monks of Saint-Denis and their abbot were valued for their special
prayers, not merely for their historiographical and administrative services
to the crown.[81]

Once more, who knows how much time Abbot Mathieu took to edit
and even instruct Saint-Denis's historiographers in their use of the collection he amassed or in supervising the production of the *Grandes Chroniques*? Who knows how much time he was simultaneously devoting to
the work of assembling evidence of miracles at Louis IX's tomb in the
abbey—interviewing recipients and witnesses and recording their stories?
And then there were the routine administrative tasks of running the great
abbey, never a mere pro forma endeavor—arranging for purchases of property, protecting dependents, defending jurisdictional claims, maintaining
immunities, keeping a tight rein over serfs, collecting tithes—the list is
endless.[82] Yet it may not be too much to suppose that the opportunity to
concentrate on these tasks was available to him precisely because he was
spending as little time as permissible on his official duties at court during
the ascendancy of the despised chamberlain.

None of this is meant to suggest that the meager scraps of evidence on
Mathieu's activities in government from the king's coronation in 1271
until Pierre de la Broce's arrest and execution in 1278 constitute anything
like a full picture of his role as a councilor, but neither do they suggest his
dominance of government in this period that Carolus-Barré imagined. In
fact, it was not until *after* Pierre de la Broce's fall that the documentary

---

[80] The relevant letters are nicely inventoried in ibid., pp. 557–59 nos. 3, 7–8, 12, and 15.

[81] The letter is published in ibid., pp. 558–59 no. 14. Sivéry, simplistically in my view, sees
Mathieu only as an administrator or councilor; *Philippe III*, p. 93.

[82] For examples in the period of Pierre de la Broce's ascendancy, see *Cartulaire blanc de
Saint-Denis*, Rueil nos. 53, 56–57, and Tremblay nos. 32a–32b; *Atlas historique de Saint-
Denis*, p. 236 no. 66, p. 388 no. 123; *Olim*, 1:936–37 no. XXX; *Actes du Parlement de Paris*,
1:177 no. 1933, 326 no. 127, 330 nos. 189–90; *Série L . . . L829 à L839B*, p. 76, L839A
no. 12.

record shows the abbot again and undeniably as a weighty presence in the administration of the kingdom. From the moment Philip III began to lose faith in Pierre, he turned to his father's old friends, like Mathieu de Vendôme.[83] Afterward it was these men, Abbot Mathieu among them, who regained prominence, although the high aristocracy's role in toppling Pierre presaged a dangerous deviation from the nobility's century-long submission to the crown. Abbot Mathieu could count on the administrative loyalty of most of the *baillis*, especially after weeding out Pierre's creatures. Simon de Nesle could count on his status as a noble himself to reassure the aristocracy, particularly with regard to military affairs, which was one of his specialties. Yet both men would have to be careful whenever crown interests, as they understood them, clashed with the interests of the aristocracy.[84]

King Henry III of England was pleased with the translation of the body of Edward the Confessor, and he entered into easy relations with Westminster Abbey after the splendid celebration. His administration was solicitous of the monastery's needs, whether for dead wood to keep its forges and workshops supplied with charcoal, or for venison to meet its obligations of hospitality, or for wine for divine service and meals.[85] The king confirmed to the constable of Windsor Castle in 1272 that there were to be no prises on firewood, corn, and other victuals brought to Westminster Abbey by land or water.[86] He acquiesced in releasing Abbot Richard from a host of minor administrative and judicial responsibilities.[87] And on the occasion of the casting of a new seal, the king issued a charter confirming the monastery's various privileges; it is dated 20 February 1271.[88]

Somewhat curiously (though perhaps Henry's expectation of perfect motives in everything touching Saint Edward explains it), there does not appear to have been an audit of the accounts of William of Gloucester, who had received huge sums to create and repair jeweled pieces in the abbey's hoard, to craft a silver image on the far side of (*ultra*) the tomb of Katherine, Henry III's daughter, in the church, to make a frontal (*spontale*) for the high altar, and to otherwise enhance the Confessor's shrine. It did become known to the king that William had never rendered account of all the monies he had received; so Henry III ultimately ordered an

---

[83] Cf. Sivéry, *Philippe III*, p. 230, who believes that the king's mother also emerged as a major councilor in the wake of Pierre's fall.

[84] Cf. ibid., pp. 216, 218–19, 241, 245–47, 285.

[85] Wood for charcoal: *Close Rolls, 1268–1272*, p. 177. Venison: *Close Rolls, 1268–1272*, pp. 209–10, 482. Wine: *Close Rolls, 1268–1272*, pp. 178, 205.

[86] *Patent Rolls, Henry III, 1266–1272*, p. 654.

[87] *Close Rolls, 1268-1272*, pp. 296, 388, 427, 551, 565.

[88] WD, fol. 61b.

audit. He was in no particular hurry, however, to have it carried out, or perhaps declining health undermined his attention to administrative work. It remained for the regents in the next reign to see to the task.[89]

Although the king treated Westminster Abbey and its abbot exceedingly well in the closing years of his life, the administrative and financial burdens that Richard de Ware had to shoulder were still heavy—heavy but not unspeakably so, as they had been in the days of baronial rule and rebellion. The flooding of fields on the abbey's estates near the Thames and its watershed was a recurrent problem, which the abbot finally had the disposable funds to deal with in 1271. By a statute enacted in chapter that year the monastery authorized the construction of a levee to prevent spillage and damage in the future.[90] Around the same time the abbey had to raise funds to support Prince Edward's plans for Crusade. The prince was borrowing 70,000 l. t. from Louis IX, but he was also receiving the return on a twentieth from the clergy. The abbot was recognized as having paid his portion on 26 October 1270, at least that portion which devolved on "his villeins in the counties of Middlesex, Essex, Hertford[shire], Surrey, Oxford[shire], Berks[shire], Gloucester[shire], Worcester[shire], and Rutland."[91] By 22 January 1271 all the assessments owed on the convent's holdings and its villeins were certified as fully paid.[92]

The warm and intimate relations between Westminster Abbey and the crown in the twilight years of Henry III's reign do not mirror the monastery's relations with other powerful people and groups. An old adversary, Pershore Abbey, under its ruler, Henry de Bideford, was at the center of one unpleasant conflict.[93] One David de la Fortheye of the village of Pershore captured three wild animals in the enclosure known as Tiddesley Park, which belonged to the abbot of Westminster (*super captione trium ferarum in parco ipsius abbatis*). He and his comrades, all armed, assaulted the abbot's men, presumably the park wardens (the act is described as an *insultum*). All of this allegedly began at the command of the abbot of Pershore.[94] Richard de Ware was enraged against this David; nothing justified an attack, even if the abbot of Pershore did supposedly encourage it.

---

[89] *Close Rolls, 1272–1279*, p. 3 (the order to initiate the previously commanded audit is dated 14 December 1272; Henry had died in mid-November).

[90] WD, fol. 642b. Some property arrangements, detailed immediately following the statute in the cartulary and permitting construction on two parcels of land (*platee*) near the Thames, may be related to the execution of the statute.

[91] *Patent Rolls, Henry III, 1266–1272*, p. 468.

[92] Ibid., p. 509.

[93] I have reconstructed this case from WAM, no. 22471, and WD, fols. 285–286, 287–287b, 295–295b. For earlier relations with Pershore, above, p. 46.

[94] I follow the index to WD on this, since the original is faded and difficult to read with confidence.

The Latin phrase used to describe his anger was *rancor animi*, a phrase well-known to students of medieval feud.[95] Thanks to the intervention of the precentor of Hereford Cathedral, Hervey de Boreham, who also had a career as a lower (*puisne*) justice of common pleas, Abbot Richard was persuaded to soften his rancorous spirit against David.[96] He did so at a meeting on the eve of Saint Dunstan's day (18 May), 1272 (*eidem David omnem animi rancorem et omnem accionem ea occasione eidem abbati competentem*). The precentor ordered David to appear on the next day, the Feast of Saint Dunstan, before the king's justices to acknowledge his responsibility for the attack (*recognoscat insultum et factum*). David was going to be fined for the crime, but the abbot of Westminster agreed to indemnify him owing to the miscreant's newfound devotion and humility toward the churchman, and to forgive the damages he otherwise would have paid to Richard. The phrasing is quite precise: "ac ob devotionem et humilitatem ipsius David renunciat ei omnem emendam dampnorum eidem abbati ea occasione illatorum competentem." David de la Fortheye in essence became the dependent—the man—of Abbot Richard of Westminster by this series of acts. His family, it would seem, did not suffer from this relationship in the long term.[97]

King Henry III's health began to show ever more serious signs of deterioration through 1270. The death of his friend and brother-in-law Louis IX must have worsened his spirits. The absence of his son Prince Edward, gone to join the French king's Crusade, was undoubtedly another burden; who could know whether Edward would return alive. Abbot Richard did what he could to bring God's mercy on the king. During a particularly severe illness that year, Westminster's monks set out barefoot in procession in the rain to the New Temple in London to invoke the divine powers in their ruler's favor. Happily, they could have commended their actions on this occasion, for Henry recovered.[98] Two small gilded silver images—one of the king and one of the queen—that were offered at the Confessor's shrine in 1271 may represent a thank offering for his recuperation.[99]

It was the death of Alphonse of Poitiers, Louis IX's brother, that compounded the difficulties of Henry III's final months. Alphonse's death— which is to say, the death of the man who was titular count of Toulouse

---

[95] Cf. Hyams, *Rancor and Reconciliation*, esp. pp. 130, 255, 297.

[96] For Hervey's judgeship, see Haydn, *Book of Dignities*, p. 226.

[97] Inferred from the transactions noted in *Descriptive Catalogue of Ancient Deeds*, 1:262 and 314, B 508 and 1051.

[98] *Flores historiarum*, 3:22.

[99] The suggestion is mine. Weiler, "Symbolism and Politics," p. 22, notes the gift and the ceremonial splendor of its offering, but makes no guess as to why the latter was appropriate at this time.

by courtesy of his wife—opened territorial questions put in abeyance by the Treaty of Paris of 1259. Had Jeanne, Alphonse's wife, outlived him by more than a few days, the whole constellation of problems surrounding the territories in question would have developed differently and perhaps without enmity. Had Louis IX lived through the Crusade, I also feel certain that the two old monarchs would have striven hard to maintain the pacific tone that had characterized French-English relations since the late 1250s. With Louis gone and Henry dying, the administrators and lawyers took over.

According to the treaty, the wearer of the English crown was to receive the region known as the Agenais, a county in dignity, if Alphonse of Poitiers died without heirs.[100] The complexities underlying this simple provision emerged from a host of factors that could be debated: (1) the precise nature of Richard I the Lionhearted's original grant of the county to the house of Toulouse in 1196, (2) the overlapping and conflicting patterns of lordship and dependence in the region, (3) residual claims and counterclaims that emerged during the various phases of the Albigensian Crusades, and (4) the fact that, although their deaths were almost simultaneous, Alphonse, as noted, actually predeceased his wife Jeanne in 1271, and it was in her that "hereditary" right to the fief actually lay (or at least this last argument was being used at the same time to contest dispositions of property in the Comtat-Venaissin where the house of Toulouse had similar claims).[101]

Though Henry III was ill when news of the deaths of Alphonse and Jeanne reached the English royal court, he appointed an embassy of four commissioners on the 12th of August 1271 to go to the French court to enter a formal claim to the Agenais. Two of the four commissioners were abbots, Richard de Ware of Westminster and Roger de Norton of Saint-Albans, and two were royal officials, Adam de Novo Mercato and John de la Lynde.[102] The two senior members of the embassy were Richard and John, and by and large they actually carried out the commission. On 20 October 1271 there are records of payments to each for expenses (fifty marks) of their overseas travel on the king's business.[103]

An entry on the Patent Rolls for the next day, besides noting the issuance of a general writ of protection for the abbot of Westminster's proper-

---

[100] Cuttino, *English Medieval Diplomacy*, pp. 10–11.

[101] Ibid. For the Comtat-Venaissin comparison, see Jordan, "Jews and the Transition to Papal Rule in the Comtat-Venaissin," p. 215.

[102] *Patent Rolls, Henry III, 1266–1272*, p. 568. Many of the documents to be cited here were published by Rymer and are conveniently inventoried in the *Syllabus* (p. 79) to the *Foedera*.

[103] *Calendar of the Liberate Rolls*, 6:184.

ties while he was abroad, specifies in great detail what the ambassadors were supposed to do while on the Continent. Acting with Henry III's full powers in this regard, they were to approach Philip III and petition for the transfer of the county of Agen and the associated lands of Saintonge and Quercy in the borderlands of the duchy of Gascony. In expectation that the terms of the Treaty of Paris, as the English understood them, were unambiguous in this matter, a proclamation was also to be published in Agen declaring the ambassadors' authority in anticipation of the transfer of lordship. While Richard and John were negotiators with the French crown and were empowered to do fealty to the French in Henry's behalf, they were also mediators between the French crown and another party, the English queen, Eleanor. For Henry III and his son, Prince Edward, had agreed before the latter left on Crusade that the lands in question would be assigned to the queen. Consequently, one of the embassy's priorities in the autumn of 1271 was to see that the territories and their inhabitants were formally accredited to the queen's proctor in her name. They also sought to have the French king certify all these arrangements.[104]

The negotiations were more protracted than the ambassadors perhaps expected, and required their trooping around the countryside to keep pace with the travels of the new French king and his entourage. Philip III kept court in Châteauneuf-sur-Loire and Montargis in the Orléanais, in December 1271.[105] Abbot Richard lodged nearby, probably at the abbey of Saint-Benoît-sur-Loire, where the relics of Saint Benedict reposed—an appropriate location for an extended visit from the head of one of the greatest Benedictine monasteries in England. The likelihood of some such arrangement derives from the fact that it was from Orléans in 1271 that Richard sent a statute (or, rather, presumably his approval of a chapter statute) for Westminster regulating the singing of hymns, proper procedures to minister to ill and dying monks, and limits on movement within the monastery, among other matters; he may also have authorized a grant to help repair chinks and fissures in the abbey precinct walls at the same time and from the same venue.[106] The 1270s were mercifully free of deferred maintenance.

---

[104] *Patent Rolls, Henry III, 1266–1272*, pp. 581–82.

[105] See Philip's itinerary; *HF*, 21:424.

[106] WD, fols. 641b–642, records the statute described and gives its provenance as Orléans and its date as 1271. Accompanying the statute (fol. 642), but not self-evidently part of it, is the record of the grant for the walls, also dated 1271. I am presuming that Richard was in or near Orléans (conjecturally at Saint-Benoît) when he sent his instructions to give the grant.

In any case, on the day after Christmas 1271 the English government paid out another one hundred pounds for the continuing expenses of the principal negotiators and proctors in France, again by name Richard de Ware and John de la Lynde.[107] And one month later, with the negotiations continuing and not seeming to move closer to resolution, the men's commission had to be renewed. At the same time, three other men were appointed to the embassy as supplementary proctors to Parlement where the technicalities being argued demanded more and more expert knowledge. For the predictable problems that accompanied overlapping lordship began to take on a more suspicious aspect in the negotiations.

Suspicion arose from the suddenness of a group of complaints from the inhabitants of Gascony. The duchy was of course already under English control, but its inhabitants sometimes tried to appeal to the French crown as their overlord when they suffered from breaches of the peace and believed or asserted that they believed the English duke's government was failing to provide them with justice.[108] Sometimes, as Pierre Chaplais remarked, the appeals were sincere; at other times they were instrumental, a means by which one party put off or stymied an unfavorable decision in the ducal court.[109] The month of February 1272 saw the English government react to just such a situation. On the 23rd of the month Henry's officials instructed Abbot Richard and John de la Lynde to run interference, as it were, and intervene to see that no justified complaint could be made to Parlement against English governance of the duchy. The directing of this order to the ambassadors, I think, was a sign to the French crown that the English suspected a link—and an improper one, at that—between the spate of Gascon allegations and the preexisting hesitancy to transfer the Agenais rather than a genuine concern on the part of the French about the quality of administration in the duchy. Of course, neither Richard de Ware nor John de la Lynde had time to spend on seeing justice done for Gascon trespasses. The order, in fact, required the seneschal of Gascony, the man who in a sense was the implied target of those who criticized English justice in Gascony, to do all the preliminary investigation for the ambassadors while they continued to negotiate in the

---

[107] *Calendar of the Liberate Rolls*, 6:194. And more generally on the information presented in this paragraph, Kicklighter, "English Gascony and the Parlement of Paris," pp. 119–36.

[108] Cf. Kicklighter, "French Jurisdictional Supremacy in Gascony," pp. 127–34; idem, "Appeal, Negotiation, and Conflict," pp. 45–59.

[109] Chaplais, *Essays in Medieval Diplomacy*. essay 6, "Les Appels gascons au roi d'Angleterre sous le règne d'Edouard Ier (1272–1307)," p. 383, and, more generally. 382–85 for appeals in the period covered by this book. See also Kicklighter, "Monastères de Gascogne et le conflit franco-anglais," pp. 121–34.

north.[110] All this effort was terribly expensive, especially considering that funds which otherwise might have been available were going to Prince Edward's Crusade. Henry III was forced once again to get help from Westminster Abbey. He asked the pope, Gregory X (1271–1276), for authorization for a special subvention to meet his needs, and a papal order was issued at Viterbo on 1 October 1272 granting the king's request. The order instructed Richard de Ware as well as the abbot of Holy Cross, Waltham, to divert their revenues temporarily to six of the king's clerks who needed the cash while they were about the king's business—not as odious an importunity perhaps as a request to pawn Saint Edward's jewels, but bad enough and a dispiriting reminder of past fiscal crises.[111]

To some extent, the French policy (or conspiracy, if English suspicions were accurate) to impede the negotiations on the Agenais and Saintonge succeeded. Perhaps if Henry III, though terribly ill and short of money, had traveled to France, the situation could still have been resolved in a trice. He and Richard could have called on their old acquaintance Mathieu de Vendôme, even though with the favorite Pierre de la Broce so prominent, the French abbot was keeping a low profile. Still, Mathieu might have been importuned with a sense of urgency to use his influence as the English king neared death. Henry would have been a living reminder to Philip III of the goodwill that had bound him and his father, Louis IX, and perhaps the English king could have called on the good offices of the queen mother, his sister-in-law, Marguerite de Provence, as well. All this is speculation—not baseless, perhaps, but in the event sadder precisely because it makes a plausible scenario. In fact, the problem of the transfer of the Agenais would not be resolved in what little remained of Henry III's time among the living.

The king of England died on 16 November 1272, a date that, as more than one chronicler noted, fell close to the saint's day of Edmund of Pontigny whose "exile" in France some of Henry's detractors attributed to him and, as a later poet noted, close to the feast of Saint Edmund the Anglo-Saxon martyr-king, after whom Henry had named his younger son.[112] The Templars claimed that his body should be consigned to them, since at various times in his long reign Henry had expressed different preferences, including the Temple, for his entombment.[113] Despite their pro-

---

[110] *Patent Rolls, Henry III, 1266–1272*, p. 628. Kicklighter, "English Gascony and the Parlement of Paris," p. 132, notes without comment Richard de Ware's service as a representative of the king-duke at Parlement.

[111] *Original Papal Documents*, no. 741.

[112] *Chronicles of the Reigns of Edward I and Edward II*, 1:82, and *Historical Poems*, p. 248. The feasts of both Edmunds are celebrated on 20 November.

[113] *Flores historiarum*, 3:28.

test, he was laid to rest four days later, on 20 November, in the tomb that had once held the Confessor's remains.[114] Chroniclers memorialized the deceased monarch with conventional praises of his piety and generosity, but they noted, too, that he was a naïf when it came to governance (*licet simplex in administratione temporalium*).[115]

Either at this time or about a decade later, when Henry's body was moved to the ornate Italianate tomb now visited at the abbey (see fig. 12a, b), Abbot Richard composed a memorial in his master's honor.[116] It was inscribed on a tablet and hung on the tomb: "Henry III lies here, the friend of piety: he razed this church, whereupon he rebuilt it. He offers the gift to Him, the Trinity, who rules."[117] This modest epitaph notwithstanding, on the day of Henry's first burial, there was not, so far as one can reconstruct, much talk of making the king's resting place into a more splendid site. There at the high altar, it was the responsibility of the greatest magnates in the kingdom, including the Earl of Gloucester as interim guardian of the realm, to swear fidelity to Henry's successor, Prince Edward, far away in the East. They did so as if they were actually in the presence of their new lord and king.[118]

A small group of men who had the administration of Prince Edward's affairs while he was on Crusade quickly moved into positions of authority upon King Henry's death. The cleric Robert Burnell was the major presence.[119] A longtime friend of the new but absent king, Burnell had intended to go on Crusade with him. Edward, however, put off this plan, hoping to have him made archbishop of Canterbury when Boniface of Savoy died in his Savoyard homeland in preparation to join the prince's Crusade in July of 1270. This attempt failed, but it testifies to the close personal ties of the prince and the English churchman.

---

[114] *Willelmi Rishanger . . . Chronica*, pp. 74, "Corpus autem ejus apud Westmonasterium honorificae traditur sepulturae," and 429, "apud Westmonasterium decentissime est sepultus." See also *Ypodigma Neustriae*, p. 166; the "Annals" of Winchester, Waverley, Dunstable, and Worcester in *Annales Monastici*, 2:112, 378; 3:254, and 4:461; *Chronicles of the Reigns of Edward I and Edward II*, 1:82.

[115] *Chronicon domini Walteri de Heminburgh*, 1:341. See also, for example, *Nicolai Triveti, Dominicani, Annales*, p. 236.

[116] On the translation of Henry's body, below, chapter 8, p. 204.

[117] *Monasticon Anglicanum*, 1:273 (citing Fabyan's *Chronicle* [early sixteenth-century]), "Tercius Henricus jacet hic, pietatis amicus: / Ecclesiam stravit istam, quam post renovavit. / Reddat ei munus qui regnat trinus et unus."

[118] *Chronicles of the Reigns of Edward I and Edward II*, 1:82, "ac si praesens esset, super majus altare Westmonasterii." See also *Flores historiarum*, 3:28; *De antiquis legibus liber*, p. 155.

[119] Huscroft, "Robert Burnell and the Government of England," pp. 61–70; idem, "Correspondence of Robert Burnell," pp. 18–19.

The regency government set up under these men was very much a care-taker government, about whose effectiveness there is a debate. Huscroft, the most recent authority, argues that if one takes the notion of a caretaker government seriously and expects it to maintain the status quo as best it can, then the Burnell-dominated regime was successful.[120] Its most stunning move was the convening of a parliament to recognize the validity of its authority in January 1273. The situation in England was very different from that in France, where the meticulous arrangements for a possible transition assured a smooth succession. The planners for a possible English succession had thought that Henry III's brother, Richard of Cornwall, or in the case of his death, his son Henry of Almain, might exercise royal power until Edward's return. Philip Basset, the justiciar, in the absence of or in concert with these great nobles, could also have been expected to help govern the realm, since the justiciarship had traditionally been conceived of as the office vested with governing England when kings visited their Continental lands. All three men, however, were dead by the time of the Parliament of January 1273. The greatest tragedy, both in the circumstances of his death and perhaps for Westminster Abbey, involved Henry of Almain. Lord Henry was a friend and recent benefactor of the abbey: in 1270 he had granted buildings, a garden, and a quay to the monastery with royal permission.[121] He would likely have been a good friend to the monks during a regency, but he was murdered in Italy in 1271 by Simon de Montfort's sons.[122] It was under these circumstances that Robert Burnell emerged as the key figure in the regency.

Meanwhile the negotiations over the Agenais dragged on. On 20 January 1273 additional protection was extended until Michaelmas for the abbot of Westminster still beyond the seas on the king's affairs.[123] Business at home that concerned the abbot had to be dealt with by his representatives. On 27 January 1273, he received the regents' authorization for him to appoint men for this purpose.[124]

Edward I, recognized as fully and legitimately possessing the dignity of kingship, like his French counterpart, even before coronation, was making a slow progress in his return to England from the Holy Land, where he had gone after Louis IX's death. He tarried for quite a bit of time in Gascony, in part exploiting his ducal demesne lands and financial rights in order to repay the 70,000 l. t. loan Louis IX had authorized for the Cru-

---

[120] Huscroft, "Robert Burnell and the Government of England," pp. 59–60, 69–70, courteously assesses the competing views.

[121] WD, fols. 355b–356.

[122] Huscroft, "Robert Burnell and the Government of England," p. 64.

[123] *Patent Rolls, Edward I, 1272–1281*, p. 3.

[124] *Close Rolls, 1272–1279*, p. 43.

sade.[125] His presence also helped move the prolonged negotiations over the Agenais forward toward conclusion. Final resolution did evade the various panels of commissioners for years, but despite this, there was still a bedrock of goodwill between the two kingdoms.[126] Edward could put off his return to English shores only so long. He finally came home, landing at Dover on Thursday (2 August) after the feast of Saint Peter in Chains, 1274.[127]

There was no lengthy period of public mourning for his father after his return. Preparations were already in train for his coronation. With his mother, the queen dowager, and many other members of his family, including both of his sisters, in attendance and in the presence of King Alexander III of Scotland, the duke of Brittany, the archbishop of York, and a host of additional notables, Edward and his consort, Eleanor of Castile, were solemnly anointed and crowned king and queen of England by the archbishop of Canterbury, Robert Kilwardby, in an atmosphere of expectancy and joy all around in the magnificent setting of Abbot Richard de Ware's abbey.[128] The day was the Sunday after Assumption, 19 August, 1274, less than three weeks after Edward disembarked at Dover.[129]

The archbishop of York, it was reported, had no serious part to play in the ceremony (*sed non apposuit manum*).[130] However disappointing this was to that prelate, it does not seem to have much dampened anyone else's spirits. But soon afterward all this changed, because, as the Worcester annalist believed, God or fate decreed that for many of those in attendance, the time of their sojourn on earth was near an end (*Sicque post magnum gaudium coronationis magnam tristitiam nobilibus reliquerunt*).[131] Young Aveline, the child-bride of King Edward's brother Edmund, was among these. She died on 10 November 1274, less than three months shy of her sixteenth birthday, and had her obsequies and interment at Westminster Abbey. The bishop of London attended Aveline's funeral, but, showing more tact than Bishop Etienne Tempier of Paris at Louis IX's obsequies, he formally stipulated that his presence did nothing to derogate "from the

---

[125] Raban, "Edward's Other Inquiries," p. 46.

[126] Cf. Glenisson, "Application de la 'Paix' de Paris," pp. 191–205, and below, pp. 206–9.

[127] *Close Rolls, 1272–1279*, p. 97; *Calendar of the Fine Rolls*, 1:26; *Patent Rolls, Edward I, 1272–1281*, pp. 55–56.

[128] *Willelmi Rishanger . . . Chronica*, p. 84. See also *Flores historiarum*, 3:44; *Ypodigma Neustriae*, p. 169; the "Annals" of Winchester, Waverley, Bermondsey, Dunstable, Oseney, and Worcester in *Annales Monastici*, 2:118, 383, 465; 3:263; 4:262, 465.

[129] *Close Rolls, 1272–1279*, p. 97; *Calendar of the Fine Rolls*, 1:26; *Patent Rolls, Edward I, 1272–1281*, pp. 55–56; *Chronicles of the Reigns of Edward I and Edward II*, 1:84.

[130] "Annals of Dunstable," in *Annales Monastici*, 3:263.

[131] "Annals of Worcester," in *Annales Monastici*, 4:467. See also *Flores historiarum*, 3:44.

rights and privileges of the Abbey as an exempt House."[132] The funerals continued. In October, Edward's son Henry died; he would be laid to rest in a Purbeck marble tomb at the abbey.[133] There was, thus, an unsettling and uncanny parallel in the transitions to new rulership in France and England in the 1270s: the multiple funerals of royal kin and the making of multiple tombs at the two greatest royal abbeys.

[132] The quotation is from Tanner, "Nature and Use of the Westminster Abbey Muniments," p. 61.

[133] Carpenter, "King Henry III and the Cosmati Work," p. 194.

VII

THE ABBEYS IN THE NEW REGIMES

T HE TRANSITION TO NEW rulership was a short episode—an extended moment fraught with singular problems—in the history of the two royal abbeys, but over the longer term the major challenge facing both institutions was the working out of a healthy and enduring relationship with their kings. Notwithstanding all the spiritual authority and economic clout they wielded, the abbeys were dependent on the monarchs to provide the optimum environment for them to flourish and in particular to successfully fend off recurrent attempts from various corners to encroach on their power. The governments' maintenance of internal peace, the effective functioning of the justice systems, and the provision of royal patronage and more general protection were necessary to prevent the erosion of the abbeys' status.

There was in theory and sometimes actively an even higher authority that safeguarded the abbeys, the papacy. Yet just as the kings demanded and expected ideological and, if necessary, material support from the abbeys in return for their protection, the popes, in return for theirs, depended on great exempt monasteries, like Westminster and Saint-Denis, to do their bidding in governing the church and exploiting the resources necessary for all aspects of the Catholic mission. This became evident very early in the new reigns. On the 30th of September 1272 Pope Gregory X (1271–1276) requested various English bishops as well as the abbot of Westminster and the abbot of Saint-Albans—representing, as it were, the exempt religious congregations of the realm—to use their influence to obtain from all the prelates continuing subventions for the Crusade.[1]

Gregory's request came with compelling insistence, given his background. He had been elected pope after a more than two-year interregnum. He was a minor churchman, in terms of rank, not even a priest, let alone a cardinal, and was in the Holy Land on pilgrimage when he received news of his election as supreme pontiff. His pilgrimage coincided with Prince Edward's truncated Crusade, truncated by Louis IX's death and the French decision to return home after they settled the peace agreement with the Tunisians. It was an agreement quite favorable to the Christian side and especially to Charles of Anjou, and thus technically a "victory."

---

[1] *Calendar of Entries in the Papal Registers*, 1:444.

The Crusade, however, had not achieved its main objectives. The ruler of Tunisia did not convert. No North African attack was launched against Egypt. Christian military forces in the Holy Land were only briefly and inadequately reinforced. As far as the distant rulers and commanders in Europe were concerned, the victory in Tunisia would someday have to be followed up by another concerted effort, but there was no particular hurry. Indeed, it is not clear that any Western rulers except the future Edward I and the future Gregory X, who had been on the spot in 1271, fully realized how precarious the situation in the Crusader States was. This was why both men were fully committed to the resumption of military campaigns as soon as possible. In the event, Edward's commitment foundered on the political torments of the British Isles and the changed leadership in France, recurrent and relentless checks to his fulfilling his hopes for the Holy Land. Gregory X did not live long enough to see his hopes fade. For the five years he was pope he worked indefatigably to marshal a new Crusade. The best way to achieve his goal, he believed, was to convene an ecumenical council as his predecessors, Innocent III and Innocent IV, had done and to inspire and mobilize churchmen and laymen alike to the challenge of securing the land of Christ's birth, ministry, and resurrection. Within days of his consecration as pope he made known his intent to call a council. Like Innocent IV's it was to be held at Lyon.

Although conceived in his mind early in his pontificate, the necessary preliminaries for Pope Gregory's meeting took an enormous length of time, and the Second Council of Lyon did not convene until 1 May 1274. It was an intensive meeting, lasting only two and one-half months and wrapping up its business on 16 July 1274. The *Dit du Concile de Lyon*, a poem contemporary with the meeting of the council, remarks that as many as four hundred abbots attended the sessions.[2] This may be a considerable exaggeration, or, more likely, the poet made no distinctions among abbots, representatives of absent abbots, and men whom the pope specifically delegated official status at the meeting.

One knows from an entry on the Close Rolls for 28 March 1274 that Abbot Richard de Ware received royal permission to appoint attorneys to see to his business while he was abroad at the meeting. The record was included in a long list of royally sanctioned arrangements for prelates who were preparing to embark for it.[3] Abbot Mathieu de Vendôme almost certainly attended the council, as Carolus-Barré argued, although the list of abbots for whom explicit evidence of attendance exists is woefully incom-

---

[2] Carolus-Barré and Payen, "Dit du Concile de Lyon," pp. 933, 956.
[3] *Close Rolls, 1272–1279*, p. 117. See also *Patent Rolls, Edward I, 1272–1281*, p. 46.

plete, including only fifteen men, and the name of the abbot of Saint-Denis is not among these.[4]

The council itself had two fundamental and interrelated goals, that is, in addition to the proclamation of a Crusade, the union of the Eastern and Western churches under papal authority.[5] Ancillary to these goals were matters like relations with the Tatar Khan, perhaps important in themselves but considered crucial at the time for their possible resonances with the two greatest aims of the council. With respect to the example invoked, that of the Tatar Khan, the desire was to assure that his realm, strategically located on the Black Sea, would not provide indirect aid to the Muslim power in Palestine by attacking the recently restored Greek Empire, thereby undermining the Crusade effort. For Michael VIII Paleologus (1261–1282), the emperor of the Greeks, had promised not only ecclesiastical union with Rome, if the appropriate formulas could be worked out, but support for the westerners' Crusade. A papal effort to preempt Tatar attacks on the Greeks was tantamount to a sign of the pope's good faith.

Even more than a decade after their reconquest of Constantinople from the Latins in 1261, the Greek rulers were still quite weak in relation to the numerous enemies on the borders of the truncated state. Also there were, by the very nature of the situation, multiple claims among the Franks to the imperial patrimony or to parts of it, and, along with the claims, there was the westerners' ever looming threat to take military action to recover the empire. The pope had to choose the best course of action: encourage a Crusade against the Paleologoi, support the dynastic claims of Latin princes, and encourage them to attack independent of or coordinated with a Crusade, or make the accommodations the Byzantine emperor desired, accommodations that might be advantageous to Rome given the vulnerability of the restored empire. In the end, the pontiff opted to pursue an alliance with Michael Paleologus.

The personal opinions of neither Richard de Ware nor Mathieu de Vendôme on these matters are known, but their official opinions can be inferred, or rather some of the views they communicated to the pope can be deduced from the positions held by their kings. Richard de Ware would have represented a king passionately committed to the Crusade, as Gregory knew, and, because of the fragility of the Crusader States, not particularly hostile to the idea of rapprochement with the restored Greek Empire. Moreover, the union of the churches was deeply desired in England and

---

[4] "L'importance de l'abbaye de Saint-Denis, dépendant directement du Saint-Siège, autorise à penser que Mathieu de Vendôme participa à ces grandes assises de la chrétienté"; Carolus-Barré, *Procès de canonisation*, p. 232. But see the documented list of attendees in idem, "Pères du IIe Concile de Lyon," pp. 415–16.

[5] In general, see Roberg, *Das Zweite Konzil von Lyon*.

throughout Roman Christendom, if negotiators could achieve it without sacrificing any of the serious aspects of papal supremacy. Mathieu de Vendôme had a more complicated royal voice to channel. The recently defunct Latin Empire was a Frankish empire; the deposed rulers were closely related biologically to the French royal house. Throughout the Greek mainland and the archipelago French aristocratic families held out against the Paleologoi. The help they needed might come from either Charles of Anjou as ruler of Sicily or Philip III (on this the two Capetians were of the same mind). Consequently, it was not self-evident among French aristocrats that the pope should acquiesce in the continuance of the Greek Empire. Only the more fundamental hope of ecclesiastical union presented a barrier to French refusal to cooperate, and I presume that Mathieu de Vendôme made this point abundantly clear to his colleagues at Lyon. Whether it was he who was instrumental in securing the French government's adherence to the pope's plans is unknown and perhaps unknowable, but if a voice as prestigious as his had been raised in opposition to the pope's efforts, it is hard to believe this would have remained unmentioned in the surviving sources.

When the council closed, union had theoretically been achieved through the formal submission of the Greek delegation. Theologians of the caliber of Eudes Rigaud and Saint Bonaventure worked out the details. Preparations for a new Crusade were also in train, but this effort, including the taxation, was vested in the bureaucrats of the papal curia and in their local agents, Italian merchant bankers.[6] Thus most prelates, like the two abbots, simply returned home. Mathieu settled easily into his routine as the administrative head of Saint-Denis. He was still leery of Pierre de la Broce's influence, even though the favorite's star, one is aware in retrospect, was beginning to set. He focused his attention on securing the fortunes of his monastery.[7] He came to be recognized as the abbot who had "much augmented Saint-Denis in rents" (*multum in reditibus augmentavit*).[8]

Saint-Denis acquired property and rights both from other ecclesiastical institutions (in the form of exchanges of property) and from the crown, aristocrats, and bourgeois as exchanges, gifts, and purchases.[9] Unlike the

[6] For the monies, often in arrears, provided by Westminster Abbey to the Italian depositories for the crusading tenths, see Lunt, *Financial Relations*, pp. 324–25, 655.

[7] On Mathieu's activities on behalf of the monastery in the 1270s and early 1280s, see *GC*, vol. 7, cols. 393–94.

[8] Ibid., col. 395 (quoting Guillaume de Nangis).

[9] Discussion of transactions with lay parties follows immediately. An example of an exchange with an ecclesiastical institution, in this instance the priory of Saint-Martin-des-Champs of Paris, in March 1282, is preserved in *Recueil de chartes et documents de Saint-Martin-des-Champs*, no. 1288; the abbot of Saint-Denis exchanged a quitrent on property opposite the church of Sainte-Croix of Saint-Denis for one held by Saint-Martin on a plot of land along the highway to Senlis.

case with most monasteries but like Westminster's the balance of out-and-out gifts was skewed in favor of the crown as patron. Noncrown gifts of real property or rights in real property were rare and perhaps increasingly so in a world that offered so many alternative targets of largesse—cathedrals and monumental collegiate churches, parish churches, family chapels, friaries, oratories, almonries, hermitages, hospitals and leprosaria, colleges and schools, béguinages, nunneries, and other monasteries. Yet the occasional outright gift does show up in the records. In June of 1279, for example, Etienne Barre, a clerk in lower orders, founded a chaplaincy in the parish church of Villepinte (department, Seine-Saint-Denis). He reserved to himself the right to appoint the incumbents during his lifetime or even to name himself, if he ever took full priestly orders. He gave the chaplaincy to Saint-Denis, that is to say, made it dependent on the abbey, which was vested with the power of naming all incumbents after Etienne's death. He appointed various rents on property in the vicinity of Roissy (department, Val d'Oise) to endow the chaplaincy and stipulated that the chaplain's duties would include celebrating daily masses, preferably at the altar dedicated to Saint Nicholas, if that was available, and commemorating Etienne, his benefactress, Marie, the late *domina* of Villepinte, his parents, and his three children, a girl and two boys.[10] Abbot Mathieu (*Matheus miseratione divina ecclesie Beati Dyonisii in Francia abbas humilis*) and his community made formal recognition of the act in a separate instrument in the same month.[11] A notice nearly a year later (8 April 1280) that also records an endowment at the altar of Saint Nicholas, and where Etienne Barre is mentioned as the executor of a testament that specified the endowment, reveals that Etienne did in fact become a priest (*presbyter*).[12]

Gifts of real property and chattels real, however, were rare. *Purchases* were not. Many were minor and appear to have been intended to consolidate holdings. On the 14th of July 1276, for example, letters of Jean Le Saunier, guard of the *prévôté* of Paris, announced the sale made by Jean du Bois-Bagnolet, a squire, to the abbey of Saint-Denis, of various revenues and parcels of land situated at Bagnolet in the present department of Seine-Saint-Denis.[13] Pierre dit Mauvoier of Gonesse and his wife Erembourg also sold land, one arpent of arable she had inherited, to Saint-Denis on 1 August 1281 for 7 l. p. This purchase was clearly an attempt at consolidation; the property was contiguous to some plots the abbey

---

[10] *Cartulaire blanc de Saint-Denis*, Tremblay no. 36.

[11] Ibid., Tremblay no. 51a.

[12] Ibid., Tremblay no. 51b.

[13] *Série L . . . L829 à L839B*, p. 68, L838 no. 1.

already owned.[14] A couple of years later in the month of September 1283 six married couples sold Saint-Denis annual quitrents of 12s. 3d. drawn from about forty arpents of land in the vicinity of Roissy for 6 l. p.[15] Apart from their value in consolidating existing estates, purchases like this were economically sound in terms of the land market: within five years Saint-Denis would have recouped the cost of the acquisition at Roissy. The purchase of a willow grove at Villepinte from a married couple on 22 December 1283 (the wife had inherited it) fits this pattern too. It was next to property already held by the abbey, and the purchase price was a modest 60 s. p.[16]

Among these smallish purchases, one recorded in February 1280 had an importance that belies its fiscal modesty in that, like all sales made by the crown to the monastery for which this transaction can stand, it potentially signaled the king's continued goodwill and solicitude. In that month Philip III for an annual rent of 20 l. t. invested Saint-Denis with approximately twelve arpents of vineyard at Charlevanne (department, Yvelines), along with the winepress there and the rights pertaining to it, including the service owed of taking the wine produced there to Saint-Germain-en-Laye. That is to say, if I understand the transaction correctly, the abbey of Saint-Denis was not to have to do that service; it was remitted.[17]

Many really major sales of property to the abbey occurred in which the king was not a party, but it is unlikely that they would have been permitted if he did not remain favorably disposed to the abbey or at least indifferent to limiting these kinds of acquisitions. On 7 October 1274, for instance, Saint-Denis purchased the fief that Gilles d'Aciaco, a knight, and Isabelle de Pomponne, his wife, held of Raoul le Bouteiller at Villepinte. The manor house was presumably impressive enough to be specifically mentioned. The fief had come to the couple through Isabelle's inheritance. Raoul, their lord, held his own rights in Villepinte from Saint-Denis, and he formally consented to Saint-Denis's purchase. The abbey paid the enormous sum of 800 l. p.[18] A few years later (7 July 1281), to provide another and related instance, Hugues Le Loup, the lord of Villepinte, and his wife sold Saint-Denis certain fiefs, arrear-fiefs, and rights they held at Villepinte, including a mill and high and low justice, for the even larger sum of 4,000 l. p. They stipulated that a range of obligations still had to be fulfilled. A nun, by the name of Aveline, was entitled to 100 s. p. yearly until her death, whereupon her interest would escheat to Saint-Denis

---

[14] *Cartulaire blanc de Saint-Denis*, Tremblay no. 35b.

[15] Ibid., Tremblay no. 49.

[16] Ibid., Tremblay no. 50.

[17] Ibid., Rueil no. 55.

[18] Ibid., Tremblay no. 30.

as the new overlord. The abbey of Yerres continued to receive each year two measures (*muids*) of grain from the lands, and the house of Saint-Lazare of Paris to receive 10 s. p. per year.[19] On the same day, 7 July, came public registration of the conveyance; and in the first few weeks thereafter (10 July, 23 July) other parties, including Hugues's mother, Isabelle de Pomponne, affected by the transaction confirmed and ratified the sale, with the sellers' overlord, Guy Le Boutellier, explicitly stipulating—for an additional 1,500 l. t. from the abbey—that Saint-Denis could hold the fiefs in mortmain.[20]

In a sense the accumulation of property in the last example remained incomplete. Nearly two years later, on 27 March 1283, one Marguerite and her husband, Renaud de Pomponne, perhaps one of Isabelle de Pomponne's relations, also sold to Saint-Denis their goods, rents, rights, fiefs, arrear-fiefs, the ban of wine, and the rights of justice that stood to escheat to them from the estate of the same nun, Aveline, in Villepinte. The purchase price was 1,515 l. t. As with the purchase of Hugues and his wife's properties two years before, there were a small number of stipulations. Saint-Denis would pay the nunnery of Yerres, where Aveline was a nun, 20 s. p. per year and another 15 s. p. annually to a number of religious whose names the sellers could not recall (*quibusdam religiosis, quorum nomina ad presens ignorant*)![21] Again, official registration of the conveyance was issued the same day, and the overlord's ratification followed the next day for an additional payment from Saint-Denis of 600 l. p. to hold the property in mortmain.[22]

These purchases of property sometimes—and where the property was fiefs and arrear-fiefs almost inevitably—carried with them rights of justice. The accumulation of such rights was an important aspect of Saint-Denis's political and economic strategy, but it was not just a question of accumulation. In the long history of the monastery, preservation was equally if not more pressing. At All Saints 1275 Mathieu successfully defended the possession of high or capital justice (the gibbet) in the *prévôté* of Marnay (department, Aube). A dispute had arisen between Lady Blanche of Navarre and the abbot and convent, but the monks had an abundance of evidence, including royal letters, proving their case. Judgment in their favor was executed later that year, in December.[23]

[19] Ibid., Tremblay no. 37.

[20] Ibid., Tremblay nos. 38 (registration), 39 (the overlord's concession), and 40 (Hugues's mother's ratification).

[21] Ibid., Tremblay no. 41.

[22] Ibid., Tremblay nos. 42 (registration by the guard of the *prévôté* of Paris) and 43 (overlord's confirmation).

[23] *Actes du Parlement de Paris*, 1:338 no. 235.

Pentecost 1276 saw the abbot of Saint-Denis and the *prévôt* of Beaune[-la-Rolande] successfully defend their joint claim to the justice of Arconville (department, Aube), Batilly (department, Loiret), and two other locations, Bois Girard and the field of Gabeval, against the crown's claims. Along with the rights of justice went the right to hunt little beasts (rabbits, hares, foxes, partridges, and *acicie* [woodcocks?]) in Arconville. They proved their case by means of a royal charter. In this instance, judgment was executed in July 1276.[24] In other disputes Saint-Denis defended its rights to woods, salt, fishponds, and grain as intensely as its rights to justice, almost though not fully with absolute success.[25]

Indeed, defense of rights was never ending. The All Saints Parlement of 1278 gave judgment in favor of the abbey against Gaucher d'Autrèches, who was a knight and the advocate of the priory of Sainte-Leocade of Vic[-sur-Aisne] near Soissons, and his wife, and against the lord of Vaux on the subject of the high justice and the seigneurial rights of the island or, rather, of all the territory situated between the River Aisne and the River Balencon, which flowed between the towns of Vic and the seigneurie of Vaux. (It would appear, however, that Gaucher and his wife sustained their claim to at least some rights.) In addition, a prohibition was issued to the inhabitants of Vaux, barring them from bringing their flocks to pasture on the island, although the prohibition did not apply to the inhabitants of Vic. The judgment was ordered executed in January of the following year.[26]

It might be wondered why there were so many disputes. The fact is that even the best-written delineations of rights and privileges, like the best-drafted laws, cannot anticipate every complication. The month of Novem-

---

[24] Ibid., 340–41 no. 258.

[25] Woods: Candlemas 1276, the abbot of Saint-Denis was accorded *bocage* in the land of Saint Merry at Paris (ibid., p. 341 no. 264). Salt: Mary Magdalene and its morrow, 22 and 23 July, 1277, the abbot was prohibited from taking one toll but confirmed in another on the salt merchants traveling by water, unless the water was so low as to increase the merchants' expenses, in which case this toll was also prohibited (ibid., p. 343 no. 273). Fishpond: February 1278, a barrage of documents proved that Lord Mathieu de Montmorency had to do homage to Saint-Denis for the fishpond that was conveyed to him at Bû (department, Eure-et-Loir) and for Chastelier and its appurtenances, and not to the king (ibid., p. 349 no. 321A). Transfers of lordship of this sort were usually easier; cf. 3 September 1275, the routine conveyance by Héloise l'Epicière to her son Louis l'Epicier of the hereditary sergeanty of Saint-Denis she held, whose pecuniary return was thirty measures (*setiers*) of grain a year (*Cartulaire blanc de Saint-Denis*, Rueil no. 67). Grain: All Saints 1278, the abbot of Saint-Denis was confirmed in his possession of one-half measure (*muid*) of wheat as rent from the lord of Mauny (department, Seine-Maritime) (*Actes du Parlement de Paris*, 1:351 no. 325).

[26] *Actes du Parlement de Paris*, 1:205 no. 2184H and 351–52 no. 331.

ber 1278, for example, also saw the issue of a charter of nonprejudice under the seal of the *prévôt* of Paris. In it the *bailli* of the lord of Marly-le-Roi (department, Yvelines) stipulated that Saint-Denis's justice at Louveciennes (department, Yvelines), which had long before been differentiated carefully from that of the lord of Marly, would remain unchallenged even if the abbey's sergeants handed over to the lord of Marly's men a thief who had escaped to the abbey's lands but who had originally been captured on the lord's lands.[27] Obviously, an incident provoked an argument over what until then had been regarded as a settled matter and ultimately necessitated a judgment from Parlement.

The early1280s witnessed Abbot Mathieu dealing with the same sorts of problems.[28] Just one further illustration: at Pentecost 1280 Parlement issued a judgment for Saint-Denis against the count of Roucy on the extent of the limits of the abbey's justice in the territory of Concevreux, lying toward Roucy. The abbey's justice was adjudged to extend from Concevreux to a road that passed in front of the local leprosarium up to the road to Hamerimont and the road to Pontanoire. The count was permitted to hang thieves from the abbey's gallows, which stood between Concevreux and the leprosarium. It all seems pretty plain, but this initial and quite detailed judgment was misunderstood or deliberately violated by the count. Consequently Abbot Mathieu sent the monastic chamberlain to complain at the royal assize of Laon. This required that an authentic copy of Parlement's judgment be brought to Laon. The assize confirmed the abbey's claim.[29]

One category of disputes reflects "lower-class" tensions in society. Serfdom was a weakening institution in the mid-thirteenth century, but it was

---

[27] *Cartulaire blanc de Saint-Denis*, Rueil no. 54.

[28] In July 1280 letters patent of Philip III promulgated Parlement's judgment of a dispute between the *bailli* of Orléans and the *prévôt* of Beaune[-la-Rolande] (in Loiret) for Saint-Denis concerning the road of Bois Girard, where a thief was arrested. The judgment sustained the justice of Saint-Denis on the road as well as confirmed its high and low justice on the manors of Barville, Arconville, and Batilly and (low) justice on that of Saint-Loup-des-Vignes in the modern departement of the Loiret (*Série L . . . L829 à L839B*, p. 70, L838 no. 15; Barville and Batilly are in the present department of Loiret). At Pentecost 1281 a man in Saint-Loup-des-Vignes had responded to a criminal complaint to the *bailli* of Orléans, even though high justice was with the abbot and church of Saint-Denis. The *bailli*, nonetheless, was allowed to keep the respondent without prejudice to the abbey rights (*Olim*, 2:181 no. XXXIV; *Actes du Parlement de Paris*, 1:225 no. 2350). On the morrow (2 November) of the feast of All Saints 1283, the abbot and convent of Saint-Denis, after diligent investigation, were confirmed in the high justice of Val-Saint-Loup, repudiating the claim of the prior of Lory. Parliamentary judgment was executed in December 1283 (*Actes du Parlement de Paris*, 1:386 no. 527).

[29] *Actes du Parlement de Paris*, 1:218 no. 2269B.

far from dead. Many lords under fiscal pressure were freeing their serfs, the payoff being the lump sums that the serfs traded for their liberty. The availability of this capital allowed seigneurs to patronize their favorite monumental projects, attend to deferred maintenance of major resources (bridges, roads, barns, etc.) and go to war, even though manumission meant the loss of the annual income in labor and money that serfs otherwise paid.[30] Abbot Mathieu and the monastery of Saint-Denis were more fortunate, economically speaking, than many of their aristocratic and institutional counterparts who used manumission to raise money. As a result, Saint-Denis's serfs were worse off. The abbey felt no fiscal pressure to manumit its *homines et femine de corpore*, so it was as relentless in preserving its rights over them as it was in preserving its rights of justice. At All Saints 1278 the abbey won a judgment against Gilles Tort-Col and his wife, who had been daring to claim to be bourgeois of Sens. While Gilles was making this claim at Grand-Puits, the almoner of Saint-Denis had him arrested, clapped him in irons, and demanded 100 l., probably *tournois*, because, as the almoner said, Gilles was born of a woman *de corps* of the almonry of Saint-Denis en Brie (a dependency of the great abbey) and had married a woman of another seigneurie. Judgment was awarded to Saint-Denis, with Gilles being obliged to compensate the almoner for having made a mixed marriage.[31] The judgment was ordered executed in the following January.[32] At Saint-Martin in the winter of 1282 the abbot and convent successfully claimed another two serfs, a married couple, Guillaume Normand and Alithie Normande.[33] And at Pentecost (28 May) 1284 Mathieu and his monks managed to quash the counterclaim of the lord of Crécy and have their justice confirmed in the castellany of Crécy over the *homines de corpore* living there. Exception was made only if any of the serfs were taken in flagrante (*nisi caperentur in presenti delicto*), in which case the lord of Crécy retained the right of adjudication. Judgment was executed June 1284.[34]

The conclusion to this discussion is fairly obvious. The royal abbey of Saint-Denis was wealthy. The realm, despite any number of problems, enjoyed domestic peace and was economically vibrant. The king, insofar as it is possible to determine, was inclined favorably to the abbey and to the abbot, perhaps not to the degree his father had been, but he was anything but hostile. Administering the abbey, preserving and enhancing its status and prestige, and exploiting its available resources effectively were fully

[30] Jordan, *From Servitude to Freedom*, pp. 26–34.
[31] *Actes du Parlement de Paris*, 1:205 no. 2184G.
[32] Ibid., pp. 354–55 no. 346A.
[33] *Olim*, 2:208 no. XVII; *Actes du Parlement de Paris*, 1:232–33 no. 2438.
[34] *Actes du Parlement de Paris*, 1:395 no. 549.

within the grasp of the abbot and those who constituted his staff. The situation in England was less happy for Mathieu de Vendôme's and Saint-Denis's counterparts, Richard de Ware and Westminster Abbey.

Robert Burnell was made chancellor of England in 1274.[35] It is possible that Richard de Ware, who was an able administrator and diplomat, also coveted a formal position in government.[36] The failure of Edward I to name him to a post, at least at this time, may be an indication that the king's appreciation of the abbot was initially less substantial than his father's had been. Indeed, soon after Edward was crowned in August 1274, a note of tension, I think, sounds from the records. The crown kept a stable within the abbey precincts, specifically within the bounds of the churchyard or cemetery. In a letter of 28 September the king ordered Abbot Richard to permit the constable of Windsor Castle, Geoffrey de Picheford, acting in the crown's behalf, to make all the necessary arrangements to sell the stable or to dispose of the property in some other way to the royal profit.[37] An inference one might draw from this letter is that there was resistance on the abbot's part to Geoffrey's (putatively initial) attempt to carry out the king's orders, but I confess that there is no proof that this is accurate. Moreover, even if Richard's obstinacy, if that is what it was, annoyed the new king, the royal order to the abbot might still be read as an implicit and very formulaic recognition of Westminster's right to be consulted on a transaction that impinged on its interests. Finally, there are instances of (minor) positive gestures in the 1270s from the crown toward the abbot and abbey that could call my suggestion about this incident into question.[38]

These concessions notwithstanding, the examination of other issues will show that a skeptical interpretation of the foregoing exchange is in order. For one thing, the abbot was publicly reprimanded during the Worcestershire eyre of 1275 for offending the crown by allowing his court at Pershore to free a thief unpunished; this was said to be "contrary to the custom of the realm," in that "any malefactor, arrested and imprisoned for any offence done against the dignity of the king's crown" should be punished appropriately. Summerson, who cites this case, notes that the matter at issue was only a petty theft.[39] The principle being stressed, how-

---

[35] Huscroft, "Robert Burnell and the Government of England," p. 70. He was made bishop of Bath and Wells in 1275 as well.

[36] See the character portrait constructed by Foster, "Context and Fabric," p. 51.

[37] *Calendar of the Fine Rolls*, 1:29.

[38] Among these gestures, a quittance for the common summons of pleas in the forest of Essex, 16 March 1277 (*Close Rolls, 1272–1279*, p. 414).

[39] Summerson, "Attitudes to Capital Punishment," p. 125.

ever, was major. The abbot exercised his secular jurisdiction at the king's pleasure, pleasure that could be revoked if he failed to exercise it in accordance with the law.

Yet most telling in the king's attitude was a situation that went back to the crowded years of the 1260s and early 1270s, with the Barons' War, the frenzied, erratic building program at the abbey, Richard's long diplomatic absences on Henry III's behalf, and his attendance at Lyon II. These factors had produced lax discipline within the walls of Westminster Abbey. To be sure, as late as 1268 the papal legate, who made a formal visitation of the monastery, seems to have given it and its abbot a clean bill of health.[40] Yet constant vigilance was necessary. In the year before, 1267, Richard de Ware together with the legate had issued regulations for Saint James's Hospital of Westminster, an institution for leprous women that was dependent on the abbey.[41] The transgressions identified, to argue back from the regulations, were legion: they centered on the failures of the eight brothers and sixteen sisters who administered the institution to adhere properly to the rule of Saint Augustine, as well as their failure to hold regular chapter meetings and to do the proper business in them when they were held. The monks and nuns were charged with too infrequent confession, communion, and attendance at mass, excessive frivolity, disobedience to the master of the hospital, drunkenness, quarreling, illicit visits paid to establishments outside the hospital precincts, violation of the vow of silence, overindulgence in food and drink (regularly claiming the double portions supposed to be given the nuns solely on the patron's feast day), avoiding communal meals, wearing inappropriate clothing, sexual lapses, and malfeasance with regard to income.

The issuance of the regulations, however, had only a temporary salutary effect, and the situation festered until the 1270s. The situation within Westminster Abbey itself also came to a crisis in these years. Laxity of adherence to the rule among the monks appears to have been the flip side of the abbot's extramural activities, and although many of these activities were on the crown's behalf, it was King Edward I who expressly complained to the abbot on 23 May 1275 about the behavior or rumors of bad behavior at the royal abbey, in particular the dissolute conduct and extravagant habits of the monks there.[42] Abbot Richard saw the justice of the complaint or at least acted as though he saw its justice.

In the matter of the Hospital of Saint James, the occasion for action probably came when the old master, Brother James, who ruled the house continuously from 1259 until well into the 1270s, either retired or died.

---

[40] Carpenter, "Ware, Richard of" (online).

[41] *Victoria History of London*, 1:543.

[42] *Fourth Report of the Royal Commission on Historical Manuscripts*, pt. 1, p. 184.

A new master, Brother William, was put in charge by 1278, probably to maintain another recently imposed reform.[43] For in 1277, the year before Brother William enters the records, the hospital was visited by Westminster in the person of its subprior and two other monks. They reissued the regulations of 1267 that Abbot Richard and Cardinal Ottobuono had laid down, but they were harsher still.[44] Fractious brothers or those who got drunk were to be summarily reprimanded and administered correction—the day after their infractions were known. The master and his brethren were told not to wait until the regularly scheduled Sunday chapter meeting. Swift punishments were to be meted out, obviously as an example but also to prevent the passage of time from leading to a softening of discipline.

The visitors also tightened restrictions on contacts between the brothers and sisters, including forbidding common meals, let alone reciprocal visits to each other's apartments. And, presumably because they were troubled by the evidence of continuing quarrelsomeness and fighting, the visitors more explicitly specified punishments for disruptive behavior. Even wakes for recently deceased brothers and sisters—occasions for the kind of reconciliation and catharsis that comes from drinking and merrymaking in recalling with (sometimes forced) fondness the quirks and kindnesses of the departed—were forbidden.

Property relations among the hospital religious and with the outside world were also regulated through a reminder to the sisters especially that they were not free to bequeath any goods without their superiors' permission. In this respect, it can be mentioned that a little before the issuance of this regulation (in 1277), specifically in 1274, an incident took place that may have influenced the subsequent Westminster Abbey investigators of the hospital. At another establishment dependent on the abbey, Kilburn Priory, a house for nuns, one Godhuda, the sister of Roger de Wyke, tried to orchestrate a property transfer that was contrary to the rules of the order. In this instance, Godhuda went so far as to pass herself off as a nonvowed woman in order to claim her brother's estate. It is hard to imagine, except in an atmosphere of loose overlordship and lax supervision, that she would have conceived of this as a possible course of action. For when Abbot Richard got wind of her claim, he intervened and produced the evidence that she had been a nun in excess of thirty years, and therefore that she had to return to Kilburn Priory, which she had left.[45]

---

[43] *Victoria History of London*, 1:545–46.

[44] For theirs and the bundle of follow-up regulations I discuss here, see ibid., pp. 543–44.

[45] For the case, see Logan, *Runaway Religious*, p. 256. For Kilburn's dependency on Westminster, see Mason, *Westminster Abbey and Its People*, pp. 63, 134, 239–41; *Documents Illustrating the Rule of Walter of Wenlok*, p. 159 n. 2.

Thus the 1270s saw Abbot Richard try to mend his image as a lax ruler of the abbey and its dependents. Indeed he successfully came to be regarded, it seems, as austere and strict.[46] And the chapter house (*capitulum*) in these years came to live up to its description in the *Customary*, where its name by an imaginative etymology is said to derive from *caput licium*, the head of strifes, "for there strifes ended. It is the workshop of the Holy Spirit, in which the sons of God are gathered together. It is the house of confession, the house of obedience, mercy, and forgiveness; the house of unity, peace, and tranquility, where the brethren make satisfaction for their faults."[47]

Thanks to the chance survival of a fragment for 24 November to 24 December 1275 of the so-called diet or daily accounts of expenditures kept by the steward for the abbot's household, one can get a sense of what the routine of life was like at Westminster and at the abbot's manors for Richard de Ware and his *familia* in the more settled years of his abbacy, coinciding with the reimposition of "good" order.[48] The patterns recoverable are equally characteristic of those of the less eventful years in the rule of other abbots.[49] There are few surprises. People who experience joy in following a routine often appreciate most the reassuring banality and comforting predictability of behavior and the absence of interruptions in the supply of goods and services used to sustain this behavior.

The abbot became a regular itinerant supervisor traveling in loops from manor to manor and then back to Westminster. Itinerancy, of course, was expected and characteristic of high-ranking ecclesiastics who had responsibility for the administration of widely scattered properties. Yet until the 1270s expectations may not have been fulfilled in the person of the often long-absent Richard de Ware. In the one week beginning Sunday, 24 November 1275 (the morrow of the feast of Pope Saint Clement I), according to the fragmentary account referred to, Richard stayed at his house in Eye (the present Eybury), Middlesex, but not the entire day, for he briefly returned to his *camera* at the abbey. On Monday the 25th, Saint Katherine's day, he visited his manor of Laleham (Middlesex). Friday saw him at

---

[46] Below, p. 201.

[47] *Customary*, 2:183–84 (the translation of this passage is Bradley's, *Annals of Westminster Abbey*, p. 62).

[48] WAM, no. 24489, dated 24 November–24 December 1275 and inventoried in Harvey, *Obedientiaries of Westminster Abbey*, p. 5 (I.1). For a somewhat pessimistic discussion, lamenting the relative scarcity of this and other "scrappy" evidence, see idem, *Westminster Abbey and Its Estates*, p. 134. Scarcity is relative; most historians of thirteenth-century France would break into Beethoven's setting of Schiller's "Ode to Joy" if they came upon evidence of this quality.

[49] Cf. Barbara Harvey's comment in the unpublished catalog for the diet account in WAM, no. 24561C.

Hurley Priory, a dependency of Westminster in Berkshire, and Saturday, at nearby Pyrton in Oxfordshire. At other times during the week, starting back on Sunday afternoon, he was carrying out his duties while being physically present at Westminster. Other entries show the abbot's steward or his deputy seeing to the purchase of everything from bread (*in pane*) to the tanning of cowhides (*pro ii coreis boum tannandis*), from horseshoe nails (*claves equorum*) to the oats (*avena*) for the horses that had to be shod in order to carry the abbot and his baggage on their travels. Since Richard de Ware needed to have his ceremonial *cathedra* on one of his journeys, his steward saw to it, carefully recording the payment made to two servants who carried the throne to the abbot's house at Islip on one such occasion (*duobus garcionibus portantibus unam cathedram de West-monasterio usque Istelep'*). His itinerancy notwithstanding, Abbot Richard also kept in contact with people whom he could not visit by paying to have letters taken to them (*cuidam garcioni portanti literas*). And on and on and on—and on.

Vigilance with regard to monastic rights was, as it was for the abbot and monks of Saint-Denis, always necessary. One could never predict when someone might intrude on Westminster's property, seize it, or cause damages. A good abbot was one who carefully monitored inheritances of property dependent on the abbey.[50] A good abbot was one who made sure monastic fairs and markets operated according to regulations, as in implementing the standardization of sizes and quality of cloth sold, and to the economic benefit of the house.[51] A good abbot was also one who used the courts effectively to counter the invasions of aristocratic usurpers, just as the abbot of Saint-Denis did. Yet one could go too far, or at least that is the impression one once again gets from the English case. There were times when compromise—some kind of compromise—might have been better than the rigorous execution of the law. Hugh d'Oddingsell came from an upper-class family and is known to have served the king in important military matters. Abbot Richard successfully got him convicted of illegal disseisin of certain of Westminster's lands. The abbot's unforgiving pursuit of the king's friend, Hugh, sat just as poorly with the king as his former laxity in the disciplining of his monks. In June of 1278 Edward pardoned Hugh the fifty marks that the court had sentenced him to pay.[52]

The abbot was nonetheless consistent in his determination and was also quite willing to employ his powers of excommunication and absolution, if he deemed their use necessary, to defend the abbey's interests. A case in

---

[50] *Calendar of Inquisitions Post Mortem*, 2:54 no. 73, 75 no. 110, 80 no. 123.

[51] *Close Rolls, 1272–1279*, p. 502. The general order was issued on 15 July 1278; the abbot received a separate copy, dated 23 October.

[52] On Hugh's service, see *Close Rolls, 1272–1279*, p. 373; on the pardon, p. 461.

point involves William, the son of Robert of Wendon, of the diocese of London. William was supposed to execute the will of one John Giffard (he was on the staff of the Exchequer and may have known the king). Despite the abbot's instructions and summons to do so, William delayed or simply refused to obey. The abbot does not seem to have asked for the king's help; perhaps he did not expect to get it. Instead, he excommunicated William for his stubbornness (*propter contumaciam*), a formulaic accusation. The supposedly contrite Londoner appeared before commissioners whom Richard appointed to receive him and begged them to restore him to communion, again a formulaic gesture. On 21 March 1277, they agreed to do so under conditions that, formulas aside, were astonishingly stiff. He personally (not by financially supporting a proxy) was to travel all the way to Rome on a penitential pilgrimage, whether on foot or by horse was indifferent to Richard de Ware's commissioners (*ire deberet personaliter Romam pedos vel equos*). He was there to receive formal curial letters attesting to his visit that would verify his fulfillment of his penance on his return.[53] This seems a high price to pay for failing to execute a will, an impression heightened fortuitously by a scribe's almost surreal employment of the dorse of a copy of the parchment order to jot down a few unrelated notes on the "rates of exchange at the principal marts of Europe and cost of the Kitchen at Westminster" and a list of the months of the year, starting with January and giving the number of days for each.[54]

In almost all the ecclesiastical cases Abbot Richard was involved in, he followed a very precise scenario. Faced with an alleged usurpation of Westminster's rights or property, he would issue a pro forma first response warning the usurper. He then endeavored to get the supervening authority, the pope, often enough a personal acquaintance, to act in his behalf.[55]

---

[53] WAM, no. 6684. I infer that the verification (*deferat litteras testimoniales de visitatione*) had to come from the papal curia, because of the requirement that William visit the "limina beatorum apostolorum Petri et Pauli," a common phrase for the institution. See also *Fourth Report of the Royal Commission on Historical Manuscripts*, pt. 1, p. 183. On John Giffard, see Rosser, *Medieval Westminster*, p. 31.

[54] The quotation is from the catalog slip, which, however, does not mention the list of months.

[55] Pope John XXI (Petrus Hispanus), for example, who sometimes employed the abbot for papal business in England (*Calendar of Entries in the Papal Registers*, 1:453–54), knew Richard from the time the former spent in the island kingdom in the entourage of the legate Ottobuono. In the example cited, the pope commissioned both the chancellor, Bishop Robert Burnell, and Abbot Richard to do his bidding, an indication that outside the realm, it was obviously still felt that the abbot was at the center of government. For another instance of appeal to the pope (against the pope's own order!) in this period (11 July 1277), see the *Syllabus* (p. 184) to Rymer's *Foedera*.

(His contacts at Rome would prove useful to the king's business too.)[56] The pontiff would issue a letter that constituted a preemptive strike of sorts, one emphasizing that no action taken in consequence of the resolution of the disputes would work any prejudice to the abbot's privileges or the immunities and franchises of Westminster. Thus, to give one example, when bishops tried to coerce the abbey's dependents by threats of suspension, excommunication, and interdiction to contribute to otherwise properly constituted levies on the English church, the papacy intervened in 1276 at Westminster's petition to restrain them and to order lifted any sentences that they had imposed.[57] On the nones of May (7 May), 1277, to give another example, Abbot Richard's procurator in Italy petitioned the pope for protection in a dispute dealing with the alleged illegal detention of goods and animals in a dispute with the Benedictine monastery of Saint Peter of Chertsey in Surrey, which imagined itself nearly as privileged as Westminster and was involved in recurrent and fractious disputes with its rival institutions.[58] The papal intervention assured that nothing prejudicial would appertain to Westminster, no matter how the technical matters at issue with Chertsey, and detailed in its abbot's bill of complaint, were resolved: "Nullum dicto abbati Westmonasterii per predictas litteras preiudicium generetur."[59] Another example, precisely similar but slightly later in date (11 July 1278), involved the English Hospitallers (*pro priore et fratribus eiusdem hospitalis in Anglia*). This time Master Edmund de Warfeld, acting as the abbot's proctor, made the formal public denunciation, invoked the legal formula defining the exempt status of Westminster, and saw to the execution of the necessary written instruments of nonprejudice.[60]

An unrelated plea between Abbot Richard and the mayor and sheriff of London occurred between these last two incidents and further exemplifies Westminster's recurrent need to be vigilant especially vis-à-vis the actions of the capital's residents. In this case (28 December 1277), the king's judges gave judgment for the abbot. As a result of a jurisdictional conflict,

---

[56] For example, on 12 October 1277 the king pardoned half of a final payment of a fifteenth, which pardoning served as part payment of the abbot's expenses at Rome on the crown's behalf; *Patent Rolls, Edward I, 1272–1281*, pp. 231, 257.

[57] *Fourth Report of the Royal Commission on Historical Manuscripts*, pt. 1, p. 195.

[58] *Victoria History of the County of Surrey*, 2:57.

[59] WAM, no. 1885.

[60] WAM, no. 9181, "Eisdem litteris magister Edmundus de Warefield clericus procurator abbatis et conventus Westmonasterii Londoniensis ad Romanam ecclesiam nullo medio pertinentis, ordinis sancti Benedicti pro ipsis et membris eidem monasterio immediate et pleno iure subiectis in audiencia publica contradixit. Quas tandem ea conditione absolvit quod dictis abbati et conventui et membris prefatis nullum per predictas litteras preiudicium generetur."

Londoners had taken sheep from the manor of Knightsbridge, illegally according to the abbot. The judges found that the suit was warranted and ordered the livestock returned. And the Londoners who had perpetrated the injury were obliged to promise to respect the abbot's jurisdiction in the future.[61]

Yet the Londoners persisted, and if there is any doubt as to Edward's coolness toward Westminster's abbot, what the monarch did in 1278 should dispel it. In that year, "desiring," it was said, "to increase the royal majesty," the king proceeded *judicialiter* or under color of juridical propriety to "deprive many famous monasteries of their ancient and customary freedoms."[62] In fact, ominous signs preceded the moves Edward made in 1278. From the time of the Michaelmas Parliament of 1275, he had made it clear that he was concerned about a number of "liberties" that were being exercised without proper permission or warrant by magnates and churches.[63] One among many of these liberties, but one of the more prized and less common, was that of *amerciamenta hominum*, "by which [the possessor] received the amercements [fines] laid against their own men by the king's justices."[64] Richard de Ware, in defense of the rights of his abbatial office, claimed this extremely valuable liberty as well as a fabulous list of others.[65] The problem at the Michaelmas Parliament of 1275 was that so many matters came before the king's council that it was impossible to deal systematically with the justice or injustice of the various franchisal claims, including Richard's. Consequently, although the abbot's possession was queried at Michaelmas 1275, adjudication of the matter was put off until the Easter Parliament of 1276—or so Edward intended.[66]

In fact when the Easter Parliament of 1276 came around, the same problem arose. A parliament was a venue and occasion for the discussion of high matters of state, including taxation and war. At this period Welsh affairs and the need to negotiate to raise the money to deal with the growing disorder on the border with and in Wales took up the lion's share of the sessions. So, once again, the abbot of Westminster's defense of his liberty of *amerciamenta hominum* against the crown's challenge was

---

[61] *Liber Niger*, fols. iiii–iiiib; *Abstract of Charters*, p. 2. no. 12.

[62] *Willelmi Rishanger . . . Chronica*, p. 92, "Rex Edwardus multa famosa monasteria sui regni judicialiter libertatibus usitatis et antiquis privavit." Rishanger dates this move to 1277 but the "Annals of Worcester" date it 1278, which the documentary evidence to be cited confirms (*Annales Monastici*, 4:475). The Worcester annalist remarks that the king's goal was "regiam dignitatem cupiens ampliare."

[63] Sutherland, *Quo Warranto Proceedings*, p. 21.

[64] Ibid., p. 4.

[65] Below, p. 177.

[66] Sutherland, *Quo Warranto Proceedings*, p. 21.

postponed, this time to the Michaelmas Parliament of 1276.[67] Perhaps some progress from the crown's point of view was made by way of clarifying the issues in the next year and a half, for at the Easter Parliament of 1278 a beleaguered Richard de Ware along with the abbot of Saint-Augustine's, Canterbury, was persuaded to consider ceding a number of liberties to the crown.

It was said that Edward indulged his vexatious behavior toward the abbot of Westminster, in particular, at the insistence of Londoners who, as neighbors and enemies of the abbey, resented its privileges, especially its immunity from writs issued by the city's magistrates.[68] This powerful alliance between municipality and crown explains why Richard submitted when faced with the king's determination: on 28 June 1278 the abbot and convent of Westminster surrendered the liberty of return of writs in their lands in Middlesex.[69] With this success, Edward was confident that his case for forcing further concessions was unassailable. He needed information, though, and required lords to present their claims to privileges to be enrolled on the Hundred Rolls. As Sandra Raban puts it, in 1279 lay lords in tandem with "a galaxy of prominent religious led by the abbots of St Albans and Westminster, the bishop of London together with the chapter of St Paul's, and the military orders, each proffered their evidence."[70] These declarations of claims, along with the king's experience of frustration in working through Parliament, contributed to a more systematic investigation of franchises, the so-called Quo Warranto campaign, that had begun in late 1278, slightly before the prelates' presentations, lasted to 1290, and operated through itinerant justices rather than through Parliament.[71]

Edward must also have believed that the abbot of Westminster accepted the justness of the crown's position with regard to the recovery of franchises, including some of those of his own monastery. In fact, Richard de Ware was deeply upset. On the one hand, he was angry at having to yield to the indirect pressure of the London burghers, the abbey's traditional antagonist. On the other, his concession in August was strategic. He had not ceded the treasured liberty of *amerciamenta hominum*, which was to remain an abbatial franchise of Westminster until the very end of the Quo Warranto campaign, long after his death.[72] The abbot's increased personal

---

[67] Ibid., pp. 21–22.

[68] *Willelmi Rishanger . . . Chronica*, p. 92, "inter quae, Westmonasterium multum vexavit, insistientibus Londoniensibus, inimicis dicti loci."

[69] *Close Rolls, 1272–1279*, p. 468. Sutherland, *Quo Warranto Proceedings*, p. 22.

[70] Raban, *Second Domesday?*, p. 44.

[71] Sutherland, *Quo Warranto Proceedings*, p. 22.

[72] Ibid., pp. 208–9.

cultivation of Edward in the wake of his strategic concession on the Middlesex privileges may explain the king's hesitation after 1278 to come down as hard as he might have on the abbey. Better relations are suggested by the fact that Richard even agreed as the campaign was set into motion to act as chief judge on the panel of justices sent to the northern circuit (Cumberland, Westmoreland, and Northumberland) to hear cases related to Quo Warranto.[73]

Closely connected to the king's initiation of the Quo Warranto campaign was his decision, enacted by statute, to forbid further unlicensed gifts in mortmain in1279.[74] After 1279 the abbot had to be concerned about this legislation.[75] The long-term effect on gift giving to religious institutions would eventually be muted by the development of clever ways around the ban, but the immediate effect, lasting about a generation, was a precipitous decline in the conveyancing of fiefs to churches.[76] Whatever worries the abbot had about the fiscal future of his monastery, the king looked upon the legislation as a necessary gesture to aristocratic overlords who had been complaining for years that they were losing their income from feudal incidents like relief, marriage, and wardship by their vassals' conveyancing of property to an entity that never died, married, or tried to avoid marriage, and was never under age.

Richard, in any case, could not devote his full attention to developing a strategy to buffer the impact on Westminster of the Quo Warranto campaign and the prohibition of conveyances in mortmain, for the years 1278 and 1279 were replete with other rather nasty and immediate problems he had to see to. Three days in July give the flavor of his burdens. On the 5th of July 1279 the abbot had William de Cumbe, one of his bailiffs, seize and impound the farm animals of Abbot Henry of Pershore for an alleged transgression of Westminster's rights, but the abbot of Pershore and his men, according to Richard's plaint, broke the pound in which the animals were being kept and led them off. Following the abbot of Westminster's charge, Henry and his associates were summoned to appear before a commission of oyer and terminer before the king in Worcestershire, the fortnight after midsummer, 7 July, only two days after the incident at issue. Why the hurry? The abbot of Westminster was being sent to further certain business of the crown, diplomatic business involving the

---

[73] The appointment is dated 16 August 1278; *Close Rolls, 1272–1279*, pp. 503–4; Sutherland, *Quo Warranto Proceedings*, "Appendix I: Select Documents," p. 194. This may explain the abbot's being excused from common summons for the eyre of Surrey on 10 May 1279; *Close Rolls, 1272–1279*, p. 564.

[74] The best discussion is Raban's *Mortmain Legislation.* Cf. Harvey, *Westminster Abbey and Its Estates*, p. 176.

[75] Harvey, *Westminster Abbey and Its Estates*, p. 183.

[76] Gervers, *Cartulary of the Knights of St. John*, pp. xlvi–xlvii.

marriage of the king's daughter Margaret to the duke of Brabant, and needed a quick resolution of the matters at issue between his house and Pershore.[77] And on the very same day, 7 July, the docket of the commission of oyer and terminer included another case involving Westminster's abbot. His adversary in this one was the abbot of Holy Cross, Waltham. Richard charged that the men of Waltham had raised sluices in Amwell and Stanstede (Hertfordshire), flooding the royal monastery's mill there and its tenants' holdings.[78]

Despite the press of other business that kept him from concentrating fully on his problems with royal policy, Richard de Ware's readiness to make concessions on some of Westminster's privileges, his willingness to serve on the Quo Warranto commission, and his continued value in diplomatic missions obviously began to influence King Edward to mollify his policies toward the abbey. Whether the abbot orchestrated his behavior deliberately to bring this about (my position) or not, it did take place. The annalist of Worcester had a different primary explanation for Edward's transformation. It was just too difficult, in his view, for Edward—who was baptized at Westminster Abbey, who was confirmed there and crowned there and whose dearest relatives, including his father and children, were buried there—to resist the entreaties of the abbot and convent.[79]

The annalist must have been brought to this opinion by the fact that the year 1280 saw Edward, in an act of filial devotion, providing for the decoration of his father's tomb at the abbey. He enhanced it with expensive green-hued stones of jasper-like luster (*de lapidibus jaspidum*) or with "slabs of porphyry," which he had obtained and brought back from one of his trips to his ducal lands in France.[80] And, of course, the annalist would have been cognizant of Richard de Ware's good offices in arranging for Cosmati work at the tomb during still another lengthy trip to Rome in 1276.[81]

Of course, as the annalist of Worcester was also aware, Westminster's hopes for beneficent royal treatment were at least partly rooted in the

---

[77] *Patent Rolls, Edward I, 1272–1281*, pp. 345–46.

[78] Ibid., p. 346.

[79] *Flores historiarum*, 3:50; "Annals of Worcester," in *Annales Monastici*, 4:475.

[80] *Willelmi Rishanger . . . Chronica*, p. 96, "Edwardus Rex Angliae, de lapidibus pretiosis jaspidum, quos secum attulerat de partibus Gallicanis, paternum sepulcrum, apud Westmonasterium, fecit plurimum honorari." What is now known as jasper, as the word quoted is usually translated, comes in many mineralogical variants and colors, but it was shiny translucent green stones, whether mineralogically jasper or not, that appear to have been intended in ancient and medieval references. The Massif Central (Auvergne) in France may have been the source of Edward's purchase. For the alternative translation, porphyry, see Binski, "Cosmati at Westminster," p. 19.

[81] Cf. Carpenter, "King Henry III and the Cosmati Work," p. 193.

volume of authentic records the monastic archives possessed and could bring forward in support of the legality of its privileges. All of these things—the abbot's overtures to Edward, Edward's own filial piety, the record evidence—had their effect in leading the king to rethink his regime's challenge to Westminster's privileges. Government officials were not so swayed, but Edward intervened directly and by his own special favor (*de speciali gratia*) caused the campaign to be abated.[82]

The 24th of November 1280 saw the king confirm eight charters granted by his father to Westminster, touching upon gifts of deer, the holding of fairs, return of writs, immunity from providing sustenance and lodging in the houses belonging to it, and any number of other privileges, most going back to before Abbot Richard's time.[83] Two days later, he confirmed a very extensive charter of liberties originally given in 1235, an act that essentially quashed the abbey's renunciation of its privileges in Middlesex, which the Londoners had earlier exacted.[84] And then, three days later, on the 29th, the king confirmed two more of Henry III's charters to Westminster (dated 1248 and 1255), the first giving the freedom to create warrens and to hold them freely in all the abbey's existing demesne lands and future acquisitions, and the second recognizing the division of properties between the abbot and the convent, and the king's rights solely over the abbot's properties during vacancies.[85]

In a sublime ceremony of restoration on 5 December 1280, each and every one of Edward's confirmations of the charters issued by his royal predecessors was read aloud in the presence of the new royal treasurer and of the barons of the Exchequer. The abbot and convent were then encouraged to exercise their liberties.[86] There would be subsequent royal confirmations of the privileges possessed by the monastery, but this occasion was special.[87] The beauty of this performance was enhanced by the fact that the new royal treasurer was none other than Abbot Richard de Ware. In June, the king had bestowed the office on him. Westminster's scribes later enrolled all of Edward's confirmations in a special list in the cartulary, distinct from the copies of the individual confirmations, which were also inscribed in the book.[88]

---

[82] *Flores historiarum*, 3:50; "Annals of Worcester," in *Annales Monastici*, 4:475.

[83] *Calendar of the Charter Rolls*, 2:239. See also WD, fol. 86b.

[84] *Calendar of the Charter Rolls*, 2:238; WD, fols. 65–66b.

[85] *Calendar of the Charter Rolls*, 2:238–39; WD, fols. 69–70.

[86] *Close Rolls, 1279–1288*, p. 72. Cf. WD, fols. 70–70b. See also *Fourth Report of the Royal Commission on Historical Manuscripts*, pt. 1, p. 185.

[87] For example, WD, fols. 70b–71, dated a few days later, 9 December, and dealing with fines and return of writs.

[88] WD, fol. 62b, "Omnes iste carte confirmantur per Edwardum filium regis Henrici III," and in a later hand, "Omnes predicte carte in textu nominate confirmantur per Edwardum filium Regis Henrici tertii." See also *Abstract of Charters*, pp. 2–3 no. 13.

It had probably been presumed since the date of Richard's appointment as treasurer, if not before, that Westminster, despite its monks' and abbot's initial apprehensions, was not going to suffer from any of the campaigns against franchises and conveyances in mortmain. The truth of the presumption was manifested immediately. Licenses for and ratifications of the alienation of property in mortmain to the monastery date from 27 May 1280 and 5 July 1281.[89] A new privilege exempted a warehouse from being commandeered for royal use freely, that is to say, without payment, except with the abbot and convent's permission. In return, the payments of merchants who leased space in this warehouse to store their goods during the abbey's fairs on the Confessor's two feasts and indeed throughout the year were assigned to support the light at the great altar of the church and, of course, the saint's shrine.[90] Another royal grant, 5 June 1281, gave the monastery the right to establish a weekly market every Monday on its manor of Stevenage in Hertfordshire and a yearly fair there on the eve, the feast day, and the morrow of the Nativity of John the Baptist (23–25 June).[91] Taken together, the evidence of reconciliation between king and abbot is overwhelming and reveals the flowering of a depth of trust, if not of intimacy, not unlike that which had existed between Richard and Henry III.

[89] *Patent Rolls, Edward I, 1272–1281*, pp. 373 (conveniently accessible also in *English Historical Documents*, 3:587), 446.

[90] *Patent Rolls, Edward I, 1272–1281*, p. 418.

[91] *Calendar of the Charter Rolls*, 2:252.

VIII

DIPLOMACY AND GOVERNANCE

T HE CAREERS OF BOTH Abbot Richard de Ware and Abbot Mathieu de Vendôme culminated in government service. In each case, the appointments made sense based on the men's prior activities, Richard's as a judge and diplomat and Mathieu's as coregent during Louis IX's final Crusade. Both men had also long served as councilors, informally and formally (the Englishman in Parliament, his French counterpart in Parlement). True, Richard's appointment as royal treasurer in 1280 followed a period of less than genial relations with Edward I, but they had resolved their differences and could look forward to working closely together. Mathieu, a little later, again accepted the office of coregent, a post that was necessitated because his own diplomatic efforts to prevent a French war with Aragon failed.

Even with the problems that Richard experienced with the crown after Edward I's return to England from Crusade in 1274, the abbot's Continental contacts, evidenced in his role in the negotiations over the transfer of the Agenais, made him an appropriate choice in future diplomatic negotiations in the king's name and also kept the door open, if his work was a success, to a more cordial relationship with the king. The later 1270s until his appointment as treasurer in June of 1280 are full of special royal protections and licensed exemptions for the abbot from routine governmental obligations as he went about the crown's business in France and Italy.[1] The substance of the business he looked after on the Continent varied greatly, from negotiating marriages to sounding out the pope on Sicilian matters; "abroad on the king's business" or words to that effect are a common refrain in records pertaining to Richard in these years.[2] Even some of the special issues he addressed while physically present in England, like the status of alien priories, were undoubtedly entrusted to him because of his expertise and experience in Continental affairs.[3]

[1] *Close Rolls, 1272–1279*, pp. 262, 324, 417; *Patent Rolls, Edward I, 1272–1281*, pp. 128, 159, 162, 171, 302–3, 308.
[2] *Close Rolls, 1272–1279*, pp. 349, 417; *Patent Rolls, Edward I, 1272–1281*, pp. 128, 159, 162, 171, 186, 302–3.
[3] *Documents . . . of the General and Provincial Chapters of the English Black Monks*, 1:119–21 no. 34A: on 2 January 1280 Richard served with the dean of Arches and the bishop of Rochester to arbitrate a dispute concerning the English alien priories of the Norman abbey of Bec and their relationship to the general chapters of Benedictine houses in the province of Canterbury.

Richard de Ware's formal appointment as treasurer in June 1280 did not decrease his travel, but it concentrated it in England. I will simply call his office that of treasurer. An alternative, offered by T. F. Tout, is "Treasurer of the Exchequer."[4] Contemporary narrative sources also give the abbot various titles, but ordinarily without making reference to the Exchequer. For instance, the *Chronica* of John of Oxnead, a Benedictine monk of the abbey of Saint-Benet of Holm in Norfolk, written circa 1293, describes Richard as the "King's Treasurer" (*Ricardus abbas Westmonasterii Regis Angliae factus est Thesaurarius*).[5] The *Historia Anglicana* of Bartholomew of Cotton, completed before the author's death in 1298, uses precisely the same words.[6] The contemporary "Annals of Dunstable" denominate the abbot as the "lord king's treasurer" (*domini regis thesaurarius*).[7] A chancery roll entry noted by the editor of John of Oxnead's *Chronica*, but dating considerably later, 19 Edward I or circa 1291, remembered the abbot as having served as "treasurer and chamberlain" (*tunc thesaurarii et camerarii*).[8]

As treasurer of the realm, Richard became a frenetically busy man. He had to see to the proper reception of fiscal records, execution (and delays in execution) of writs for distraint and collection of debts, and other administrative matters at the Exchequer.[9] Fairly frequently, too, Edward ordered him, typically as part of a tiny delegation, to represent the crown officially when he could not be present. A couple of examples will establish how important these assignments were. On 5 January 1283, the archbishop of Canterbury, John Pecham, and other prelates were ordered to listen in convocation to a three-man panel consisting of the king's nephew and zealous supporter Earl Edmund of Cornwall; John de Kirkby, archdeacon of Coventry and deputy chancellor; and the treasurer a.k.a. abbot of Westminster as it offered the king's observations on the matters before the ecclesiastical assembly. Hostilities with Wales and the collecting of money needed to deal with the problem were high on the agenda. The members of the panel or just two of them were empowered to speak the king's words (*ea quae ipsi omnes vel duo eorum vobis nomine nostro dicent*).[10]

---

[4] Tout, *Chapters in Mediaeval Administrative History*, 2:13, and 6:19.

[5] *Chronica Johannis de Oxenedes*, p. 234. On the author, his village of origin (Oxnead is about ten miles from Saint Benet Holme), and the date of his work, see pp. iii, xxxiv.

[6] *Bartholomaei de Cotton*, p. 160 (on the author, p. xvii). Other sources that employ this usage include the *Chronicle of Bury St Edmunds*, p. 71.

[7] "Annals of Dunstable," in *Annales Monastici*, 3:305. See also the "Annals of Worcester," in *Annales Monastici*, 4:489.

[8] *Chronica Johannis de Oxenedes*, p. 310.

[9] See, for example, *Close Rolls, 1279–1288*, p. 131 (dated 12 July 1281); Rokéah, *Medieval English Jews*, p. 278 no. 942 (27 April 1283); *Registrum domini Johannis de Pontissara*, pp. 408–9 (11 May 1283) and pp. 409–10, for evidence of the delays mentioned.

[10] *Registrum . . . Johannis Peckham*, 2:501–2. On Earl Edmund, see Vincent, "Edmund of Almain," in *ODNB*; on John of Kirkby's career, Richardson and Sayles, "King's Ministers in Parliament," pp. 532–35, and Prestwich, "Kirkby, John," in *ODNB*.

As will become evident presently, listening to the treasurer speaking with royal authority was bad enough, as far as the archbishop of Canterbury was concerned.[11] But it is clear that the meeting also outraged Pecham because he had to command the presence of his suffragans in the beastly dead of winter: "we must obey the royal majesty, insofar as we are able in accord with the law of God, although the manifold unfitness of the roads and the weather and other inconveniences would seem very much to militate against holding this meeting."[12] Scarcely three months later, on Easter, 18 April 1283, with King Edward burning hot with rage as he led his army through insurgent Wales, he again ordered the English clergy, who were to meet in convocation three weeks from then, to be attentive to his needs. He entrusted the mission of explaining the situation that he was facing to the same group of three men—Earl Edmund, John de Kirkby, Richard de Ware. The clergy were to give credence to anything they said as a group or, as before, if one of them could not attend, to the entreaties and counsel of any two of them.[13]

Working for the king in these onerous and sensitive matters had its payoff for the abbot and his monastery. An arbitration took place at the beginning of September 1281. Men of the abbot of Holy Cross of Waltham had erected a lock (*loccum*) on one of the rivulets near Abbot Richard's manor at Amwell, the result of which was to damage the meadows and a mill wheel belonging to him. The arbiters included the chancellor, Robert Burnell, who was bishop of Bath and Wells, the archdeacon of Coventry (not exactly a stranger to Richard de Ware, with whom as deputy chancellor, he regularly worked), other royal councilors, and two king's clerks. The panel decided that Waltham was responsible for the injury and was to expedite the restoration of the meadows and the repair of the mill wheel to the satisfaction of another panel of inspectors of the work. This second panel was to consist of five men, two chosen by the abbot of Waltham, two by Abbot Richard, and one by the king himself. If problems persisted and no resolution could be reached, the king reserved the right to intervene without the mediation of the original arbiters or the inspectors. Edward made plain that he would act in such a way as to compel the restoration and repairs, and he obliged Waltham's ruler, though exempt, to confirm the royal right to do so.[14] The lag time here was considerable,

---

[11] Below, pp. 187–90, 193–99.

[12] He expressed himself in this way in a letter of 18 December 1282 to the bishop of Winchester; *Registrum domini Johannis de Pontissara*, pp. 241–43 and 396–98. My translation is a little free, "Quia igitur Regie majestati tenemur quantum secundum Deum possumus obedire, quamvis viarum et temporum et aliorum gravaminum multiplex importunitas videatur huic negotio plurimum adversari."

[13] *Calendar of Various Chancery Rolls: Supplementary Close Rolls*, p. 269.

[14] *Close Rolls, 1279–1288*, p. 132.

but the second panel was commissioned on 28 October 1283 to inspect the restoration and repairs.[15]

The king's care to defend Westminster's legitimate rights and their exercise was balanced by an austere insistence on his part that the abbot and monastery live up to their obligations. If monasteries had criminal jurisdiction, then they were supposed to have strong prisons to incarcerate those accused and convicted of crimes within their jurisdiction. Yet monastic prisons were proverbially porous. When Roger de Hertford, an infamous felon—a thief and killer (*fur et homicida . . . notorius*)—was convicted of homicide and robbery perpetrated in dwellings belonging to the prior and brothers of the Carmelite convent near Fleet Street in London, the king firmly reminded the abbot of his duty. On 11 May 1282 Richard received a note reminding him that Roger was never to be permitted to escape (*vos liceatis quod a prisona vestra nequaquam evadit quoquomodo*).[16]

The admonition was in no way a return to the bad feelings between abbot and king of the period before the former's ascension to the treasurership. It was just a reminder from a sometimes hyperconscientious king. A little more than a week later, 19 May 1282, Edward committed the manor of Pyrton (Oxfordshire)—which had been held by Robert de Gresley, a tenant in chief—to the abbot of Westminster at the royal pleasure.[17] The farm of the manor was to be paid, according to an order of 13 June 1282, to Amadeus de Savoy, *custos* during the minority of the heir.[18] Amadeus, of the house of Savoy, was a royal familiar and would aid Edward in the suppression of the Welsh before returning to his homeland and assuming the countship there.[19] Less profitable, but still a nice gesture was the king's order of 9 October 1282 to the keeper of the forest of Lithewode to permit the abbot of Westminster three leafless oak trunks for fuel as Edward's gift.[20] In 1283, the royal family offered the abbey the diadem of the rebel Llewellyn of Wales and a mass of jewels to further enhance Edward the Confessor's shrine.[21]

Into this almost refreshing final phase of Richard de Ware's career and his relations with King Edward I came the Franciscan friar, professor, poet, hagiographer, and theologian John Pecham to trouble it. John was appointed archbishop of Canterbury in 1279 while he was in Rome ostensibly to secure the position for another man, Chancellor Robert Burnell,

---

[15] *Patent Rolls, Edward I, 1281–1292*, p. 103.

[16] WAM, no. 17459.

[17] *Close Rolls, 1279–1288*, p. 156. On the manor, and arguments surrounding it, see Richardson and Sayles, "King's Ministers in Parliament," p. 535 n. 3.

[18] *Patent Rolls, Edward I, 1281–1292*, p. 24.

[19] Taylor, "Letter of Lewis of Savoy," pp. 60 n. 4, 62.

[20] *Close Rolls, 1279–1288*, p. 170.

[21] "Annals of Waverly," in *Annales Monastici*, 2:401.

the bishop of Bath and Wells. Pope Nicholas III, it has been surmised, doubted the chancellor's suitability and devotion to the papacy. In January 1279 he decided to appoint John Pecham himself, who had been teaching under a papal commission in Viterbo. Nicholas formally confirmed the Franciscan in February. It was on 8 October of the same year that John's ceremonial enthronement took place back at Canterbury Cathedral.[22] The new prelate invited a number of bishops and abbots, including Richard de Ware, to the enthronement, the invitation requesting them to furnish the festal occasion with venison and wild fowl (*venationibus scilicet et aucupationibus*) for the meat eaters who would be in attendance.[23] Almost from the beginning John was a dynamic presence in the archbishopric, holding a synod at Reading in July, for instance, even before his enthronement; yet one unsympathetic chronicler, William Rishanger, considered him a busybody and intimated that his feverish activity was more a performance than anything necessary for the good of the church in the ecclesiastical province of Canterbury.[24] The archbishop's seemingly purposeless zeal was not especially pleasing to the king either.[25]

John Pecham learned quickly that his suffragan bishops, like the future saint, Thomas Cantilupe of Hereford, were sensitive to Canterbury's claimed prerogatives over them and were willing to fight him tooth and nail to preserve their privileges. By the end of 1282 he found that he had to compromise with regard to the *exercise* of those aspects of his authority that were resisted by these powerful men, although he never yielded on his claims.[26] He also learned that Westminster Abbey was singularly vigilant as to whether any of the archbishop's apparently almost manic activities might intrude on its exempt status. On the one hand, the elite—royal ladies and magnates—wanted to meet the archbishop and wished to have him present at the ceremonies that united them as an aristocracy, including masses in honor of their ancestors, their and their kinsmen's weddings and funerals, and the like. They wanted the primate of England there even when the ceremonies were held not at his great cathedral church at Canterbury but at the royal abbey of Westminster. On the other hand, the abbot and monks of Westminster did not wish the archbishop's regular presence at rites in their sanctuary to become an entitlement that compromised the monastery's independence. On the 16th of November 1279, only a few weeks into his archiepiscopate, John found

---

[22] Powicke, *Thirteenth Century*, pp. 469–72.

[23] *Registrum . . . Johannis Peckham*, 1:37–38.

[24] *Willelmi Rishanger . . . Chronica*, p. 96.

[25] This is my interpretation of some of Benjamin Thompson's remarks in the *ODNB*, 43:364–65.

[26] *Medieval Court of Arches*, pp. xxii–xxvi, xxxix–xl, 66, 145 n. 269.

himself formally acknowledging that his visits would in no way derogate the abbey's exemption.[27]

Movement, actions, dramatic and caring gestures for his flock, frequent attendance at ceremonies dear to the aristocracy—all these typed John Pecham as a man living up to his calling as a good pastor. William Rishanger asserted that because John never wanted to give the appearance of doing nothing, the Franciscan even went so far as to call another synod for Lambeth for October 1281.[28] This would be the third major meeting of the clergy of the province (including his enthronement) since he arrived in England. And it caused a great stir, for when a number of churchmen who the archbishop believed ought to attend this synod did not send proctors, he was quite unsurprisingly annoyed. The annoyance may have been exacerbated by the relative recency of his appointment. To tolerate this defiance of his authority so early in his archiepiscopate would negatively mark his rule and set an unhappy precedent. He therefore immediately issued letters, which were read publicly in all the sees of the province of Canterbury and became famous or notorious, expressing his consternation and displeasure.[29]

In the course of these letters he instructed the bishops under his jurisdiction to order exempt institutions that had rights of patronage over nonexempt churches to appear before him.[30] Failure to obey their bishops' orders, he informed them, would result in the seizure of the goods of these lesser institutions, even those goods "pertaining to" (*pertinentia ad*), that is to say, held of or, in any of several complicated ways, dependent on the exempt institutions.[31] Resentment against the privileges of the exempt was widely shared and strong, of course.[32] But that only encouraged the exempt all the more to defend their immunities. The heavyweights among the abbots of exempt houses—Westminster, Saint-Albans, Bury-Saint-Edmunds, and Waltham—which the archbishop had targeted, immediately and forcefully appealed.[33] The Cistercians made ceaseless angry

[27] WAM, no. 12771.

[28] *Willelmi Rishanger ... Chronica*, p. 96.

[29] "Annals of Waverley" (dated before 1291, under the year 1280), in *Annales Monastici*, 2:395, "qui contra exemptos, ad dictum concilium venire nolentes libellum famosum in forma subscripta edidit, et per omnes episcopatus suae jurisdictioni subjectos publicari demandavit." See also the "Annals of Worcester" (early fourteenth-century), in *Annales Monastici*, 4:481–83.

[30] "Annals of Waverley," in *Annales Monastici*, 2:395–96, "ratione saltem ecclesiarum non exemptarum, quas in proprios usus, permittente Domino, detinent occupatas."

[31] *Willelmi Rishanger ... Chronica*, p. 96.

[32] "Annals of Waverley," in *Annales Monastici*, 2:396, "viscera multi ex eis [the exempt] plus onerant quam honorant."

[33] *Registrum ... Johannis Peckham*, 1:276–80; *Willelmi Rishanger ... Chronica*, p. 96; "Annals of Waverley," in *Annales Monastici*, 2:397; "Annals of Worcester," in *Annales Monastici*, 4:483. Prior John of Lewes, immune by the dependence of his priory on Cluny, set

noises of protest too.[34] Others protested as well, but with less intensity (*tepide*), presumably owing to the archbishop's vigorous (and well-meant?) behind-the-scenes efforts to reassure them as to the legality and the very limited intent of his actions.[35]

The notarial instrument recording the four great abbots' indignation, dated 7 December 1281, quoted their joint proctor's public declaration of their appeal (*Instrumentum appellationis*) at Saint Paul's, London. The abbots' proctor spoke of slurs (*diffamaciones*), wrongs (*injurie*), and oppressions (*gravamina*) laid on his clients, but not just on them. It may be useful to quote him in full on this point, if only to emphasize how far the defenders of exemption asserted that it extended: according to the proctor exemption from the archbishop's summons protected the "abbots and each of them and, in their name, their monasteries, priories, cells, churches, priors, convents, monks, canons, clerics, servants, familiars, dependents [*hominum*], parishioners and those adhering to them."[36] The proctor appealed to the holy Roman church, as to a mother whose paps nourish the faithful, to safeguard her children, to be to them as David was to those who fled from the madness and torments of Saul.[37] Five days later the proctor appeared in the diocese of Winchester at a manor belonging to the bishop of Worcester and made the same impassioned and very public appeal.[38] The witness lists indicate that an impressive number of clerics heard these declarations.[39]

---

out for Rome. The pope, Martin IV, from Orvieto on 9 February 1282, instructed the abbot of Westminster to annul any actions (of Pecham's, presumably) that might have been taken against the prior since he set out; *Original Papal Documents*, no. 833.

[34] "Annals of Waverley," in *Annales Monastici*, 2:397, "Cistercienses vero per se constanter appellarunt."

[35] Ibid., "alii autem quidam exempti appellarunt, suam tamen appellationem tepide prosequentes, pro eo quod archiepiscopus dissimulavit, quoad quosdam, executioni suam sententiam demandare." See also the "Annals of Worcester," in *Annales Monastici*, 4:483.

[36] WAM, no. 12784, "predictis abbatibus et pro quolibet eorumdem et in nomine eorum et monasteriorum, prioratuum, cellarum, ecclesiarum, priorum, conventuum, monachorum, canonicorum, clericorum, servientium, familiarium, hominum, parochianorum suorum et aliorum sibi adherentium vel adherere volentium et nomine cuiuslibet predictorum." See also *Fourth Report of the Royal Commission on Historical Manuscripts*, pt. 1, p. 184.

[37] His exact words were "sancta ecclesia Romana cunctarum sit domina et magistra ad quam tamquam piam matrem est appellandum et recurrendum ut eius uberibus nutriantur, auctoritate defendantur et a suis oppressionibus releventur quia non potest nec debet mater oblivisa filios suos sicut antiquitus legitur quod omnes qui gemebat et vexabat a Saul fugiebat et veniebat ad David."

[38] WAM, no. 12785 (12 December 1281 was when the self-styled *appellacio* was *facta*). See also *Fourth Report of the Royal Commission on Historical Manuscripts*, pt. 1, p. 184.

[39] For the first (WAM, no. 12784) six clergy appear by name, followed by the catchall phrase "et plures alii testes vocati et rogati." For the second (WAM, no. 12785) eight appear by name, followed by the same catchall phrase. Among the named clergy were four *magistri* (Bartholomew *de Lardario* [not *Lardano*, as on the catalog slip], Roger *de Saxinghirst*, William of Saint-Augustine's, Canterbury, and Adam *de Hales*), as well as Archdeacon Emman-

Archbishop John Pecham was not successful in his attempts to bring the heads of the exempt houses over to his way of thinking, although they did not wish to ruin themselves in long and expensive litigation and were willing to leave the matter in abeyance.[40] Richard de Ware demurred on this (*excepto abbate Westmonasterii*), thereby expressing his willingness to fight to the bitter end, if the challenge to his abbey's immunity continued.[41] Pecham seems to have suspected that Abbot Richard was not above transgressing his legitimate jurisdiction in retribution for his challenges to Westminster's privileges. On 22 January 1282, for example, he requested the dean of Arches, which is to say, Canterbury's judge delegate, to investigate how and what certain men to the prejudice of his tenants at Lambeth had been doing, as the archbishop had been led to believe, at the instigation of none other than Richard de Ware, the abbot of Westminster (*de voluntate et mandato abbatis, ut dicitur*).[42] Scarcely more than a month later, on 25 February, in a general letter to his proctors in Italy the irate archbishop brought them up to date on the state of affairs in the province of Canterbury and in particular on his justification for the jurisdictional challenges he had launched against the exempt houses. They were instructed, although it seems to have availed nothing, to make his case before the supreme pontiff, Martin IV.[43]

The abbot and the archbishop faced off on another issue in mid-1282. The latter addressed Richard in his capacity as treasurer in a letter of 8 June but collaterally appealed to his responsibility as a comrade (*ut amicus*), one who shared, as a churchman himself, Pecham's desire to protect the freedom of the church. The issue was Bogo de Clare's pending suit against the prior of Merton in the Exchequer, contrary, in the archbishop's words, to the canons of the church (*in casu per Spiritum Sanctum in canonibus condemnato*). The soft word, *amicus*, meant to smooth over John's earlier dispute with Richard soon yielded to a threat. How mighty, the archbishop averred, would be his own complaint against the treasurer until and unless Richard blocked the suit.[44] Archbishop John had little or no tolerance or respect for this Bogo, even though Bogo, as the Earl of Gloucester's brother, was an influential man, and also even though the Earl of Gloucester was himself Pecham's personal friend. The problem was that Bogo was a notorious pluralist. At their greatest extent, his possessions included thirty-one rectorships of churches or parts of churches and

---

uel of Cremona, Prior William of Saint-Augustine's, Canterbury, and another William, a clerk from Saint-Albans.

[40] *Gesta abbatum monasterii sancti Albani*, 1:458.

[41] Ibid.

[42] *Registrum . . . Johannis Peckham*, 1:283–84.

[43] Ibid., pp. 306–10.

[44] Ibid., pp. 370–71. Archbishop John uses the phrase "great complaint" (*magnam querelam*).

prebends in six cathedrals. Thanks to his influential family he had started accumulating these holdings and incomes at the age of six.[45]

The archbishop excoriated Bogo in a letter of the same day, 8 June, for pursuing his legal action in a secular court and for other practices the prelate found repugnant. Bogo was, in Sir Maurice Powicke's vivid summation of the archbishop's denunciation, a "pestilent dilettante, luxuriating on the proceeds of his neglected benefices . . . openly hostile," a man who "wagged his scurrilous tongue without restraint."[46] Richard de Ware, for all one knows, may have been sympathetic to John Pecham's plea. If so, he appears to have been as stymied as the archbishop. It is also possible that he felt no more urge to censure Bogo than his former royal master felt. After all, the abbot would have known of and may have been in attendance at Henry III's pardon of Bogo for each and every one of the numerous forest offenses that the noble cleric's retinue had committed against the crown and the fines they had incurred over the years. The infirm Henry granted the pardon in Westminster (Palace) on 26 May 1272, only a few months before his death.[47]

To be sure, Bogo was neither beloved or tolerated in all circles nor invincible. One suit in which he was involved over his claims in the Yorkshire church of Adlingfleet, and to which his lawyers devoted twenty years of effort, ended in his loss in 1288.[48] Yet this would have been cold comfort at best for the archbishop; and it was none to Abbot Richard who, if he shared John Pecham's opinion of Bogo, was long deceased by the time that trial came to an end. The point is that Richard did not act in 1282, and by failing to do so sealed the enmity between himself and John Pecham.

As preoccupied as Abbot Richard was with the routine duties of heading Westminster, the obligations and new work demands he had as treasurer, and what he regarded as the archbishop of Canterbury's niggling attempts to test the boundaries of his monastery's exemption and his loyalty as a cleric, he faced at the same time a new and extraordinary legal struggle with Italian merchants to whom he was in debt as a result of loans he had contracted during his ultimate trip to Rome in 1276.[49] The sums at issue were huge, for even though Westminster was fiscally secure in 1276, no one traveled with the kind of funds needed to sustain an entourage such as Richard's. The easy way was to take loans from Italians on the spot and repay them at their branch offices in London.

---

[45] *ODNB*, 11:742–43.

[46] Powicke, *Thirteenth Century*, p. 475.

[47] *Oxfordshire Forests*, p. 52 no. 4.

[48] *ODNB*, 11:743, and 43:365.

[49] For the details and references for what will now be narrated, see Jordan, "Westminster Abbey and Its Italian Bankers," pp. 348–53.

Simple as this procedure may sound, its execution was fraught with problems. The disputes were similar to earlier ones. Had the abbot and convent made installment payments in a sufficiently timely manner to avoid penalty payments beyond the interest the merchant companies charged? Were such penalty payments collectible anyway; did they not constitute a form of usury? Had representatives of the companies accepted partial payments of or in lieu of installments in a spirit of fellowship, implying that no penalty payments would be charged as long as partial payments continued at intervals? Did making payments to one part of the consortium of merchants in this spirit compel the other parties to the consortium to withdraw their suits? To what authority were the abbot and convent justiciable? What proof did the Italians or the judges have that summonses had actually been served on the abbot or his representatives or, if they were served, had been done properly? Did the abbot or his proctor have to answer before legatine courts convened at a greater distance than two days' ride from Westminster? On and on, ad nauseam.

To all of the answers favored by the monastery to these questions, the Italians had just as punctilious responses. Thus for three years, litigation and the inevitably recurring postponements went on in a frenzied way and have left a thick parchment trail. Because Abbot Richard was overwhelmed with work, he left most of the hands-on business to proctors who dealt with branches of the merchant companies in London and at their home offices in Italy. The papacy as usual tried to negotiate without alienating either the great abbey or the wealthy Italian merchant bankers it needed to finance its missions. As the chief creditor in the dispute, one Aldebrando Brunetti, grew ill, however, in 1283, power in the consortium migrated into the hands of less angry men, willing to compromise and cede, as a gesture of goodwill, some of the penalty payments that Aldebrando had demanded.

When Aldebrando Brunetti died, the members of his consortium quickly resolved the matters in dispute with the abbot of Westminster, but Richard continued to be plagued by his enemies, or those he constructed as enemies, men bent, in his reckoning, on undermining his status and that of his monastery. He seems to have trusted almost no one on this issue.[50] Yet another villain who emerged to prominence in these years was the bishop of Worcester, Godfrey Giffard by name. Godfrey claimed to have the right of visitation, literally the right to enter and investigate the common life, of the priory of Great Malvern, one of three Benedictine

---

[50] See, for example, his suspicions of the treasurer of the cathedral of York, Amaury de Montfort, whom Richard set his proctor at Rome, a certain Master Peter, canon of Assisi, to watch, during a visit of Amaury to Rome in 1283; WAM, nos. 1492, 6681. See also *Fourth Report of the Royal Commission on Historical Manuscripts*, pt. 1, p. 183.

houses dependent on Westminster Abbey, but a sizable establishment in its own right.[51] The claim arose because Great Malvern's founding had preceded its affiliation with the exempt abbey of Westminster, which had initiated a reform there in the mid-twelfth century. One could argue that the affiliation had left Great Malvern's jurisdictional subjection to the see of Worcester intact, since even the more general question of the effect of a mother house's exemption on priories originally founded by it was contested (by John Pecham, for instance).[52] The discussion among the various bishops of Worcester, abbots of Westminster, and priors of Great Malvern was in fact continuous through the early part of the thirteenth century, and every interim resolution of the discussion was later tendentiously construed by one side or another.[53]

More to the point, the bishops of Worcester regularly visited Great Malvern in the first half of the century, and as late as 1242 one of them installed a prior at Great Malvern on the death of the incumbent, an act prejudicial to Westminster, although not permanently.[54] This does not mean that the monks of Great Malvern were necessarily having good relations with the great abbey that claimed their house as a dependency. For one finds in 1264, one of the most confused years of the Barons' War, that the dean of Powick, which neighbored Great Malvern and where it and Westminster both had rights in a manor, was solemnly warning the priory on the abbey's behalf to pay a fine for contumacious behavior (resistance to the royal monastery's authority) on pain of public excommunication of the priory leadership.[55] Westminster Abbey tried to have it both ways, disciplining Great Malvern through the dean's threat while at the same time trying to prevent this from being interpreted as an infringement of the mantle of immunity its dependency supposedly shared with Westminster.[56]

It was the bishop of Worcester's pretended right of visitation of Great Malvern that on more than one occasion softened the fractiousness be-

---

[51] Besides having Great Malvern (Worcestershire) as a dependency, Westminster was the mother house of the priories of Hurley (Berkshire) and Saint-Bartholomew's Sudbury (Suffolk); Heale, *Dependent Priories*, pp. xvii, 289–90. For further information on these other priories, and the extent of their autonomy, along with references to sources for their history, see pp. 84 n. 73, 86, 206 n. 60, 234 n. 15.

[52] Cf. ibid., pp. 79, 100; Lunt, *Financial Relations*, pp. 111–13; *English Episcopal Acta*, vol. 13, no. 75 note.

[53] *Victoria History of the County of Worcester*, 2:138.

[54] Ibid. Evidence from 1267 demonstrates that the election of a new prior proceeded under the mandate of Westminster; WAM, nos. 32631–32, and WD, fols. 307–307b.

[55] WAM, no. 32629 (in the end, this order, dated the Friday before the feast of the Purification, 1264 n.s., or 1 February, appears to have been canceled, as Great Malvern capitulated; two large holes have been cut in the parchment instrument).

[56] WAM, no. 32630; this is dated 14 March 1264.

tween the monks of the two communities, propelling the priory and the abbey into alliance. It was this prelate's attempts to exercise that right which caused the rulers and inmates of Great Malvern to assert most vigorously and unequivocally that the priory constituted a privileged cell of its "mother house," exempt from all except papal jurisdiction. Unmoved by their clamor, Bishop Godfrey visited anyway, and in 1282 upon hearing scurrilous stories about the prior, he attempted to depose this longtime monk and much maligned man, William de Ledebury, for general incompetence, including tolerating irregularities at the house (the claim of twenty well-kept mistresses on the premises seems more like a slur than a serious charge, but who knows?).[57]

Both the abbot of Westminster and William de Ledebury as well as some priory monks protested the bishop's visitation and intervention.[58] Word reached Archbishop John Pecham. Godfrey's actions pleased him, and so the archbishop supported his suffragan, if not all the particulars of the charges of William de Ledebury's enemies.[59] Using the bishop of Bath and Wells, Chancellor Robert Burnell, as his conduit, Godfrey also managed to convey his version of events and his justifications for acting as he did to Edward I, who, however, was unimpressed. The monarch even made some overtures toward intervening, but not yet decisively, since he was preoccupied with the war in Wales.[60]

The bishop of Worcester's deposition of the prior or, seen from the other side, his illegal attempt to depose him had ugly repercussions. The dismissed and angry prior and his supporters left the house to the bishop's agents and grumbled from a distance. The monks who remained behind elected a new prior, a William de Wykewane, in the wake of Bishop Godfrey's action and with that bishop's approval.[61] The new man was immedi-

---

[57] I follow the *Victoria History of the County of Worcester*, vol. 2, for my reconstruction of events. (On the specific point, see 2:138 n. 14.) Often I have provided additional primary source notation from episcopal registers and WAM. (For example, the allusion to William de Ledebury as a longtime monk derives from his presence in a charter pertaining to Great Malvern as early as 1267; WAM, no. 32632.) Many of the original charters in WAM are also well recorded in the cartulary, WD, fols. 307b–308, 310b–311b, 312b–314. See also Heale, *Dependent Priories*, p. 82.

[58] See the badly damaged notarial instrument, WAM, no. 32633, dated 1282, with the notation on the dorse "contra episcopum W[igornensis]."

[59] For a brief summary of the archbishop's role in this continuing dispute, see Douie, *Archbishop Pecham*, pp. 161–62. I am arguing back from a letter (26 October 1282) published in the *Registrum ... Johannis Peckham*, 2:423, "tam super dilapidatione rerum dictae domus et irregularitatis nota, quam aliis quampluribus criminibus enormiter ut dicitur irretitum."

[60] *Victoria History of the County of Worcester*, 2:139.

[61] This William, as far as I know, had no relation to the thirteenth-century archbishop of York of the same name.

ately buffeted by gale-force winds of recrimination and aggression. He and some confreres who supported him traveled to Shrewsbury for the customary formal confirmation by Westminster's abbot, who happened to be staying there at the time, but Abbot Richard had no intention of confirming William or of tolerating monks from a dependency of his monastery who willingly accepted episcopal discipline instead of defending their exemption. Consequently, in the name of his abbey and of its cell's privileged status, he had William and his companions arrested, put in irons, sent to Westminster, and incarcerated in the monastic prison there.[62]

John Pecham, upon being informed, was incensed; in a letter in support of Bishop Godfrey's deposition of William de Ledebury, dated 26 October 1282, he insisted that the abbot of Westminster release the imprisoned delegation from Great Malvern.[63] Archbishop John's information on the events had not come directly from Bishop Godfrey Giffard, who, in fact, did not apprise him in full detail of these happenings and their supposedly infamously prejudicial nature to the see of Worcester (*praejudicio et offensa notaria*) earlier than his dispatch of a communication dated 10 November 1282, more than two weeks after his superior's reproof to Abbot Richard.[64]

Then, in a letter dated 7 February 1283, John Pecham went further. He appointed commissioners to go to Westminster Abbey to examine and assess the evidence said to be in favor of the priory of Great Malvern's exemption.[65] The archbishop himself traveled to Great Malvern around the same time. He preached to the assembled monks, about twenty-five or so in all, less those jailed at Westminster, but the truncated community, relieved of having to obey the incarcerated William de Wykewane and his supporters, and instrumentally invoking the priory's alleged exemption, refused to let either the archbishop of Canterbury or his commissioners follow up the sermon by making a formal visit.[66] Archbishop John had not quite reached the limit of his patience. His chief judicial agent, the *officialis* of the archdiocese, even issued letters, based on the evidence available to him, against the bishop of Worcester on the 7 Kalends of March (23 February). He ordered Bishop Godfrey to cease his actions against the prior and convent of Great Malvern because of their exemption (*ab omni iurisdictione ordinarii adeo sunt exempti*).[67] He was trying to initiate a kind

---

[62] *Registrum . . . Johannis Peckham*, 2:423, "fecistis . . . ipsos sub vinculis ferreis detineri."

[63] Ibid., pp. 423–24.

[64] Ibid., pp. 747–48.

[65] Ibid., pp. 516–18.

[66] Ibid., p. 748 (extracted from the Register of Bishop Godfrey Giffard). See also *Victoria History of the County of Worcester*, 2:139. On the size of the Great Malvern community, see Moorman, *Church Life in England*, p. 403.

[67] WAM, no. 32634.

of cooling-off period. Time and an opportunity were needed to investigate the matter more fully.

And so, in this interval, while the bishop of Worcester's candidate remained imprisoned and the bishop legally challenged, the prior whom the prelate had accused of irregularities and incompetence reemerged as a force at Great Malvern. In a letter dated 24 February 1283, William de Ledebury made known his complicity in the keeping of the usurper and his coconspirators (*complices, per suos complices et conspirationis sue fautores*) under arrest for their attempt to subvert Great Malvern's exemption (*a . . . exemptione eidem*), as he saw it. And it is also from this letter that one learns that the men who went to seek Abbot Richard's confirmation were suspected—or were smeared with the charge—of stealing the priory's charters of privilege from the archives and of helping themselves to 200 marks of coin, along with some silver cups, spoons, other silver vessels, and precious goods worth another 60 marks. They allegedly also took four horses, valued at 5 marks, three books, valued at the same price, and other (unspecified) goods worth 100 marks. More dangerous still, Bishop Godfrey's puppet, the now jailed William de Wykewane, was said to have provided himself with three blank but presealed charters (*tres albas cartas sibi fieri procuravit et sigillo predicto latenter signari*).[68] An enormous number of other charges were launched against Bishop Godfrey himself around the same time.[69] And they were accompanied by orders to the bishop to desist from interfering with the priory, because the exemption of Great Malvern from his authority, alleged Westminster's conservators, the abbots of Waltham and Saint-Albans, had been recognized since time out of mind (*a tempore cuius memoria non existit hac exemptione gaudeat*).[70] Although he, too, was a conservator pledged to defend Westminster's rights, the bishop of Lincoln, Oliver Sutton—whether because of incapacity or in an act of dissent—begged off from joining his voice to this order and the others that were prepared for possible future use.[71]

William de Wykewane, although sitting miserably in jail, was well connected. He was the nephew of the English cleric Hugh Atratus of Evesham, cardinal-priest of Saint Lawrence in Lucina and a prolific medical

---

[68] WAM, no. 22944.

[69] Cf. WAM, no. 32636, which is a list of complaints from 1283 under sixteen heads: Bishop Godfrey was said to have allowed certain parish chaplains to use violence to enter the priory choir, to have lanced improper excommunications at the priory, to have appointed one of his clerks as the guard of both temporalities and spiritualities, etc., etc., etc.

[70] WAM, no. 32637 (undated). Many such orders of the same import but with date deliberately left empty to be filled in later, if necessary, were prepared, WAM, nos. 32638–39.

[71] WAM, nos. 32637–39. I have not found any reason for the bishop of Lincoln's withdrawal in the voluminous published records of his episcopate; cf. *Rolls and Register of Bishop Oliver Sutton*.

writer, biblical exegete, and author of sermons, and this may help explain why a papal commission appears to have taken a somewhat tolerant view of Bishop Godfrey's intervention at Great Malvern and his endorsement of William, although nothing else much came of the commission's work.[72] In any case, William's friends and supporters also had the ear of the queen dowager, King Edward's mother, Eleanor of Provence. On the 26th of February 1283, she wrote her son, describing what she had heard from the bishop of Worcester and the archbishop of Canterbury about William de Wykewane's fate. The poor man, she pleaded, was being treated like a common criminal or, in her evocative phrase, was "in hard confinement" (*en dure prison*). The two monks who accompanied William on the ill-starred effort to secure Abbot Richard de Ware's confirmation of his election as prior of Great Malvern were confined in the same manner, and worse, as she heard, one of them had died in custody (*dunt lun est mort en prison, si com nus avoms entendu*). The queen dowager wanted her son to bring an end to the unspeakable horrors.[73] Less than two weeks later, on 10 March, John Pecham, now confident that he had the necessary support to succeed in his attempt, claimed jurisdiction over the dispute between Worcester, on the one side, and Westminster together with Great Malvern, on the other; he would judge the case.[74] Whether he was fully aware of how terrible—or allegedly terrible—the conditions for the prisoners were, as described by the queen dowager, is doubtful, as one can discern from the next stage in the story.

Bishop Godfrey Giffard did write to the archbishop on the 23rd of March to bring him up to date on the situation. The clapping of the prisoners in irons particularly riled the Worcester prelate.[75] But his letter also acknowledged (*recepimus*) an earlier one that he had received from John Pecham, and he quoted it directly. In that letter the archbishop claimed that most of his knowledge hitherto had come from rumors (*fama publica referente*). If what the archbishop had heard was creditable (*Quod si ita est*), the treatment meted out by the abbot of Westminster's deputies to William de Wykewane and his party was nothing short of a willful transgression of the freedom of the church (*contra censuram ecclesiasticam in contemptum ecclesiasticae libertatis*) and incurred automatic excommunication. Godfrey Giffard now assured his superior that the rumors were all true. The whole mess constituted a *scandalum manifestum*. And, yes, the worst had happened; one of the Great Malvern monks had died in captivity

---

[72] *Victoria History of the County of Worcester*, 2:140.

[73] The letter is transcribed and translated as an ancillary document for the *Registrum . . . Johannis Peckham*, 2:749, 761.

[74] Ibid., p. 750.

[75] Ibid., pp. 750–53.

because of the severity of the conditions of imprisonment (*prae nimii do-loris angustia jam viam universae carnis ingresso*). Yet none of this, the angry bishop reported, moved the abbot of Westminster to modify his position; indeed, Richard de Ware became more severe still.

Meanwhile, rather than let John Pecham exercise any pretended judicial right over the dispute, Richard de Ware made his own move and claimed the authority of deciding the dispute, a claim that enraged the archbishop of Canterbury. The commissioners the Franciscan prelate had appointed in February had already concluded that the abbot of Westminster had no right to be a judge in the matter; Archbishop John confirmed their judgment on 30 April.[76] Through June and July the evidence is fairly strong that he was determined to see the struggle through to the bitter end and, if necessary, to try to humiliate Abbot Richard, royal treasurer though he was. On the 17th of June he explicitly bestowed on Bishop Godfrey Giffard the power of placing the priory of Great Malvern under interdict.[77] And a month later (13 July 1283) there is evidence of another bishop, Salisbury's Robert de Wykehampton, instituting measures to prevent those living in his diocese and owing tithes to the priory from paying them, a measure presumably intended to induce a full capitulation or at least a negotiated settlement.[78] By the 19th of the month on the archbishop's instructions his suffragans, including the bishop of Winchester, were preparing wholesale excommunications of the restored prior and all the defenders of his immunity from episcopal jurisdiction.[79]

As matters thus stood, John Pecham was perfectly prepared to believe that his enemies would strike back at him and in unsavory ways, and he acted on this belief on 23 July 1283 when he condemned the sacristan of Westminster Abbey for trying to prevent the inhabitants of several parishes from paying obventions that the archbishop insisted they owed to his see.[80] The sacristan grew so angry that he traveled, uninvited, to the bishop of Rochester's consecration ceremony at Canterbury Cathedral and interrupted the service in order to protest Archbishop John's actions. The archbishop regarded the furious sacristan as no better than Satan's errand boy (*in angelum Sathanae transformatus*) and excommunicated him on 29 September.[81]

Meanwhile at the Michaelmas Parliament held at Acton Burnell in Shropshire where the king was settled temporarily, to wrap up Welsh af-

---

[76] Ibid., p. 754.
[77] Ibid., pp. 754–56.
[78] Ibid., pp. 756–57.
[79] *Registrum domini Johannis de Pontissara*, pp. 268–70.
[80] *Registrum . . . Johannis Peckham*, 2:588–89.
[81] Ibid., pp. 617–18.

fairs, which had concluded successfully, a day was given, in the legal parlance of the time, to settle the dispute between Abbot Richard and Bishop Godfrey.[82] In fact, the two men or rather their representatives, in concert with the monks of Great Malvern, had already reached a tentative agreement; it was ratified by their restored prior, William de Ledebury, on 15 September, two weeks before Archangel Michael's feast day. It provided for the grant of a manor to the bishop of Worcester with the license of the abbot and convent of Westminster.[83] Bishop Godfrey, as a consequence of the concession of the manor, Knightwick by name, recognized Great Malvern's immunity as a dependency of Westminster Abbey from the jurisdiction of the see of Worcester.[84] This agreement, which the king brokered, received more formal confirmation from Prior William on the 7th of the ides, which is to say, the 9th, of October, 1283, in an instrument that recognized Edward I's authority to enforce it.[85] Four days later, on 13 October, Prior William and Abbot Richard de Ware together acknowledged the restoration of peace between them and Bishop Godfrey Giffard. The king swore that if they contravened it, he would move against the offending party or parties, even to the extent of imposing forfeitures. The prior and abbot in their appearance before the royal court promised not to contravene the peace and affirmed Edward's right to act against them if they did.[86] A few final details were worked out in the month following.[87] And, then, a comprehensive and conclusive peace was solemnly declared on 15 November, with the crown confirming all the parties' agreement to it.[88]

Although the outcome of this struggle was the upholding of the exemption of his priory and the privileges of his office, the illegally deposed and now fully restored William de Ledebury did not benefit personally from it. The formal and ultimately successful claim made by the abbot of Westminster that the bishop of Worcester had no authority to depose the prior did not imply that William de Ledebury was an able or morally upstanding monk. Abbot Richard de Ware did have the authority to depose him and promptly exercised it after achieving concord with Bishop Godfrey.[89]

---

[82] *Rotuli Parliamentorum Anglie*, p. 13 (*Parliament Rolls*, 1:148 no. 7).

[83] *Close Rolls, 1279–1288*, p. 238.

[84] *Victoria History of the County of Worcester*, 2:140.

[85] WAM, no. 504. The ratification was affirmed in different circumstances the next day; WAM, no. 32635.

[86] *Close Rolls, 1279–1288*, p. 242.

[87] A record of 15 November makes reference to the bishop of Worcester's remaining rights despite his remission (on the eve, 5 November, of the feast of Saint Leonard the Abbot; WAM, nos. 32640–41) of his claim to visitation; *Patent Rolls, Edward I, 1281–1292*, p. 90.

[88] *Patent Rolls, Edward I, 1281–1292*, pp. 90–91; WAM, nos. 32642–43. *Victoria History of the County of Worcester*, 2:140.

[89] *Victoria History of the County of Worcester*, 2:140.

John Pecham felt betrayed both by the content of the agreement and by the very process by which it had been reached. The so-called peace (*pax*), as he wrote on 15 November, was polluted. The bishop of Worcester, one of those suffragans who had been so obstreperous at the onset of John's archiepiscopacy and with whom the Franciscan had had to reach an unhappy modus vivendi, had simply sold out.[90] The pact to which Godfrey gave his assent could be likened to simony, the crime and sin of selling church offices, and was repellent to the same degree: "Give me a manor and you can keep the priory." The process of reaching the compromise raised an equally bad stench, for it bypassed Canterbury completely—and this despite the fact that intelligent and informed men knew that every legal system recognized that no agreement or contract could be made affecting the rights of any party if that party did not approve of it. Adapting the legal maxim then current, especially as a justification for the negotiations that took place in secular politics in Parliament, that what touches all had to be approved by all, the archbishop castigated his suffragan bishop mercilessly.[91] And, although Bishop Godfrey promptly explained his reasons for settling and attempted to deflect the peculiarly nasty charge of simony, John Pecham would not be appeased.[92]

Probably it was Abbot Richard de Ware's passing away suddenly a few days later, around the feast of Saint Andrew the Apostle, 30 November 1283, and the interval between his obsequies and the settling into place of a new abbot that delayed the archbishop from expeditiously following up on his verbal censure of Bishop Godfrey with further measures and threats against Great Malvern and Westminster.[93] Yet, as he made known in February of the next year to Cardinal Hugh of Evesham, he had forgotten neither the suffering of that ecclesiastical prince's kinsman, William de Wykewane, and his associates nor the humiliating pact, the "illicit transaction," that was so soon followed by the abbot of Westminster's "unex-

---

[90] The role of Godfrey in these early disputes (above, p. 186) is addressed in *Medieval Court of Arches*, pp. xxii, xxv, 66, 145 n. 269.

[91] *Registrum . . . Johannis Peckham*, 2:757–58, "praesertim cum juxta civiles et canonicas sanctiones, quod omnes tangit, ab omnibus merito debeat approbari."

[92] For Godfrey Giffard's reply, see ibid., p. 758.

[93] On the abbot's death, see the "Annals of Worcester," in *Annales Monastici*, 4:489, and Pearce, *Walter de Wenlok*, p. 2 (for further discussion). Permission to elect a new abbot was granted on 11 December 1283; *Patent Rolls, Edward I, 1281–1292*, p. 107. The election of Walter de Wenlok, "by way of compromise," took place on 31 December; "Annals of Worcester," p. 489, "in vigilia Circumcisionis per viam compromissi frater W[alterus] de Wenlac concorditer est electus" (see also *Flores historiarum*, 3:60). Papal confirmation was issued on 24 April 1284 and reached England by 20 June (*Calendar of Entries in the Papal Registers*, 1:472; *Patent Rolls, Edward I, 1281–1292*, p. 124).

pected death."[94] Indeed, Archbishop John Pecham continued until 1289, long after Richard de Ware had gone to his eternal sleep with his predecessors, to vex the bishop of Worcester and the monks of Westminster Abbey, even claiming, though always unsuccessfully, the right of visitation of Great Malvern for Canterbury itself.[95]

Did Abbot Richard go to his rest in peace, sensing his victory, sensing that he had won his last great struggle with the episcopate? Perhaps, but whether his accomplishment was fully appreciated by those who should have appreciated it most may be doubted. The king remembered the abbot fondly.[96] The king's officials and Richard's successor at Westminster, Walter de Wenlok, both during the vacancy and thereafter, assiduously saw to the memorials of his life and death.[97] They arranged payment for his burial.[98] They authorized the epitaph.[99] They saw to the execution of his bequests to his personal servants and the transfer of the insignia of the

[94] These words are used in a letter of 23 February 1284; *Registrum . . . Johannis Peckham*, 2:676, "quem post contractum transactionis illicitae mors [abbatis Westmonasterii] sustilisse dicitur improvisa."

[95] Pearce, *Walter de Wenlock*, p. 33; *Victoria History of the County of Worcester*, 2:140.

[96] *Close Rolls, 1279–1288*, p. 330: on 27 June 1285 Edward I informed the new abbot of Westminster that he would pardon him from furnishing military service for a year on account of his predecessor's good service.

[97] Custody of the vacant abbey was vested in the royal clerk, Malcolm de Harleye, appointed on the 8th of December 1283, who was occupied, to some degree, with the abbey down to 1285 and, with regard to some lingering issues, even into the next decade (*Patent Rolls, Edward I, 1281–1292*, pp. 107, 112, 222–23; *Close Rolls, 1279–1288*, pp. 254, 282; WAM, nos. 9467, 28953; Harvey, *Obedientiaries of Westminster Abbey*, pp. 12–13 [I.133]; Pearce, *Walter de Wenlok*, p. 44). He had the assistance of the royal escheator who removed fifty pounds from the abbot's personal treasure, which included coffers of precious vessels and jewels as well as coin, for the king's use as protector of the dead abbot's property during the vacancy (*Close Rolls, 1279–1288*, p. 247, and Harvey, *Obedientiaries of Westminster Abbey*, pp. 12–13 [I.133]).

[98] *Close Rolls, 1279–1288*, p. 247: on 9 December 1283 the money for the burial was ordered to be turned over to Robert de Dymmok, Richard's clerk. He was laid to rest in a stone coffin on the north side of the presbytery (east of the transept) but still under the Cosmati pavement according to the report of excavations in 1866; Stanley, *Historical Memorials of Westminster Abbey*, 2:131, and Harvey, *Westminster Abbey and Its Estates*, p. 375 n. 14.

[99] The mid-fifteenth-century historian and monk of Westminster John Flete (*History of Westminster Abbey*, p. 115), recorded the inscription, "Abbas Richardus de Wara qui requiescit hic portat lapides quos hoc portavit ab urbe" ("Abbot Richard de Ware who rests here is supporting the stones which he brought hither from the City [Rome]"). Scholars have generally accepted Flete's transcription as accurate (see the notes of the Victorian restorer of Westminster Abbey, Sir Gilbert Scott, WAM, no. 61083C [further on Scott, Cole, *Work of Sir Gilbert Scott*], and Binski, "Cosmati at Westminster," p. 13), although the original has been effaced since at least 1713 (Crull, *Antiquities of St. Peter's*, pp. 8–9). Foster (*Patterns of Thought*, p. 20) believes that the brevity of the inscription points to Westminster's monks' dislike of their abbot.

royal treasurer to John de Kirkby, the man with whom Richard had served as king's spokesman in the 1280s.[100] They set about arranging for anniversary masses in his honor and according to his wishes.[101] Yet Richard's monks, if one can believe the late thirteenth-century annalist of Dunstable, little mourned his sudden passing.[102] In his efforts to please his king and establish regularity after the chaos of the years of baronial rule and rebellion, he had become too strict, too austere, in his enforcement of the rules governing their lives.

The major construction of the thirteenth-century church of Saint-Denis was completed in 1281, but the building complex was vast, and there seems never to have been a moment when Mathieu de Vendôme could truly declare that nothing remained to be achieved or repaired. In the fiscal year 1282–1283 expenditures were made to repair the subprior's *studium* or workroom and to upgrade the convent oven, washhouse, and baths; to secure the equipment for raising the bells; to make the abbey prison secure—an endless list. And these tasks went along with others affecting Saint-Denis's property in the town.[103] Every relevant surviving fiscal account of the monastery in the last years of Mathieu's abbacy records these and similar expenses. In the fiscal year 1282–1283 the total was more than 488 l. In fiscal 1284–1285, it was only slightly less, 472 l. (probably *parisis*). The last year of Mathieu's abbacy these expenses, recorded as ever with meticulous care, reached 315 l. and covered new windows for the refectory, repairs in the kitchen, and work in the sleeping and/or working quarters of the *infirmarius*, the prior, and the subprior.[104] For comparison, the Lendit fair was producing income of 1,035 l. a year at around the same time (1285).[105]

---

[100] The bequests included money, cloth, and brass and wooden plates and cups; *Close Rolls, 1279–1288*, p. 247. For the transfer of the keys and other paraphernalia of the treasurer's office, see *Patent Rolls, Edward I, 1281–1292*, p. 109.

[101] WD, fols. 638–639: "Memorandum quod anno domini millesimo ducentesimo octagesimo tercio die veneris proxima post natale domini vacante Abbatia Westmonasterii per mortem bone memorie Ricardi de Ware Abbatis. . . . Item anniversarium Ricardi de Ware Abbatis cum V capis in choro annis singulis celebretur. Datum in capitulo nostro in crastino circumcisionis domini. Anno gratie millesimo ducentesimo octogesimo tercio." See also *Documents Illustrating the Rule of Walter de Wenlok*, p. 232 n. 1, and Pearce, *Walter de Wenlok*, p. 144.

[102] "Annals of Dunstable," in *Annales Monastici*, 3:305, "Abbas de Westmonasterio Londoniae, tunc domini regis thesaurarius, obiit, quasi repente; propter austeritatem parum planctus a conventu suo." Bradley, *Annals of Westminster Abbey*, p. 63, accepted the accuracy of the remark.

[103] *Atlas historique de Saint-Denis*, pp. 143–44.

[104] Ibid., pp. 143–45.

[105] Ibid., p. 389.

All this said, and to repeat, it was the year 1281 that witnessed the completion of major architectural work at Saint-Denis. The edifice was perfectly prepared for the solemn recognition of Louis IX as a saint.[106] In the event, this recognition came sixteen years later, in 1297, but it is not surprising, as has been noted before, that most people thought it would come much sooner. For Abbot Mathieu had been assiduously having his scriptorium record miracles at the king's tomb and reports of them happening elsewhere since the early 1270s. Moreover, from May 1282 to March 1283 three investigators, papal commissioners designated by Martin IV, heard testimony, including the abbot's, concerning Louis IX's life and the miracles that reputedly occurred through the late king's intermediation.[107] From 12 June 1282 the three commissioners held their sessions at Saint-Denis, and they invited Abbot Mathieu, then about sixty years old, to give his testimony on the first day of the opening session.[108] The little abbatial town must have been atwitter with excitement since some of the miracles being weighed for authenticity involved natives and longtime residents, Gile, the daughter of the local butcher, for instance, and Luce, a Norman woman who had moved to the town a few decades before.[109]

What has been reconstructed of this testimony suggests that Mathieu concentrated on three themes from Louis IX's life, with the self-evident implication that these demonstrated the late king's holiness.[110] The first was his annual visits to the abbey of Saint-Denis on the principal feast day of the patron saint, 9 October. The abbot related with relish the king's experiences, for they reflected well not only on the monarch but on the monks of his community. Traditionally on the evening of the feast, the monks chanted almost the entire night, a custom that garnered the king's enthusiastic praise. Louis declared that he loved this dedication to the patron and to the glory of God, and he processed with his own clerks and chaplains as part of the solemn reverencing of the martyr.

The second theme that the abbot developed was closely related. There were times when the king could not be present at the annual feast day solemnities at Saint-Denis, as, for example, when he was on Crusade, but he made up for his absences in subsequent visits to the altar dedicated to the saint. According to Mathieu's description a finely orchestrated drama was often played out on these occasions. King Louis brought his eldest son with him to watch as his father knelt bareheaded in prayer before the

---

[106] Cf. Brown, *Saint-Denis*, p. 313.

[107] Le Goff, *Saint Louis*, p. 304.

[108] *HF*, 20:61, 122. Carolus-Barré, *Procès de canonisation*, p. 233.

[109] *HF*, 20:125, 174–76.

[110] I follow Carolus-Barré's reconstruction of the testimony in *Procès de canonisation*, pp. 118–19.

high altar. Then the pious king commenced the well-established ritual of the four *besants d'or*. (France did not produce its own gold coins, *écus*, until Louis IX completed a number of monetary reforms very late in his reign, more precisely in 1266.)[111] He placed the *bésants* on his head and then laid them gently on the altar, simultaneously putting his lips to the altar in a kiss of devotion to the martyr. Seven times during the Crusade of 1248–1254, Mathieu informed the commissioners, the king was absent from France during the annual feast day commemorations of Saint Denis at the abbey, but when he first resumed his visits to the altar after his return, he recompensed the saint with seven times the usual offerings of four *bésants*. The gold—the abundance of gold—and the abundance of kisses must have made for an arresting vision.

A third theme of Mathieu's testimony was Louis IX's justice. The king was willing to take risks to do justice. He particularly wished to do justice for those most vulnerable, women and children. This is why he confronted Lord Enguerran IV de Coucy when that noble summarily executed three boys he had taken with toy bows and arrows for "poaching" in his forest. Mathieu knew this because the king had asked him to get firsthand information on what had transpired. And Mathieu had delighted in the king's heavy punishment of the arrogant aristocrat—a punitive fine, obligation to go on Crusade as a penance (or the purchase of redemption), and the erection of sanctuaries for perpetual masses to the boys' memory.

The atmosphere surrounding the commissioners' investigations, Mathieu's recollections and those of other witnesses, the splendor of the newly completed church, and the near certainty (although it proved transitory) that the king would soon be canonized helps explain why in 1282 the decision was taken to decorate Louis's hitherto simple tomb with precious metals and the royal effigy.[112] All of this is gone now, of course, but Mathieu must have felt that it would be cared for until the end-time, a perpetual testimony to the holiness of the monarch and the abbey, and a response, as well, to the lovely but a little over-the-top Cosmati works and mystical inscription at Westminster.[113]

It is true that following King Henry III's death on 16 November 1272 and his interment on the 20th before the high altar at Westminster, rumors began to circulate that miracles were occurring at his tomb.[114] These seem

---

[111] Jordan, *Louis IX*, pp. 206–13.

[112] Cf. Brown, *Saint-Denis*, p. 396.

[113] I am extending Lillich's argument, which itself draws on the work of Georgia Sommers, that Louis's enhanced tomb was Philip III and Mathieu de Vendôme's response to Edward the Confessor's; *Armor of Light*, p. 244.

[114] *Flores historiarum*, 3:28. Carpenter, "Meetings of Kings Henry III and Louis IX," pp. 28–29.

never to have numbered very many, although Abbot Richard de Ware would have been heartened by them. What may be evidence of one such miracle is the bequest to Westminster Abbey in 1275 of a certain Philip, a cleric serving the church of Saint-Maxentius of London, of the proceeds from the sale of houses he owned in the London parish of Saint Peter the Less to honor the late king, possibly for his saintly intercession, and also to remember the cleric's parents, Odor and Alexia Russell.[115]

In any case, not long afterward, Abbot Richard commemorated the beautiful Cosmati work of the abbey by composing an inscription that thereafter adorned it: "In the year 1280, this work, which Peter citizen of Rome commenced, was accomplished; man, know the reason, if you desire. The king was Henry, friend of the saint here."[116] Yet Henry III's cult, despite Abbot Richard de Ware's and Edward I's efforts, including the translation of the king's body in 1290 to the ornate Italianate tomb now visited at the abbey, never really flourished. Pilgrims undoubtedly hoped that visiting the shrine would trigger miraculous interventions.[117] But in fact Mathieu de Vendôme's king, not Richard de Ware's, became the incarnation and symbol of holy rulership in medieval Europe.[118]

The consensus among the chroniclers appears to be that after Pierre de la Broce's fall, Abbot Mathieu reemerged as the most prominent member of government.[119] He continued in the late 1270s and 1280s as a judge or master of Parlement. In one case in the latter part of this period, at the feast of Saint Martin in the Winter (11 November) 1282, one sees him helping decide the extent of the immunity of a certain Jew from a tallage of 60,000 l.p. levied on his coreligionists.[120] At All Saints 1283 he and an associate heard an appeal from the county of Champagne. It was a complicated affair whose very hearing in Parlement might have been regarded as diminishing the juridical authority of the heir, Jeanne de Navarre, to the county, had not the judges made clear that the decision to hear and decide the appeal respected the heir's rights.[121] In two cases from

---

[115] For the gift, see Harvey, *Westminster Abbey and Its Estates*, p. 392; the speculation about the intercession is my own.

[116] *Monasticon Anglicanum*, 1:273 note n (citing Fabyan's *Chronicle* [early sixteenth-century]), "Anno Milleno Domini cum septuageno / Et bis centeno cum completo quasi deno, / Hoc opus est factum quod Petrus duxit in actum, / Romanus civis; homo, causam noscere si vis / Rex fuit Henricus, Sancti presentis amicus."

[117] Cf. Binski, "Cosmati at Westminster," pp. 19–22, 27.

[118] Hughes, "Monarch as the Object of Liturgical Veneration," pp. 384–86, 413–18; Jordan, "Representation of Monastic-Lay Relations," pp. 225–39; Folz, "Sainteté," pp. 31–45.

[119] Sivéry, *Philippe III*, p. 198, citing chroniclers like Guillaume de Nangis and Girart de Frachet.

[120] *Olim*, 2:218 no. XLV; *Actes du Parlement de Paris*, 1:234 no. 2467.

[121] *Olim*, 2:228 no. VI; *Actes du Parlement de Paris*, 1:237 no. 2490.

1285 Abbot Mathieu served as a judge in a case involving a dispute over rights in the Fairs of Champagne (by this time the heiress to the county had married Philip III's son and heir, Philip the Fair). We get some indication of how difficult the case was from the time, eighteen days, that the abbot and a clerk of Parlement allotted to it.[122]

Occasionally Mathieu served more as an arbitrator than as a judge.[123] In this capacity he usually acted in concert with other dignitaries, like the very senior royal administrator, the *bailli* of Vermandois, Gautier Bardin, in various disputes involving lay aristocrats, prelates, and towns.[124] His selection was sometimes owed to the request of the parties in dispute, as in two cases concerning jurisdictional rights in the 1270s, one involving the Hôtel-Dieu, or hospital of Paris, and the bishop and cathedral chapter of Paris in 1272 and the other involving the count and countess of Dreux and the priory of Saint-Martin-des-Champs of Paris in 1279.[125] At other times, the crown formally designated or confirmed him as an arbitrator in cases that came before or might potentially come before the Parlement of Paris. One sees evidence of this in 1275, 1278, 1282, 1283, and 1284.[126] Since the abbot was also regularly present among the masters who sat in Parlement throughout Philip III's reign, his voice was heard on nearly all significant political issues, like Charles of Anjou's futile attempts to "inherit" his brother Alphonse of Poitier's rights in the latter's appanage, and on administrative and regulatory matters leading to the enactment of royal ordinances and statutes.[127]

The records of Parlement, of course, are laconic and often formulaic, but occasionally they provide the opportunity to see Mathieu asking ques-

---

[122] Longnon, *Documents relatifs au comté de Champagne*, 3:29: the payment was 8 l. 5 s. (*provinois?*) "por les besoignes des foires."

[123] *GC*, vol. 7, cols. 393–94.

[124] *Actes du Parlement de Paris*, 1:379 no. 510, 386 no. 526, and Langlois, *Règne de Philippe III*, pp. 434–35 no. XV. Carolus-Barré, *Procès de canonisation*, pp. 232–33, cites instances from 10 August 1272, 3 July 1275, and April 1282/3 (see also, *GC*, vol. 7, col. 393). The last two involved Gautier Bardin, on whose long career see Carolus-Barré, "Baillis de Philippe III," pp. 162–65.

[125] Carolus-Barré, *Procès de canonisation*, p. 232; *Recueil de chartes et documents de Saint-Martin-des-Champs*, no. 1277.

[126] To the evidence cited in Langlois, *Règne de Philippe III*, pp. 254–55, and Carolus-Barré, *Procès de canonisation*, pp. 232–33, add that in *Olim*, 2:121 no. XLIV; *Actes du Parlement de Paris*, 1:202–3 no. 2165; and *Recueil de chartes et documents de Saint-Martin-des-Champs*, nos. 1293, 1300.

[127] In addition to the evidence adduced in the last two paragraphs on his activities in Parlement, see *Actes du Parlement de Paris*, 1:388–89 no. 53, and Carolus-Barré, *Procès de canonisation*, pp. 232–34. For Charles's case (finally resolved against his claim on 1 March 1284), see *Actes du Parlement de Paris*, 1:388–89 no. 537 (Mathieu's attendance is noted explicitly). For a list of the legislative acts known from Philip III's reign, see Carolus-Barré, *Procès de canonisation*, pp. 230–32.

tions or otherwise taking an active—or, as Carolus-Barré insisted, a leading—part in the proceedings. One thing is sure: the abbot of Saint-Denis was not a mere ornamental presence in Parlement, no matter, it seems, how arcane the legal issues became. If a felony occurred on a town's, in this case, Aurillac's, walls, or in its boundary ditches or along other built-up boundary limits (not otherwise in private ownership or occupation), where did jurisdiction lie, with the abbey of Aurillac or the town consuls?[128] That Mathieu asked such a question may not establish that his intervention had a particular authority, exceeding that of other parlementaires, but it does suggest that he was very active and *attentive*.[129]

Yet in the period of the late 1270s and early 1280s it was really one aspect of government, namely, diplomacy, that Mathieu dominated. In this area, to paraphrase Carolus-Barré in somewhat milder language, his authority was of the weightiest sort and close to determinative (*prépondérante et véritablement souveraine*). On matters of diplomacy, Abbot Mathieu was both an important contributor to policy and a main executor of that policy, although *chef réel du gouvernement royal*, Carolus-Barré's formulation, is exaggerated.[130] He could not—given the military zeal of Philip III and the increasing presence at court of youthful adventurers, many the king's kinsmen on his wife's side—prevent aggressive posturing on all occasions.[131] His greatest failure in this regard was his inability to prevent the war known as the Crusade against Aragon (1285). When the war came, Abbot Mathieu did his duty.[132] Fortunately, diplomacy until then was more firmly in his control.

The last gasp of the dispute with England over the Agenais was heard not long after Pierre de la Broce's execution. On 23 May 1279 a meeting took place at Amiens between Philip III and Edward I during which the two kings discussed the already much discussed concession of the Agenais.[133] At the time of Edward's return from Crusade through France in 1273, he had insisted on the validity of the English claim, as put forth by the official delegation, headed in part by Richard de Ware, and he did a form of homage using words that presumed the imminent return of lands "promised" by the Treaty of Paris. But Edward did not obstruct the lawyerly debates that were slowing down the finalization of the transfer of

---

[128] Carolus-Barré, *Procès de canonisation*, p. 234.

[129] For Carolus-Barré, the abbot's question was a "détail prouvant que Mathieu de Vendôme intervenait clairement (et avec autorité) dans un débat qui sans doute s'embrouillait et risquait de s'éterniser"; ibid.

[130] Ibid., pp. 234–35.

[131] Cf. Sivéry, *Philippe III*, p. 198.

[132] Below, pp. 209–13.

[133] On the earlier negotiations, see above, pp. 150–54, 157.

lordship.[134] It was rather the meeting at Amiens in 1279, recalling the place at which Louis IX in 1264 had upheld Henry III's prerogative, that was the concluding chapter—the recognition of Edward's lordship—in this long-drawn-out tale, even though the delivery to the English of copies of all the documents in the French royal archives relevant to the administration of the territory was not completed until 18 August 1286![135] Nonetheless, the territory was ceded to Edward long before the documentation was fully duplicated and transferred. Carolus-Barré believed that Abbot Mathieu was the moving force behind Philip III's concession.[136] That, despite technical issues, Edward I also smoothly acceded to the countship of Ponthieu, within the realm of France, through his wife's inheritance in 1279 also owed a lot to sensible men, like Mathieu de Vendôme.[137]

The abbot was simultaneously directing his attention to another thorny difference between the English and French kings. Edward I's officials were sensitive to their master's status as duke of Aquitaine. On the French side, Philip III's officials were equally sensitive to the status of the French king. A nasty dispute broke out over what words or formula was appropriate to use in official charters issued by Edward as duke, words that could be understood as describing his authority in Aquitaine. In 1282 the French royal seneschal of Toulouse, Eustache de Beaumarchais, one of the senior officials in the administration, instructed his administrative counterpart, Edward's seneschal of Gascony, Jean de Grailly, to have the latter's clerks employ a particular protocol. They were to make reference in all official correspondence to the reigning French king (*regnante Philippo, rege Francie*), from whom the duke held his fief, rather than, as was the practice, to Duke Edward's kingship (*regnante Edwardo, rege Anglie*), a dignity that was juridically irrelevant to the status of the fief.[138] Jean de Grailly was distressed with the order and sought to have it overturned. Addressing himself to Philip III and his counselors, including Abbot Mathieu, Jean offered a compromise, a formula that mentioned Edward's ducal position so as not to imply that he had royal rights in Aquitaine, but still referred to Edward as a king: *Actum fuit Edwardo, rege Anglie, duce Aquitanie.*

The French remained dissatisfied and rejected the offer. It was then Abbot Mathieu who devised a fourth formula. Clerks would invoke the royal status of each man as long as these words were followed by an explicit reference to the Englishman's "holding" the duchy of Aquitaine: *Actum*

---

[134] Cuttino, *English Medieval Diplomacy*, p. 61.

[135] Delaborde, "Archives royales," p. 290.

[136] Carolus-Barré, *Procès de canonisation*, p. 233.

[137] Parsons, "Beginnings of English Administration in Ponthieu," pp. 371–403.

[138] For this and the discussion that follows, see Carolus-Barré, *Procès de canonisation*, p. 234, and Langlois, *Règne de Philippe III*, pp. 224–25.

fuit regnante Philippo, rege Francie, Edwardo, rege Anglie, tenente ducatum Aquitanie. The dispute threatened to continue, however, because Edward's councilors in England gagged at the sequence of the names, that is, at the French king's being mentioned first in the new formula. An order went out to Jean de Grailly to repudiate the offer. He was upset by his masters' stance and argued against the repudiation, urging reconsideration and acceptance of Mathieu's compromise wording. Faced with Jean's stance, the English royal council, on which Abbot Richard sat as treasurer, relented and accepted the formula. On 1 August 1282 Jean ordered his clerks to henceforth use the new formula, with the French king's name in the first place in official documents.

English sensitivities with regard to Aquitaine were not limited to issues of protocol like that just described. The relation of the duke to the French crown was fraught, because anytime a party in the duchy felt aggrieved, it might turn to the French king or rather his judges for redress as the representatives of the duke's overlord. The English therefore were always alert and had been alert since the 1250s to the potential erosion of the duke's authority that successful appeals might lead to or imply, and not without reason.[139] For even Mathieu de Vendôme, cautious, careful, and courteous as he usually was, could speak out of character in the heat of the moment or in exasperation at English fastidiousness. Once he declared that Parlement could accept appeals from any aggrieved Gascon party, only to have to back down and clarify that what he meant to say was that appeals could come from any petitioner who could not otherwise exhaust his legitimate redress. Put positively, that is, such petitioners could appeal only for defect of justice.[140]

Within a few months of the resolution of the dispute over the formula to be used in Aquitaine's administrative correspondence, a case arose, though not technically an appeal, that shows some of the care that needed to go into the treatment of issues straddling the conceptual boundary of Gascon and French royal jurisdiction. In this case, the complaint came from the abbey of Saint-Benoît-sur-Loire. The abbey had a dependent priory, La Réole, situated in the lands of the duchy of Aquitaine on the banks of the Gironde River to the southwest of Bordeaux; when the prior and monks of La Réole claimed to suffer injury at the hands of the duke's government, the abbey naturally pursued the case, since it could claim to be injured through its dependent's injury. At the Parlement of Pentecost

---

[139] Above, pp. 153–54. Cf. Chaplais, *Essays in Medieval Diplomacy*. essay 6, "Les Appels gascons," pp. 382–84.

[140] Mathieu's outburst in Parlement, 11 November 1284, and his subsequent clarification are remarked in Langlois, *Règne de Philippe III*, pp. 280–81, and Carolus-Barré, *Procès de canonisation*, p. 234.

1283, in which Mathieu de Vendôme had a dominant voice, the masters gave judgment to the abbey, but Duke Edward's procurators succeeded in having their lord's jurisdiction over and "guard" of La Réole confirmed in the duchy, so that his authority remained otherwise undiminished.[141]

While the two abbots, Mathieu and Richard, lived or, rather, while councilors like these men, representing the aspirations to peace of their ancient masters, Louis IX and Henry III, remained vital presences in the royal retinues, problems and concerns of this sort continued to be resolvable. They were to some extent brakes on their new sovereigns, especially Mathieu, who was friendly with Edward I, on the hotheaded Philip III.[142] Indeed, despite strains in the relationship between the two kingdoms, the French persisted in looking upon the English as friends, and Philip's closest councilors felt nothing odd in calling upon the good offices of London. There were often good structural reasons for having recourse to the English. The vassalic relationship of Edward as duke of Aquitaine meant that Philip expected not only military support but counsel from him when needed.

Edward, however, wanted to stay out of Philip's wars. For example, when problems between the French and the Castilians became, if only ephemerally, a hot war in the late 1270s and early 1280s, Edward offered his good offices because the tenure of his Continental lands in the southwest created competing obligations for him to the two hostile kings.[143] The *oriflamme* solemnly received by Philip III from Abbot Mathieu availed nothing.[144] The war led instead to a crisis. The incompetence of French military preparations indeed helped bring down the royal favorite, Pierre de la Broce.[145] Edward's offer of arbitration in the circumstances ran the considerable risk of being interpreted by the French as reluctance to support them at a very precarious time. And yet the situation never developed into a real confrontation between the English and the French because a much more terrifying diplomatic nightmare, Paris's involvement in Mediterranean politics, displaced the Castilian crisis and everything related to it in importance. So a truce was possible with Castile and diplomatic courtesy with England, but neither of these was possible, it seemed, with the new enemy of the 1280s, Aragon.

This situation owed its genesis to circumstances that in the 1250s were central to English history, namely, King Henry III's failure to fulfill his

[141] Carolus-Barré, *Procès de canonisation*, p. 233, attributes the leading role to Abbot Mathieu based on the order of the masters' names ("Furent présents à ce jugement l'abbé de Saint-Denis, dont le nom précède ici celui de l'évêque de Dol, et plusieurs autres").

[142] Cf. Langlois, *Règne de Philippe III*, p. 191.

[143] Chaplais, *Essays in Medieval Diplomacy:* essay 3, "Duché-Pairie de Guyenne," p. 20.

[144] *HF*, 20:540.

[145] Above, p. 141.

promise to wage war on the papacy's behalf against the heirs of Emperor Frederick II. Charles of Anjou, Louis IX's brother, ultimately picked up the baton, as it were, invaded Italy, and destroyed the last vestiges of Hohenstaufen power in the 1260s. Thereafter, for a decade and a half, Charles of Anjou was an imposing, if brutal, presence in the central Mediterranean and developed grandiose plans to extend his reach into the eastern Mediterranean and reconquer the Byzantine Empire for Latin Christendom. Implementation of his plans, however, was several times stymied because of the success of the restored Greek emperor, Michael VIII Paleologus, in convincing a succession of popes that he was making a good faith effort to unite the churches under Roman sovereignty as mandated at the Second Council of Lyon in 1274.

Nevertheless, by the early 1280s it became clear that the emperor was meeting extraordinary resistance in his effort to persuade the reluctant Greek clergy and monks to accept the union on the council's terms. And it was also evident that in looking around for people to blame, many influential westerners came to distrust the emperor, believing that if he genuinely wanted the union to succeed, he would use more draconian measures against the opposition. This created the opening Charles of Anjou prayed for, but the execution of his plans to invade, which had fully matured by 1282, was prevented by the Sicilian uprising later known as the Vespers on 31 March in that year.

The revolt took place in Sicily and was carried out by Sicilians, but Charles and his French nephew and admirer, Philip III, came to blame the Crown of Aragon for the mire into which Charles's foreign policy had sunk. For the ruler of Aragon, Peter III, was the husband of Constance of Hohenstaufen, the daughter of Manfred, Emperor Frederick II's bastard son. With all her close male relatives in the Staufer connection now dead, she was the heiress to their claims to the kingdom of Sicily. The evidence was fairly strong from early on and it mounted over time that the Aragonese had long intended to exploit unrest in Sicily caused by Charles's exacting rule. To what extent, however, the Crown of Aragon was party to the rebels' councils or had advance knowledge of their uprising is shrouded by the mists of time and the very nature of conspiratorial politics. What was not lost on the Aragonese was the opportunity the rebellion presented to assert Constance's hereditary claim.

The situation steadily deteriorated after March 1282, as the French gathered evidence of and confirmed to their satisfaction Aragon's ultimate intention to seize Sicily. The Aragonese invasion of the island commenced on 30 August. An absurd and unfulfilled proposal, ridiculed by the pope, to prevent full-scale war between Charles of Anjou's forces and those of Peter III was to accept a decision by single combat between the two men and equal companies of one hundred knights. But the two sides showed up at different times, and each king proclaimed the other in default. And then the two kings wrote peevish notes to each other. The whole mess was the talk of Europe.[146]

It became evident to Charles and his supporters that the only appropriate response was the invasion of Aragon, an invasion approved and hallowed by the papacy, Charles's ally in the matter, and therefore known as the Crusade against Aragon. As late as March 1284, however, diplomacy was not entirely exhausted. Many influential French personages were opposed to war, including Abbot Mathieu de Vendôme, now in his sixties.[147] Also opposed was the queen dowager, Marguerite de Provence, Louis IX's widow. Marguerite had particular reasons for disliking Charles of Anjou, with whom she had had a bitter dispute over the rule of the county of Provence following the death of her sister, Charles's wife. In 1282 she began to mobilize forces for war with the support of another of her sisters, the English queen dowager (and behind his mother potentially stood Edward I).[148] Calmer heads prevailed, however, and, although there were lingering resentments, the antagonists reached a negotiated monetary settlement, which compensated Marguerite for her ceded jurisdictional claims in the county.

Moreover, since the Treaty of Corbeil, Louis IX's attempt in 1258 to establish permanent peace between France and Aragon, the two kingdoms had been on fairly good terms. There were close personal relations between members of the two ruling houses. Philip III's first wife and the beloved mother of his putative heir, Philip the Fair, had been the Aragonese princess, Isabella. She had died in 1270 while accompanying her husband and her father-in-law, Louis IX, on Crusade to Tunisia. Her son, only three at the time of his mother's death, nevertheless cherished her memory, partly as a counterweight to his dislike of his stepmother after 1274, Marie de Brabant. An adolescent by the time of the diplomatic and military crises of 1282, Philip the Fair had no stomach for war against his mother's family and his favorite cousins, but he had no power to prevent it.

At the beginning of the year 1284, Pope Martin IV excommunicated Peter III of Aragon, even though Edward I was urging, through the abbot of Saint-Denis, further negotiations among Philip III, Charles of Anjou, and Peter III.[149] On the 21st of February the French royal council, bring-

---

[146] This explains why documents relating to the failed combat show up, for example, in the register of an English bishop, like Winchester's Jean de Pontoise; *Registrum domini Johannis de Pontissara*, pp. 403–6.

[147] Langlois, *Règne de Philippe III*, p. 149; Sivéry, *Philippe III*, p. 245.

[148] Sivéry, *Philippe III*, pp. 258–61.

[149] Edward's letter to Mathieu is dated 12 January 1284; *Syllabus* (p. 98) to Rymer's *Foedera*.

ing to a conclusion a series of discussions that had been going on for some time among the elite of the church and the aristocracy, held a final set of debates on whether to endorse this action and to pursue a military policy appropriate to it. There was much rancor, but two days later clergy and barons decided in favor of aligning France with the papal initiative and giving it military bite. A month later followed a ceremony presided over by papal representatives signaling the formal deposition of the Aragonese ruler and the investiture of his realms to Charles of Valois, a younger son of Philip III.[150] Yet, according to one piece of evidence dated 2 March 1284—that is, as fiscal and material preparations for the French invasion of Aragon shifted into high gear—Abbot Mathieu de Vendôme secretly approached the English at Philip's order, to seek their help in persuading the Aragonese to make the kind of concessions that might prevent the opening of full-scale hostilities. His old acquaintance and diplomatic partner, Richard de Ware, could play no role in this last-ditch effort, having died suddenly in December, and in any case, though not for lack of trying, Mathieu's effort came to nothing.[151]

So Philip III had a new version of his will drafted, one in which he named Abbot Mathieu as an executor, in fact the third in the list.[152] On 24 March 1285, he received the royal battle standard, the *oriflamme*, from the abbot of Saint-Denis and underwent all the rituals appropriate to a crusader at the monastery and at the other appropriate sites.[153] Arrangements taken with respect to the government and administration of the realm during the king's absence on the Aragonese campaign were uncannily similar to those made in 1270 before Louis IX departed on his final Crusade. Philip selected the same two men his father had selected as coregents, Lord Simon de Nesle and Abbot Mathieu.[154] Jean de Joinville, the hereditary seneschal of Champagne and Louis IX's old friend and future biographer, was specifically charged, however, with the office of guarding the Capetians' rights in the county of Champagne, for Philip III's son and heir was married to the heiress of the county and was, therefore, titular count himself.[155] The king along with his eldest son then departed the north, and Simon and Mathieu began to exercise their regnal powers in April.[156]

The war was, militarily speaking, short and humiliating. The invasion bogged down in the Pyrenees. Diseases decimated the army. The heir pre-

---

[150] For the events of early 1284, see Carolus-Barré, *Procès de canonisation*, pp. 234–35.
[151] Sivéry, *Philippe III*, pp. 264, 272–73; Carolus-Barré, *Procès de canonisation*, p. 235.
[152] *GC*, vol. 7, col. 394; Carolus-Barré, *Procès de canonisation*, p. 235.
[153] Carolus-Barré, *Procès de canonisation*, p. 235.
[154] *GC*, vol. 7, col. 394; Carolus-Barré, *Procès de canonisation*, p. 235.
[155] Carolus-Barré, *Procès de canonisation*, p. 235.
[156] Ibid.

sumptive hated every minute of it and kept hoping for an out for his father and the army and the realm. With the French effectively beaten both on land and at sea, a sad retreat began, culminating in King Philip III's death in Perpignan on 5 October 1285 and his son's assumption of power as Philip IV (1285–1314).[157] The dead king's body made its way back to Paris and burial at Saint-Denis on 3 December 1285.[158] The royal heart, however, was interred with the Dominicans of Paris, as the late king had wished. Sivéry, in the absence of evidence but with a characteristic rhetorical question, intimated that this fulfillment of his father's wish by the new king, Philip IV the Fair, was a slap at Saint-Denis and in the face of its abbot, since, he assumes, the monks wanted the entire corpse.[159]

Mathieu de Vendôme and Simon de Nesle's formal regency was therefore fairly short, if one dates its end from Philip the Fair's assumption of power while he was in Languedoc, and, indeed, even if one adds the period until the old king's burial in December or his son's coronation at Reims on 6 January 1286. A smattering of surviving records indicate that Mathieu and Simon had no evident hesitation in exercising full powers in these months on matters as diverse—and weighty—as taxation for the war, disputes over river transport on the Loire, and requests by urban corporations for privileges and concessions of various sorts, like a free port for Niort.[160] They also closely monitored Jean de Joinville's guard of the county of Champagne, since Philip the Fair's accession was another step in the process of the fief's *rattachement* to the crown.[161] The latest few of their acts are dated the week before Christmas, a fact suggesting that the still teenaged Philip the Fair left the day-to-day administration of the realm in their hands until at least his formal consecration.[162]

Soon after the regency began, Simon de Nesle asked Abbot Mathieu to serve with several others as the executor of his will. This was in June 1285. Perhaps the abbot's willingness to be named in this capacity reflects merely his habit of responding in the affirmative to other supplicants who had requested it. After all, Mathieu served as an executor of Louis IX's testament (1270), Philip III's (both the version of 1270 and that of 1285),

---

[157] Ibid., p. 236.

[158] Sivéry, *Philippe III*, p. 282; Carolus-Barré, *Procès de canonisation*, p. 235; Erlande-Brandenburg et al., *Gisants et tombeaux*, p. 16.

[159] Sivéry, *Philippe III*, p. 285.

[160] *HF*, 22:672; Carolus-Barré, *Procès de canonisation*, pp. 235–36.

[161] On the monitoring of Jean de Joinville's guard of Champagne, see Carolus-Barré, *Procès de canonisation*, p. 235. The *rattachement* was completed only later. In 1305 Philip the Fair's heir, Prince Louis, succeeded on his mother's death to the countship, and in 1314, on his own accession to the crown as Louis X, Champagne formally became property of the crown.

[162] Carolus-Barré, *Procès de canonisation*, pp. 235–36.

and those of at least two other powerful personages, Renaud de Nanteuil, the bishop of Beauvais (April 1283) and one of Philip III's physicians in August 1284.[163] And yet it was probably close friendship and profound trust (the phrase describing the abbot as an honest man and a dear friend is not likely to have been a mere formula) as well as a sense of time running out that were more significant factors in Simon's decision. For by the time they began formally to exercise their regnal powers in April 1285, neither Mathieu nor Simon was a young man. The abbot was about sixty-two and Simon at least seventy-five years old. It was only two months later that the older man's scribe placed Abbot Mathieu's name on the list of his executors. He was probably already ill. Indeed, if one takes the coronation of the new king on 6 January 1286 as the latest possible date for the end of the coregency, Simon barely lived to complete his work. He died less than four weeks afterward, on 1 February.[164]

Mathieu de Vendôme returned to his duties at Saint-Denis full-time around Christmas 1285. This last phase of his long career was interrupted only by his participation in the coronation ceremony. He must have felt fairly healthy, because, among his other activities, he carried out a visitation of the abbey's dependent priories, including the house at the present Beaune-la-Rolande (department, Loiret). Beaune-la-Rolande has become infamous in modern history, first as the site in 1870 of a disastrous defeat of the French army in the Franco-Prussian War and then as a major railway depot during the Second World War for the Vichy government's transfer of thousands of French Jews to Auschwitz. It was a quiet little castle-priory town in the Gâtinais in the late thirteenth century, probably already noted for its exquisite honey. During his visitation of the priory the old abbot died, 25 September 1286.[165] His body was immediately brought back to the monastery he had ruled for twenty-eight years. On the 27th a copper vault, prepared to receive his remains, was placed in the spot chosen for his burial, hard by the great iron gate along the passage from the choir to the cloister.[166]

Little remained of Abbot Mathieu's body or his burial attire by the time his tomb was opened in 1699, but written memorials of his greatness have kept his name alive. He was recalled—essentially—as the man who made things work at his abbey and in the realm.[167] "[P]rincipal counselor of the king and kingdom of France," a man "by whom the whole

---

[163] GC, vol. 7, col. 394; Carolus-Barré, Procès de canonisation, p. 236.
[164] On Simon, see Carolus-Barré, Procès de canonisation, pp. 168–75.
[165] GC, vol. 7, col. 394; Carolus-Barré, Procès de canonisation, p. 236.
[166] GC, vol. 7, col. 394; Carolus-Barré, Procès de canonisation, p. 236.
[167] GC, vol. 7, col. 395.

kingdom of France was ruled," an abbot of "great virtue" and "exceedingly religious," the builder of a "marvelous and sumptuous" church—these are the kinds of phrases scattered throughout the sources, whether epitaphs or chronicles or letters.[168] From a medieval Christian's point of view, they represented high and, as far as can now be ascertained, quite well-deserved praise.

[168] Ibid., cols. 394–95.

IX

EPILOGUE

THE INTERWOVEN STORIES of Mathieu de Vendôme and Richard de Ware and of the monasteries they ruled, Saint-Denis and Westminster, have provided an alternative route through the history of France and England in the thirteenth century. I neither do nor wish to insist that it is a better route than any others. Nevertheless, as a detour reveals new landscapes to a driver, it does bring into focus the effect of the great national rivalries on aspects of political, social, economic, and cultural life in each realm that have sometimes been neglected or treated without reference to other major themes.

Of course, the personal stories of the two abbots are interesting in themselves and uncannily similar. Both men came from modest backgrounds. There was nothing very special about the status of either family so far as historians have been able to tell. Yet, as an arresting testimony to medieval social mobility, both rose to become rulers of monasteries that were in a very real sense the repositories of the national patrimony—the tombs of its royal saints—and centers of the cult of monarchy. They had a keen eye for the value of ornamentation and display, as their refurbishment of their churches manifestly demonstrates. They tried doggedly to maintain their institutions' wealth. And they were fastidious about protocol, partly because they shared another trait, implicit in their status as heads of exempt ecclesiastical institutions, a deep suspicion of bishops. This suspicion was most evident in Mathieu's case in his relations with Etienne Tempier, the bishop of Paris, whom he calculatedly humiliated before Louis IX's funeral for a transgression of protocol. In Richard's case it manifested itself most vigorously in his bitter jurisdictional struggles with the Franciscan archbishop of Canterbury, John Pecham. At base, the issue for both abbots was their and their monasteries' right not to be judged or even interfered with on spiritual matters by any authority on earth save the supreme pontiff.

Both Mathieu de Vendôme and Richard de Ware also lived through and were parties to momentous changes in government dictated, in the English case, largely by the aristocracy; in the French, by the crown. To a certain extent, given when the great reforms occurred (the mid- to late 1250s to the mid-1260s), the administrative and political context in which the reforms emerged constituted the learning laboratory for the two men early in their careers as abbots. For Richard the laboratory tested him metaphorically in a trial by fire, the baronial seizure of power and the civil war. Londoners' support of the barons coupled with their long-standing resentment of Westminster's privileges put the abbey in terrible danger. The barons' attempt to co-opt Westminster, to make it into a monument to their ideal of governance, ultimately failed but was no less threatening in its way than the Londoners' assault on its privileges.

There was no violence of this sort in France, but men and women knew that Louis IX's insistence on *his* standards of justice did not always go down well with the lay aristocracy. Mathieu de Vendôme saw this vividly manifested when he was commissioned to look into Enguerran de Coucy's execution of three boys and observed the sequel in the king's ferocious condemnation of the baron. For him—for Mathieu—the king's facing down and humiliation of the powerful nobleman would be remembered as being at the very core of his master's sanctity. Louis's arbitral judgment in the Mise of Amiens, though rejected by the English barons in 1264, emanated from a lofty ideology of rulership that underlay every reform in the midcentury.

Matters of delicacy fell to the abbots rather frequently, as their skills became familiar to their masters. Richard would have first met Mathieu in the context of the negotiation of the Treaty of Paris and in the wake of the settlement of the Deerhurst affair, which restored the English alien priory of that name to Saint-Denis's control. Later among his many missions the Englishman was sent to France to reassure the French king, Louis IX, about the safety of his royal brother-in-law and his family after Simon de Montfort's victory at Lewes, and still later, following the death of Louis IX's brother, Alphonse, to negotiate the restoration of the Agenais according to the spirit and letter of the Treaty of Paris. Mathieu carried out the inquiry into Pierre de la Broce's relations with the so-called Flemish prophetesses, the women whose alleged rants about Philip III's sins against nature and his second wife's determination to murder her stepchildren were at the core of the greatest scandal of that king's reign. He subsequently played a vigorous but unsuccessful role in the early 1280s in trying to prevent war between France and the Crown of Aragon. Their administrative expertise, their negotiating abilities, and their unwavering loyalty led inexorably to the abbots' selection as high officers of state, Mathieu as regent and Richard as royal treasurer.

Neither man is remarkable for his personal literary output. They did not themselves write learned theological or philosophical tomes, polemical works, sermon collections, or poetry. Yet books commanded their interest, sufficiently to elicit commissions. These were either for worship, the very first books whose production Mathieu authorized as abbot, or in Richard's case for recording the customs of his monastery. Mathieu's fascination, of course, went beyond this in that Saint-Denis was responsible for writing the history of the kings of France. The abbot delegated the final work, the *Grandes chroniques*, to a gifted monk and equally gifted illustrators, but contributed semiofficial materials from his first regency for it and took a keen interest in its compilation. Richard may have been more than passingly interested in history, too, if the migration of the *Flores historiarum* from Saint-Albans to Westminster in 1265 can be attributed to his impulse, but this remains unproved. Mathieu, of course, also relished being able to oversee the assembly in written form of the miracles of his saintly patron Louis IX after the king's burial in the abbey church in 1271. Undoubtedly Richard de Ware would have enjoyed supervising such a literary enterprise as well if his late patron Henry III's cult had taken off, but it never did.

There were differences, naturally, in the two men's personalities that affected their careers. One thinly documented difference involves their relations with the widowed queens of Henry III and Louis IX, the sisters Eleanor and Marguerite of Provence. Toward the end of his life, Richard de Ware's position in his dispute over the immunity of Great Malvern reveals this difference. The bishop of Worcester and the man the bishop tried to impose as prior of Great Malvern had powerful friends in and around government. Having them proved insufficient to overcome Richard's claim to the ecclesiastical lordship of Great Malvern or to invalidate the priory's immunity from episcopal jurisdiction. Nonetheless, the swiftness and unmitigated manner in which the queen dowager Eleanor intervened, urging her son Edward I to take action against the abbot of Westminster, are astonishing. She seems not to have doubted for a moment that this religious man, whom she had known for a quarter of a century and who had been her husband's consistent supporter, was capable of the savagery imputed to him—imprisoning monks opposed to him in horrifying, even lethal, conditions—in order to secure his jurisdictional rights. In contrast, there are hints, admittedly few, that despite differences Mathieu de Vendôme and Marguerite of Provence in her widowhood shared in general a similar vision. The abbot of Saint-Denis and Louis IX's widow counted on each other as allies at court, especially during the period leading to the Aragonese war, quite unlike the abbot of Westminster and the queen dowager of England, insofar as the Great Malvern incident is representative of their relations. One would like to know more about the abbots and the queen dowagers.

A better-documented and equally striking difference between the two abbots emerges from a recognition of how little of Richard de Ware's wanderlust Mathieu de Vendôme had. True, Mathieu remembered his boyhood in Vendôme and inspired some of his Capetian patrons to succor the great Benedictine monastery there, La Trinité, where he probably professed. But after becoming a monk of Saint-Denis, he traveled little except to do his abbatial duties as a visitor to his monastery's dependencies and estates. When offered a bishopric in Normandy, he declined. His attendance at the Second Council of Lyon, presuming he did attend, proceeded without fanfare, and he was back at work at Saint-Denis in a trice. He was Louis IX's friend, but unlike Archbishop Eudes Rigaud, who was also the king's friend and joined the king on Crusade in 1270, Mathieu stayed behind to rule the kingdom in Louis's name. He was not much of a personal friend of Philip III and appears to have had little confidence in the new king's political sense. He had no incentive to travel with him on the Crusade against Aragon, once again staying behind to govern the realm in the king's name. Mathieu de Vendôme gives the impression of a man supremely comfortable in just staying put.

Not so Richard de Ware. We find few if any truly warm remembrances of him. Henry III assuredly held him in high esteem for his support and probably regarded him affectionately, but Edward I treated Richard and his monastery quite harshly in the 1270s, at least with respect to their jurisdictional privileges. He regretted this after he came to know Richard better, restoring and confirming the privileges and rewarding the abbot with the office of royal treasurer. Edward's commendation of his treasurer following his death seems genuine, although not particularly expressive. The word "love" does not leap to mind to characterize their relationship. I am inclined to think that Richard came across as being a hard man with a disciplined and cautious personality; he was a dependable and useful man but scarcely endearing to those he served or to those he ruled. There is more than a hint of this in his fiscal and jurisdictional relations with the men and institutions dependent on him and his monastery. On those occasions when he defended them, even pugnaciously, it was not out of any particular *dilectio* for them but because any infringement of their privileges was an infringement of his. To suggest that he was friendless (Henry III excepted) is to argue from silence, but the silence is deafening in its way. Not a single person appears to have asked Richard de Ware to serve as an executor of his will, and even if this judgment does not hold up under future research, the contrast with Saint-Denis's abbot is obvious. Men lined up to request this favor of Mathieu de Vendôme, known affectionately by his nicknames, Maci and Mahé.

There is no doubt—and this adds to the impression of his lack of close relations in the kingdom he called home—that Richard, like many of his countrymen of the time, enjoyed being away from England. Possibly his enjoyment was augmented by the opportunity absence gave him to be free from the fiscal problems, including the importunities of Henry III, that faced Westminster in the 1260s and to avoid the tedium of exercising monastic correction (itself a factor contributing to the laxity of life at the monastery that Edward I censured in the early 1270s and Richard belatedly but effectively remedied). The abbot's consent to the pawning of the monastic treasure may have endeared him to Henry III, but it also made spectacularly clear the invidious contrast between Saint-Denis's solvency and Westminster's fiscal vulnerability. So, on his frequent trips abroad, ostensibly devoted to maneuvering in the heady and exhausting world of international diplomacy, where men hung on his every utterance, Richard lingered—there is no better word to describe his leisurely progress through the Romagna, in the French countryside, and in Paris. He liked and adopted the Continental styles he encountered, whether the latest fashion in depicting powerful men on their seals or the ornamental pavements shimmering in the soft sunlight that filtered through the windows of Italy's ornate chapels. Being royal treasurer of England in the last few years of his life was a great honor, no doubt, but it came at a price in making travel abroad to France and Italy out of the question. In the Cosmati pavement, Richard had a little bit of Italy present at Westminster to remind him of what he was missing.

The underlying theme throughout Mathieu's and Richard's abbacies was competition, always competition. In the early years their kings competed with one another as supporters of papal policy, Louis IX as a crusader, Henry III as the potential deliverer of the Holy See from its mortal Hohenstaufen enemy. As time went by, this competition transformed itself into a virtual race in which sanctity was the laurel. Still later, after the old kings' deaths, the nature of the competition was transformed once more, this time into political posturing, posturing with a kind of immature silliness about it on Philip III's side, as compared with the behavior of Edward I.

Through it all, the abbeys were showcases of what some historians would be willing to call an emerging national spirit. It is not clear that every comparison scholars make between the great sanctuaries is a comparison that contemporaries would have made or would have made with the specific intent of denigrating one or the other monument. But enough evidence survives to show that Westminster kept an eye on Saint-Denis (and homegrown rivals) and vice versa. The magnificent tombs of the Confessor and Henry III were paralleled by the rearrangement and refurbishment of the royal inhumations at Saint-Denis to emphasize the Carolingian lineage of the dynasty, the fabrication of an elegant new reliquary for Saint Denis's head, and the installation of an elaborately ornate second tomb for Louis IX. The rebuilding at Westminster had its counterpart in the completion of the church at Saint-Denis in the latest style. Westminster's monopoly over coronation provoked the envy of Saint-Denis's monks, who still had not given up fully on their claim to the coronation in the thirteenth century. And Saint-Denis's special honor as the royal necropolis provoked, in its turn, the envy of Westminster's monks.

The middle years of the thirteenth century were eventful for the kings and kingdoms of France and England. They constituted a privileged interval of peace between two long periods of war, an era in which some of the greatest and most long-lasting institutions—Parliament and Parlement, to name only two—were created. The years were equally eventful for the royal abbeys of Saint-Denis and Westminster. Both monasteries became jewels in the architectural and ideological treasury of the two realms. True, the French Revolution simply overwhelmed Saint-Denis as it did the sacred monarchy that the abbey celebrated. No restoration of the buildings or the dynasty has ever quite recaptured the medieval magic that was the institution under Mathieu de Vendôme. On the other side of the Channel, though, Westminster, despite the iconoclasm of the Protestant Reformation, continues to claim its architectural and symbolic status. The evidences of that status nowadays, however, make an odd touristy stew that would perplex and would probably be distasteful to its medieval monastic inmates, not least Richard de Ware. If he were miraculously to return, I think he might swiftly retire to the vibrant cities, the sunny valleys, and the verdant uplands of the Italy he so obviously enjoyed.

BIBLIOGRAPHY

Primary Sources: Manuscripts

AN. See Paris, Archives Nationales
BL. See London, British Library.
BnF. See Paris, Bibliothèque nationale de France.

London

    British Library (BL)

        Cotton Faustina A III, "Registrum Cartarum ecclesiae B. Petri
           Westmonasteriensis"
        Royal 5 B VIII, "Jerome, 'De viris illustribus'; Augustine, 'Retracti-
           ones'; etc."

    Lambeth Palace Library, MS 761, "Vita S. Edwardi"
    Westminster Abbey

        Westminster Abbey Muniments, by number (WAM):
           504, 1202, 1492, 1667, 1692, 1808, 1874, 1885, 4226–4227, 4242,
           4269, 4907, 5400, 5673, 6681, 6684–6685, 8578, 8581–8585,
           8589–8590, 9181, 9467, 9468, 12733, 12771, 12784-12785,
           12796–12877, 12890, 17459, 22471, 22944, 24489, 24561A–C,
           28953, 32629–32643, 61083C
        Westminster Abbey Muniments Book no. 1 (= *Liber Niger*)
        Westminster Abbey Muniments Book no. 11 (= Westminster Domesday;
           WD)

Paris

    Archives Nationales
    Bibliothèque nationale de France

WAM. See London, Westminster Abbey

Primary Sources: Printed

*Abstract of Charters and Other Documents Contained in a Cartulary of the Abbey
of St. Peter Westminster in the Possession of Samuel Bentley.* London: Privately
printed, 1836.
Actes du Parlement de Paris. Ed. Edgar Boutaric. 2 vols. Paris: H. Plon, 1863–
1867.
Annales Monastici. Ed. Henry Luard. 5 vols. London: Longman, Green, Longman, Roberts, and Green, 1864–1869.
Atlas historique de Saint-Denis: Des origines au XVIIIe siècle. Comp. Michaël Wyss
et al. Paris: Editions de la Maison des Sciences de l'Homme, 1996.

Bartholomaei de Cotton, monachi Norwicensis, Historia anglicana (A.D. 449–1298). Ed. Henry Luard. London: Longman, Green, Longman, and Roberts, 1859.

Calendar of Entries in the Papal Registers relating to Great Britain and Ireland. Vol. 1, *Papal Letters, A.D. 1198–1304*. Ed. W. H. Bliss. London: Her Majesty's Stationery Office, 1893.

Calendar of Inquisitions Post Mortem. Vol. 1, *Henry III*. Vol. 2, *Edward I*. London: His Majesty's Stationery Office, 1904–1906.

Calendar of the Charter Rolls. Vol. 1, *Henry III, A.D. 1226–1257*. Vol. 2, *Henry III–Edward I, A.D. 1257–1300*. London: His Majesty's Stationery Office, 1903–906.

Calendar of the Close Rolls Preserved in the Public Record Office. London: Her/His Majesty's Stationery Office, 1892–.

Calendar of the Fine Rolls. Vol. 1, *Edward I, A.D. 1272–1307*. London: His Majesty's Stationery Office, 1911.

Calendar of the Liberate Rolls. Vol. 4, *Henry III, 1251–1260*. Vol. 5, *Henry III, 1260–1267*. Vol. 6, *Henry III, 1267–1272*. Reprint. London: His Majesty's Stationery Office, 1959–1964.

Calendar of the Patent Rolls Preserved in the Public Record Office, Edward I. 4 vols. Nendeln, Liechtenstein: Kraus Reprints, 1971.

Calendar of Various Chancery Rolls; Supplementary Close Rolls, Welsh Rolls, Scutage Rolls, A.D. 1277–1326. London: His Majesty's Stationery Office, 1912.

Carolus-Barré, Louis, comp. *Le Procès de canonisation de saint Louis (1272–1297): Essai de reconstitution*. Rome: Ecole Française de Rome, 1994.

Carolus-Barré, Louis, and Jean-Charles Payen, eds. "Le Dit du Concile de Lyon (ms. Zagreb MR 92)." In *1274, Année charnière: Mutations et continuités*, pp. 917–66. Paris: Editions du Centre National de la Recherche Scientifique, 1977.

Cartulaire blanc de Saint-Denis. Comp. Olivier Guyotjeanin. Editions en ligne de l'Ecole de Chartes, no. 3: http://elec.enc.sorbonne.fr/cartulaireblanc.

Cartulaire de Marmoutier pour le Vendomois. Ed. Charles de Tremault. Paris: A. Picard et Fils, 1893.

Charmasse, A. de, ed. *Cartulaire de l'évêché d'Autun*. Paris: Durand, 1880.

Chronica Johannis de Oxenedes. Ed. Henry Ellis. London: Longman, Brown, Green, Longmans, and Roberts, 1859.

The Chronicle of Bury St Edmunds, 1212–1301. Ed. Antonia Gransden. London: Thomas Nelson and Sons, 1964.

The Chronicle of William de Rishanger of the Barons' Wars. Ed. James Halliwell. London: Camden Society, 1840.

Chronicles of the Reigns of Edward I and Edward II. Ed. William Stubbs. 2 vols. London: Longman, 1882–1883.

Chronicles of the Reigns of Stephen, Henry II, and Richard I. Vol. 2. Ed. Richard Howlett. London: Longman, 1885.

Chronicon domini Walteri de Heminburgh. Ed. Hans Hamilton. 2 vols. London: English Historical Society, 1848–1849.

Chronik des Saba Malaspina. Ed. Walter Koller and August Nitschke. *Monumenta Germaniae Historica, Scriptores*, 35. Hanover: Hahnsche Buchhandlung, 1999.

Close Rolls. See *Calendar of the Close Rolls*.

Colvin, Howard, ed. *Building Accounts of King Henry III.* Oxford: Oxford University Press, 1971.

Crouch, David, ed. *Llandaff Episcopal Acta, 1140–1287.* Cardiff: South Wales Record Society, 1988.

Curia regis Rolls. Vol. 19, *33 to 34 Henry III (1249–1250).* Ed. David Crook. Woodbridge, UK: Boydell Press, 2002.

Curia regis Rolls. Vol. 20, *34 to 35 Henry III (1250).* Ed. David Crook. Woodbridge, UK: Boydell Press, 2006.

Customary of the Benedictine Monasteries of Saint Augustine, Canterbury, and Saint Peter, Westminster. Ed. Edward Thompson. 2 vols. London: Henry Bradshaw Society, 1904.

De antiquis legibus liber: Cronica maiorum et vicecomitum Londoniarum. Ed. Thomas Stapleton. London: Camden Society, 1846.

Descriptive Catalogue of Ancient Deeds in the Public Record Office. Vol. 1. London: Her Majesty's Stationery Office, 1890.

Documents Illustrating the Activities of the General and Provincial Chapters of the English Black Monks, 1215–1540. Ed. William Pantin. Publications of the Camden Society, 3rd series, no. 45. 3 vols. London: Camden Society, 1931.

Documents Illustrating the Rule of Walter de Wenlok, Abbot of Westminster, 1283–1307. Ed. Barbara Harvey. Publications of the Camden Society, 4th series, no. 2. London: Royal Historical Society, 1965.

Documents of the Baronial Movement of Reform and Rebellion, 1258–1267. Ed. Reginald Treharne and Ivor Sanders. Oxford: Clarendon Press, 1973.

English Episcopal Acta. Vol. 13, *Worcester 1218–1268.* Ed. Philippa Hoskin. Oxford: Oxford University Press, 1997.

English Historical Documents, 1189–1327. Vol. 3. Ed. Harry Rothwell and David Douglas. Oxford: Oxford University Press, 1975.

Flete, John. *The History of Westminster Abbey.* See below under "Secondary Sources."

Flores historiarum. Ed. Henry Luard. 3 vols. London: Her Majesty's Stationery Office, 1890.

Gallia christiana in provincias ecclesiasticas distributa. 16 vols. Paris: V. Palmé, etc., 1856–1899.

GC. See *Gallia christiana in provincias ecclesiasticas distributa.*

Gervers, Michael, ed. *The Cartulary of the Knights of St. John of Jerusalem in England.* Oxford: Oxford University Press for the British Academy, 1982.

Gesta abbatum monasterii sancti Albani, a Thoma Walsingham. Vol. 1, *A.D. 793–1290.* Ed. Henry Riley. London: Longmans, Green, Reader, and Dyer, 1867.

HF. See *Recueil des historiens des Gaules et de la France.*

Historical Poems of the XIVth and XVth Centuries. Ed. Rossel Robbins. New York: Columbia University Press, 1959.

The Historical Works of Gervase of Canterbury. Vol. 2, *Minor Works.* Ed. William Stubbs. London: Longmans, 1880.

Layettes du Trésor des chartes. Ed. Alexandre Teulet et al. 5 vols. Paris: H. Plon, 1861–1909.

Longnon, Auguste, ed. *Documents relatifs au comté de Champagne et de Brie, 1172–1361.* 3 vols. Paris: Imprimerie Nationale, 1901–1914.

Mason, Emma, ed. *Westminster Abbey Charters, 1066–1214*. London: London Record Society, 1988.

Matthew Paris. *Chronica majora*. Ed. Henry Luard. 7 vols. London: Her Majesty's Stationery Office, 1872–1883.

Medieval Court of Arches. Ed. F. Donald Logan. Woodbridge, UK: Boydell Press (for the Canterbury and York Society), 2005.

Monasticon Anglicanum. New ed. Vol 1. London: James Bohn, 1846.

Montgomery, Edward, ed. *Le Chastoiement d'un père à son fils: A Critical Edition*. Chapel Hill: University of North Carolina Press, 1971.

Nicolai Triveti, Dominicani, Annales sex regum Angliae. Ed. Antony Hall. Oxford: Theatrum Sheldonianum, 1719.

Olim, ou, Registres des arrêts rendus par la Cour du roi. Ed. Arthur Beugnot. 3 vols. Paris: Imprimerie Royale, 1839–1848.

Original Papal Documents in England and Wales from the Accession of Pope Innocent III to the Death of Pope Benedict XI (1198–1304). Comp. Jane Sayers. Oxford: Oxford University Press, 1997.

Oxfordshire Forests, 1246–1609. Ed. Beryl Schumer. Oxfordshire Record Society Series, 64. Oxford: Oxfordshire Record Society, 2004.

The Parliament Rolls of Medieval England, 1275–1504. Vol. 1, *Edward I, 1275–1294*. Ed. Paul Brand. Woodbridge, UK: Boydell Press; London: The National Archives, 2005.

Patent Rolls, Edward I. See *Calendar of the Patent Rolls*.

Patent Rolls, Henry III. See *Patent Rolls of the Reign of Henry III*.

Patent Rolls of the Reign of Henry III, Preserved in the Public Record Office. 6 vols. Nendeln, Liechtenstein: Kraus Reprints, 1971.

Recueil de chartes et documents de Saint-Martin-des-Champs: Monastère parisien. Ed. Joseph Depoin. Paris: Jouve, 1912. (Available also online.)

Recueil des historiens des Gaules et de la France. Ed. Martin Bouquet et al. 24 vols. Paris: V. Palmé, 1840–1904.

The Register of Eudes of Rouen. Trans. Sydney Brown. New York and London: Columbia University Press, 1964.

Registrum domini Johannis de Pontissara quondam episcopi Wyntoniensis. London: Surrey Record Society, 1913–1924.

Registrum epistolarum fratris Johannis Peckham, archiepiscopi Cantuariensis. Ed. Charles Martin. 3 vols. London: Longman, 1882–1885.

The Riverside Chaucer. Ed. Larry Benson. 3rd ed. Boston: Houghton Mifflin, 1987.

Rokéah, Zefira, comp. *Medieval English Jews and Royal Officials: Entries of Jewish Interest in the English Memoranda Rolls, 1266–1293*. Jerusalem: Hebrew University Press, 2000.

Rolls and Register of Bishop Oliver Sutton, 1280–1299. Ed. Rosalind Hill. 8 vols. Lincoln: Lincoln Record Society, 1948–1986.

Rotuli Parliamentorum Anglie hactenus inediti, MCCLXXIX–MCCCLXXIII. Ed. H. G. Richardson and George Sayles. Publications of the Camden Society, 3rd series, no. 51. London: Camden Society, 1935.

Salimbene de Adam. *Cronica*. Ed. Giuseppe de Scalia. 2 vols. Bari: Laterza, 1966.

Select Documents of English Constitutional History. Ed. George Adams and H. Morse Stephens. New York: Macmillan, 1935.

Série L, Monuments ecclésiastiques, titre VII, ordres monastiques: Abbaye de Saint-Denis—Inventaire analytique des cartons L829 à L839B. Comp. Bernard Ahieu and Ghislain Runel. Online typescript: 1950–2003.

Sharpe, Richard, et al., eds. *English Benedictine Libraries: The Shorter Catalogues.* London: British Library, 1996.

Syllabus (in English) of the Documents relating to England and Other Kingdoms Contained in the Collection Known as "Rymer's Foedera." Comp. Thomas Hardy. London: Longmans, Green and Co., 1869.

Willelmi Rishanger, quondam monachi s. Albani, et quorundam anonymorum, Chronica et annales, regnantibus Henrico tertio et Edwardo primo. Ed. Henry Riley. London: Longman, Green, Longman, Roberts, and Green, 1865.

Wright, Thomas, ed. and trans. *The Political Songs of England, from the Reign of John to That of Edward II.* 1839. New York and London: Johnson Reprint Corporation, 1968.

Ypodigma Neustriae, a Thomas Walsingham, quondam monacho monasterii s. Albani, conscriptum. Ed. Henry Riley. London: Longman and Co., 1876.

Secondary Sources

Abou-El-Haj, Barbara. "The Structure of Meaning: Architectural Representations in the Later Middle Ages." *Studies in Iconography* 25 (2004): 129–71.

Abulafia, David. *Frederick II: A Medieval Emperor.* New York and Oxford: Oxford University Press, 1988.

Alexander, Jonathan, and Paul Binski, eds. *Age of Chivalry: Art in Plantagenet England 1200–1400.* London: Royal Academy of Arts, 1987.

Aveling, Hugh. "Westminster Abbey—The Beginnings to 1474." In *A House of Kings: The History of Westminster Abbey,* ed. Edward Carpenter, pp. 3–84. London: John Baker, 1966.

Baaken, Gerhard. "Die Verhandlungen von Cluny (1245) und der Kampf Innocenz' IV. gegen Friedrich II." *Deutsches Archiv* 50 (1994): 531–79.

Baldwin, John. *The Government of Philip Augustus.* Berkeley and Los Angeles: University of California Press, 1986.

———. *Paris, 1200.* Paris: Flammarion, 2006.

Barber, Malcolm. "The Crusade of the Shepherds." In *Proceedings of the Tenth Annual Meeting of the Western Society for French History,* pp. 1–23. Lawrence: University Press of Kansas, 1984.

———. *The Trial of the Templars.* 2nd ed. Cambridge: Cambridge University Press, 2006.

Barron, Caroline. *London in the Later Middle Ages: Government and People, 1200–1500.* Oxford: Oxford University Press, 2004.

Barthélemy, Dominique. *Les deux âges de la seigneurie banale: Pouvoir et société dans la terre des sires de Coucy (milieu XIe–milieu XIIIe siècle).* Paris: Publications de la Sorbonne, 1984.

Bartlett, Robert. "The Impact of Royal Government in the French Ardennes: The Evidence of the 1247 *Enquête.*" *Journal of Medieval History* 7 (1981): 83–96.

Beaune, Collette. "Messianesimo regio e messianesimo popolare in Francia nel XIII secolo." In *Poteri carismatici e informali: Chiesa e società medioevali*, ed. Agostino Paravicini Bagliani and André Vauchez, pp. 114–36. Palermo: Sellerio, 1992.

Bedos-Rezak, Brigitte, ed. *Polity and Place: Regionalism in Medieval France.* (= *Historical Reflections / Reflexions historiques* 19 [1993]).

Bémont, Charles. *Simon de Montfort, comte de Leicester.* Paris: Alphonse Picard, 1884.

Berg, Beverly. "Manfred of Sicily and Urban IV: Negotiations of 1262." *Mediaeval Studies* 55 (1993): 111–36.

Berkhofer, Robert. *Day of Reckoning: Power and Accountability in Medieval France.* Philadelphia: University of Pennsylvania Press, 2004.

Billot, Claudine. "Les Saintes-Chapelles (XIIe–XVIe siècles): Approche comparée de fondations dynastiques." *Revue d'histoire de l'église de France* 73 (1987): 229–48.

Binski, Paul. "The Cosmati and *Romanitas* in England: An Overview." In *Westminster Abbey: The Cosmati Pavements*, ed. Lindy Grant and Richard Mortimer, pp. 116–34. Aldershot, UK: Ashgate, 2002.

———. "The Cosmati at Westminster and the English Court Style." *Art Bulletin* 77 (1990): 6–34.

———. *Westminster Abbey and the Plantagenets: Kingship and the Representation of Power, 1200–1400.* New Haven and London: Yale University Press, 1995.

Blair, John. "Purbeck Marble." In *English Medieval Industries: Craftsmen, Techniques, Products*, ed. John Blair and Nigel Ramsay, pp. 41–56. London and Rio Grande, OH: Hambledon Press, 1981.

Boullé, Jules. "Recherches historiques sur la maison de Saint-Lazare de Paris." *Mémoires de la Société de l'histoire de Paris et de l'Ile-de-France* 3 (1876): 126–91.

Boutoulle, Frédéric. "La vigne et le négoce du vin en Bordelais et Bazadais (fin XIe–début XIIIe siècle)." *Annales du Midi* 112 (2000): 275–98.

Bove, Boris. *Dominer la ville: Prévôts des marchands et échevins parisiens de 1260 à 1350.* Paris: Editions du CTHS, 2004.

Bradley, E. T. [= Mrs. A. Murray Smith]. *Annals of Westminster Abbey.* London and elsewhere: Cassell and Co., 1898.

Bridbury, Anthony. "Thirteenth-Century Prices and the Money Supply." *Agricultural History Review* 33 (1985): 1–21.

Brown, Elizabeth. *Saint-Denis: La Basilique.* Trans. Divina Cabo. Saint-Léger-Vauban: Zodiaque, 2001.

Brussel, Nicholas. *Nouvel examen de l'usage général des fiefs en France pendant le XIe, le XIIe, le XIIIe et le XIVe siècle, pour servir à l'intelligence des plus anciens titres du domaine de la Couronne.* 2 vols. Paris: C. Prud'homme and C. Robustel, 1727.

Bruzelius, Caroline. *The 13th-Century Church at Saint-Denis.* New Haven and London: Yale University Press.

Buc, Philippe. *L'ambiguïté du Livre: Prince, pouvoir, et peuple dans les commentaires de la Bible au moyen âge.* Paris: Beauchesne, 1994.

Buisson, Ludwig. "Saint Louis et l'Aquitaine." *Actes de l'Académie nationale des sciences, belles-lettres et arts de Bordeaux,* 4th series, 26 (1970–1971): 1–19.

Butler, Alban. *Lives of the Saints.* Rev. ed. Tunbridge Wells, UK: Burn and Oates, 1995–2000.

Cam, Helen. *The Hundred and the Hundred Rolls: An Outline of Local Government in Medieval England.* London: Methuen, 1930.

Cambridge Urban History of Britain. Vol. 1, *600–1540.* Cambridge: Cambridge University Press, 2000.

Carlin, Martha. "Shops and Shopping in the Early Thirteenth Century: Three Texts." In *Money, Markets and Trade in Late Medieval Europe: Essays in Honour of John H. A. Munro,* ed. Lawrin Armstrong et al., pp. 492–537. Leiden: Brill, 2007.

Carolus-Barré, Louis. "Les baillis de Philippe III le Hardi." *Annuaire-Bulletin de la Société de l'histoire de France* (1966/1967): 109–244.

———. "Les pères du IIe Concile de Lyon (1274): Esquisses prosopographiques." In *1274, Année charnière: Mutations et continuités,* pp. 377–423. Paris: Editions du Centre National de la Recherche Scientifique, 1977.

———. "Un recueil épistolaire composé à Saint-Denis sur la Croisade (1270–1271)." *Académie des Inscriptions et Belles-Lettres: Comptes rendus des séances* (November–December 1966): 555–68.

———. "Le service militaire en Beauvaisis au temps de Philippe de Beaumanoir: L'estaige à Gerberoy et à Beauvais (1271–1277); l'ost de Navarre (1276)." *Actes du 101e Congrès National des Sociétés Savantes* (1978): 73–93.

Carpenter, David. "The Fall of Hubert de Burgh." *Journal of British Studies* 19 (1980): 1–17.

———. "Gold and Gold Coins in England in the Mid-Thirteenth Century." *Numismatic Chronicle* 147 (1987): 106–13.

———. "The Gold Treasure of King Henry III." In *The Reign of Henry III,* pp. 107–36. London and Rio Grande, OH: Hambledon Press, 1996.

———. "The Household Rolls of King Henry III of England (1216–72)." *Historical Research* 80 (2007), 22–46.

———. "King Henry III and the Cosmati Work at Westminster Abbey." In *The Cloister and the World: Essays in Medieval History in Honour of Barbara Harvey,* ed. John Blair and Brian Golding, pp. 178–95. Oxford: Clarendon Press, 1996.

———. "King Henry III's 'Statute against Aliens': July 1263." In *The Reign of Henry III,* pp. 261–80. London and Rio Grande, OH: Hambledon Press, 1996.

———. "King, Magnates, and Society: The Personal Rule of King Henry III, 1234–58." *Speculum* 60 (1985): 39–70.

———. "The Meetings of Kings Henry III and Louis IX." *Thirteenth Century England* 10 (2005): 1–30.

———. *The Minority of Henry III.* London: Methuen, 1990.

———. "Simon de Montfort and the Mise of Lewes." *Bulletin of the Institute of Historical Research* 58 (1985): 1–11.

———. *The Struggle for Mastery: Britain, 1066–1284.* London: Allen Lane, 2003.

Carpenter, David. "An Unknown Obituary of King Henry III from the Year 1263." In *The Reign of Henry III*, pp. 253–60. London and Rio Grande, OH: Hambledon Press, 1996.

———. "Ware, Richard of." In *Oxford Dictionary of National Biography* (online edition only; http://www.oxforddnb.com).

———. "Westminster Abbey and the Cosmati Pavements in Politics, 1258–1269." In *Westminster Abbey: The Cosmati Pavements*, ed. Lindy Grant and Richard Mortimer, pp. 37–48. Aldershot, UK: Ashgate, 2002.

———. "Westminster Abbey in Politics, 1258–1269." *Thirteenth Century England* 8 (2001): 49–58.

Chaplais, Pierre. *Essays in Medieval Diplomacy and Administration*. London: Hambledon Press, 1981.

Clanchy, Michael. "Did Henry III Have a Policy?" *History* 53 (1968): 203–16.

———. *England and Its Rulers, 1066–1272*. 2nd ed. Oxford: Blackwell, 1998.

Clark, William. "Saint-Denis." In *Medieval France: An Encyclopedia*, ed. William Kibler and Grover Zinn, pp. 836–38. New York and London: Garland, 1995.

Claussen, Peter. *Magistri Doctissimi Romani: Die Römischen Marmorkünstler des Mittelalters*. Stuttgart: Franz Steiner Verlag, 1987.

Cohen, Meredith. "An Indulgence for the Visitor: The Public at the Sainte-Chapelle." Forthcoming.

Coldstream, Nicola. *Medieval Architecture*. Oxford: Oxford University Press, 2002.

Cole, David. *The Work of Sir Gilbert Scott*. London: Architectural Press, 1980.

Coss, Peter. "Sir Geoffrey de Langley and the Crisis of the Knightly Class in Thirteenth-Century England." In *Landlords, Peasants and Politics in Medieval England*, ed. Trevor Aston, pp. 166–202. Cambridge: Cambriedge University Press, 1987.

Crosby, Sumner. *The Royal Abbey of Saint-Denis: From Its Beginnings to the Death of Suger, 475–1151*. Ed. Pamela Blum. 2nd ed. New Haven: Yale University Press, 1987.

Crouch, David. "A Norman 'Conventio' and Bonds of Lordship in the Middle Ages." In *Law and Government in Medieval England and Normandy: Essays in Honour of Sir James Holt*, ed. George Garnett and John Hudson, pp. 299–324. Cambridge: Cambridge University Press, 1994.

———. *William Marshal: Court, Career, and Chivalry in the Angevin Empire*. London: Longman, 1990.

[Crull, Jodocus]. *The Antiquities of St. Peter's or the Abbey-Church of Westminster*. London: J. Nutt, 1713.

Cuttino, George. *English Medieval Diplomacy*. Bloomington: Indiana University Press, 1985.

Davis, Adam. *The Holy Bureaucrat: Eudes Rigaud and Religious Reform in Thirteenth-Century Normandy*. Ithaca, NY, and London: Cornell University Press, 2006.

Davy, Christian. "La connaissance de la peinture murale romane de la vallée du Loir, un siècle après la synthèse de Henri Laffillée." *Bulletin de la Société archéologique, scientifique et littéraire du Vendômois* (1998): 35–41.

Delaborde, Henri-François. "Les archives royales depuis la mort de saint Louis jusqu'à Pierre d'Etampes." *Bibliothèque de l'Ecole des chartes* 69 (1908): 289–302.

Demurger, Alain. *Les Templiers: Unie chevalerie chrétienne au moyen âge.* Paris: Editions du Seuil, 2005.

Denholm-Young, Noël. *Richard of Cornwall.* New York: William Salloch, 1947.

De Ville, Oscar. "John Deyville: A Neglected Rebel." *Northern History* 34 (1998): 17–40.

Dianoux de la Perrotine, Hugues de. "Saint Louis à Chypre." *Praktikōn tou prōtou diethnous kyprologikou synedriou* 2 (1972): 13–16.

Douie, Decima. *Archbishop Pecham.* Oxford: Clarendon Press, 1952.

Duby, Georges. *Legend of Bouvines: War, Religion and Culture in the Middle Ages.* Trans. Catherine Tihanyi. Cambridge: Polity Press, 1990.

Dunbabin, Jean. *France in the Making, 843–1180.* Oxford: Oxford University Press, 1985.

Elwes, Dudley. *A History of the Castles, Mansions, and Manors of Western Sussex.* London: Longmans, 1876.

Erlande-Brandenburg, Alain, et al. *Gisants et tombeaux de la basilique de Saint-Denis.* Saint-Denis: Archives Départementales de la Seine-Saint-Denis, 1975.

Field, Sean. *Isabelle of France: Capetian Sanctity and Franciscan Identity in the Thirteenth Century.* Notre Dame, IN: University of Notre Dame Press, 2006.

First Report of the Royal Commission on Historical Manuscripts. 2 vols. in 1. London: Her Majesty's Stationery Office, 1870.

Flete, John. *The History of Westminster Abbey.* Ed. J. Armitage Robinson. Cambridge: Cambridge University Press, 1909.

Folz, Robert. "La sainteté de Louis IX d'après les textes liturgiques de sa fête." *Revue d'histoire de l'église de France* 57 (1971): 31–45.

Fossier, Robert. *L'histoire économique et sociale du moyen âge occidental: Questions, sources, documents commentés.* Turnhout: Brepols, 1999.

Foster, Richard. "The Context and Fabric of the Westminster Abbey Sanctuary Pavement." In *Westminster Abbey: The Cosmati Pavements,* ed. Lindy Grant and Richard Mortimer, pp. 49–71. Aldershot, UK: Ashgate, 2002.

———. *Patterns of Thought: The Hidden Meaning of the Great Pavement of Westminster Abbey.* London: Jonathan Cape, 1991.

Fourth Report of the Royal Commission on Historical Manuscripts. Pt. 1, *Report and Appendix.* London: Her Majesty's Stationery Office, 1874.

Fuller, Thomas. *The History of the Worthies of England.*1662. London, 1840. Ed. P. Austin Nuttall. 3 vols. Reprint. New York: AMS Press, 1965.

Gavrilovitch, Michel. *Etude sur le Traité de Paris de 1259 entre Louis IX, roi de France, et Henri III, roi d'Angleterre.* Paris: Librairie Emile Bouillon, 1899.

Geary, Patrick. *Furta Sacra: Thefts of Relics in the Central Middle Ages.* Rev. ed. Princeton: Princeton University Press, 1990.

Gelsinger, Bruce. "A Thirteenth-Century Norwegian-Castilian Alliance." *Medievalia et Humanistica,* new series, 10 (1981): 55–80.

Glenisson, Jean. "L'application de la 'Paix' de Paris (1258) en Saintonge, de 1273 à 1293." *Actes du 111e Congrès national des sociétés savantes: Histoire médiévale et philologie* (1986): 191–205.

Graboïs, Aryeh. "L'abbaye de Saint-Denis et les juifs sous l'abbatiat de Suger." *Annales: ESC* 24 (1969): 1187–95.

Grant, Lindy. *Architecture and Society in Normandy, 1120–1270.* New Haven and London: Yale University Press, 2005.

Greatrex, Joan. "Monastic Charity for Jewish Converts: The Requisition of Corrodies by Henry III." In *Christianity and Judaism,* ed. Diana Wood, pp. 133–43. Cambridge, MA: Published for the Ecclesiastical History Society, 1992.

Groot, Roger. "The Early-Thirteenth-Century Criminal Jury." In *Twelve Good Men and True: The Criminal Trial Jury in England, 1200–1800,* ed. Thomas Green and James Cockburn, pp. 3–35. Princeton: Princeton University Press, 1988.

Guest, Gerald. "The People Demand a King: Visualizing Monarchy in the Psalter of Louis IX." *Studies in Iconography* 23 (2002): 1–27.

Guillot, Olivier, Albert Rigaudière, and Yves Sassier. *Pouvoirs et institutions dans la France médiévale.* 2 vols. Paris: Armand Colin, 1994.

Hallam, Elizabeth. "Royal Burial and the Cult of Kingship in France and England, 1060–1330." *Journal of Medieval History* 8 (1982): 359–80.

Hamilton, Bernard. "Eleanor of Castile and the Crusading Movement." *Mediterranean Review* 10 (1995): 92–103.

Harvey, Barbara. *Living and Dying in England, 1100–1540: The Monastic Experience.* Oxford: Clarendon Press, 1993.

———. *The Obedientiaries of Westminster Abbey and Their Financial Records, c. 1275 to 1540.* Woodbridge, UK: Boydell Press, 2002.

———. *Westminster Abbey and Its Estates in the Middle Ages.* Oxford: Clarendon Press, 1977.

Haydn, Joseph. *Book of Dignities.* London: Longman, Brown, Green, and Longmans, 1851.

Heale, Martin. *The Dependent Priories of Medieval English Monasteries.* Woodbridge, UK: Boydell Press, 2004.

Hedeman, Anne. *The Royal Image: Illustrations of the Grandes Chroniques de France, 1274–1422.* Berkeley and Los Angeles: University of California Press, 1991.

Hélary, Xavier. "Pierre de la Broce, seigneur féodal et le service militaire sous Philippe III. L'ost de Sauveterre (1276)." *Journal des savants* (July–December 2006): 275–305.

Hershey, Andrew. "Justice and Bureaucracy: The English Royal Writ and '1258.'" *English Historical Review* 113 (1998): 829–51.

Heslop, T. A. "English Seals in the Thirteenth and Fourteenth Centuries." In Alexander and Binski, *Age of Chivalry,* pp. 114–17.

Hillgarth, Jocelyn. *The Spanish Kingdoms, 1250–1516.* 2 vols. Oxford: Clarendon Press, 1976–1978.

The History of the King's Works. Vol. 1, *The Middle Ages.* Ed. R. Allen Brown, H. M. Colvin, and A. J. Taylor. London: Her Majesty's Stationery Office, 1963.

Holt, James. *Magna Carta.* 2nd ed. Cambridge: Cambridge University Press, 1992.

Howell, Margaret. *Eleanor of Provence: Queenship in Thirteenth-Century England.* Oxford: Blackwell, 1998.

———. *Regalian Right in Medieval England*. London: University of London, Athlone Press, 1962.

Howlett, David. "The Inscriptions in the Sanctuary Pavement at Westminster." In *Westminster Abbey: The Cosmati Pavements*, ed. Lindy Grant and Richard Mortimer, pp. 100–110. Aldershot, UK: Ashgate, 2002.

Hughes, Andrew. "The Monarch as the Object of Liturgical Veneration." In *Kings and Kingship in Medieval Europe*, ed. Anne Duggan, pp. 375–424. London: Centre for Late Antique and Medieval Studies, King's College, 1993.

Huscroft, Richard. "The Correspondence of Robert Burnell, Bishop of Bath and Wells and Chancellor of Edward I." *Archives* 25 (2000): 16–39.

———. "Robert Burnell and the Government of England, 1270–1274." *Thirteenth Century England* 8 (2001): 59–70.

Hyams, Paul. *Rancor and Reconciliation in Medieval England*. Ithaca, NY: Cornell University Press, 2003.

Iglesia-Rábade, Luis. "The Multi-Lingual Pulpit in England, 1100–1500." *Neophilologus* 80 (1996): 479–92.

Iogna-Prat, Dominique. "Constructions chrétiennes d'un espace politique." *Le Moyen âge* 107 (2001): 49–69.

Jackson, Richard. *Vive le Roi! A History of the French Coronation from Charles V to Charles X*. Chapel Hill and London: University of North Carolina Press, 1984.

Jehel, Georges. *Aigues-Mortes: Un port pour un roi*. Roanne: Horvath, 1985.

Jones, Michael. "Les Bretons et les croisades." *Mémoires de la Société d'histoire et d'archéologie de Bretagne* 71 (1994): 367–80.

Jordan, Alyce. "Seeing Stories in the Windows of the Sainte-Chapelle: The *Ars Poetriae* and the Politics of Visual Narrative." *Mediaevalia* 23 (2002): 39–60.

———. *Visualizing Kingship in the Windows of the Sainte-Chapelle*. Turnhout: Brepols, 2002.

Jordan, William. "The Case of Saint Louis." *Viator* 19 (1988): 209–17.

———. "Communal Administration in France, 1257–1270: Problems Discovered and Solutions Imposed." *Revue belge de philologie et d'histoire* 59 (1981): 292–313.

———. "Cutting the Budget: The Impact of the Crusades on Appropriations for Public Works in France." *Revue belge de philologie et d'histoire* 76 (1998): 307–18.

———. "The English Holy Men of Pontigny." *Cistercian Studies* 43 (2008): 63–75.

———. *The French Monarchy and the Jews from Philip Augustus to the Last Capetians*. Philadelphia: University of Pennsylvania Press, 1989.

———. "A Fresh Look at Medieval Sanctuary." In *Law and the Illicit in Medieval Society*, ed. Ruth Karras, Joel Kaye, and Ann Matter, pp. 17–32. Philadelphia: University of Pennsylvania Press, forthcoming.

———. *From Servitude to Freedom: Manumission in the Sénonais in the Thirteenth Century*. Philadelphia: University of Pennsylvania Press, 1986.

———. "Isabelle d'Angoulême, by the Grace of God, Queen." *Revue belge de philologie et d'histoire* 69 (1991): 821–52.

Jordan, William. "The Jews and the Transition to Papal Rule in the Comtat-Venaissin." *Michael* 12 (1991): 213–32.

———."Jews, Regalian Rights, and the Constitution in Medieval France." *AJS Review* 23 (1998): 1–16.

———. *Louis IX and the Challenge of the Crusade: A Study in Rulership*. Princeton: Princeton University Press, 1979.

———. "Marian Devotion and the Talmud Trial of 1240." In *Religionsgespräche im Mittelalter*, ed. Bernard Lewis and Friedrich Niewohner, pp. 61–76. Wiesbaden: Otto Harrassowitz, 1992.

———. "The 'People' in the Psalter of Saint Louis and the Leadership of Moses." In *Medieval Paradigms: Essays in Honor of Jeremy Duquesnay Adams*, ed. Stephanie Hayes-Healy, 2 vols., 1:13–28. New York: Palgrave Macmillan, 2005.

———. "The Psalter of Saint Louis (BN MS. Lat. 10525): The Program of the Seventy-Eight Full-Page Illustrations." *ACTA* 7 (1980): 65–91.

———. "The Representation of Monastic-Lay Relations in the Canonization Records for Louis IX." In *Religious and Laity in Western Europe, 1000–1400: Interaction, Negotiation, and Power*, ed. Emilia Jamroziak and Janet Burton, pp. 225–39. Turnhout: Brepols, 2006.

———. "The Struggle for Influence at the Court of Philip III: Pierre de la Broce and the French Aristocracy." *French Historical Studies* 24 (2001): 439–68.

———. *Unceasing Strife, Unending Fear: Jacques de Thérines and the Freedom of the Church in the Age of the Last Capetians*. Princeton: Princeton University Press, 2005.

———. "Westminster Abbey and Its Italian Bankers during the Abbacy of Richard de Ware, 1258–1283." *Revue bénédictine* 118 (2008): 334–54.

Kaeuper, Richard. *Bankers to the Crown: The Riccardi of Lucca and Edward I.* Princeton: Princeton University Press, 1973.

Kantorowicz, Ernst. *The King's Two Bodies: A Study in Mediaeval Political Theology.* Princeton: Princeton University Press, 1957.

Keene, Derek. "London *circa* 600–1300: The Growth of a Capital." *Franco-British Studies*, no. 17 (spring 1994): 23–31.

Kerov, Vsevelod. *Narodnye vosstaniia i ereticheskie dvizheniia vo Frantsii v kontse XIII–nachale XIV veka.* Moscow: Izdatel'stvo Universiteti druzhby narodov, 1986.

Kicklighter, Joseph. "Appeal, Negotiation, and Conflict: The Evolution of the Anglo-French Legal Relationship before the Hundred Years War." *Proceedings of the Annual Meeting of the Western Society for French History* 18 (1991): 45–59.

———. "English Gascony and the Parlement of Paris: A Study of Anglo-Gascon Legal Representatives, 1259–1337." In *Documenting the Past: Essays in Medieval History Presented to George Peddy Cuttino*, ed. J. S. Hamilton and Patricia Bradley, pp. 119–36. Wolfeboro, NH: Boydell Press, 1989.

———. "French Jurisdictional Supremacy in Gascony: One Aspect of the Ducal Government's Response." *Journal of Medieval History* 5 (1979): 127–34.

———. "Les monastères de Gascogne et le conflit franco-anglais (1270–1327)." Trans. Philippe Wolff, *Annales du Midi* 91 (1979): 121–34.

Kienast, Walther. *Deutschland und Frankreich in der Kaiserzeit (900–1270)*. 3 vols. Stuttgart: Hiersemann, 1974–1975.

Knowles, David, David Smith, and Vera London. *The Heads of Religious Houses, England and Wales*. 2 vols. Cambridge: Cambridge University Press, 1972–2001.

Lambert, Malcolm. *The Cathars*. Oxford: Blackwell, 1998.

Lancaster, R. Kent. "Henry III, Westminster Abbey, and the Court School of Illumination." In *Seven Studies in Medieval English History and Other Historical Essays Presented to Harold S. Snellgrove*, ed. Richard Bowers, pp. 85–95. Jackson: University Press of Mississippi, 1983.

Langlois, Charles-Victor. *Le Règne de Philippe III le Hardi*. Paris: Hachette, 1887.

Lawrence, Clifford. *Medieval Monasticism: Forms of Religious Life in Western Europe in the Middle Ages*. London and New York: Longman, 1984.

Le Gall, Jean-Marie. "La nécropole dynastique des Bourbons à Saint-Denis ou l'impossible corps du roi." *Revue historique*, no. 637 (January 2006): 61–80.

Le Goff, Jacques. "A Coronation Program for the Age of Saint Louis: The Ordo of 1250." In *Coronations: Medieval and Early Modern Monarchic Ritual*, ed. János Bak, pp. 46–57. Berkeley and Los Angeles: University of California Press, 1990.

———. "Le roi dans l'Occident médiéval: Caractère originaux." In *Kings and Kingship in Medieval Europe*, ed. Anne Duggan, pp. 1–40. London: Centre for Late Antique and Medieval Studies, King's College, 1993.

———. "Royauté biblique et idéal monarchique médiéval: Saint Louis et Josias." In *Les juifs au regard de l'histoire: Mélanges en honneur de Bernhard Blumenkranz*, ed. Gilbert Dahan, pp. 157–67. Paris: Picard, 1985.

———. *Saint Louis*. Paris: Gallimard, 1996.

———. "Saint Louis and the Mediterranean." *Mediterranean Historical Review* 5 (1990): 21–43.

———. "Saint Louis et la prière." In *Horizons marins, itinéraires spirituels (Ve–XVIIIe siècles)*, ed. Henri Dubois et al., 2 vols., 1:85–94. Paris: Publications de la Sorbonne, 1987.

Le Goff, Jacques, et al. *Le sacre royal à l'époque de saint Louis d'après le manuscrit latin 1246 de la BNF*. Paris: Gallimard, 2001.

Lewis, Suzanne. "Henry III and the Gothic Rebuilding of Westminster Abbey: The Problematics of Context." *Traditio* 50 (1995): 129–72.

Leyser, Henrietta. "Cultural Affinities." In *The Twelfth and Thirteenth Centuries*, ed. Barbara Harvey, pp. 167–200. Oxford: Oxford University Press, 2001.

Lillich, Meredith. *The Armor of Light: Stained Glass in Western France, 1250–1325*. Berkeley and Los Angeles: University of California Press, 1994.

Lives of the Saints. Ed. Herbert Thurston and Donald Attwater. Comp. Alban Butler. Rev. ed. 12 vols. London: Burns, Oates and Washbourne, 1926–1938.

Lloyd, Simon. *English Society and the Crusade, 1216–1307*. Oxford: Clarendon Press, 1988.

———. "King Henry III, the Crusade and the Mediterranean." In *England and Her Neighbours, 1066–1453: Essays in Honour of Pierre Chaplais*, ed. Michael Jones and Malcolm Vale, pp. 97–119. London and Ronceverte, WV: Hambledon Press, 1989.

Lloyd, Terrence. *The English Wool Trade in the Middle Ages.* Cambridge: Cambridge University Press, 1977.

Lodge, R. A. "Language Attitudes and Linguistic Norms in France and England in the Thirteenth Century." *Thirteenth Century England* 4 (1992): 73–83.

Logan, F. Donald. *Runaway Religious in Medieval England, c. 1240–1540.* Cambridge: Cambridge University Press, 1996.

Lombard-Jourdan, Anne. "La confrérie de Saint-Denis des origins à 1785." In *Saint-Denis, lieu de mémoire,* pp. 377–406. Etudes et documents, no. 5. Paris: Fédérations des Sociétés historiques et archéologiques de Paris et de l'Ile-de-France, 2000.

———. *Fleur-de-lis et oriflamme: Signes célestes du royaume de France.* Paris: Presses du CNRS, 1991.

———. "Les foires de l'abbaye de Saint-Denis: Revue des données et revision des opinions admises." In *Saint-Denis, lieu de mémoire* (as above), pp. 99–159.

———. *"Montjoie et saint Denis!": Le centre de la Gaule aux origines de Paris et de Saint-Denis.* Paris: Presses du CNRS, 1989.

———. "'Montjoies' et 'Montjoie' dans la Plaine Saint-Denis." In *Saint-Denis, lieu de mémoire* (as above), pp. 65–98.

———. "'Munjoie!', montjoie et monjoie: Histoire d'un mot." In *Saint-Denis, lieu de mémoire* (as above), pp. 35–64.

———. "La naissance d'une légende parisienne: Le miracle du Lendit." In *Saint-Denis, lieu de mémoire* (as above), pp. 161–78.

Lunt, William. *Financial Relations of the Papacy with England to 1327.* Cambridge, MA: Mediaeval Academy of America, 1939.

Lyon, Bryce. *A Constitutional and Legal History of Medieval England.* 2nd ed. New York: Norton, 1980.

Maddicott, J. R. "The Mise of Lewes, 1264." *English Historical Review* 98 (1983): 588–603.

———. *Simon de Montfort.* Cambridge: Cambridge University Press, 1994.

———. "'1258' and '1297': Some Comparisons and Contrasts." *Thirteenth Century England* 9 (2003): 1–14.

Maier, Christoph. *Preaching the Crusades: Mendicant Friars and the Cross in the Thirteenth Century.* Cambridge and New York: Cambridge University Press, 1994.

Mason, Emma. *Westminster Abbey and Its People, c. 1050–c. 1216.* Woodbridge, UK: Boydell Press, 1996.

Matthew, Donald. *The English and the Community of Europe in the Thirteenth Century.* Reading: University of Reading, 1997.

McKechnie, William. *Magna Carta.* 2nd ed. Glasgow: James Maclehose and Sons, 1914.

Menache, Sophia, and Jeannine Horowitz. "Quand le rire devient grinçant: La satire politique aux XIIIe et XIVe siècles." *Le Moyen âge* 102 (1996): 437–63.

Mercuri, Chiara. *"Stat inter spinas lilium:* Le lys de France et la couronne d'épines." *Le Moyen âge* 110 (2004): 497–512.

Moorman, John. *Church Life in England in the Thirteenth Century.* Cambridge: Cambridge University Press, 1955.

Mortimer, Richard. *Angevin England, 1154–1258.* Oxford: Blackwell, 1994.

Mundill, Robin. *England's Jewish Solution: Experiment and Expulsion, 1262–1290.* Cambridge: Cambridge University Press, 1998.

Murray, Stephen. *Notre-Dame Cathedral of Amiens: The Power of Change in Gothic.* Cambridge: Cambridge University Press, 1996.

Nebbiai dalla Guarda, Donatella. *La bibliothèque de l'abbaye de Saint-Denis en France du IXe au XVIIIe siècle.* Paris: Editions du CNRS, 1985.

———. "Des rois et des moines: Livres et lecteurs à l'abbaye de Saint-Denis (XIIIe–XVe siècles)." In *Saint-Denis et la royauté: Etudes offertes à Bernard Guenée,* ed. Françoise Autrand et al., pp. 355–74. Paris: Publications de la Sorbonne, 1999.

New, Chester. *History of the Alien Priories in England to the Confiscation of Henry V.* Chicago: Privately printed, 1916.

Nisse, Ruth. "'Your Name Will No Longer Be Aseneth': Apocrypha, Anti-martyrdom, and Jewish Conversion in Thirteenth-Century England." *Speculum* 81 (2006): 734–53.

Norton, Christopher. "The Luxury Pavement in England before Westminster." In *Westminster Abbey: The Cosmati Pavements,* ed. Lindy Grant and Richard Mortimer, pp. 7–27. Aldershot, UK: Ashgate, 2002.

O'Callaghan, Joseph. *A History of Medieval Spain.* Ithaca and London: Cornell University Press, 1975.

ODNB. See *Oxford Dictionary of National Biography.*

Oxford Dictionary of National Biography. 60 vols. Oxford and New York: Oxford University Press, 2004. Electronic version, 2004–.

Panofsky, Erwin. *Abbot Suger on the Abbey Church of St.-Denis and Its Art Treasures.* Ed. Gerda Panofsky-Soergel. 2nd ed. Princeton: Princeton University Press, 1979.

"Parish Church of Eaton: High Onn." *Staffordshire Historical Collections* 4 (1883): 52–63.

Parsons, John. "The Beginnings of English Administration in Ponthieu: An Unnoticed Document of 1280." *Mediaeval Studies* 50 (1988): 371–403.

———. *Eleanor of Castile: Queen and Society in Thirteenth-Century England.* New York: St. Martin's Press, 1995.

Pearce, Ernest. *Walter de Wenlock, Abbot of Westminster.* London: Society for Promoting Christian Knowledge, 1920.

Pegg, Mark. *The Corruption of Angels: The Great Inquisition of 1245–1246.* Princeton: Princeton University Press, 2001.

———. *A Most Holy War: The Albigensian Crusade and the Battle for Christendom.* Oxford: Oxford University Press, 2008.

Petit-Dutaillis, Charles. *Etude sur la vie et le règne de Louis VIII (1187–1226).* Paris: E. Bouillon, 1894.

Phillips, Jonathan. "The Latin East, 1098–1291." In *The Oxford Illustrated History of the Crusades,* ed. Jonathan Riley-Smith, pp. 112–40. Oxford: Oxford University Press, 1997.

Platt, Colin. *The Abbeys and Priories of Medieval England.* London: Secker and Warburg, 1984.

Powicke, Frederick (later Sir Maurice). *The Loss of Normandy, 1189–1204: Studies in the History of the Angevin Empire.* Manchester: University Press, 1913.

Powicke, Frederick (later Sir Maurice). *The Thirteenth Century, 1216–1307.* Oxford: Clarendon Press, 1953.

Prestwich, Michael. "Kirkby, John." In *ODNB.*

———. *Plantagenet England, 1225–1360.* Oxford: Clarendon Press, 2005.

Raban, Sandra. "Edward I's Other Inquiries." *Thirteenth Century England* 9 (2003): 43–57.

———. *Mortmain Legislation and the English Church, 1279–1500.* Cambridge: Cambridge University Press, 1982.

———. *A Second Domesday? The Hundred Rolls of 1279–80.* Oxford: Oxford University Press, 2004.

Ramsay, Nigel. "Alabaster." In *English Medieval Industries: Craftsmen, Techniques, Products,* ed. John Blair and Nigel Ramsay, pp. 29–40. London and Rio Grande, OH: Hambledon Press, 1981.

Rasmussen, Linda. "Monastic Benefactors in England and Denmark: Their Social Background and Gender Distribution." In *Religious and Laity in Western Europe, 1000–1400: Interaction, Negotiation, and Power,* ed. Emilia Jamroziak and Janet Burton, pp. 77–91. Turnhout: Brepols, 2006.

Richard, Jean. *Saint Louis: Roi d'une France féodale, soutien de la Terre sainte.* Paris: Fayard, 1983.

Richardson, H. G., and George Sayles. "The King's Ministers in Parliament, 1272–1377." *English Historical Review* 46 (1931): 529–50.

Ridgeway, H. W. "The Ecclesiastical Career of Aymer de Lusignan, Bishop Elect of Winchester, 1250–1260." In *The Cloister and the World: Essays in Medieval History in Honour of Barbara Harvey,* ed. John Blair and Brian Golding, pp. 148–77. Oxford: Clarendon Press, 1996.

Riley-Smith, Jonathan. *The Crusades: A Short History.* New Haven and London: Yale University Press, 1987.

Roberg, Burkhard. *Das Zweite Konzil von Lyon [1274].* Paderborn: Ferdinand Schöningh, 1990.

Robertson, Anne. *The Service Books of the Royal Abbey of Saint-Denis: Images of Ritual and Music in the Middle Ages.* Oxford: Clarendon Press, 1991.

Robinson, J. Armitage, and Montague James. *The Manuscripts of Westminster Abbey.* Cambridge: Cambridge University Press, 1909.

Rodríguez García, José. "Henry III (1216–1272), Alfonso X of Castile (1252–1284) and the Crusading Plans of the Thirteenth Century (1245–1272)." In *England and Europe in the Reign of Henry III (1216–1272),* ed. Björn Weiler, pp. 99–120. Aldershot, UK: Ashgate, 2002.

Rosser, Gervase. *Medieval Westminster, 1200–1540.* Oxford: Clarendon Press, 1989.

Roux, Simone. *Paris au moyen âge.* Paris: Hachette Littératures, 2003.

Ruggiu, François-Joseph. "Westminster, nécropole royale, ou la disparition des trois corps du roi." *Revue historique,* no. 637 (January 2006): 81–112.

Saint-Venant, R. *Dictionnaire topographique, historique, biographique, généalogique et héraldique du Vendômoise.* Vol. 3, *O<n->U.* Blois: C. Migault, 1914–1915.

Sayles, George. *The Medieval Foundations of England.* New York: A. S. Barnes, 1961.

Schneidmüller, Bernd. *Nomen Patriae: Die Enstehung Frankreichs in der politisch-geographischen Terminologie (10.–13. Jahrhundert)*. Sigmaringen: J. Thorbecke, 1987.

Scott, Edward. ["Notice,"] *Athenaeum* (1897): 635.

Sivéry, Gérard. *Les Capétiens et l'argent au siècle de saint Louis: Essai sur l'administration et les finances royales au XIIIe siècle*. Villeneuve d'Ascq: Presses Universitaires du Septentrion, 1995.

———. *Louis VIII le Lion*. Paris: Fayard, 1995.

———. *Marguerite de Provence: Une reine au temps des cathédrales*. Paris: Fayard, 1987.

———. "Le mécontentement dans le royaume de France et les enquêtes de saint Louis." *Revue historique*, no. 545 (January–March, 1983): 3–24.

———. *Philippe III le Hardi*. Paris: Fayard, 2003.

Sloane, Barney. "Archaeology in London: Annual Round-Up and News for 1855/6." *Transactions of the London and Middlesex Archaeological Society* 55 (2004): 9–16.

Spiegel, Gabrielle. *The Chronicle Tradition of Saint-Denis: A Survey*. Brookline, MA, and Leyden: Classical Folia Editions, 1978.

———. "The Cult of Saint Denis and Capetian Kingship." *Journal of Medieval History* 1 (1975): 43–69.

Stacey, Robert. "Anti-Semitism and the Medieval English State." In *The Medieval State: Essays Presented to James Campbell*, pp. 163–77. London and Rio Grande, OH: Hambledon Press, 2000.

———. "The Conversion of Jews to Christianity in Thirteenth-Century England." *Speculum* 67 (1992): 263–84.

———. "Crusades, Crusaders, and the Baronial *Gravamina* of 1263–64." *Thirteenth Century England* 3 (1991): 137–50.

———. *Politics, Policy and Finance under Henry III, 1216–1245*. Oxford: Oxford University Press, 1987.

———. "Royal Taxation and the Social Structure of Medieval Anglo-Jewry: The Tallages of 1239–1242." *HUCA* 56 (1985): 175–249.

Stanley, Arthur. *Historical Memorials of Westminster Abbey*. 2 vols. Philadelphia: George W. Jacobs and Co., 1899.

Stearns, Justin. "Exceptional Footnotes: Ibn al-Khatib's Description of the Kings of Christian Spain." Unpublished.

Stern, Derek. *A Hertfordshire Demesne of Westminster Abbey: Profits, Productivity and Weather*. Ed. Christopher Thornton. Hatfield, UK: University of Hertfordshire Press, 2000.

Stone, Lawrence. *Sculpture in Britain in the Middle Ages*. Harmondsworth, UK: Penguin, 1955.

Strayer, Joseph. *The Albigensian Crusades*. Ann Arbor: University of Michigan Press, 1992.

Studd, Robin. "The 'Privilegiati' and the Treaty of Paris, 1259." *Actes du 111e Congrès national des sociétés savantes* (1986): 175–85.

———. "Reconfiguring the Angevin Empire, 1224–1259." In *England and Europe in the Reign of Henry III (1216–1272)*, ed. Björn Weiler, pp. 31–41. Aldershot, UK: Ashgate, 2002.

Summerson, Henry. "Attitudes to Capital Punishment in England, 1200–1350." *Thirteenth Century England* 8 (2001): 123–33.

———. "Kingship, Government, and Political Life, c. 1160–c.1280." In *The Twelfth and Thirteenth Centuries,* ed. Barbara Harvey, pp. 201–42. Oxford: Oxford University Press, 2001.

Sumption, Jonathan. *The Albigensian Crusade.* London and Boston: Faber, 1978.

———. *Pilgrimage: An Image of Medieval Religion.* London: Faber and Faber, 1975.

Sutherland, Donald. *Quo Warranto Proceedings in the Reign of Edward I, 1278–1294.* Oxford: Oxford University Press, 1963.

Symes, Carol. *A Common Stage: Theater and Public Life in Medieval Arras.* Ithaca, NY, and London: Cornell University Press, 2007.

Tanner, Lawrence. "The Nature and Use of the Westminster Abbey Muniments." *Transactions of the Royal Historical Society,* 4th series, 19 (1936): 43–80.

Tanz, Sabine. "Saint-Michel contra Saint-Denis—Mentalitäts- und National-geschichtliche Aspekte spätmittelalterlicher Heiligenverehrung." In *Mentalität und Gesellschaft im Mittelalter: Gedenkschrift für Ernst Werner,* ed. Sabine Tanz, pp. 107–26. Frankfurt am Main: Peter Lang, 1993.

Tatlock, J.S.P. "The Dragons of Wessex and Wales." *Speculum* 8 (1933): 223–35.

Taylor, A. J. "A Letter of Lewis of Savoy to Edward I." *English Historical Review* 68 (1953): 56–62.

Teyssot, Josiane. "Le mouvement communal en Auvergne, XIIe–XVe siècles." *Annales du Midi* 109 (1997): 201–10.

Titow, Jan. *English Rural Society, 1200–1350.* London: Allen and Unwin, 1969.

Tout, Thomas. *The Beginnings of a Modern Capital: London and Westminster in the Fourteenth Century.* London: Oxford University Press, 1923.

———. *Chapters in Mediaeval Administrative History.* 6 vols. Manchester: Manchester University Press, 1937.

Treharne, R. F. *The Baronial Plan of Reform, 1258–1263.* Manchester: Manchester University Press, 1971.

Turner, Ralph. *The King and His Courts.* Ithaca, NY: Cornell University Press, 1968.

Tyerman, Christopher. *England and the Crusades, 1095–1588.* Chicago: University of Chicago Press, 1988.

Vale, Malcolm. *The Princely Court: Medieval Courts and Culture in North-West Europe, 1270–1380.* Oxford: Oxford University Press, 2001.

Valente, Claire. "The Provisions of Oxford: Assessing/Assigning Authority in Time of Unrest." In *The Experience of Power in Medieval Europe, 950–1350: Essays in Honor of Thomas N. Bisson,* ed. Robert Berkhofer et al., pp. 25–41. Aldershot, UK: Ashgate, 2005.

———. "Simon de Montfort, Earl of Leicester, and the Utility of Sanctity in Thirteenth-Century England." *Journal of Medieval History* 21 (1995): 27–49.

———. *The Theory and Practice of Revolt in Medieval England.* Aldershot, UK: Ashgate, 2003.

Victoria History of London. Vol. 1. Ed. William Page. London: Constable, 1909.

Victoria History of the County of Surrey. Ed. H. E. Malden. 4 vols. Westminster: A. Constable, 1902–1912.

Victoria History of the County of Worcester. Ed. J. Willis-Bund and William Page. 4 vols. Reprint. Folkestone: University of London Institute of Historical Research, 1971.

Vincent, Nicholas. "Edmund of Almain." In *ODNB.*

———. "England and the Albigensian Crusade." In *England and Europe in the Reign of Henry III (1216–1272)*, ed. Björn Weiler, pp. 67–97. Aldershot, UK: Ashgate, 2002.

———. *The Holy Blood: King Henry III and the Westminster Blood Relic.* Cambridge: Cambridge University Press, 2001.

———. "Isabella of Angoulême: John's Jezebel." In *King John: New Interpretations*, ed. Stephen Church, pp. 165–219. Woodbridge, UK: Boydell, 1999.

———. *Peter des Roches: An Alien in English Politics, 1205–1238.* Cambridge: Cambridge University Press, 1996.

———. "The Pilgrimages of the Angevin Kings of England 1154–1272." In *Pilgrimage: The English Experience from Becket to Bunyan*, ed. Colin Morris and Peter Roberts, pp. 12–45. Cambridge: Cambridge University Press, 2002.

Wakefield, Walter. "Heretics and Inquisitors: The Case of Le Mas-Saintes-Puelles." *Catholic Historical Review* 69 (1983): 209–26.

Waldman, Thomas. "Denis." In *Medieval France: An Encyclopedia*, ed. William Kibler and Grover Zinn, pp. 292–93. New York and London: Garland, 1995.

Wander, Steven. "The Westminster Abbey Sanctuary Pavement." *Traditio* 34 (1978): 137–56.

Waugh, Scott. *The Lordship of England: Royal Wardships and Marriages in English Society and Politics, 1217–1327.* Princeton: Princeton University Press, 1988.

———. "Marriage, Class, and Royal Lordship in England under Henry III." *Viator* 16 (1985): 181–207.

Wayno, Jeffrey. "An Instance of Pawning: King Henry III and the Westminster Jewel Collection." Unpublished senior thesis, Princeton University, 2007.

Weiler, Björn. "Henry III and the Sicilian Business: A Reinterpretation." *Historical Research* 74 (2001): 127–50.

———. *Henry III of England and the Staufen Empire, 1216–1272.* Woodbridge, UK: Boydell, 2006.

———. "Henry III through Foreign Eyes—Communication and Historical Writing in Thirteenth-Century Europe." In *England and Europe in the Reign of Henry III (1216–1272)*, ed. Björn Weiler, pp. 137–61. Aldershot, UK: Ashgate, 2002.

———. "Symbolism and Politics in the Reign of Henry III." *Thirteenth Century England* 9 (2003): 15–41.

Weiss, Daniel. "Architectural Symbolism and the Decoration of the Ste.-Chapelle." *Art Bulletin* 77 (1995): 308–20.

———. "Biblical History and Medieval Historiography: Rationalizing Strategies in Crusader Art." *MLN* 108 (1993): 710–37.

———. "The Three Solomon Portraits in the Arsenal Old Testament and the Construction of Meaning in Crusader Painting." *Arte medievale*, 2nd series, 6, no. 2 (1992): 15–36.

West, Francis. *The Justiciarship in England, 1066–1232.* Cambridge: Cambridge University Press, 1966.

Williams, Gwyn. *Medieval London: From Commune to Capital.* London: Athlone Press, 1963.

Wilson, Christopher. "The English Response to French Gothic Architecture, c. 1200–1350." In Alexander and Binski, *Age of Chivalry*, pp. 74–82.

Wood, Charles. *French Apanages and the Capetian Monarchy, 1224–1328.* Cambridge, MA: Harvard University Press, 1966.

———. "The Mise of Amiens and Saint Louis' Theory of Kingship." *French Historical Studies* 6 (1970): 300–10.

INDEX

Medieval persons are indexed alphabetically by their first name; titles are supplied for monarchs and consorts, aristocrats and prelates. At times, consistency, with regard to phrases, yields to convention: so, the Ordinance of Melun is indexed under "Melun, Ordinance of," but the Provisions of Oxford under "Provisions of Oxford" and the Treaty of Meaux-Paris under "Treaty of Meaux-Paris.